TRANSATLANTIC PIETIES

Holland Museum
Docent Library
Spring 2014

The Historical Series of the Reformed Church in America
no. 76

TRANSATLANTIC PIETIES
Dutch Clergy in Colonial America

Leon van den Broeke
Hans Krabbendam
Dirk Mouw, editors

Van Raalte Press
Holland, Michigan

William B. Eerdmans Publishing Company
Grand Rapids, Michigan / Cambridge, UK

© 2012 Reformed Church Press
All rights reserved

Wm. B. Eerdmans Publishing Co.
2140 Oak Industrial Drive SE, Grand Rapids, Michigan 49503
PO Box 163, Cambridge CB3 9PU UK
www.eerdmans.com

Van Raalte Press
Hope College
Theil Research Center
9 East 10th Street, Holland, Michigan 49423
www.hope.edu/vri

Printed in the United States of America
ISBN: 978-0-8028-6972-2

Library of Congress Cataloging-in-Publication Data

Transatlantic pieties : Dutch clergy in colonial America / Leon van den Broeke, Hans Krabbendam, Dirk Mouw, editors.
   pages cm. -- (The historical series of the Reformed Church in America ; no. 76)
  Proceedings of conferences held at the First Reformed Church, New Brunswick, N.J., and at Hope College, Holland, Mich.
  Includes bibliographical references and index.
  ISBN 978-0-8028-6972-2 (pbk. : alk. paper) 1. Reformed Protestant Dutch Church (U.S.)--Clergy--Biography--Congresses. 2. Reformed Protestant Dutch Church (U.S.)--History--Congresses. 3. Church development, New--Reformed Protestant Dutch Church (U.S.)--Congresses. I. Broeke, Leon van den. II. Krabbendam, Hans, 1964- III. Mouw, Dirk.
  BX9541.D88 2012
  285.7092'33931073--dc23
  [B]
                                   2012039240

This volume grew out of an idea planted by Gerald De Jong, tended by Russell Gasero, and brought into full bloom by conference participants led by Leon van den Broeke. A significant grant from the Collegiate Church of New York City and additional financial support from the Roosevelt Study Center in the Netherlands and the Van Raalte Institute of Holland, Michigan, made possible the two conferences at which the essays found in this volume were originally presented. Barbara Fillette, director of the Reformed Church Center, coordinated the process and logistics. The first Reformed Church in New Brunswick, New Jersey, hosted the first conference. Jacob E. Nyenhuis, director of the Van Raalte Institute, hosted the second conference at Hope College, Holland, Michigan.

To Russell L. Gasero, archivist extraordinaire.

The Editors

The Historical Series of the Reformed Church in America

The series was inaugurated in 1968 by the General Synod of the Reformed Church in America acting through the Commission on History to communicate the church's heritage and collective memory and to reflect on our identity and mission, encouraging historical scholarship which informs both church and academy.

www.rca.org/series

General Editor
    Rev. Donald J. Bruggink, PhD, DD
    Western Theological Seminary
    Van Raalte Institute, Hope College

Associate Editor
    George Brown Jr., PhD
    Western Theological Seminary

Production Editor
    Russell L. Gasero

Commission on History
    Douglas Carlson, PhD, Northwestern College, Orange City, Iowa
    Hartmut Kramer-Mills, MDiv, DrTheol, New Brunswick, New Jersey
    David M. Tripold, PhD, Monmouth University
    Audrey Vermilyea, Bloomington, Minnesota
    Linda Walvoord, PhD, University of Cincinnati
    Lori Witt, PhD, Central College, Pella, Iowa

Contents

Contributors ix
List of Illustrations xi
Preface xiii
    Leon van den Broeke, Hans Krabbendam, Dirk Mouw

INTRODUCTION

Dutch Clergy in Colonial North America
    Dirk Mouw   1

PIONEERS
Church Planters in the Early Seventeenth Century

1. Bastiaen Jansz Krol (1595–1674): New Netherland's First Church Servant
    Willem Frijhoff   37
2. Jonas Michaëlius (1584–c. 1638): The Making of the First Minister
    Jaap Jacobs   59
3. Everardus Bogardus (1607–1647): A Dutch Mystic in the New World
    Willem Frijhoff   79

STABILIZERS
Laying the Foundations of the Church in the Late Seventeenth Century

4. Gideon Schaats (1607–1694): Old World Dominie in a New World Setting
    Firth Haring Fabend   103
5. Henricus Selijns (1636–1701): Churchman with a Steady Hand
    Jos van der Linde   119
6. Petrus Tesschenmaecker (ca. 1642–1690): Atlantic Preacher and Adventurer
    Dirk Mouw   147

DIVERSIFIERS
Clerical Triumphs and Tragedies in the Seventeenth Century

7. Rudolphus van Varick (1645–1694): Mild, Mobile, and Mistreated Pastor
    Leon van den Broeke   173

8. Guiliam Bertholf (1656–1726): Irenic Dutch Pietist in
   New Jersey and New York
       Earl Wm. Kennedy   197
9. Laurentius van den Bosch (c. 1660?–1696): Scandalous Founder
       Evan Haefeli   217

MEDIATORS
Dutch-Americans and Their Neighbors in the Transitional Eighteenth Century

10. Archibald Laidlie (1727–1779): The Scot Who Revitalized New York City's Dutch Reformed Church
        Joyce D. Goodfriend   239
11. Gerrit Lydekker (1729–1794): A Tory Among Patriots
        Firth Haring Fabend   259
12. Eilardus Westerlo (1738–1790): From a Colonial to an American Pastor
        Robert Naborn   275

SUCCESSORS
The Colonial Legacy for the New Denomination and the New Immigration in the Nineteenth Century

13. John Henry Livingston (1746–1825): Interpreter of the Dutch Reformed Tradition in the Early American Republic
        John W. Coakley   295
14. Cornelius van der Meulen, 1800–1876: Builder of a New Dutch-American Colony
        Hans Krabbendam   315

Index   333

Contributors

John W. Coakley is Feakes Professor of Church History at New Brunswick Theological Seminary in New Brunswick, New Jersey, and author of *Women, Men and Spiritual Power: Female Saints and Their Male Collaborators* (New York: Columbia University Press, 2006). E-mail: jcoakley@nbts.edu

Firth Haring Fabend is an independent historian. Her most recent book-length work is *Zion on the Hudson: Dutch New York and New Jersey in the Age of Revivals* (New Brunswick, NJ: Rutgers University Press, 2000). E-mail: fhfabend@verizon.net

Willem Frijhoff is Professor of Early Modern History Emeritus at the Vrije Universiteit in Amsterdam, the Netherlands, and author of *Fulfilling God's Mission: The Two Worlds of Dominie Everardus Bogardus (1607-1647.)* (Leiden & Boston: Brill, 2007). E-mail: willem.frijhoff@gmail.com

Joyce D. Goodfriend is Professor of History at the University of Denver in Denver, Colorado, and author of "Practicing Toleration in Dutch New Netherland" in Chris Beneke and Christopher S. Grenda, eds., *The First Prejudice: Religious Tolerance and Intolerance in Early America* (Philadelphia, PA: University of Pennsylvania Press, 2011). E-mail: jgoodfri@du.edu

Evan Haefeli is Associate Professor of History at Columbia University and author of "A Scandalous Minister in a Divided Community: Ulster County in Leisler's Rebellion, 1689-1691," *New York History* 88:4 (Fall 2007): 357-389. E-mail: eh2204@columbia.edu

Jaap Jacobs is the Erasmus Lecturer in the History and Civilization of the Netherlands and Flanders at Harvard University and author of *The Colony of New Netherland: A Dutch Settlement in Seventeenth-Century America* (Ithaca, NY: Cornell University Press, 2009). E-mail: Jacobs640@zonnet.nl

Earl Wm. Kennedy is Senior Research Fellow at the A.C. Van Raalte Institute at Hope College, Holland, Michigan, and editor of the *Minutes of the Classis of Holland of the Reformed Church in America, 1848-1876* (forthcoming). E-mail: kennedye@hope.edu

Hans Krabbendam is Assistant Director of the Roosevelt Study Center in Middelburg, the Netherlands and author of *Freedom on the Horizon: Dutch Immigration to America 1840-1940* (Grand Rapids, MI: Eerdmans, 2009). E-mail: jl.krabbendam@zeeland.nl

Dirk Mouw is a Fellow of the Reformed Church Center in New Brunswick, New Jersey. He received the 2010 Hendricks Manuscript Award from the New Netherland Institute (Albany, NY) for his dissertation, "*Moederkerk* and *Vaderland*: Religion and Ethnic Identity in the Middle Colonies, 1690-1772." E-mail: dirk.mouw@earthlink.net

Robert Naborn is Director of the Dutch Studies Program at the University of Pennsylvania in Philadelphia. In 2011 he defended his doctoral dissertation at the Vrije Universiteit in Amsterdam, the Netherlands, *Eilardus Westerlo (1738-1790): From Colonial Dominee to American Pastor*. E-mail: rob.naborn@gmail.com

Leon van den Broeke is Assistant Professor Religion, Law & Society/Church Polity and Chair of the Centre for Religion and Law at the Vrije Uiversiteit in Amsterdam, the Netherlands, and author of *Een geschiedenis van de classis: classicale typen tussen idee en werkelijkheid (1571-2004)* (Kampen: Kok, 2005). E-mail: **clvandenbroeke@hotmail.com**

Jos van der Linde is Director of Administration at the New England Conservatory of Music in Boston. In 2007-08 he reviewed the transcription and translation that Francis Sypher was making of Henricus Selijns's *Liber A, 1628-1700* (Grand Rapids, MI: Eerdmans, 2009). E-mail: **josvdl@verizon.net**

Illustrations

Map 1: Present-day Netherlands with the location of the places mentioned in this collection	xii
Montanus's view of New Amsterdam, c. 1650	2
Map 2: New Amsterdam/New York City and surrounding area	33
Map 3: New Netherland	34
Fragment of Bastiaen Krol's *Troost der vromen*	38
Albert Eekhof	60
Reverend Everardus Bogardus	80
Old Stone Church in Albany c. 1715	104
Henricus Selijns's house and surrounding streets	120
Signature of Petrus Tesschenmaecker	148
Artist's rendition of Schenectady	163
Rudolphus van Varick Tombstone	174
Rudolphus van Varick handwriting	174
Guiliam Bertholf's signature	198
Map of the mouth of the Mississippi River and the Gulf Coast	218
Archibald Laidlie	240
Gerrit Lydekker, c. 1775	260
Pulpit in the Albany Dutch Reformed Church, c. 1657	276
John Henry Livingston	296
Cornelius van der Meulen	316
Map 4: Nineteenth-century Dutch settlements in the American Midwest	323

Map 1: Present-day Netherlands with the location of the places mentioned in this collection.

PREFACE

Leon van den Broeke
Hans Krabbendam
Dirk Mouw

On the surface this collection of essays on the lives of Dutch-American clergy might seem to be an outmoded type of denominational history celebrating dead white males and singing the praises of bilateral virtues. This is by no means the intent of the planners. Granted, it fits the category of ethnic denominationalism, which is a significant phase in the revived field of denominational history.[1] The hope, however, is that these fourteen short biographies foster cohesion in the narrative of an institution that moved from the center to the margin in the course of two centuries, a history that is still relevant today.

The idea to collect these biographies arose when Leon van den Broeke explored the colonial holdings of the Reformed Church Archives at the Sage Library at New Brunswick Theological Seminary in New Brunswick, New Jersey, as the Albert A. Smith Visiting Research Fellow of the Reformed Church Center on that campus. His main focus was the relationship of the Classis of Amsterdam and the congregations in the Middle Colonies. Research in the minutes and letters of consistories,

---

[1] Russell E. Richey, "Denominationalism," in Philip Goff, ed., *Blackwell Companion to Religion in America* (Chichester: Blackwell Publishing, 2010), 90-104.

classes, and ministers suggested that there must be a method to the ministry of Dutch Reformed clergy in the New World. This observation led to the idea of collecting a series of biographies of clergy who served in the (Dutch) Reformed churches in North America. Since Dirk Mouw had just completed his comprehensive survey of Dutch American clergy in the eighteenth century and Hans Krabbendam had helped map out the contours of the Dutch presence in North America on the occasion of the commemoration of the quadricentennial of Dutch-American relations in 2009, the combination of these three areas of expertise offered an ideal occasion to assess the forces that had shaped one of the enduring institutions created by the Dutch-American relationship: the Reformed Church in America.[2] This collection crosses both borders by putting flesh and bones on the patterns of this relationship.

The plan was embraced by the Reformed Church Center with the encouragement of minister and scholar, the Reverend Allan Janssen and Reformed Church archivist Russell Gasero. This series would document the latest research on the religious relationship between the Low Countries and North America and would enhance the current interest in Dutch-American relations.

A number of very able scholars paved the way for this collection. American church historian Gerald F. De Jong wrote a valuable and complete colonial history of the Reformed Church in 1975. James Tanis concentrated on theological development; Randall Balmer and Dirk Mouw wrote about clerical recruitment and social relationships in the eighteenth century; and Firth Fabend concentrated on the nineteenth century. From the Dutch side of the Atlantic, Jaap Jacobs researched the ministers of the Dutch period until 1664, and Albert Eekhof and Willem Frijhoff followed the whereabouts of Dutch clergy in the early history of Dutch New Amsterdam. A new body of literature on the ethnic minister in the nineteenth and early twentieth centuries repeated those themes in the next phase. The rich material remained separated by time periods and geographical boundaries.[3]

---

[2] Fred van Lieburg's chapter on the Dutch and their religion in Hans Krabbendam, Cornelis A. van Minnen and Giles Scott-Smith, eds., *Four Centuries of Dutch-American Relations, 1609-2009* (Amsterdam/New York: Boom/State University of New York Press, 2009), 154-65.

[3] Gerald F. De Jong, *The Dutch in America, 1609-1974* (Boston: Twayne Publishers, 1975); James Tanis, *Dutch Calvinistic Pietism in the Middle Colonies: A Study in the Life and Theology of Theodorus Jacobus Frelinghuysen* (The Hague: Martinus Nijhoff, 1967); Randall H. Balmer, *A Perfect Babel of Confusion: Dutch Religion and English Culture in the Middle Colonies*, (New York: Oxford University Press, 1989); Dirk Mouw,"*Moederkerk* and *Vaderland*: Religion and Ethnic Identity in the Middle Colonies, 1690-1772" (Ph.D., University of Iowa, 2009; revised July 2011); Jaap Jacobs, *New Netherland:*

Far from repeating familiar stories, this collection seeks to reexamine some of the movers and shakers in this historical arena and to deepen our knowledge of the period. Through the selection of fourteen ministers covering two hundred fifty years, the essays shed light on the high and low tides, the promises and disappointments, and the factors within and beyond the control of a new society in the making.

The subjects selected for the biographies were chosen to be spread evenly over time, from periods of both ease and difficulty. Each of these individuals had one foot in the Netherlands and the other in the New World. They came from a variety of backgrounds and diverse life trajectories, with an array of theological preferences. They had prepared for their roles in different ways and then faced a myriad of new situations in North America. The selection process resulted in portraits of a few comparatively well-known clerics such as Dominies Everardus Bogardus and John Henry Livingston, as well as many more of lesser fame, such as Dominies Gideon Schaats and Laurentius van den Bosch. The lesser-knowns were nevertheless influential in their own spheres and/or changed the course and development of churches in important ways. Some belonged to the elite, others rose to that status, and still others slipped down the social ladder. The period covered here begins with Dominie Bastiaen Krol, arguably the leader of the first official Dutch worship services in seventeenth-century North America, and ends with Dominie Cornelius van der Meulen, a representative of the new wave of organized immigration comprised of people with high religious expectations.

By returning to original sources on both sides of the Atlantic, researchers have uncovered a rich and surprising history. This volume humanizes and contextualizes the lives of fourteen men who served not only as religious leaders and cultural mediators in colonial communities, but also as important connective tissue in the Dutch Atlantic world.

All the contributors were requested to explore the ways in which the lives and careers of the protagonists illuminate important aspects of European or colonial life and society of their times. They were asked

---

A Dutch colony in Seventeenth-Century America (Boston: Brill, 2005); Albert Eekhof, *De Hervormde Kerk in Noord-Amerika, 1624-1664*, 2 vols. (The Hague: Nijhoff, 1913); Willem Frijhoff, *Fulfilling God's Mission: The Two Worlds of Dominie Everardus Bogardus, 1607-1647* (Leiden: Brill, 2007); Victor Greene, *American Immigrant Leaders, 1800-1910: Marginality and Identity* (Baltimore: Johns Hopkins University Press, 1987); Hartmut Lehmann, ed., *Migration und Religion im Zeitalter der Globalisierung* (Göttingen: Wallstein Verlag, 2005); Richard Alba, Albert J. Raboteau, and Josh DeWind, eds., *Immigration and Religion in America: Comparative and Historical Perspectives* (New York: NYU Press, 2008).

to consider a number of facets of the lives of the subjects both before and during their North American service, as far as their sources allowed.

First, researchers considered the process by which the subjects were selected for North American pulpits and the reasons behind their decisions to serve in the New World. How did they learn about vacancies in America? What were their hopes and expectations? How and by whom were they selected? What role did familial connections play in their decisions to return or to prolong their tenures after they reached their destinations?

Second, these scholars examined the backgrounds of the ministers and considered whether their experiences and training in the Old World had prepared them for their colonial roles. This included theological education, of course, but also included linguistic and other skills as well.

Third, authors were asked to delve into the character and mindsets of their subjects, considering the roles played by such factors as personality traits, their positions on the spectrum of Calvinist theology, and their responses to tense or difficult times during their New World tenures.

Fourth, the biographers attempted to evaluate the subjects' relationships with Europeans and non-Europeans in both the Old World and the New, considering the extent to which such interactions influenced decisions to remain in North America for an extended term or to return to the Netherlands.

Likewise, the biographers looked for clues regarding the role the ministers saw for themselves in a culturally diverse environment, seeking the subjects' views about the proper responsibilities and functions of the church, the state, and/or the company.

Finally, researchers attempted to take a broad view and shed some light on the degree to which the ministers succeeded in achieving their personal and professional ends as well as on their legacies in the Netherlands and/or North America.

Dirk Mouw's introductory essay provides the necessary context regarding the work of these ministers in North America and offers answers to these questions based on the scholars' findings—but without divulging all of the treasures hidden in these essays. Much more could be derived from the original and insightful research reflected in these biographies. The essays are arranged in chronological order and are subdivided into five categories. These labels should not be taken as definitions of the ministers' characters, since the subtitles of each biography do that job. The categories characterize the phase of church and society and then place the ministers in this context. Most played multiple roles, of course, and would fit under other flags as well, but in general this was the situation in which they operated:

Bastiaen Krol, Jonas Michaëlius, and Everardus Bogardus represent the pioneers, the church planters in the early seventeenth century. The next group of ministers—Gideon Schaats, Henricus Selijns, and Petrus Tesschenmaecker—contributed to stabilizing the church in the late seventeenth century. During the same time period the lives and ministries of Rudolphus van Varick, Guiliam Bertholf, and Laurentius van den Bosch revealed the diversity among the clergy. Archibald Laidlie, Gerrit Lydekker, and Eilardus Westerlo acted as mediators between the Dutch and other groups in the eighteenth century, a time of major transitions. The final section addresses the legacy of the colonial Dutch Reformed for the denomination and the new immigration in the nineteenth century through the lives of John Henry Livingston and Cornelius ver Meulen.

The most obvious contributions of this volume are new insights and correctives offered about men who have figured prominently in local, regional, congregational, and denominational histories as well as in more general works on the history of religion in America. Collectively, these essays also offer a variety of perspectives that will enrich other fields of research and will provide opportunities for conversation among professional and avocational historians who are too often isolated from each other by geography or the narrow foci of their research and interests.[4]

In addition to the fact that most of these essays draw on sources and historical literature in two or more languages, they also bring together questions posed by a wide variety of scholars. These include community, institutional, church, and congregational historians; those interested in religious, cultural, associational, ethnic, and political developments and conflicts in early American history; scholars with interests in various strains of Reformed theology; and others whose research focuses on the character and professionalization of lay and ordained worship leaders in the early modern era in both the Netherlands and North America.

This volume should also be of interest to scholars in the growing area of "Atlantic" or "transatlantic" studies. This is a field which, in its weakest form, explores the connections between the people of Old

---

[4] Randall J. Stephens, ed., *Recent Themes in American Religious History: Historians in Conversation* (Columbia: University of South Carolina Press, 2009).

and New England. Even in its more robust manifestations it seldom extends the "Atlantic" much farther than the British colonies south of New England and, on occasion, to the nations of the Iberian Peninsula and their New World colonies. A related group of scholars interested in transnational history will find much interesting and challenging material in these essays as regards the transcending or perpetuating role of religion in the construction of national narratives.[5]

A final word about institutional support. This project was blessed with strong support from a number of backers. The assistance of the Van Raalte Institute at Hope College in Holland, Michigan, and the Reformed Church Center and First Reformed Church, both of New Brunswick, New Jersey; and funding from the Collegiate Church in New York City and the Roosevelt Study Center in Middelburg, the Netherlands, enabled a group of experts from Europe and North America to meet and explore these pastors' lives and subsequently underwrote the publication of this book.

---

[5] For the importance of the early history for later perspectives, see Charles Hirschman, "The Role of Religion in the Origins and Adaptations of Immigrant Groups in the United States," in Alejandro Portes and Josh DeWind, eds., *Rethinking Migration: New Theoretical and Empirical Perspectives* (New York: Berghahn, 2007), 391-418. James C. Kennedy, "Religion, Nation, and European Representations of the Past," in Stefan Berger and Chris Lorenz, eds., *The Contested Nation: Ethnicity, Class, Religion and Gender in National Histories*. Writing the Nation Series (New York: Palgrave Macmillan, 2008), 104-34.

INTRODUCTION

Dutch Clergy in Colonial North America

Dirk Mouw

A Snapshot from Rural New Jersey

In the late 1730s the Reverend Theodorus Jacobus Frelinghuysen Sr. (1692- c. 1747) was intermittently ill and unable to perform all his duties without help. The consistories[1] of his four Dutch Reformed congregations in the Raritan valley (New Jersey) united in an urgent appeal for help to two men in the Netherlands: Gerardus van Schuijlenburg, a minister in Tienhoven, and Jan Stockers, probably a merchant in Amsterdam. The consistories authorized the men to form a committee, choosing one or two members of the Classis of Amsterdam to join them. The colonists empowered the committee so formed to select a colleague for their ailing dominie and issue a call[2] on behalf of their consistories. Their description of what would be expected of

---

I am grateful to co-editors Leon van den Broeke and Hans Krabbendam for their thoughtful input.

[1] A consistory is the ruling body of a Dutch Reformed congregation, consisting of the minister(s), elders, and, in some cases, the deacons.
[2] "Calling" a minister is Dutch Reformed terminology for recruiting or hiring a pastor.

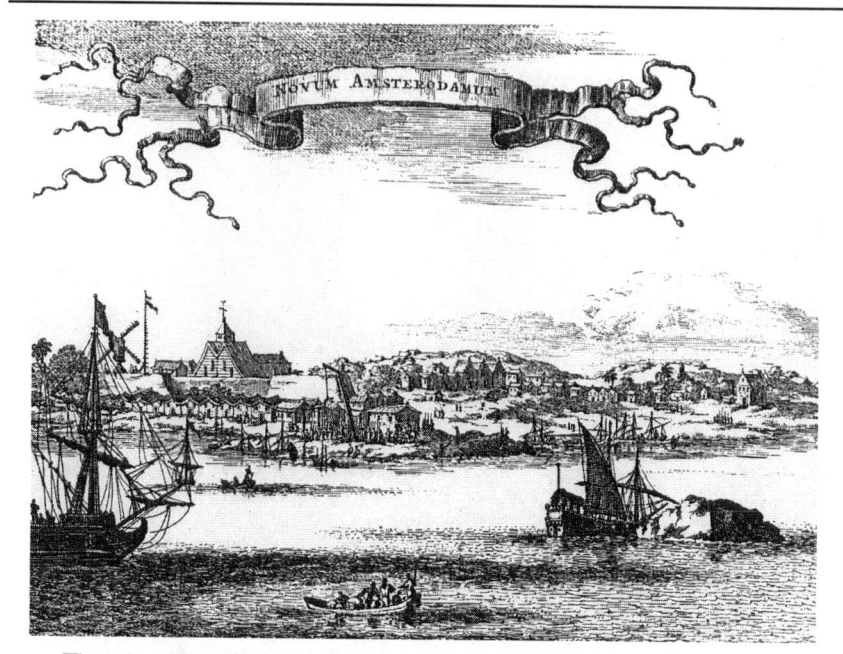

The so-called Montanus view of New Amsterdam, about 1650, showing the Dutch Reformed Church in the fort, built in 1642.

[Reproduced after I.N. Phelps Stokes, The Iconography of Manhattan Island 1498-1909, vol. I (New York, 1915), plate 6]

the man to be called on their behalf underscores the importance and manifold functions of a minister in their communities. He was

> to preach the Holy Gospel with power, so that our flock may be fed with pure fodder, to administer the Holy Seals of the Covenant faithfully after the manner in which they were established by Christ and the practice of the Apostles, to catechize the youth, to exercise discipline carefully with the Consistory, to visit the sick, and in a trustworthy manner to undertake all the duties of the Office of Minister, [and] to do the work of an Evangelist...

The consistories had consulted with Frelinghuysen, and their letter reports his endorsement of the call. Using a familiar biblical passage that Puritans had put in the mouth of an American Indian on the Great Seal of the Massachusetts Bay Colony more than a century earlier, Frelinghuysen had said "longingly" and "yearningly" to the as yet unknown man who would be chosen to be his colleague by Van Schuijlenburg and Stockers, "Brother, come over... and help us."[3]

---

[3] Consistories of Raritan, Six Mile Run, Three Mile Run, and North Branch to

Introducing a volume of biographical essays about Dutch Reformed ministers in North America with this story of the actions of a particular group of consistories—a story in which a minister plays only a minor role—may, on the surface, seem odd; particularly so when one considers that neither the minister nor the consistories figure at all prominently in the essays that follow. Indeed, some readers will know that the oft-told story of Frelinghuysen and his Raritan valley congregations was itself in many ways unusual.

The foregoing story nonetheless offers an instructive backdrop to this collection of biographies in a number of respects. Most notably, it points to a common occurrence in colonial North America: colonial congregations routinely finding themselves in need of a minister from the Netherlands. The manner in which the Raritan colonists went about trying to meet that need was commonly employed as well. Like many Dutch colonists before and after them, they worked through an ecclesiastical "mail-order" system. By the 1730s this system had become quite sophisticated. Colonists deployed networks of friends (or friends of friends), family, trusted merchants, and ministers or professors who, because of their reputations or the posts they occupied, seemed to the colonists to be well suited to choose a minister for them. Thus, the Raritan consistories took care to word and direct their letter carefully. Writing of their need for "pure fodder," emphasizing church discipline, and employing numerous tell-tale biblical allusions and turns of phrase, they made sure that the readers of that letter would understand that they wanted a minister of a particular theological style: a Dutch Reformed pietist. To make it absolutely certain that Frelinghuysen's "brother, co-worker, and fellow combatant [*mede-Broeder, mede-Arbeider, en mede-Strijder*]" would indeed have the theological style they felt their communities needed, they addressed their letter to Van Schuijlenburg, a minister who embraced a particularly robust strain of Dutch pietism.

The story of the efforts of the congregations of the Raritan valley to procure a minister is an instructive introduction to this collection of biographies in a number of other ways as well. Securing a minister was as serious a matter as it was costly. If the effort resulted in the arrival of a minister who was able and well matched to his flock, many people would reap the benefits; if not, the consequences could be disastrous

---

the Classis of Amsterdam, n.d., c. 1738. Manuscript copy in Minute Book of the Readington Reformed Church, Archives of the Reformed Church in America, New Brunswick, New Jersey. For his health during the 1730s, see Peter Hood Ballantine Frelinghuysen, *Theodorus Jacobus Frelinghuysen* (Princeton, NJ: privately printed, 1938), 51-52. The biblical quotation is from Acts 16:9.

for congregations. And whether harmonious or not, the relationship between shepherd and flock was likely to be long-lasting. Thus, we see in the words and deeds of Raritan valley colonists not only the importance placed upon recruiting capable ministers, but we can also discern some questions they were asking of themselves and of each other. These questions echo recurring themes in the biographies that follow: What qualities would a minister need in order to serve effectively in their congregations? By what means were they most likely to succeed in attracting such a man to their communities? Many of the colonists also undoubtedly wondered what sort of a man would answer their call, willingly exchanging the relative comforts of life in the Dutch Republic for a pulpit in a distant colonial outpost; and what might his motives be for doing so? The case studies in this volume seek to answer similar questions from a historical perspective.

Of course, no single church, nor any individual minister can be taken as perfectly emblematic of Dutch congregations or clergy in the colonies. The first Dutch minister arrived in North America and organized the first congregation in 1628. By the beginning of the American Revolution there were nearly one hundred organized Dutch Reformed congregations in North America, served by about three dozen ministers.[4] The fourteen biographies that follow, however, serve as useful case studies. Individually they shed light on the lives of specific figures and on communities in which they lived and worked. Collectively, these case studies also offer a fresh perspective on the history of the Dutch in colonial America and a host of related fields.

A capable minister, whose gifts and manner were well matched to the laity he served, was important for a myriad of reasons. As readers will see in Jaap Jacobs's biography of Jonas Michaëlius, it was left to the minister (as there were no broader ecclesiastical assemblies in the colonies) to choose elders when he arrived in a community where no consistory had yet been organized. Thereafter, the minister, together with the other members of the consistory,[5] would decide who was fit to receive communion and be received into church membership; the minister and elders would also exercise church discipline over that membership. It was the minister who would marry them and bury them, baptize (or, occasionally, refuse to baptize), and later catechize

---

[4] For the numbers of ministers and congregations, see Dirk Mouw, "*Moederkerk* and *Vaderland*: Religion and Ethnic Identity in the Middle Colonies, 1690-1772" (Ph.D., University of Iowa, 2009; revised April 2011), 62-85, 623-37.

[5] Consistories were, not incidentally, self-perpetuating bodies, each electing the replacements of members whose terms ended.

their children, and to whose long sermons all would listen each week. The minister served other functions in these communities as well: as occasional arbiter, political commentator and chief champion of morality. The fear was often expressed that without such leadership, communities might "grow wild" or the lack thereof bring about the "desolation of the country." Indeed, readers will find in Evan Haefeli's research that the presence of a minister ill-suited to religious or moral leadership could be disastrous for a colonial community, while, as seen in Joyce Goodfriend's study, a particularly good match could augment the strength and vitality of a congregation considerably.[6]

Moreover, for Dutch Reformed congregants between the English conquest of 1664 and the immigration waves of the nineteenth century, ministers were more than emissaries of the gospel. If, as one historian has suggested, the Reformed minister in the Netherlands was a "cultural mediator, someone who passed the norms, values, morals, habits, and above all the knowledge of the 'elite' on to common people," then the Dutch clergy of the New World served double duty as cultural mediators.[7] Ministers were increasingly representatives of a fatherland most colonists had never seen and were envoys from a mother church whose outposts in their communities were not only important religious institutions, but were vital ethnic and cultural bastions as well. One could even argue that Dutch Reformed leaders and institutions in North America were not only important for sustaining and replicating Dutch culture, language and ethnic identity; in many communities they also served as a force for *batavianization*—the process by which newcomers from France, Germany, or the British Isles, as well as the progeny of the "perfect Babel" of New Netherland, came to think of themselves as Dutch or Dutch-American.

The effort of the consistories of the Raritan valley in the 1730s to procure a minister serves as an instructive context for these essays in one final respect: no one answered the call. In this, the experience of the

[6] Article 16 of the Church Order of Dordrecht stipulated that the initial selection of consistory members was to be done only with the advice of the appropriate classis. With no proximate classis, however, the selection in the colonies routinely fell to the clergy. Quotes are from Vice-Director Alrichs to the Commissioners of the Colony on the Delaware River, December 12, 1659, in E. B. O'Callaghan, et al, eds., *Documents Relative to the Colonial History of the State of New York*, 15 vols. (Albany: Weed, Parsons and Co., 1856-1887), 2:114. See also Albany consistory, acts, February 5 and May 23, 1699, in E. T. Corwin (trans. and ed.), *Ecclesiastical Records of the State of New York*, 7 vols. (Albany: Lyon, 1901-1916), 2:1307 (hereafter cited as *ERNY*).

[7] Quote is from Fred A. van Lieburg, "Profeten en hun Vaderland: De Geografische Herkomst van de Gereformeerde predikanten in Nederland van 1572 tot 1816" (PhD diss., Vrije Universiteit te Amsterdam, 1995), 103. My translation.

Raritan congregations was hardly unusual. Though it is impossible to establish precisely the degree of the shortage of clergy in the Mid-Atlantic colonies, the fact that there *was* a shortage of Dutch Reformed clergy in colonial North America is indisputable. While recent scholarship points to a sustained surplus of candidates for the Reformed ministry in the Netherlands until the final quarter of the eighteenth century, this surplus did not extend to North America.[8] The biographies here of Guiliam Bertholf, Petrus Tesschenmaecker, and Laurentius van den Bosch are testimony to this fact: even men with murky pasts, incomplete educations, Anglican ordinations—or no ordination at all—could find congregations eager to call them.

The Route to a New World Pulpit

Among the matters on which these case studies shed light are the varied means by which Dutch Reformed ministers were recruited for North America and the changing roles of various institutions in that process. In the earliest years the important decisions were made by company officials and the consistory (and later the classis) in Amsterdam. The ministers they sent were company employees. Indeed, in the correspondence between New World and Old World colonial officials, clergy seem to have been considered by officials to be basic infrastructure. (Among the "necessaries" one such official requested were materials for building a "storehouse; also suitable boats and a minister, all of which are the greatest necessity.")[9]

The career of Gideon Schaats, whose story is told by Firth Fabend, exemplifies important changes in the way ministers were called to North America during the New Netherland period—including changes in the relationships of colonial congregations to Old World church assemblies, changes in the relationships of congregations to the ministers who served them, and changes in the relationships of clergy and churches to secular authorities. By the time of Schaats's first call to Rensselaerswijck in the early 1650s, ecclesiastical supervision and administration of the North American congregations had shifted from the Amsterdam consistory to the classis, a regional assembly composed of delegations

---

[8] On the surplus of men qualified for the ministry in the Dutch Republic, see Lieburg, "Profeten", 78-83, 268; Peter T. van Rooden, *Religieuze regimes: Over godsdienst en maatschappij in Nederland, 1570-1990* (Amsterdam: Bert Bakker, 1996), 51-68.

[9] Vice-Director Alrichs to the Burgomasters of Amsterdam, May 7, 1657, in O'Callaghan, et al, eds., *Colonial Documents*, 2:9. At the time, the Dutch colony on the Delaware was under the direction of Amsterdam rather than of the West India Company.

of ministers and elders from congregations in and around the city. The classis, in turn, had entrusted some of its duties to a subcommittee, a few ministers serving in rotation. The Deputies for Indies' (or Foreign, or Maritime) Affairs, as they were known, maintained correspondence with churches in colonial and commercial outposts, attended to minor matters of church administration, and produced summaries of the voluminous correspondence for the classis. The deputies nevertheless referred weighty matters, such as the approval of Schaats's contract with the patroon of Rensselaerswijck, to the full classis.

In 1657, when the term of Schaats's second contract with the patroon came to an end, he accepted a call to the nearby town of Beverwijck. A sanctuary had been constructed there, provision had been made for a parsonage, and the congregation had agreed to share responsibility for his salary with the patroon. In this we see two important developments. First, there was little or no involvement by the classis. Second, Schaats had accepted a call that was far more similar to calls received by ministers to congregations in the fatherland than had been his contract with the patroon. The influence of patroon and company in local ecclesiastical matters diminished (as did their share in the financial support of churches) over the last decade and a half of Dutch rule, while the role of the colonial consistory grew.[10]

After the English conquest of 1664 the new political landscape presented colonial congregations and consistories with new opportunities to assert more control over the selection process, thus bringing it more closely into line with church order and practice in the fatherland. This change is discernable in the biography of Henricus Selijns. It had been the Classis of Amsterdam and the Dutch West India Company that had selected and approved him for a four-year term on Long Island in 1660 (after which he returned to the fatherland), but when he agreed in 1682 to return to North America, it was in response to a request from the consistory of New York City. Though that consistory worked with the classis as it attempted to recruit him, it was the colonial consistory, not the classis, that had selected him. Indeed, in the biographies of Van den Bosch and Tesschenmaecker, one finds colonial consistories exerting even greater influence over the selection process: the churches of Kingston and New Castle (on the Delaware) issued calls to those men unhindered by commercial or secular authorities and

---

[10] The patroon guaranteed half of Schaats's salary, though it was understood that most of this would be paid by the congregation. See Dutch West India Company Directors to Petrus Stuyvesant, May 20, 1658, in *ERNY* 1:424.

with little more than a post-facto acquiescence or confirmation by the Classis of Amsterdam.[11]

Until at least 1772 the Classis of Amsterdam and its deputies assumed responsibility for the supervision of and care for the North American congregations, but its monopoly in this regard was never entirely secure. It is important to note that not all ecclesiastical bodies in the fatherland fully acquiesced in this matter—most notably the Classis of Walcheren in the province of Zeeland. As we see in the biography of Guiliam Bertholf, that classis, arguably the second most important in the Netherlands, was willing in 1693 to challenge Amsterdam's ecclesiastical hegemony and ordain Bertholf for service in North America.[12] Amsterdam's assertions were also challenged in North America on a number of occasions. Not the least of these is the striking example in the biography of Eilardus Westerlo. The consistory of Albany, though it had no particular candidate in mind, decided to exclude the Classis of Amsterdam from the calling process entirely instead authorizing faculty at the University of Groningen to select and ordain a minister for them.[13] The so-called Coetus-Conferentie[14] dispute, which arose in the second half of the eighteenth century over Amsterdam's role in the affairs of the North American congregations, underscores the fact that after the departure of the Dutch West India Company from the scene the association of the congregations of North America with Amsterdam was largely voluntary.

The High Cost of a Call

The cases of both Westerlo and Van den Bosch shed light on a chief cause for the chronic shortage of ministers in the North American colonies. An eighteenth-century colonial minister succinctly described the reservations many colonists had about calling ministers from the

---

[11] Article 5 of the Church Order of Dordrecht required the advice or consent of the classis for calls of this sort.

[12] For more on the relationship between the Classes of Walcheren and Amsterdam, see Frans Leonard Schalkwijk, *The Reformed Church in Dutch Brazil (1630-1654)* (Zoetermeer: Boekencentrum, 1998), 95-96; Peter Blom, "'Een predicant isser hoochnodich': Bronnen in het Zeeuws Archief voor de kerkelijke geschiedenis van West-Indië," *Transparant: Tijdschrift van de Vereniging van Christen-Historici* 17 (April 2006): 14-18; Cornelis van den Broeke, *Een geschiedenis van de classis: classicale typen tussen idee en werkelijkheid (1571-2004)*, *Theologie en geschiedenis* (Kampen: Kok, 2005), 88, 90.

[13] In his dissertation, Rob Naborn sheds yet more light on the process through which Westerlo was called to Albany than appears in his essay in this volume.

[14] Pronounced SEE-tuss and Kon-fer-EN-tsee.

Old World: "It costs too much to get [ministers] from Holland, and even then, we do not know what we are going to get." Almost a century earlier, Henricus Selijns had written to a colleague about representatives of a congregation who had come to him seeking counsel. They wanted a minister and evidently had secured the necessary commitments to pay the salary; perhaps they had even raised money for transportation. When, however, Selijns told them that for "the Rev. Classis to examine him as to his knowledge; ... it would cost one hundred and fifty florins, Holland currency, they looked at each other without saying anything." Quite apart from the barrier presented by the need to raise funds for a salary, congregations had to lay out considerable funds in hard currency to get a minister to their pulpits in the first place. In the case of Westerlo, this amounted to the remarkable sum of nearly ƒ900 or £165 (New York currency). This was undoubtedly far more than the annual salary pledged by the congregation. Westerlo's call was hardly the norm, but in the well-documented 1730 call of Cornelis van Schie to two mid-Hudson valley congregations, the nearly £77 (New York currency) in procurement costs exceeded the promised annual salary by more than one tenth. Classical and recruiting-related expenses accounted for 16 percent of the total; travel, lodging, and expenses for travel within and between the Netherlands and England, 35 percent; the transatlantic voyage, 45 percent; and travel within New York, 3 percent. In this light, the fact that congregations like Kingston embraced ministers like Van den Bosch is quite understandable; though his credentials and reputation were imperfect, he was already in their midst and available for call without potentially prohibitive procurement costs. The willingness of a large congregation like Albany to invest tremendous sums to procure a minister from the Netherlands is evidence of their eagerness to have a minister in their pulpit who was well matched to their congregation; Kingston's call to Van den Bosch demonstrates that smaller congregations were also eager to call ministers—indeed, lacking the resources necessary to call one from the Netherlands, they were even willing to take a chance on a minister like Van den Bosch.[16]

Why Did Some Answer the Call?

More than one hundred men served as ministers in Dutch Reformed congregations in North America before the Revolution,

---

[15] Quotes are from Johannes Ritzema to Winoldus Budde, July 5, 1764, and Selijns to Gisbertus Oostrum, September 20, 1685 in *ERNY*, 6:3932, 2:907. The costs in New York currency for recruiting Westerlo are from promissory note, Albany

and this stream did not run dry after American independence.[16] It is impossible to resurrect from the surviving record all of the considerations which went into the decisions of these men to answer calls to colonial pulpits. One of the few avenues open to researchers in this regard is the case study, and the biographies here offer individual windows into factors involved in those personal decisions.

It is evident that few were easily induced to accept colonial pastorates. Writing in Rotterdam in the last quarter of the eighteenth century, the Reverend Petrus Hofstede (1716-1803) observed that the Dutch Reformed Church found it difficult to fill all of the pulpits in its commercial and colonial outposts around the world. Most Dutch ministers and theology students did not want to leave the fatherland. Hofstede explained that "An Icelander would rather drink a mug of fresh whale oil with his blood-relatives and those he knows well in his snowy homeland, than drink a frothy muscadel [wine] from a golden bowl in a strange land."[17]

The chief motive for leaving the fatherland was almost certainly the tight ecclesiastical labor market. As noted above, recent scholarship suggests that there was an almost continual oversupply of ministers in the Netherlands until the last quarter of the eighteenth century. Even those who did finally succeed in being called to a congregation in the Netherlands had generally spent years—often nearly a decade—"candidating," that is, accepting invitations to preach in various communities to earn a very modest income, hone skills, and exhibit their gifts to churches that were seeking ministers. For most of the ministers examined here, impatience and dissatisfaction with their prospects in the Netherlands were foremost among their motives for considering a colonial pulpit.

The essays in this volume, however, reveal other factors as well that likely made religious service outside the Low Countries attractive. For men like Krol, Bogardus, Schaats, and Bertholf, for instance, colonial pulpits offered the opportunity for gospel service to men unable or disinclined to complete the full course of formal education generally required for entrance to the Dutch Reformed ministry in the

---

Consistory, November 10, 1760, in *ERNY* 5:3800. The Van Schie figures are from A. P. Van Gieson, *Anniversary Discourse and History of the First Reformed Church of Poughkeepsie* (Poughkeepsie [NY]: First Reformed Church, 1893), 44. There is a clerical, mathematical, or typographical error of one pound.

[16] See pp. 14-18 below.

[17] Petrus Hofstede, *Oost-indische kerkzaken zoo oude als nieuwe: meest alle, uit oorspronkelijke en ongedrukte stukken by een versameld, in orde gebragt, en beredeneerd*, 2 vols. (Rotterdam: J. Bosch en R. Arrenberg, 1779-80), 2:69. My translation.

Old World. Over the decades after the Synod of Dordrecht (1618-19) this path was increasingly restricted, though it remained more common for those seeking pulpits outside the fatherland.[18] Indeed, for Bogardus and Bertholf, service in the capacity of an unordained worship leader and teacher in a distant outpost, served as both on-the-job training and a time for independent studies that were accepted by Old World ecclesiastical assemblies as an adequate alternative to a university degree.

Willem Frijhoff's research on Bogardus suggests that some aspirants to the ministry may also have been drawn to foreign and colonial pulpits out of a desire for greater autonomy. A congregation far from the broader assemblies of the mother church may have appealed to people who were something like early modern Dutch religious equivalents of twenty-first-century small business owners. They were willing to trade the security and predictability of employment with a large corporation and to accept the risks and frequent privations of running a small business in order to be relatively free from accountability and direction. Though the sphere in which a colonial minister could wield influence would likely be small, it may have been more complete and intense, with less supervision and fewer competitors for authority—and the potential for a larger number of hearers—than the average pastorate in an Old World village.

Finally, these essays suggest that distant congregations were in general attractive to candidates who were adventurous, xenophilic, and/or had been quite mobile before their colonial service. Tesschenmaecker had traveled widely both on the continent and the British Isles and then to South America before his North American tenure. Before and after his time in Kingston, Van den Bosch roamed and wandered considerably—though perhaps as a result of his habit of quickly wearing out his welcome. There are, of course, more: Bogardus, Michaëlius, Schaats, Bertholf, Rudolphus van Varick, and Archibald Laidlie had all exhibited mobility—having relocated more than once in Europe and/or to African or Asian colonies prior to their arrivals in North America. The sheer proportion of the well-traveled among the ministers examined here strongly suggests that a history of mobility was, while perhaps not a

---

[18] For an introduction to controversies over the ordinations performed in Dutch colonies (particularly in Asia), which often involved men without degrees from universities in the fatherland, see Carel Wessel Theodorus van Boetzelaer van Dubbeldam, *De Gereformeerde Kerken in Nederland en de zending in Oost-Indië in de dagen der Oost-Indische Compagnie* (Dissertation, Rijks Universiteit Utrecht, 1906), 126-83.

reliable predictor, at least a characteristic commonly shared among colonial ministers. Indeed, it appears to be a pattern that persisted into the nineteenth century; Cornelis van der Meulen had served as a sort of circuit rider among scattered congregations in Zeeland before he embarked for North America.

These factors help us to understand why some aspirants to the Dutch Reformed ministry were attracted to maritime, colonial, and commercial posts. They do not, however, offer insight into the question of why any particular individual ended up as a minister in service to the Dutch West India Company or to one or another Reformed congregation in New Netherland or British North America rather than in any of the other numerous Dutch Reformed posts around the world. The evidence presented in this volume suggests that there were several factors involved—at least after the English conquest.

Before 1664 New Netherland was like other Dutch colonies: decisions regarding the staffing of its pulpits were made by ecclesiastical and company officers in the Dutch Republic, and ministers were chosen from among those who were qualified and willing so to serve. Typically, willing candidates presented their credentials to the Classis of Amsterdam, requesting to be received as "recommended" for service in a colonial, commercial, or maritime post. When company officials announced an opening, the classis (sometimes with input from the company) chose from among the "recommended" candidates the person it deemed the most qualified and presented that candidate to company officials for approbation. A candidate could, of course, decline one post and hope that another more to his liking would come along later, though few did.

In fact, accepting a Dutch colonial pulpit was more of a commitment to a corporate entity than to a particular colonial community. Company officials could relocate ministers as they saw fit, a right they exercised regularly.[19] Thus, to the extent to which aspirants to the colonial ministry did register their geographic preferences, they expressed little more than their inclination toward a particular region of the globe and/or a particular company. Though these two matters were closely related, the reputations of the Dutch companies were undoubtedly taken into account by some who considered colonial service. The Dutch West India Company was notoriously delinquent in making payroll; it also had the reputation of being more staunchly

---

[19] Michaëlius, for instance, was transferred a number of times by the company—eventually to New Netherland, as we see in the biography by Jacobs in this volume.

Reformed than the East India Company.[20] It is not surprising, in this light, that the West India Company's New Netherland colony was supplied with Calvinists like Krol, who were willing and perhaps eager to engage Roman Catholics (and sympathizers) on various evangelistic, rhetorical, military, economic, and territorial fronts. While it is thus unlikely that many ministers served in New Netherland because it was their destination of choice, New Netherland was among the Dutch colonies more likely to attract people for whom a theological agenda was an important factor and the prospect of a promptly paid salary less so.

With the English conquest, however, company authority evaporated, and through the course of the following century the influence of the Classis of Amsterdam ebbed (though the decline was neither precipitous nor steady). For a ministerial candidate this meant that a decision to serve in North America became much less of a matter of accepting or declining a pulpit for which he had been chosen by commercial and ecclesiastical committees, and more a matter of evaluating the prospects and terms of a call to a particular New World congregation. Put another way, after 1664 those who left the Old World to minister in the New World were increasingly *attracted* to North American congregations rather than *sent* to them. The clearest example of a minister who decided to serve a congregation in North America because he found that post appealing is that of Laidlie's call to the New York City congregation. Laidlie had probably left his homeland of Scotland to minister in Zeeland in 1759 because it had been the most attractive of the few doors open to him. The handsome salary offered him by the New York City congregation in 1763—which compared well even to that of a prestigious pulpit in Amsterdam—must have been a significant factor in his decision to accept a call even further afield than Zeeland. Similarly, Westerlo's salary in Albany must have been appealing to a theological student. Though it was much smaller than Laidlie's, it almost certainly exceeded that of a pastorate of a Dutch village, comparing favorably with that of mid-sized city in the fatherland.[21]

---

[20] See Frijhoff's description of the way in which the West India Company represented itself and of its reputation for meeting payroll in his biography of Krol in this volume. See also A.Th. Boone, "Zending en gereformeerd Piëtisme in Nederland: Een historisch overzicht," *Documentatieblad Nadere Reformatie* 14 (1990): 4.

[21] It was most often the larger and wealthier North American congregations that were able to attract clergy from the Netherlands because they were able to offer larger salaries. Salary comparisons are based on Old World figures from Jonathan Israel, *The Dutch Republic: Its Rise, Greatness, and Fall, 1477-1806*, (New York: Oxford University Press, 1995), 353; Rooden, *Regimes*, 61. Laidlie's salary is from "Call of

In these biographies we also find hints of some less tangible impetuses behind decisions to answer calls to congregations in British North America. Personal relationships, for example, were evidently sometimes a factor. Van Varick's decision to minister on Long Island seems to have been at least partly shaped by kinship connections. Bertholf's decision to leave his Zeeland home for New Jersey might well have been guided, at least in part, by the presence there of other Zeelanders as well as colonists who were Bertholf's theological kinfolk. And while the indecision Selijns exhibited as he wrestled with the question of whether to return to North America reflected a reluctance to leave his homeland for a second time, it also demonstrated an obvious concern and affection for the people of New York, many of whom were people he knew personally.

Geographic, Educational and Social Backgrounds

This discussion has thus far obscured the fact that two of the subjects of these biographies were not, in fact, from the Old World at all, and two others were Netherlanders by birth but did not arrive in the New World called or appointed to serve as worship leaders. The inclusion of such individuals in a volume about Dutch Reformed clergy in the New World is quite appropriate. Dutch-born Tesschenmaecker and American-born Gerrit Lydekker, whose biographies appear here, were among at least sixteen ministers ordained in the colonies by Dutch Reformed clergy, eight under the authority of (or with subsequent confirmation by) the Classis of Amsterdam, and eight against the wishes of the classis (during the contentious years of the Coetus-Conferentie schism). There were another eight American-born men who traveled to Amsterdam (and a ninth to Utrecht) for ordination. And as we see in the biography of Bertholf, there was even one Dutch-born colonist who traveled back to Walcheren for ordination.[22] Those whose stories

---

Rev. Archibald Laidlie," July 20, 1763, in *ERNY* 6:3879. Westerlo's salary was raised to £135 (New York currency) in 1768 (e-mail, Rob Naborn to author August 13, 2010) and was therefore probably about £125 (New York currency) in 1759. All conversions between New York currency and Dutch currency are based on the tables in John J. McCusker, *Money and Exchange in Europe and America, 1600-1775: A Handbook* (Chapel Hill: University of North Carolina Press for the Institute of Early American History and Culture, 1978), 52-55, 162-67. In guilders at the time, Laidlie's initial salary was worth about ƒ1700 and Westerlo's about ƒ800.

[22] In addition to Tesschenmaecker and Lydekker, those ordained in North America with the blessing of the classis include Johannes Schuyler in 1738; Johannes Casparus Fryenmoet in 1744; Johannes Henricus Goetschius, Johannes Leydt, and Benjamin van der Linde in 1748; Samuel ver Brijck in 1749; and David Marinus

are told here reflect some of the diversity that characterized the Dutch clergy of colonial North America.

Indeed, it is worth noting that the editors of this volume have not defined "colonial Dutch minister" in terms of places of ordination or education—nor even of birthplace or ancestry. To define "Dutch" ministers in those terms would require the exclusion of the biographies of ministers like Laidlie, Lydekker, and John Henry Livingston from this volume. More appropriate is to accept as "Dutch" ministers those who were called by colonial congregations who identified themselves as Dutch Reformed. By this criterion it is possible to identify ninety-nine Dutch Reformed ministers who served in North America between 1628 and 1776. Like the sample represented by these biographies, they were a diverse lot, but mostly Dutch-born. Of those for whom country of birth is known (or can be surmised), forty-eight were born in the Netherlands, twenty-seven were born in North America, seventeen were born in German or Swiss areas, and two hailed from the British Isles.[23]

---

in 1752. Both Goetschius and Fryenmoet were ordained twice after their first ordinations were judged unlawful. To this list one could arguably add Paulus van Vleck, who aligned himself with the Philadelphia Presbytery while serving nearby Dutch congregations after his ordination was declared unlawful by the Dutch; Johannes van Driessen, whose New England ordination was never officially confirmed in Amsterdam, though he served in Dutch Reformed congregations for more than two decades; and Jonathan Du Bois, who was ordained by the Pennsylvania (German Reformed) Coetus in 1752 and served without challenge in Dutch Reformed congregations. Those ordained by the Coetus against the wishes of the classis were Henricus Frelinghuysen in 1757 and Johannes Martinus Goetschius c. 1757, Jacob Rutsen Hardenbergh and Jacobus van Nist in 1758, Henricus Schoonmaker c.1763, Benjamin du Bois c. 1764, Martinus Schoonmaker c. 1765, and Dirck Romeyn in 1766. The North American-born men ordained in Amsterdam include Theodorus Frelinghuysen in 1745, Johannes Frelinghuysen in 1749, and Thomas Romeyn Sr. as well as Ferdinandus and Jacobus Frelinghuysen in 1752 (though both Frelinghuysens died on the return voyage), Johannes Schuneman in 1753, Wilhelmus Jackson in 1757, and Johannes Martinus van Harlingen in 1761. Barent Vrooman was ordained in Utrecht in 1752. In addition to these the Dutch-born Samuel Megapolensis left New York for education and eventual ordination in 1656.

[23] More specifically, I argue for defining Dutch ministers as clergy who were called to organized congregations (having elders and deacons) that kept their records in Dutch (or where congregational records cannot be found, other evidence indicates that the records were kept in Dutch), and referred to themselves as "Reformed" and/or who made reference to the Canons and/or Post-Acta of Synod of Dordrecht (1618-1619) as authoritative documents. Geographical origins of ministers compiled from Edward Tanjore Corwin, *A Manual of the Reformed Church in America (Formerly Ref. Prot. Dutch Church), 1628-1902*, 4th ed. (New York: Board of Publication of the Reformed Church in America, 1902); Frederick Lewis Weis, *The Colonial Churches and the Colonial Clergy of the Middle and Southern Colonies, 1607-1776* (Lancaster, MA: Society of the Descendants of the Colonial Clergy, 1938);

In terms of educational attainments and family backgrounds these biographies are also a good introduction to the Dutch colonial ministry in general. Indeed, they seem roughly to reflect conditions and trends in both North America and in the Dutch Republic. Early in the course of the Reformation in the Netherlands, the ouster of Roman Catholic priests unmoved by the theological revolution resulted in a large number of vacant pulpits. As such, devout schoolmasters, lay worship leaders, catechism teachers, and other literate people found parsonage doors open to them, even though they had no university training and could not read Latin, Greek, or Hebrew. Ministers so exempted from the university requirement have variously been called "Dutch clerics [*Duitse klerken*]," "*idiotae*" (the Greek root of which can translate "layman"), "special-gifts" ministers, or "octavists" (the last two appellations alluding to the wording and the number of the relevant [eighth] article of the 1619 Church Order of Dordrecht). Though the erstwhile shortage of Protestant clergy in the Netherlands eased by the early seventeenth century, and though the ministerial class in the Dutch Republic professionalized and raised barriers to prevent less qualified and lower class people into its ranks, the practice of admitting candidates to the ministry who lacked university training continued in the Netherlands for more than a century. Given the absence of any provision for "accredited" Dutch Reformed higher education in North America until the late eighteenth century, it is not surprising that colonists who lacked formal university education continued to receive ordinations for New World pulpits at a higher rate than in the Old World. It is worthy of note, however, that the two Dutch Clerics examined in this volume, Schaats and Bertholf (in addition to Bogardus whose university education was incomplete), were ordained by classes in the Netherlands.[24]

The fact that most of the ministers examined here did, in fact, have "proper" academic credentials is also worthy of attention. Indeed, there is a certain symmetry to the essays here in this respect. The first

---

Russell L. Gasero, *Historical Directory of the Reformed Church in America, 1628-1992*, The Historical Series of the Reformed Church in America, Gen. Ed. Donald J. Bruggink, no. 23 (Grand Rapids, MI: Eerdmans, 1992). See also Mouw, "*Moederkerk* and *Vaderland*," 62-85, 623-37.

[24] Schalkwijk, *Reformed Church Brazil*, 131-32; Willem Frijhoff, "The West India Company and the Reformed Church: Neglect or Concern?," *de Halve Maen* 70 (Fall 1997): 64; T. Brienen, "Theodorus Gerardi à Brakel (1608-1669)," in T. Brienen, et al, eds, *De Nadere Reformatie en het gereformeerd piëtisme* ('s-Gravenhage: Boekencentrum, 1989), 124. An excellent summary of scholarship on the state of the Dutch ministry as well as patterns and trends in its ranks, as discussed in this and the following three paragraphs, can be found in Lieburg, "Profeten," 97-107.

essay about an ordained minister in this volume describes an orphan who only reached university by means of significant financial and personal sponsorship and then dropped out to pursue his studies in a less formal way. This largely self-taught minister served in a colony where broader assemblies and formal theological education were as yet unthinkable. The penultimate essay examines Livingston—a man of considerable educational accomplishments—and his contributions to the institutionalization of theological education and church government in the Mid-Atlantic Dutch Church. And in the final essay we find a representative of a new wave of immigration, himself of modest educational attainment and familial background, who was nevertheless a leader in efforts to foster pan-congregational unity and ecclesiastical institutionalization among his fellow newcomers. In an important sense Van der Meulen was thus following in the footsteps of—while also securing assistance from and cooperation with—the "old Dutch" of North America and the ecclesiastical institutions that had been nurtured by Livingston.

Other aspects of the backgrounds of colonial ministers in these case studies demonstrate continuity, not only through the history of the Dutch Reformed Church in North America, but between the New World and the Old. It is fitting, for example, that at least four of the subjects of study here were from ministerial families. As the ministerial class in the Netherlands began policing the requirements for entry into its ranks and standardizing the practices and comportment of its membership, it also began, quite literally, to reproduce itself. Slightly more than a third of the colonial ministers for whom information about familial background is reported in these biographies were from such families. That seems to reflect fairly accurately the situation in the fatherland in the same period.[25]

Finally, two other closely related continuities between the Old World and the New World emerge from these biographies: a discernable hierarchy of both pulpits and ministers. In the Netherlands most candidates for the ministry could expect that their first call would be to a village congregation (or a group of village congregations), though some from well respected and well connected urban families might receive their first call to larger communities. And while many would remain in the congregation to which they had been first called for their entire careers, those who distinguished themselves in the pulpit were

---

[25] Among those whose biographies appear here, Michaëlius, Schaats, Selijns, and Westerlo were from ministerial families. It is likely that Tesschenmaecker was as well. For ministerial families in the Netherlands, see Lieburg, "Profeten," 101-2.

often called to larger towns or even the great cities of the Netherlands. A similar pattern of mobility prevailed in colonial North America. Bertholf, for example, who was from a family whose social position in the Netherlands seems to have been near the border between craftsman and small merchant—and was a man without university credentials—could not have expected his first call to be to a much more prestigious Dutch pulpit than the rural New Jersey village which called him. After he distinguished himself there, however, he did receive a call to more prosperous farming communities on Long Island. Selijns, on the other hand, was born into the ministerial class and had a solid university education; he accepted as his first call the prosperous Long Island agricultural communities and later (after an interim serving a church in the Netherlands) received a call to the most prestigious Dutch pulpit in North America: New York City.

From Sojourning Preachers to Settled Pastors

The first Dutch Reformed minister to lead worship in North America was an ecclesiastical contractor employed by the Dutch West India Company. He served out the four years of his contract and went "home." So it was with about half of the clergy who came before the English conquest.[26] We learn from the essay on Schaats that in 1657 he, too, "longed" to leave. Over the course of Schaats's long career, however, expectations changed: colonists did not want ministers wayfaring in their pulpits; they wanted long-term commitments. Barely a decade and a half after New Netherland became New York at least some colonists had become insistent: their ministers should be called on the same terms as ministers were called in the fatherland. The magistrates of Albany spelled this out clearly as they wrote to the Classis of Amsterdam in 1681 asking for a colleague for the aging Schaats, insisting that "the coming of such a minister here as we have described, is not only for the term of five or six years, but durantiae vitae." Schaats, writing to his colleagues in Amsterdam, underscored this point:

> [At] present it is not as it was formerly. . . . Preachers are no longer engaged for a term of years, but for life, and with the promise of receiving a salary in their old age, which is an important consideration in a foreign land.

It is certainly not the case that all who were called to North America before 1664 arrived with the intention of serving for only a

---

[27] Jaap Jacobs, *The Colony of New Netherland: A Dutch Settlement in Seventeenth-Century6America* (Ithaca, NY: Cornell University Press, 2009), 147.

short tour of duty. The account in this volume of Bogardus's tenure makes that point well: he did not view himself as a temporary sojourner but rather as a transplant to a new homeland. And one does find instances of ministers eager to leave North America in the decades after 1681—as we see in the biographies of Van Varick, Van den Bosch, and Lydekker—but these seem uniformly to have been ministers who had become embroiled in controversy and had come to feel unwelcome in their adoptive communities. With the end of company control had come an end to ministers serving on fixed-term company contracts. Even before that, however, with the growth and maturation of colonial communities and congregations, ministers and churches had begun to view their relationships much as their counterparts in the Dutch Republic did.[27]

The roles Dutch ministers saw for themselves in North America came into closer alignment with those of their colleagues on the other side of the Atlantic in other ways as well. During the first half-century, ministers had seen themselves foremost in terms of their relationships to individual communities. To be sure, ministers did early accept the responsibility to travel to pastorless churches and preaching stations to deliver sermons and administer sacraments, and some congregations did occasionally provide financial assistance to others. There were not, however, moves to form permanent pan-regional or institutional bonds in the seventeenth century. That had been almost unthinkable when there were but a few ministers under contract to serve a small number of congregations. As the number of ministers and organized congregations grew, however, clergy and consistories evinced the same impulse toward building institutions and forming assemblies that had long been exhibited by the Dutch Reformed in Europe and in colonies around the globe. In the *ad hoc* assembly that ordained Tesschenmaecker in 1679 and in the ecclesiastical hearings regarding Van den Bosch's behavior in 1689 we see a willingness—when faced with pressing needs— to form temporary ecclesiastical assemblies in the form of those of the mother church. This impulse emerged more fully in the second half of the eighteenth century. Throughout the colonial period, however, these remained efforts to organize locally *in accordance with* Dutch Reformed church order and, indeed, *within* the ecclesiastical structure of the church of the Netherlands. The biographies of Livingston and Van der Meulen may fairly be viewed as both the culmination of this

---

[27] Albany magistrates to Amsterdam Classis, June 7, 1681, and Schaats to classis, June 25, 1681, in *ERNY* 2:669, 771. See also Jaap Jacobs, *New Netherland: A Dutch colony in Seventeenth-Century America* (Boston: Brill, 2005), 271.

trend and a departure. To a greater degree than most of their North American forebears, these men were committed to promoting and building pan-regional inter-congregational cooperation, structures, and institutions—in addition to serving the congregations to which they were called. After the establishment of the American republic, however, the institutions and structures they cultivated came to be correspondent to, rather than constituent extensions of, the structures and institutions of the fatherland.

Theological Styles

The theological styles that have played a prominent role in histories written about efforts to build Dutch Reformed institutions and structures in eighteenth and nineteenth century North America were very important at the local level as well. It is evident from these biographies that the theological style of a minister—that is, where he fit on the pietism-orthodoxy spectrum—was often a significant factor in determining the warmth of the reception he would receive in a particular congregation. Historian Joris van Eijnatten has observed that the Dutch Reformed Church in the seventeenth and eighteenth centuries was "a semi-state church in a loosely organized republic." It is not surprising in this light that, although the Synod of Dordrecht (1618-19) established certain limits to theological orthodoxy, the church's organizational framework and foundational documents allowed for considerable diversity across the spectrum of theological styles.[28]

It is important to observe, however, that some of the terminology used to indicate theological styles is misleading. Dutch Reformed pietists would have considered the word "pietist" to be an insult. They would also have been offended if they had known that in later centuries their non-pietist neighbors would be called "orthodox," with its implication that they, as pietists, were not orthodox Dutch Calvinists. The orthodox, on the other hand, would not be happy with the pietist-versus-orthodox terminology either, particularly as it seems to suggest that the orthodox were somehow lacking in piety. Church leadership in the Dutch Republic occasionally took action against the most radical of the Dutch pietists, particularly those who were divisive or schismatic. But church assemblies also took action against members and clergy who were impious. It is thus worth noting that representatives of orthodoxy and pietism alike could be found among the ranks of admired church leaders in the Netherlands.

---

[28] Quote is from Joris van Eijnatten, *Liberty and Concord in the United Provinces: Religious Toleration and the Public in the Eighteenth-Century Netherlands* (Boston: Brill, 2003), 59.

In general terms, one can say that the school of thought led by the influential university professor, Gisbertus Voetius (1579-1676), was the principal seventeenth-century form of Dutch Reformed pietism, while the wing of the church which historians call "orthodox" was the school led by another influential university professor, Johannes Cocceius (1603-1669). The two schools differed in a wide variety of arenas. Philosophically, Voetians[29] were more resolutely Aristotelian while Cocceians[30] were somewhat warmer than were Voetians to aspects of Cartesian thought and terminology. In the theological realm, a central difference lay in the understanding of the covenant: Voetians believed that the covenant of grace had been in effect continuously since the time of the Fall; Cocceians argued that God's covenant with Abraham had operated differently than the covenant of the Christian era. On a more practical level, Voetians tended to place a greater emphasis on religious experience and moral living, while Cocceians tended to place stronger emphasis on Christian freedom.

To modern ears, such differences sound academic, but the differences between Voetianism and Cocceianism had important implications for the lives of people in the pew as well as for the clergy. Indeed, these theological and behavioral differences were not only articulated in universities and sanctuaries; they had political and social dimensions as well. Cocceians, for example, considered the fourth commandment to be a ceremonial yoke that had been lifted at the advent of the Christian era, while Voetians held Sunday to be the Christian Sabbath. This meant that a woman who sat on a Sunday afternoon just inside the front window of her house reading a pious text was making a theological statement. The same was true of the neighbor who hung laundry out to dry that same afternoon. Both were making declarations that were "heard" and easily understood by passersby.

The *Nadere Reformatie*, the movement most frequently associated with Dutch Reformed pietism, and closely related to the Voetian school of thought, took shape in the Netherlands in the latter part of the seventeenth century. The Dutch term, *Nadere Reformatie,* literally translates as the "Closer" or "Further Reformation" and is often referred to as the Dutch "Second Reformation," though Anglophonic scholars have also used looser but more descriptive translations such as "Dutch Puritanism" and "Dutch Precisionism." Historians have described four central characteristics or dimensions of the *Nadere Reformatie*: it had an

---

[29] Pronounced FOO-tsee-ens.
[30] Pronounced kok-SAY-ens.

"experiential, mystical dimension," which directed believers "toward true piety"; it had a "social-cultural" dimension, which directed "this piety ... toward a 'precise' faithfulness to biblical norms in all areas of social life"; it had an "ecclesiastical" dimension, which strove "toward a continuing reformation of church life" and worship; and it had a "political, theocratic" dimension, which called upon the government to spread the Reformed faith and to rule according to Reformed principles "in order to establish a 'Dutch Israel.'"[31]

Over the course of the eighteenth century, the *Nadere Reformatie* and Dutch Reformed pietism became less programmatic and political, and less optimistic about a general reformation of the Dutch Republic. The Dutch pietist movement became less visible in Dutch society, largely transforming itself into a network of local groups which, though they remained within the national church until the nineteenth century, gathered in "conventicles" of likeminded people to read devotional texts and discuss sacred matters and personal experiences. Dutch Reformed pietists nonetheless continued publicly to issue calls to greater godliness while privately engaging in devotional exercises and rigorously examining themselves for signs of regeneration. Its more robust practitioners also carefully differentiated various categories of believers and unbelievers and even turned their impulse toward self-scrutiny outward, seeking to discern from words and behavior the spiritual states of those around them—in some cases denying access to the sacraments or even attempting to separate themselves socially from those whom they believed were unregenerate.[32]

Some who read these biographies will be surprised to learn that Theodorus Jacobus Frelinghuysen Sr. was not the first Dutch pietist minister in North America. Still more will be surprised to learn that the man who was arguably the first Dutch pietist among the clergy of New Netherland, Everardus Bogardus, arrived in New Amsterdam (later New York City) nearly a century before Frelinghuysen and barely a dozen years after the first Puritans—close theological kin to Dutch pietists—founded the Plymouth Colony. Indeed, these essays suggest that a significant proportion of those who left the fatherland in

---

[31] Willem Frijhoff, *Wegen van Evert Willemsz.: Een Hollands weeskind op zoek naar zichzelf, 1607-1647* (Nijmegen: Sun, 1995), 359-60. Frijhoff is summarizing here the structural analysis of Fred van Lieburg. My translations.

[32] For an English-language overview of the history of the *Nadere Reformatie*, see Fred A. van Lieburg, "From Pure Church to Pious Culture: The Further Reformation in the Seventeenth-Century Dutch Republic," in W. Fred Graham, ed., *Later Calvinism: International Perspectives* (Kirksville: Sixteenth Century Journals and Publishers, 1994), 409-30.

answer to a call to a colonial pulpit were Dutch pietists of one stripe or another. They also demonstrate that Dutch pietist clergy were well received—even sought out—by laity across the region, from Albany to Manhattan and Long Island to the Delaware Valley (and later in the interior of North America). In this respect, these essays point to the need for further research into the reasons behind the pietists' strong representation among the Dutch clergy in the colonies.[33] A reassessment may also be in order of the relationship between Dutch pietism and its colonial proponents with the Great Awakening of the eighteenth century Anglophonic world, in light of the sort of evidence readers will find here regarding the early and enduring influence of Dutch pietism in the New World.

Language

From the early seventeenth century through the early nineteenth, the cultural, demographic, and political changes that transformed the world inhabited by the North American Dutch were reflected in changing attitudes among them about the Dutch language. This was particularly so in the realm of religion. In a region with such a strong historical reputation for cultural diversity, it would seem logical that the ability to communicate in more than one language would have been a useful skill in the pulpit, and that multilingual preachers would have been highly sought after commodities. These case studies suggest that it was more complicated than that in the Dutch congregations of North America.

It is possible to discern three phases in the linguistic history of the colonial Dutch Reformed Church, though it is much more difficult to pin dates on those phases. Not only did change occur at different paces in different communities; congregations themselves were not monolithic, so these stages even overlapped within communities.

In the first phase, which began with the arrival of Krol and continued well into the eighteenth century in some locales, multilingual worship leaders were a necessity for a diverse society. Such ministers could bring the Reformed message to those who could not (or would not) avail themselves of Dutch-language worship. They also

---

[33] My own research indicates that through much of the eighteenth century there was a concerted effort by correspondents in both the New World and the Old to recruit Dutch pietists for North American pulpits. More research is, however, needed on this network and on the reasons behind the strong representation of pietists among North American clergy in the seventeenth century. See, Mouw, "*Moederkerk* and *Vaderland*," 544-54.

served as centripetal forces, acculturating and integrating non-Dutch immigrants into New Netherland society. From the start, because of the early influx of Walloon colonists, the ability to lead worship in both Dutch and French was important to the success of worship leaders such as Krol and Michaëlius. Competence in French continued to be useful long after the conquest in places like Staten Island and in the area around Kingston and New Paltz, as the biography of Van den Bosch demonstrates. Ministers able to preach in both Dutch and German also found themselves in demand in a number of New York communities in the eighteenth century. The region was never so diverse, however, that Dutch Reformed ministers who, like Van Varick, could communicate in "exotic" languages like Portuguese, found their linguistic abilities in demand.

As congregations were increasingly forced to rely on voluntary contributions from their own communities for the support of their ministers in the 1650s and beyond, multilingual ministers became valuable in another way. Not only could their ability to lead worship in another language be a force for social cohesion in diverse communities, it could broaden the base of contributors to clerical salaries. Readers of Tesschenmaecker's biography will see that, at the time of his arrival in North America in the late 1670s, his ability to preach in both Dutch and English attracted more interest than his abilities to preach in other languages. The Dutch language remained dominant long after the conquest in most Hudson valley communities; and newcomers to many areas in New York and New Jersey, as well as established families of French-speaking locales, adopted Dutch as their language of worship—a pattern that continued well into the eighteenth century. Nevertheless, the English-speaking population was growing, and while many communities possessed the resources to support a minister, some of these communities could not raise adequate funds solely among those favorably disposed toward Dutch-language worship. In such places, multilingual ministers could serve (and garner financial commitments from) what were essentially two congregations in the same town. The experiment in New Castle, in which both Dutch and English churchgoers engaged themselves to pay for Tesschenmaecker's services, did indeed fail—but only partly due to ethnic tensions. Van den Bosch's tenure in Kingston—preaching in Dutch, French, and English—did not last long either, though if there was conflict between cultural groups, it was obscured by the cloud of controversy surrounding the minister's scandalous behavior.

In the second phase, English-language worship became anathema (though French and German did not). As perceived threats from the ever-increasing numbers of Anglophonic neighbors and the English government grew, Dutch sanctuaries became fortresses for the defense of Dutch language, culture, and identity. Ironically, it is in the biography of Laidlie—the first minister called to preach in the English language in the Dutch church of New York City—that we see this development most clearly. It is apparent that many of the Dutch in that city welcomed the introduction of regular worship services in the English language. That this "innovation" angered so many, however, is a sign of just how important the church had become to others as a bastion—not only of the theology of the mother church—but as a bulwark of Dutch culture and ethnic identity. The battle that raged in Manhattan for much of the eighteenth century would be repeated in smaller skirmishes and debates in other North American congregations on into the nineteenth century.

In the biographies of Laidlie, Livingston, Westerlo, and Lydekker, we see the beginnings of a third chapter in the linguistic history of the Dutch Reformed Church in North America. In this phase the treasured documents from the Dutch fortress-sanctuaries were translated—both literally and figuratively—and issued from both presses and pulpits. Dutch clergy and laity alike thus made the cherished teachings contained in Dutch-language devotional, theological, and ecclesiastical texts accessible to those who would otherwise have been unable to benefit from them, both among their "Dutch" sons and daughters and their non-Dutch neighbors, much as Krol and Bogardus had done for Walloon worshippers more than a century and a half earlier.

In a sense, one can see a repetition of a portion of this cycle, in compressed form, in the life of Van der Meulen. Van der Meulen, a leader among the waves of new Dutch Reformed immigrants in the nineteenth century, did not learn English; he nevertheless viewed language and culture as matters indifferent, accepting that which he found good and useful in the religious and cultural milieu of his adopted homeland and encouraging others to do the same, while also nurturing connections and unity among the Dutch in North America, both "old" and "new." Like the translation efforts of earlier ministers such as Westerlo and Lydekker, however, Van der Meulen's energies seem to have been directed primarily toward the transmission of cherished beliefs rather than toward vocational success as a minister.

Material Success

Colonial ministers and laity wanted much the same thing: sanctuaries crowded with churchgoers who were both satisfied with, and edified through, services led by worship leaders who served long tenures, free of conflict. Ministers, however, also wanted another kind of success: a comfortable living coupled with a social standing in their communities commensurate with their office and salary. By one contemporary account, ministers from the fatherland who served in distant outposts "without exception, draw larger salaries than they do who serve in the churches at home."[34] In this respect the desires of ministers were at odds with those of colonists, who wanted more clergy. High salaries undoubtedly contributed to the scarcity of Dutch Reformed ministers in North America; unable to raise the funds necessary to maintain a minister, many communities were forced to do without.

Early in the history of New Netherland, ministers were employees of the Dutch West India Company, and their salaries and board were therefore paid by the company. Over the final decade and a half before the English conquest of 1664, the burden for ministers' salaries was increasingly shifted toward colonists through voluntary subscriptions and, when necessary, taxes. This circumstance did not change immediately in the decade or so after the conquest (though ministers reported that pledges became harder to collect), but the trend toward increasing reliance on voluntary pledges continued. By the end of the seventeenth century, Dutch churches in the colonies relied solely upon contributions and income from real estate or other investments to pay their ministers.

Ministers' salaries evidently varied quite widely, but it is difficult from our perspective to quantify them with precision. The trend from the English conquest to the American Revolution was away from in-kind remuneration and toward salaries paid in hard currency, though throughout the period (and even after the Revolution) some ministers received at least part of their pay in less liquid forms. This included titles to land or the use of church-owned farms, firewood, livestock, pelts, grain, or peas—even tobacco and butter. Excluding the value of firewood and housing—for which colonial congregations appear to have universally provided—but including other in-kind remuneration, eighteenth-century salaries (or at least pledged salaries) ranged from about £80 (New York currency) to the extraordinary annual sum of £300 (New York currency) paid Archibald Laidlie. It is not surprising that, in general, larger congregations appear to have paid higher salaries. More striking is that ministers from the Netherlands appear to have been able to command higher salaries than those born in the colonies or

---

[34] Classis of Amsterdam to consistories of Long Island, April 2, 1680, in *ERNY* 1:741.

German-speaking parts of Europe. In any event, those salaries could be exchanged at London for about ƒ500 to nearly ƒ1,700, suggesting that the salaries of ministers in the colonies were not a great deal different from those of their colleagues in the Netherlands.[35]

The salary alone put the minister above the middle of the income distribution in most communities, but many ministers had other sources of income as well. A low-end minister's salary would have probably been almost double the amount a day-laborer in Poughkeepsie could earn in a year if the laborer was able to find work six days each week.[36] Free firewood and lodging were not insignificant additions; by one estimate a typical New England household consumed thirty to forty cords of firewood (roughly four- to five thousand cubic feet) per year; even if Dutch ministers consumed only a fraction of that, it still represented a significant investment of labor.[37] Furthermore, it appears that over the eighteenth century an increasing number of congregations instituted fees for the registration of baptisms and marriages in church record books, sums that often went directly to the minister.[38] As ministers supplied the growing number of vacant pulpits (and almost all did), the combination of such registration fees and payments for leading worship significantly augmented their regular salaries.

The biographies in this volume suggest that the ministers, whatever their actual wealth, associated with families in the upper social strata of their communities. Indeed, it appears that ministers typically married into such families (particularly after the English conquest). Congregations—especially the smaller ones—often sought out young, single men to fill their pulpits. Such men cost less to transport and did not require (or command) salaries as high as men with families.[39]

---

[35] For an example of a low-end salary, see Consistories of Catskill and Coxsackie, NY to Johannes Schuneman, November 12, 1751, in *ERNY* 5:3199-3200. For more on eighteenth-century salaries, see Gerald F. De Jong, *The Dutch Reformed Church in the American Colonies* (Grand Rapids, MI: Eerdmans, 1978), 116-18. See also footnote 27.

[36] For the wages of day laborers, see Francis Filkin, *Account Book of a Country Store Keeper in the 18th Century at Poughkeepsie*, ed. Henry Booth ([Poughkeepsie, NY]: Vassar Brothers' Institute, 1911). Currency conversions based on tables in McCusker, *Money and Exchange*, 52-55, 162-67.

[37] William Cronon, *Changes in the Land: Indians, Colonists, and the Ecology of New England* (New York: Hill and Wang, 1983), 120.

[38] Mouw, "*Moederkerk* and *Vaderland*," 94-95.

[39] One call was even modified when a minister made plans to marry. See Port Jervis, NY and Montague, NJ consistories, minutes, January 7, 1742, in W. H. Nearpass, ed., *Old Dutch Records of the Machackemech and Menissinck Churches: Port Jervis, N.Y. and Montague, N.J.* (Port Jervis, NJ: Port Jervis Gazette, 1899), 9.

Thus, it was common for ministers to arrive in the colonies as single men and then marry women—often widows—of high social standing and significant financial means (though the undocumented accounts concerning Tesschenmaecker's late-life marriage plans mention only the bodily endowments of his betrothed, not her wealth or social standing). Ministers like Van den Bosch, Laidlie, Livingston, and Westerlo were not only thus able to solidify their status among the colonial elite; their advantageous marriages also brought them a measure of the financial success they sought.

African Americans and Native Americans

Whatever material success colonial Dutch Reformed ministers achieved as they ministered to Euramericans, few achieved even modest success among African Americans and Native Americans in the spiritual realm. Neither did any significantly exceed the beliefs and attitudes that pervaded Euramerican society regarding non-whites. Detailed insight into colonial Dutch Reformed attitudes and behavior toward people of other races is notoriously difficult to wrest from the surviving records, and there is much more work to be done in this area of research. The biographies in this volume do, however, support the thesis that colonial Dutch Reformed clergy were not unusually enlightened for their times in their attitudes toward people of other races.

With respect to evangelizing Native Americans, the biographies suggest widespread indifference. Krol may well have invested some effort; Michaëlius expressed an interest in missions to Native people but came to hold such a negative view of Native American society that he concluded that the only possible avenue for evangelization was through the schooling of children removed from the negative influences of their families and communities. The biography of Bogardus, on the other hand, does not tell us what he thought or did with respect to the conversions of native peoples, but it is certain that he believed some among the Dutch regarded Native American lives—whether Christian or not—too casually: he fought the Dutch governor over what the minister viewed as their unwarranted and immoral slaughter. To twenty-first-century ears the ideas of people like Michaëlius sound like cultural imperialism of the worst sort, while the apparent lack of interest in Christianizing Native Americans exhibited by many other Dutch Reformed clergy seems a laudable precursor to cultural relativism. It should be noted, however, that in the world view of Reformed ministers, indifference regarding the conversion of Native Americans must either have indicated a lack of concern for their eternal fate or a denial that they were humans endowed with souls by a common maker.

The biographies contain a similar variety of attitudes toward African Americans. At least two of the ministers studied in this volume, Tesschenmaecker and Schaats, used some of the resources they accumulated to buy slaves. Fabend's research suggests that Lydekker probably owned slaves as well, and Goodfriend has found that Laidlie had both African-American and Euramerican servants (though it is not clear that the African Americans were slaves). The New York City consistory itself accepted a slave as payment from a delinquent lessee while Laidlie and Livingston chaired that assembly. That a minister was a slave owner, however, is not evidence that he was unusually wealthy; neither did it make him unusual among the Dutch of North America.[40]

Condoning slavery and indifference regarding the souls of enslaved people did not necessarily go hand-in-hand. Before arriving in New Netherland, Bogardus had probably served as schoolmaster to indigenous children at a Dutch outpost in West Africa. Optimistic about the prospects for the conversion of Africans and African Americans, he baptized a significant number of slaves in North America. On the other hand, we see in Van der Linde's research on Selijns that the minister was unwilling to baptize the children of slaves. Selijns does not seem to have parted ways with Bogardus in the belief that African Americans had souls and eternal destinies. Instead, he refused to administer the sacrament to slaves because he doubted the theological understanding of slave parents who sought baptism for their children; he feared that beneath their expressed desire lay hope for freedom rather than a love of God and an understanding of the Bible.

These case studies do not significantly alter the assessments of previous scholarship. Indeed, they offer only a modest contribution to important fields of research that are gaining attention from a growing number of scholars. They do, however, point to the promise of the approach of careful research on individuals as a means of gaining greater insight into broader patterns.

The Keys to a Successful New World Ministry

Like many before and after them, the consistories of the Raritan valley in the late 1730s strove to get a minister with the qualities they believed necessary for effective service among the Dutch in their

[40] For Tesschenmaecker, see the biography in this volume. For Schaats's slave, see Thomas E. Burke, Jr., *Mohawk Frontier: The Dutch Community of Schenectady, New York, 1661-1710* (Ithaca, NY: Cornell University Press, 1991), 132. On the frequency of slaveholding in 1665 NYC, see Joyce D. Goodfriend, "Burghers and Blacks: The Evolution of a Slave Society at New Amsterdam," *New York History* 59 (1978): 142-43.

communities. They focused their attention on the theological style of the minister they believed their communities needed. The essays here suggest that this emphasis of the Raritan valley consistories was, to some extent, well placed, but that other qualities may have been more important to success in a colonial pulpit. It is true, for instance, that the theological orientation that had nurtured Laidlie in Edinburgh, combined with the generous portion of Dutch pietist fare he had imbibed in Zeeland, contributed significantly to his success in New York City. It is also true, however, as the biography of Selijns suggests, that his sharp intellect and sound education contributed more significantly than his theological style to the esteem he had held in that same city six decades earlier.

Overwhelmingly, however, these essays suggest that it was personal qualities of another sort that most often laid the basis for the successes and failures of colonial pastorates. The most recurrent theme through all of these biographies is that ministers who were able to adapt themselves to changing circumstances, who were inclined and able to steer clear of local or regional disputes, and who were measured and circumspect in their words and actions, found that their labors brought fruit. For those who were sources of contention or became entangled in arguments or disputes—whether willfully or inadvertently—the prospects were less promising. The results were particularly tragic for ministers like Van Varick and Lydekker, who not only found themselves drawn into heated conflicts but also committed the grave "sin" of taking the "wrong" side in those disputes (that is, the side less popular in their communities). In such cases even moderate temperaments and irenic instincts did not suffice.

Clerical Biographies as Case Studies: Fresh Perspectives on Familiar Historical Events

The biographies in this volume offer more, of course, than just insight into broad patterns regarding cultural attitudes and beliefs, the ways in which colonial pulpits were filled, and the qualities that occupants of those posts needed to achieve professional or material success. There is also much to learn from these essays concerning the changing relationships of laity to the ministers in their communities, the colonists' relationships to the assemblies and institutions of the mother church, and the ways they expressed their beliefs and preferences

---

More on Dutch Reformed thought and practice with regard to slavery can be found in Gerald Francis De Jong, "The Dutch Reformed Church and Negro Slavery in Colonial America," *Church History* 40 (1971): 423-36.

in areas such as theology and worship. But these biographies are also the stories of people who experienced and took part—sometimes eagerly, sometimes reluctantly—in events, some of which had significance stretching well beyond the walls of sanctuaries, the bounds of individual communities and colonies, and their own lifetimes.

The period during which Jacob Leisler assumed administrative authority in the colony of New York in the wake of the Glorious Revolution in England, in what is commonly known as Leisler's Rebellion, stands out as an event about which myths and misperceptions persist. The essays on Schaats, Tesschenmaecker, and Van Varick may significantly alter some readers' understanding of that conflict. Notably, an influential 1989 account of the rebellion by historian Randall Balmer characterized the Dutch ministers of the colony at the time of the rebellion as uniformly anglicized and wealthy men who consorted with the colonial elite and were therefore bitter enemies of Jacob Leisler. Readers of these case studies will find that the two ministers who had been in the colonies the longest did not, in fact, oppose Leisler. A third minister, Van Varick, also supported Leisler initially, though some of the actions of the Leislerians caused him to change his mind. These facts clearly demonstrate that some analyses of the rebellion have oversimplified the role of religion in general and of Dutch clergy in particular.[41]

Some readers will also gain new insight into the Coetus-Conferentie dispute, the English-language debate, and the American Revolution through the biographies of ministers who served during the 1760s and 1770s. Fabend's research on Lydekker portrays a man with evangelical theological leanings, who through much of the Coetus-Conferentie schism supported the Coetus, but then—abruptly—switched to the Conferentie side. This indicates that traditional assessments of the causes of that schism may not fully explain the choices made and positions taken by all of the participants. Likewise, John Coakley's reassessment of Livingston's role in the creation and implementation of the plan that brought a formal end to the Coetus-Conferentie schism, suggests that later chapters of that story, as it has

---

[41] Randall H. Balmer, *A Perfect Babel of Confusion: Dutch Religion and English Culture in the Middle Colonies*, Religion in America Series (New York: Oxford University Press, 1989), 38. Numerous myths and misperceptions about the rebellion persist, despite decades of careful research and publication by David William Voorhees, director of the Jacob Leisler Project at New York University. See David William Voorhees, "The 'fervent Zeale' of Jacob Leisler," *William and Mary Quarterly* 51 (1994): 447-72; David William Voorhees, "Family and Faction: The Dutch Roots of Colonial New York's Factional Politics," in Martha Dickinson Shattuck, ed., *Explorers, Fortunes and Love Letters: A Window on New Netherland* (Albany, NY: Mount Ida Press for the New Netherland Institute, 2009), 129-47.

most often been told, need substantial revision.

As case studies, these biographies also put human faces on major cultural and military clashes of the period. Goodfriend's essay makes it clear just how complex matters of cultural and ethnic identity were in eighteenth-century New York. In her examination of Laidlie, the Scot who had sought to adapt himself to Dutch culture while he ministered in the Netherlands, is a case in point. He found success among New York City's Dutch Reformed community by *downplaying* his Scottish roots as *well* as his Dutch background. Collectively, through the juxtaposition of biographies of men like Lydekker, Westerlo, Livingston and Laidlie, these case studies also offer readers a sampling of the wide variety of convictions and experiences of the Dutch during the American Revolution, from those of fervent Tories, to moderates, to ardent revolutionaries.

Each of these biographies is, of course, a study of an individual who has captured the interest and inspired the industry of one of the contributing scholars; as such, each can stand alone as a contribution to the field. Together, however, they are more than the sum of their parts: a series of case studies from the history of the Dutch Reformed Church in North America through the course of more than two centuries. Taken as a whole, the following essays knit together some of the important strands of the history that historians too often leave to dangle separately. By bringing together in one volume the biographies of ministers from Michaëlius to Schaats and from Westerlo through Livingston and Van der Meulen, three stories are reconnected: the history of the founding of the Dutch Reformed Church in New Netherland with its growth and maturation during the first decades under British rule; the controversies and institution building by the "old Dutch" during the Revolutionary era; and the subsequent arrival of Dutch Reformed immigrants in the nineteenth century. Indeed, the reader who is acquainted with the history of the Reformed Church of the Dutch Republic and its outposts throughout the world will find many of the recurrent themes in these biographies to be familiar ones. These essays point to important continuities in the histories of the Dutch Reformed Church in Western Europe, North America, and in colonies around the globe, as well as between the Dutch of the Mid-Atlantic colonies and the *Kolonie* of the American Midwest. This is particularly so with parallel and related developments and patterns in matters of theological style, the geographic and social mobility of clergy, relationships between Old World ecclesiastical assemblies and the churches of distant Dutch Reformed outposts, and relationships between secular and civil authorities, as well as tensions among ethnic, national, and religious identities.

Not all of the ministers whose stories have been told here were uniformly well received in the colonial communities they were called to serve. Some ministers, like the elder Frelinghuysen mentioned at the outset of this essay, were reviled by some and lauded by others. In the opinions of the contributing scholars, however, it appears that most served ably among the seventeenth-, eighteenth-, and nineteenth-century Dutch of North America, even though we might wish they had thought and taught more clearly about some important human realities. Readers will find all fourteen of these ministers serving well yet again, now as historical case studies.

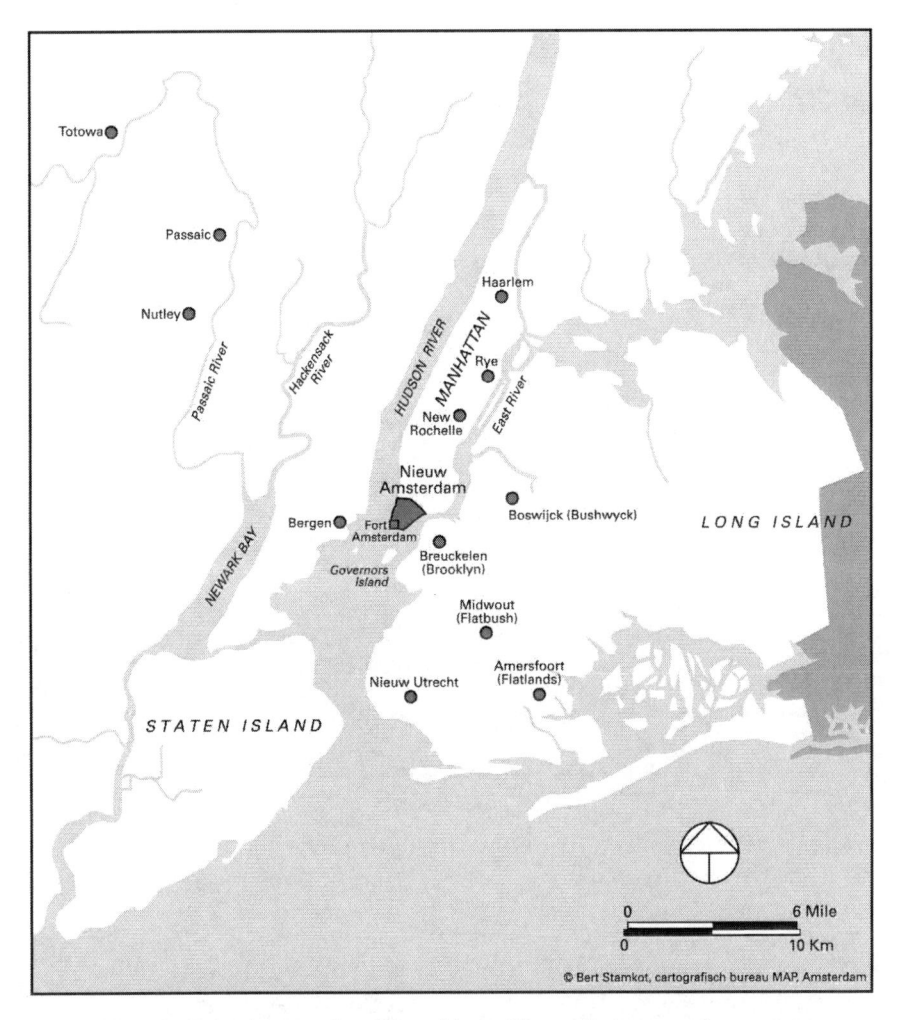

Map 2: New Amsterdam/New York City and surrounding area.

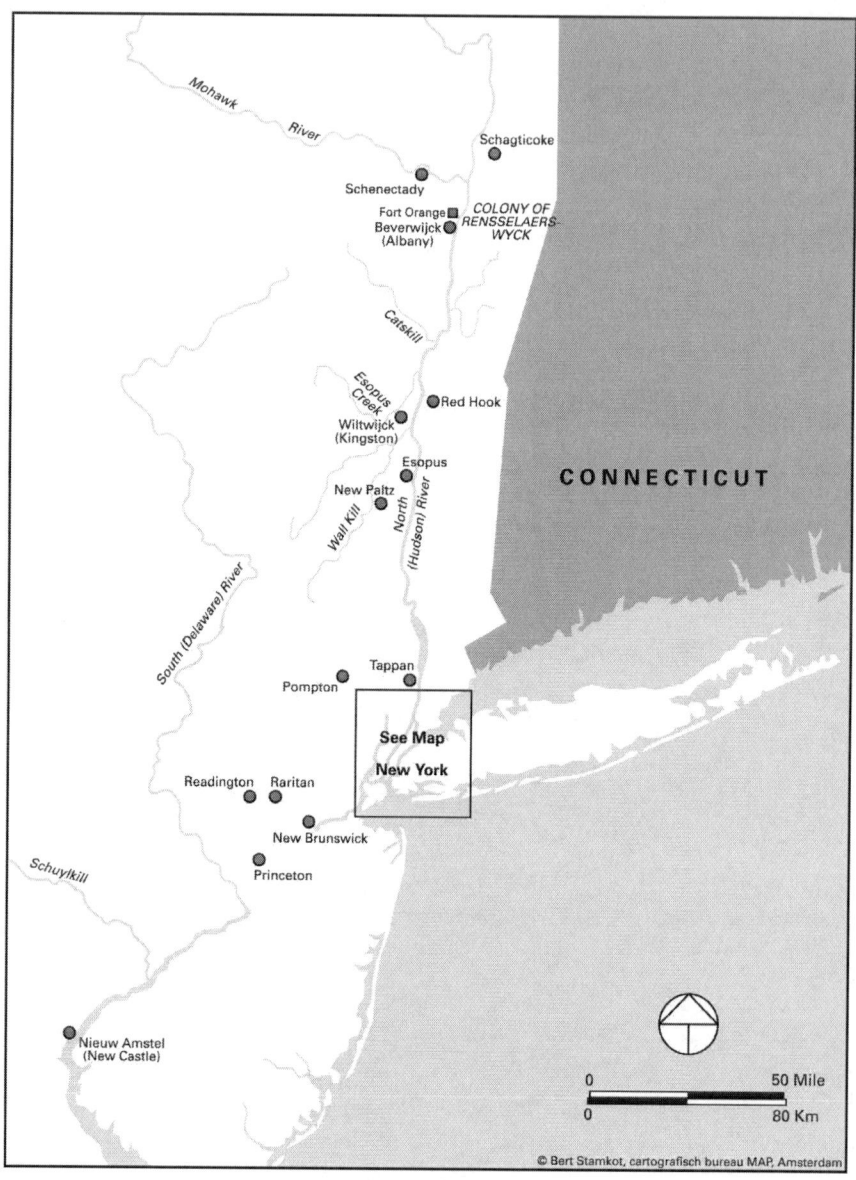

Map 3: New Netherland

PIONEERS

Church Planters in the Early Seventeenth Century

CHAPTER 1

Bastiaen Jansz Krol (1596-1674): New Netherland's First Church Servant

Willem Frijhoff

The year 2009 marked the four hundredth anniversary of Henry Hudson's voyage to the east coast of North America and the beginnings of Dutch dominion in that region,[1] but it was not until 1623 that the first Dutch settlement was established. Consequently, the Dutch Reformed Church remained absent as well. Indeed, the person to whom the honor of "founder" of the Dutch Reformed Church in North America is due has been a matter of historical disagreement. If we consider the faith of the first inhabitants of New Netherland and how religion was practiced in the colony's daily life, the title of founder of the Reformed *community* would certainly go to Bastiaen Jansz Krol.

---

[1] I am grateful to Benjamin Roberts for the translation of the original version of this article and for his excellent suggestions. An earlier, shorter version was published in Dutch: Willem Frijhoff, "Een miskende Calvinist: de religieuze opties van Bastiaen Jansz Krol, eerste kerkdienaar in Nieuw Nederland," in Jan W. Steutel, Doret J. de Ruyter & Siebren Miedema, eds., *De gereformeerden en hun vormingsoffensief door de eeuwen heen* [*Liber amicorum* voor Leendert F. Groenendijk] (Zoetermeer: Meinema, 2009), 26-46. A longer version "A Misunderstood Calvinist: The Religious Choices of Bastiaen Jansz Krol," including a full translation of the 1623 pamphlet was published in the *Journal of Early American History* 1 (2011): 62-95.

Fragment of Krol's *Troost der vromen*

[University Libraries of Amsterdam and Leiden (Bibliotheca Thysiana)]

On December 7, 1623, well before the nomination of the first minister of the Reformed Church, the Amsterdam consistory appointed Krol as "comforter of the sick" (*kranckbesoecker*).[2] The council initially commissioned him to work in the "West Indies," a term the Dutch generally used for their American possessions.[3] However, due to a turn of events, Krol arrived in the newly founded colony of New Netherland in the spring of 1624 as an employee of the Dutch West India Company. He landed on Nooten Eylandt (now Governor's Island), just off the coast

---

[2] For the occupation of comforter of the sick, see: Johan de Niet, *Ziekentroosters op de pastorale markt 1550-1880* (Rotterdam: Erasmus Publishing, 2006); Gerald F. De Jong, "De *Ziekentroosters* or Comforters of the Sick in New Netherland," *New York Historical Society Quarterly* 54 (October 1970): 339-60.

[3] Stadsarchief Amsterdam [City Archive of Amsterdam] (hereafter cited as SAA), Archief Nederlandse Hervormde Kerkenraad [Archive of Dutch Reformed Consistory] (PA 376), inv. n° 5, p. 157.

of Manhattan, where the Dutch colonists had first settled, and joined them in their 1625 resettlement on the southern tip of Manhattan.

For those who take the official standard of the Dutch Reformed *Church* as a starting point, the title of founder would probably go to the Reverend Jonas Michaëlius. In 1628 Michaëlius was appointed and sent out as the first minister of New Netherland. He was commissioned to establish a congregation and consistory of the Dutch Reformed Church in the colony. His biographer, the church historian Albert Eekhof, titled him as the real "founder of the Church in New Netherland."[4] However, if Krol's name had not been lost to obscurity, he might have been deemed worthy of the title. Like many of the servants of the West India Company who worked in New Netherland, Krol's legacy was tarnished. Several historians have suggested that his religious knowledge was limited and that his orthodoxy and behavior were less than impeccable. According to George L. Smith in *Religion and Trade in New Netherland*, Krol "was a curious figure, who was never finally certain whether his master was God or Mammon, though he clearly gravitated toward the latter."[5]

Krol's Historical Debut

In the beginning of the twentieth century Albert Eekhof researched Bastiaen Krol's early history twice.[6] Though Eekhof's research includes important data about Krol's life course, much more can be added. The earliest source regarding Krol is his application for a marriage license at Amsterdam on February 7, 1615.[7] In Amsterdam couples were required to register to marry at the city hall (*ondertrouw*),

---

[4] A. Eekhof, *Jonas Michaëlius, Founder of the Church in New Netherland. His Life and Work* (Leiden: Sijthoff, 1926), IX-148.

[5] George L. Smith, *Religion and Trade in New Netherland: Dutch Origins and American Development* (Ithaca & London: Cornell University Press, 1973), 160. In her recent biographical note, Firth Haring Fabend depicts Krol more favorably. See: "Bastiaen Jansz Krol," in *American National Biography* (New York: Oxford University Press, 1999) 12:933-934.

[6] A. Eekhof, *Bastiaen Janszoon Krol: Krankenbezoeker, Kommies en Kommandeur van Nieuw-Nederland, 1595-1645* (The Hague: Nijhoff, 1911). A. Eekhof, *De Hervormde Kerk in Noord-Amerika (1624-1664)*, 2 vols. (The Hague: Nijhoff, 1913), 1:28-32; *Nieuw Nederlandsch Biografisch Woordenboek*, 15 vols. (Leiden: Sijthoff, 1911), 1:1252-54. Also in Willem Frijhoff, *Wegen van Evert Willemsz. Een Hollands weeskind op zoek naar zichzelf 1607-1647* (Nijmegen: SUN, 1995), 587-89; idem, "The West India Company and the Reformed Church: Neglect or Concern?" *De Halve Maen* 70:3 (Fall 1997): 59-68.

[7] SAA, Doop-, Trouw- en Begraafregisters [Baptism, Marriage, and Burial Records] (hereafter cited as DTB) 418, 320 (f. 162v°). All the primary sources pertaining to Krol's age indicate 1595 as his year of birth.

which usually took place three weeks before the church marriage, but in Krol's case there is no mention of a subsequent church ritual. Krol's occupation was listed as "caffa worker,"[8] and his place of origin was the town of Harlingen, in Friesland. He was twenty years old and had already been living near the Regulierspoort in Amsterdam for ten years. His mother, Annetje Egberts, was present at the registration. His bride, Annetjen Stoffels(dochter) registered herself as having been born in Eesens, a town in the district of Harlingerland, in the county of East-Friesland. Annetjen had been living at the same place as Krol for nine years, and she was twenty-one years old. Her parents were not present at the registration. Bastiaen signed the marriage license with a bold, yet simple cross mark, which has led scholars to believe that he was illiterate. Despite her unsteady hand, his wife signed the document with a legible signature: Anneken Christouel.

Six and half months later, on August 16, 1615, the couple's first son, Thonis, was baptized.[9] The reason the couple married is obvious: Anneke was with child. By then, they may have known each other for years and may even have lived in the same boarding house, as so many immigrants did. The couple had more children hereafter, three of them named Ytje (suggesting that the first two died). The last one was baptized on August 25, 1624, when Bastiaen was already in New Netherland.[10] That child was apparently conceived just before Bastiaen shipped out, without his wife and children. Most likely he had hoped to get a temporary position in the Caribbean or on the northern shore of South America, which the merchant-shareholders of the West India Company aimed to settle. The woolen draper Jesse de Forest (c. 1575-1624), a charismatic Walloon from Avesnes (Hainaut) who had settled at Leiden, had organized an expedition to that area with a group of Walloons, but he died prematurely. The remaining colonists of this group would later settle in New Netherland, constituting Krol's first congregation.[11]

---

[8] Caffa was a damasked cloth made from silk combined with cotton or wool.
[9] SAA, DTB 5, p. 153 (Oude Kerk), p. 153. He is registered as being a son of Bastejaen Janss, caffa worker, and Anne Krijstoffelsdr.
[10] SAA, DTB 39 (Nieuwe Kerk), p. 486: IJtje, January 30, 1618; DTB 5 (Oude Kerk), p. 281: IJtje, 7 April 1619; DTB 40 (Nieuwe Kerk), f. 134r°: Ytje, August 24, 1624. Ytje was most likely the name of Annetjen's mother.
[11] See Mrs. Robert de Forest, *A Walloon family in America: Lockwood de Forest and his forebears, 1500-1848; together with A Voyage to Guiana, being the Journal of Jesse de Forest and his colonists, 1623-1625*, 2 vols. (Boston: Houghton Mifflin Co., 1914); J. Peters, "Volunteers for the wilderness: The Walloon petitioners of 1621 and the voyage of the Nieu Nederlandt to the Hudson River in 1624," *Proceedings of the Huguenot Society of London* 24 (1987): 421-33.

Bastiaen Krol was baptized as an adult, twenty-one years old, on February 23, 1616, in the Nieuwe Kerk (New Church) of Amsterdam, a year after his marriage and half a year *after* the baptism of his own son![12] This was a puzzle that Eekhof could not solve. However, historical research has revealed that in the early period of the Dutch Republic, many people from the northern Netherlands and the Frisians in particular remained quite distant from the established churches. Not being baptized was not unusual. Does that mean that, as a young adult, Krol saw himself as correcting the decades-old omission of his parents? I shall come back to this matter soon. In any event, not long after Krol's baptism in 1616 he became an active member of the Dutch Reformed Church. On October 12, 1623, shortly after the West India Company was founded, Krol appealed to the consistory for the position of comforter of the sick in the West Indies.[13] At the time he was still a caffa worker but had moved to the Bloemgracht in the Jordaan, a new, popular workers' neighborhood to which he would return many times throughout his life. His appeal must have been convincing. A week later he was among a number of men asked to take an examination for two available positions overseas. Alas, he was not one of the two fortunate ones. However, because one of the two who had been selected became sick, the consistory returned to Krol and offered him a position. On December 7 he was appointed comforter of the sick for the West Indies and received his instructions. In the meantime he became sick himself but recovered quickly before he took ship. Thus, initially, the consistory had reservations about Krol, which we will look into shortly.

New Netherland

Krol's congregation consisted of the first immigrants who sailed with him in January 1624 on board the ship *De Eendracht* [The Concord], as well as thirty families, mostly Calvinist Walloons from the Southern Netherlands, who sailed in March 1624 with the ship *Nieu Nederlandt* [New Netherland], arriving in May of that year. In the vast territory that had to be colonized, the colonists were thinly spread over four settlements far from each other, ostensibly because the West India Company wanted to make its claims to the whole territory visible. On March 24, 1624, the company issued a Provisional Order for the colony. It stipulated that the Reformed religion would be the only

[12] SAA, DTB 39 (Nieuwe Kerk), f. 207v°.
[13] SAA, Kerkenraad [Consistory], 5, p. 142 (12 October), 144 (19 October), 155 (30 November), 157 (7 December).

faith for which public worship would be tolerated, but that it would respect the freedom of conscience for all inhabitants who had been secured in 1579 by the Union of Utrecht (article 13), the foundational charter of the Dutch Republic. The Walloons, one of the few groups of refugees that emigrated to New Netherland for religious reasons, were more austere in their practice of the Reformed faith than the colonists who came later. Krol probably felt more at home with them. He must have been able to speak French, or at least to understand it, and may have said prayers in that language, although the Walloons, who had previously lived in Holland, may also have understood Dutch.[14] Some years later he was credited with having an excellent knowledge of the Indian languages. Therefore, he probably accompanied the earliest colonists who settled near Fort Orange on the Upper Hudson River, in the Mohican territory to which he would return soon as commissioner of the West India Company.

But first Krol returned to Amsterdam, in October 1624. As a comforter of the sick, Krol was not allowed to baptize, but several Walloon immigrant women were pregnant. Among them was Catelina Trico, who later claimed to be the mother of the first European baby born in New Netherland, Sarah Rapalje.[15] On November 14, 1624, Krol addressed the consistory, informing them that the inhabitants in the colony needed a minister and that provision had to be made for baptizing the children of the expectant mothers. After serious discussion the consistory decided that there were not enough families to warrant a minister, but they allowed Krol to conduct weddings and baptize. He was also given permission to read passages from the scriptures and commentaries from a few Reformed theologians such as Heinrich Bullinger. The only condition was that Krol had to read the unaltered text of the named postils and was not permitted to improvise or elaborate in his own words.[16] In January 1625 Krol, reconfirmed as comforter of the sick, returned to New Netherland on board the *Den Orangen Boom* [The Orange Tree], together with the colony's new director, Willem Verhulst. According to Verhulst's instructions, Krol

[14] For an assessment of multilingualism in the Dutch Republic, see Willem Frijhoff, *Meertaligheid in de Gouden eeuw: Een verkenning* (Amsterdam: KNAW Press, 2010), accessible at www.knaw.nl/publicaties/pdf/20101019/pdf.
[15] George Olin Zabriskie, "The Founding Families of New Netherland. No. 4: The Rapalje-Rapelje Family," *De Halve Maen* 46 (January 1972): 7-8, 16; 47 (April 1972): 11-13; 47 (July 1972): 11-14; Russell Shorto, *The Island at the Center of the World: The Epic Story of Dutch Manhattan and the Forgotten Colony That Shaped America* (New York: Doubleday, 2004), 37, 40-41.
[16] SAA, Kerkenraad [Consistory], 5, p. 231 (14 and 21 November).

was also to educate the Indians in the word of God.[17] Given his linguistic abilities, he may well have tried to involve himself in that mission.

Krol proved to be an active and successful comforter of the sick who adapted to the needs of the colonial congregation. He gained little satisfaction from his position, however. When his three-year contract came to an end in 1626, Krol did not ask for a prolongation. In the meantime another comforter of the sick had arrived: Jan Huygen, a brother-in-law of the new director, Peter Minuit, who settled on Manhattan Island.[18] Instead, Krol was appointed commissioner (*commies*) or director of Fort Orange, the military and mercantile stronghold near present-day Albany, where he was probably already living. Besides his obvious management skills, Krol was also given this position because of his previous knowledge of the Indian languages. At Fort Orange he now became responsible for the administration of stores and supplies and for maintaining contacts with the Indians. Therefore, Krol must have had already distanced himself from his church role some time before a formal minister was sent to New Netherland in 1628. In 1629 he started to work simultaneously for Kiliaen van Rensselaer, who had founded a patroonship (manor) in the region of Fort Orange, which he managed from Amsterdam.[19]

Van Rensselaer, prominent among those directing the colonial affairs of the West India Company, initially had great plans, but his colony only developed in two arenas: as a gathering place for the trade in beaver furs and for agriculture. He appreciated the manner in which Krol worked and apparently saw a good local ally in him. In February 1632, at Van Rensselaer's request, Krol was named director of New Netherland as successor to Peter Minuit, a decision that testifies to his excellent reputation as an administrator.[20] But in that very year, 1632, the newly appointed directors of the West India Company headquarters at Amsterdam radically changed the orientation of the company's

[17] Text in: F.C. Wieder, *De stichting van New York in juli 1625. Reconstructies en nieuwe gegevens ontleend aan de Van Rappard documenten* (orig. 1925; 2d printing Zutphen: Walburg Pers, 2009), 121-22.
[18] Nic. van Wassenaer, *Historisch verhael alder gedenck-weerdigste geschiedenissen* (Amsterdam, 1622-1635), XII, f. 38-39 (November 1626).
[19] Van Rensselaer's instructions to him, January 12, 1630, in: Arnold J.F. van Laer, ed., *New York State Library. Van Rensselaer Bowier Manuscripts, being the letters of Kiliaen van Rensselaer, 1630-1643, and other documents relating to the colony of Rensselaerswyck* (Albany: University of the State of New York, 1908), 158-61; Janny Venema, *Kiliaen van Rensselaer (1586-1643): Designing a New World* (Albany: SUNY Press, 2010), 220, 246.
[20] Van Laer, *Van Rensselaer Bowier Manuscripts*, 217-18 (Van Rensselaer to Krol, July 20, 1632). The brevity of his directorate has led many authors to erroneously consider him an "interim director."

policy, favoring commerce over settlement. All company administrative employees in New Netherland were called home, including the new director Krol and minister Michaëlius. They were replaced in March 1633 by Van Rensselaer's nephew, Wouter van Twiller, and the Reverend Everardus Bogardus respectively—young men without much experience, both being twenty-six years old. Between the two periods that he served as clerk of the West India Company at Fort Orange (1626-1632 and 1638-1644) and his directorship (1632-1633), Krol had returned to Amsterdam, possibly as a merchant or in Van Rensselaer's service.[21]

After 1626 Krol never again held office in the Reformed Church, unless it was as an elder or a deacon. Immediately after his arrival in 1628 Michaëlius formed a consistory, to which three members were chosen: Krol, rarely present because of the distance between New Amsterdam and Fort Orange, and two new elders, director Minuit and the former comforter of the sick Jan Huygen, now commissioner of the company store.[22] That turning point is less surprising than it appears. Despite the fact that Krol must have been a religious man, he did not have the makings of a minister. He belonged to a group of enthusiastic believers, many of whom were simple artisans who in the early days of the West India Company offered to work as comforters of the sick on ships and in newly colonized territories. In the minutes of Amsterdam's consistory, especially in the period after the Synod of Dort (1618-19), we find numerous similar cases of young men who were eager to serve God but had little education. These men were either motivated by missionary zeal or had a deep-seated hatred of the Spanish enemy. They were excited by seafaring and must have regarded this as an adventure that would offer them new opportunities.[23]

Return to Holland

By the end of 1644 Krol had returned to the Dutch Republic permanently. The house on the *Anjeliersdwarsstraat* that he had bought

---

[21] According to Krol himself, the chronology of his New Netherland sojourn was as follows: the first stay as comforter of the sick for a period of seven and a half months; a second trip of fifteen months in the same capacity, and thereafter three years followed by an additional period of two years as director (commissioner) of Fort Orange. He spent the last thirteen months as director-general of New Netherland. See SAA, Notarieel archief [Notarial Archive abbreviated: NA], inv. n° 1039, p. 151-156 (June 30, 1634; in Eekhof, *Krol*, XXV-XXXI). Also Van Wassenaer, *Historisch verhael*, XII, f. 38 (November 1626); XVI, f. 13v° (October 1628).

[22] Eekhof, *Jonas Michaëlius*, 117 (letter to Reverend Adrianus Smoutius, August 11, 1628).

[23] Frijhoff, *Wegen*, 521-22.

for 1,700 guilders during a short return visit to Amsterdam on February 6, 1630, was at that time rented out. He and his wife and children lived now a few streets away on the *Lindengracht* next to a house known as *De Drie Goudsbloemen* [The Three Marigolds].[24] On November 8, 1644, Krol and his wife drafted a mutual will.[25] The couple decided that whoever survived the other would care for their youngest son Jan and send him to school, just as they had done for their eldest son Thonis, who by that time was already thirty years old. In fact, Bastiaen's two sons followed in his American footsteps, but neither of them finally became a settler in New Netherland. Thonis joined his father in New Netherland, where in October 1643 he appears as co-owner of the frigate *La Garce* [The Wench], first with Captain Willem Albertsz Blauvelt and then with Philip Janse Ringo. After some misfortunes with other ships he finally returned to the fatherland in August 1649.[26]

Krol's youngest son Jan was born in 1634 after Bastiaen had returned from New Netherland.[27] According to a debt receipt dated June 16, 1655, for the amount of 260 guilders and 12 *stuivers* to a Jacob van Leeuwen of Amsterdam, we know that Jan was living in New Netherland at that time.[28] Two years later he was still in New Netherland, this time as mediator in the settlement of debts for the amount of 572 guilders for goods that were to be shipped to Amsterdam.[29] Eventually he was employed as head surgeon for the Dutch East India Company. He died on board *De Schelvis* [The Haddock] in August 1668 and was laid to rest in Makassar on the island of Celebes (Sulawesi, in present-day Indonesia).[30]

In 1645 Krol's wife Annetje died. She was buried on January 21 in the cemetery of the *Noorderkerk,* which was near their home. In that year Krol must have done something to cause a row with the consistory,

---

[24] SAA, NA 302, f. 63-64 (February 6, 1630); 316, f. 260 (September 7, 1637).
[25] SAA, NA 324, f. 187-88.
[26] A.J.F. van Laer, ed., *New York Historical Manuscripts: Dutch. Vol. II: Register of the Provincial Secretary, 1642-1647* (Baltimore: Genealogical Publishing Company, 1974), 162, 270, 346, 348-50; *Vol. III: 1648-1660* (1974), 167. See also http://www.ringofamilyhistory.com, and SAA, NA 2279-IV, f. 72-73 (April 24, 1652).
[27] He must be the Ian Bastiaansz Krol, who in 1652, during the first Anglo-Dutch War, published in Middelburg (Zeeland) the cartoon *Engels-Kuiper* [English Cooper], poking fun at the domestic disputes within Holland of which the English made generous use: Koninklijke Bibliotheek [Royal Dutch Library], pamphlet Knuttel 7330. Cf. Frederik Muller, *Beredeneerde beschrijving van Nederlandsche historieplaten, zinneprenten en historische kaarten,* I (Amsterdam: F. Muller, 1863), 290, n° 2034
[28] SAA, NA 561, f. 70 (June 16, 1655); 2708, f. 139 (September 25, 1655).
[29] SAA, NA 2711, f. 769 (April 12, 1657), and f. 209 (April 9, 1658).
[30] SAA, NA 3107, f. 233 (August 12, 1670); Eekhof, *Michaëlius,* 11.

which discussed his situation on September 21, 1645.[31] For some period Krol had been barred from communion, and now he requested to be readmitted.[32] The brothers who were responsible for his district found no problems with his "current conduct," but the consistory as a whole continued to have reservations about him and requested further inquiry. A week later, on September 28, Krol was allowed to receive communion again. The matter was urgent, because on October 7 Krol remarried. This time the marriage license recorded his occupation as "seafarer" and his residence as the *Reaelstraat* near the *Haarlemmerpoort*.[33] His new bride was Engeltje Baerents from Norden, again in East-Friesland.[34] She was recorded as residing in the *Haarlemmerstraat* and thirty-seven years old, and therefore somewhat younger than Bastiaen, who was then fifty. Engeltje's first husband was Abraham Valentijn, a surgeon who, according to the testimony of at least seven people (including his own brother Isaac), had died overseas, far from home. Engeltje Baerents was considered "abandoned." As with his first wife, Bastiaen was probably intimate with her before they married. Before the death of Engeltje's first husband was confirmed, Krol had already moved into her house in the *Haarlemmerstraat*. This explains the statement made on April 3 by some of his former neighbors to the clerk of the Orphan Chamber (*Weeskamer*) that Krol had moved but they did not know where.[35] To the relief of the consistory, the scandal was resolved when the couple married.

Before Krol could remarry, an inventory of his household was made on October 15, 1645, in order to determine the rightful inheritance of his two sons who by law were entitled to a share of their mother's belongings.[36] The inventory was an appendix to the marriage contract that was drafted ten days later on October 25. Engeltje was accompanied by her uncle, Harpert Jansen, who was a surgeon.[37] According to that document, Engeltje did not have any assets. If the couple had

[31] SAA, Kerkenraad, 8, p. 45 (September 21, 1645), 46 (September 28).
[32] For church discipline as practiced by Amsterdam's consistory: Herman Roodenburg, *Onder censuur. De kerkelijke tucht in de gereformeerde gemeente van Amsterdam, 1578-1900* (Hilversum: Verloren, 1990).
[33] SAA, DTB 462, f. 161v° (p. 322) lists the declarations about Abraham's death. Krol had difficulty affixing his signature and Engeltje did not endorse the document.
[34] Engeltje Baerentss married for the first time in the nearby village of Sloterdijk on June 8, 1631 (marriage license registered in Amsterdam May 10, 1631). She was then called Engeltje Biewis; SAA, DTB 437, f. 200.
[35] SAA, Begraafregister Weeskamer [Burial Register Orphan Chamber], 2 (cited by Eekhof, *Michaëlius*, 8, footnote 2).
[36] SAA, NA 328, f. 64.
[37] SAA, NA 2037, f. 13-14.

no children and Bastiaen should die first, then the household goods would be inherited by his sons as part of their mother's inheritance, and Engeltje would inherit one-third of all of the other possessions. And indeed, no children from this union can be found in the baptismal records. Engeltje would not have to worry too much, however, because her uncle was well-off. He owned property in the *Egelantierstraat*, across from *De Kalckoensche Haen*, which Engeltje inherited after Harpert's death. With this inheritance Bastiaen and Engeltje built a house on the property. She also inherited her uncle's household possessions, such as furniture, porcelain, and silverware—which a were a significant contrast to the meager belongings that Krol and Engeltje combined in 1645 when they married. The couple named their new house *'t Eeuwige Leven* [The Eternal Life].[38] Apparently, Krol's religious passion was still alive.

Krol endorsed the inventory with a real signature instead of the cross mark he had used for his first marriage license. The signature is nevertheless shaky. Besides two mortgage deeds worth 3,200 guilders in total of which one for 2,200 guilders had just been issued on June 30, 1645—the inventory only sums up the standard household effects. It reflects a scant and sparse interior that did not include many items. We find six shirts of diverse quality, six jabots, five bed sheets, a bed and bolster, six handkerchiefs, nine porcelain saucers and cups, a bedpan, seven chairs of "poor quality," seven paintings, a mirror, two trunks, eleven books, an iron chain, a pair of tongs and a shovel for the fireplace, a fire pit, a flatiron, a skimmer, a roaster, a copper kettle, a psaltery,[39] a chopping knife, nine wooden plates, six napkins, a green and white blanket, a hatrack, a *preeckstoel* (discussed below), a bucket for the market with a basket, and a poke for the fireplace. Unfortunately, no details about the books and paintings were specified. Clearly, the couple was poor. However, we do learn from the inventory that Krol played music on a psaltery, probably religious music.

Like many employees of the West India Company, Krol was entitled to back wages from the company after his return. The company had a reputation for being one of the worst in the Republic for paying its employees, and after 1645 when the company began gradually to lose its possessions in Brazil, the situation only worsened. A year after

---

[38] SAA, NA 3109, f. 26 (February 9, 1673).
[39] A *scharrebord*, i.e., a psaltery, a musical instrument (probably a flat box with strings spanning across it), according to Willem Sewel, *Volkomen Woordenboek der Nederduitsche en Engelsche Taalen / A Complete Dictionary Dutch and English* 2 vols. (Amsterdam: Kornelis de Veer, 1766), 2:697.

Krol's return he authorized surgeon Abraham Riddersbach to get as much back salary from the company as possible. Riddersbach's reward would be 25 percent of everything he retrieved. Krol was apparently in financial need.[40] Krol's second wife also endorsed this document with a cross-mark because she could not write. On March 11, 1663, Krol drafted a new will. This time his assets included 1,800 guilders of salary in arrears due him from the company.[41]

On May 10, 1669, Krol registered for a third time to marry. By this time he was seventy-four years old, and his bride was again a Frisian woman, named Wige Baerents (also called Ytje), from the village of Anjum, in the district of Dongeradeel. Wige was forty-eight years old and a generation younger than Krol. She was the widow of Denijs Leendertse of Sint-Truiden (St.-Trond) in the prince-bishopric of Liege, himself a widower who, given his place of origin, may have been a Roman Catholic. Wige also lived on the *Egelantiersgracht*.[42] Perhaps she had already been living with Bastiaen as his housekeeper. In 1673 Bastiaen had a stroke that paralyzed him and left him unable to write.[43] On March 14, 1674, he was buried in the Noorderkerk cemetery. He was almost eighty years old and was registered as a resident of the *Egelantiersgracht*.[44] By the time of his death the positions he had held as administrator and commander had long passed and New Netherland had already become New York. For Krol, however, they represented his pride and joy because they helped shape his identity.[45]

Eekhof believed that the *preeckstoel* listed in Krol's inventory of 1645 was the old pulpit he had used as a comforter of the sick. He took the word in its present-day sense. In the vocabulary of the Dutch used in that era, a *preeckstoel* referred, however, to a "church stool," a folding chair that women brought with them to the church so that they could sit during the long sermons.[46] The misunderstanding of *preeckstoel*, together with the poor furnishings of his household, led Eekhof to draw negative conclusions about Krol. "This Krol was not the 'hero'

---

[40] SAA, NA 1746, f. 438 (November 28, 1645).
[41] SAA, NA 2070, f. 132.
[42] SAA, DTB 493, f. 328. Neither bride nor groom endorsed the document. At the time of her first marriage on July 21, 1650 she used the name Ytgie (Ytje) Barentss. She was twenty-nine years old and was recorded as living in the Tuinstraat; SAA, DTB 467, p. 689.
[43] SAA, NA 3885, d.d. January 18, 1673.
[44] SAA, DTB 1079, p. 61. Eekhof initially believed that he died in 1645 but rectified that in Eekhof, *Michaëlius*, 1-13.
[45] SAA, NA 3760, f. 180: statement by Yfje Barends, 57 years old, housewife of Bastiaen Crol, known as "former commander of Fort Orange in New Netherland".
[46] Sewel, *Volkomen Woordenboek*, 2, 650.

which anyone had hoped to discover as the founder of the Reformed Church."[47] Krol's poor image as an illiterate, a common laborer, baptized late in life, a horse-trader in his later years, and in addition to that a problem for the consistory, made Michaëlius a more suitable candidate for "founder" of the church in New Netherland.

A Converted Mennonite?

However, new facts about Krol's life restore his place as an appropriate church founder. The first enigma that needs to be unraveled is his late baptism at the age of twenty-one. One plausible hypothesis could be that he was baptized late in life because of the religious leanings of his parents. His mother and father were most likely Mennonites, who did not believe in childhood baptism but believed that baptism should be reserved for adults who fully understood its meaning. In Harlingen, where Krol was born, there were many Mennonites who worked as skippers or seafarers. They were about 20 percent of the population.[48] During the years 1551-1582 at least 1,180 people were baptized at Harlingen by a wandering Mennonite preacher who counted the converts in his diary.[49] Unfortunately, research is difficult for the period of Krol's birth because the Mennonites were divided into many rival groups, making the associations of individuals and families difficult to discern.[50]

For this proposition we have available a supplementary argument. Bastiaen's mother's name is known from his first marriage license: Annetje Egberts. Most probably, then, Bastiaen Jansz was the son of Jan Bastiaensz and Annetje Egberts, who according to the baptismal register of the Reformed Church in Amsterdam had five children baptized in that city between 1606 and 1614. They were Trijntje and Sijmon (both baptized on May 14, 1606), Grietje on January 19, 1610, and (after the death of the first Sijmon[51]) a second Sijmon on December

---

[47] Eekhof, *De Hervormde Kerk*, 1:32.
[48] For the relationship between the Reformed and the Mennonites in the province of Friesland: Wiebe Bergsma, *Tussen Gideonsbende en publieke kerk. Een studie over het gereformeerd protestantisme in Friesland, 1580-1650* (Hilversum: Verloren, 1999), 142-46; Samme Zijlstra, *Om de ware gemeente en de oude gronden. Geschiedenis van de dopersen in de Nederlanden 1531-1675* (Leeuwarden/Hilversum: Fryske Akademy/Verloren, 2000).
[49] K. Vos, "De dooplijst van Leenaert Boumans," *Bijdragen en Mededeelingen van het Historisch Genootschap* 36 (1915): 39-80.
[50] With appreciation to René Attema en Yde Elsinga of Harlingen for their information.
[51] Presumably this was the child of Jan Bastiaensz, who was buried on June 24, 1611 in the Nieuwe Kerk; SAA, DTB 1053, p. 132.

28, 1614, who was baptized in de Nieuwe Kerk (New Church). Geesjen was baptized on May 23, 1613, in the Oude Kerk (Old Church).[52] In 1613 the occupation of Bastiaen's father, Jan Bastiaensz, is registered as a *kleinschuitenvoerder* or small barge operator: a skipper. When the first Sijmon was baptized in 1606, Trijntje's name was recorded above his own name and listed as being "2 years" old. Apparently Trijntje was baptized at an older age, her parents having used the occasion of her brother's baptism to have her baptized as well.

I surmise that the following took place: Bastiaen Jansz was born around 1595. At the time of his birth his parents were of the Mennonite faith and resided in Harlingen.[53] Circa 1605—and no later than May 1606—his parents must have joined the Reformed Church and settled in Amsterdam, which was a logical choice for a skipper. Perhaps they had already started going to the Reformed Church in Harlingen, but most likely the couple changed their religious affiliation when they moved to Amsterdam. They may have been members of the Reformed Church, but they could also have been just "adherents" (*liefhebbers,* or sympathizers). At the baptism of their youngest child they also presented two-year-old Trijntje for baptism. Her religious status became regularized, and the children born afterwards were baptized consistently in the Reformed Church. One fact is certain: in 1606 their eldest son, Bastiaen, was not baptized with his two younger siblings. In fact, when he was eleven years old he was not living at home anymore. While his parents were still at Harlingen, he had become an apprentice caffa worker in Amsterdam. Indeed, according to his marriage license, he had been living in that city since 1605.

Around 1600 many barge operators like Bastiaen's father lived in the Reguliersbuurt, which was a convenient location for barge travel between Amsterdam, Utrecht, and Leiden.[54] But this was also a neighborhood where many caffa workers settled. Under this scenario, Bastiaen probably lived at the home of his employer or in a boardinghouse as a daytime apprentice. Most caffa workers and other workers employed in the luxury cloth industry were immigrants from the Southern Netherlands and were predominantly Calvinist Walloons. When in the 1610s the town was enlarged with the Jordaan extension, many of the Walloon caffa workers took up residence in that new district, in particular on the Bloemgracht and the Egelantiersgracht.

---

[52] SAA, DTB 5, p. 65; 39, p. 95, 208 and 370.
[53] Their marriage has not been found in the Amsterdam register.
[54] Erika Kuijpers, *Migrantenstad. Immigratie en sociale verhoudingen in 17^e-eeuws Amsterdam* (Hilversum: Verloren, 2005), 171.

Krol's family had lived there since 1630. Thus, as an apprentice in the caffa industry, Krol was most likely trained and influenced by Reformed Walloons who dominated that craft. They may have influenced him in his decision to become a member of the Reformed Church and made him familiar with the French language.

Bastiaen postponed becoming Dutch Reformed until after he married. Because it probably was a mixed marriage, there is no registration of the marriage on record in the Reformed Church. One reason for his conversion may have been that Bastiaen was not cut out for the strict discipline of the Mennonites. For one, he engaged in premarital sex with his future wife. That would explain the unusual chronology of baptisms in his family: first his son, and then himself, after he was married. The pressure from the Reformed consistory could have persuaded him to leave the Mennonite congregation. And his conversion may have motivated the Reverend Gosuinus Geldorpius (1563-1627) to have a favorable opinion of Krol when he examined him in Amsterdam on November 30, 1623. Before Geldorpius came to Amsterdam in 1612, he had served for sixteen years as a minister in the Frisian city of Sneek, where he had fiercely opposed the Mennonites.[55]

Nonetheless, something else must have stimulated Krol's religious zeal for the Reformed faith. During the unsettled early days of the Dutch Republic, when the Reformed church was laying its foundation, it was not uncommon for people to experience life-altering changes after their conversion to the new faith.[56] We should consider Krol's sudden change in 1623 within the broader context of the religious élan of those who founded the West India Company in 1621. The company asserted itself in popular propaganda as anti-Spanish and anti-Catholic, much more so than did the East India Company. The West India Company had an explicit mission to conquer and to convert. The company had a massive number of recruits, and in July 1623 the Amsterdam consistory made an appeal to find comforters of the sick to man the company's ships. Many religiously motivated young artisans jumped at the opportunity. The element of adventure must also have been an important motive for young single men who wanted to get away from their jobs that were

---

[55] R.B. Evenhuis, *Ook dat was Amsterdam*, 5 vols. *De kerk der hervorming in de gouden eeuw* (Amsterdam: W. ten Have, 1965), 1:214.

[56] A similar example from the same period was the apprentice-tailor Evert Willemsz Bogaert from Woerden. Bogaert later became known as Everardus Bogardus. As the second Reformed minister of New Netherland, he was a contemporary of Bastiaen Krol and must have known him well as a commissioner at Fort Orange in 1638-1644. See: Willem Frijhoff, *Fulfilling God's Mission: The Two Worlds of Dominie Everardus Bogardus, 1607-1647* (Leiden: Brill, 2007), and his biography in this volume.

probably quite mundane; volunteering for the West India Company was an opportunity to travel to remote destinations around the world. It must have been so for Bastiaen as well. Surprisingly, he was even willing to leave his wife and young child for the unknowns of the New World.

But was he really qualified for the job? Did he have enough education? The marked cross in lieu of a signature on his marriage license and the later unsteady signatures on documents do not point to learning, but neither do they automatically mean he was illiterate. As an apprentice craftsman he most probably had only limited opportunity for schooling. When assessing the level of educational attainment of individuals in the early modern era, however, a clear distinction should be made between learning *to read* and learning *to write*. It is quite possible that Krol could read flawlessly but did not have much training in how to write. In the Dutch Republic learning to read was crucial. Protestants deemed it foundational to their religion that everyone could read the Bible. Writing, however, was another matter. This skill, for which pupils often had to pay extra, was normally taught after one had learned how to read. In general, writing was considered less important than reading.[57] Most likely, Bastiaen learned this skill at a later age, after he realized his spiritual calling. This squared with Krol's supposed Mennonite background, which focused on Bible reading, even though the Mennonites remained leery of the intentions of the Reformed education that had become the basis of public schools. Nevertheless, eight years after his baptism Krol's level of literacy must have been adequate for him to pass the consistory's exam for the position of comforter of the sick. There were plenty of craftsmen like Krol who had additional schooling in the workplace. In November 1624 at the latest he must have been able to write neatly enough for keeping record of the baptisms as required by church order. According to the few books in Krol's household inventory from 1645, however, we can only guess that he was not a scholar, but just a man of practical piety.

Comfort for the Dutch Reformed

Recently a pamphlet written by Krol has been discovered. His anti-Spanish and anti-Catholic views were clearly echoed in this document, which had been written in the aftermath of the Twelve-Year Truce (1609-1621). Moreover, the pamphlet is a revealing testimony of his religious convictions. It is a simple, eight-page pamphlet entitled

---

[57] See R.A. Houston, *Literacy in Early Modern Europe. Culture and Education 1500-1800* (2d ed.; Harlow etc,: Longman, 2002); and for the daily practice in the Netherlands: Jeroen Blaak, *Literacy in Everyday Life: Reading and Writing in Early Modern Dutch Diaries*. Trans. Beverley Jackson (Leiden: Brill, 2009).

Troost der vromen die in desen tegenwoordigen staet der kercke Gods becommert zijn [Comfort for the godly who are troubled about the present state of God's church]. It was anonymously published in 1623, the year in which he volunteered for a mission as comforter of the sick. The publisher was Gerrit Hendricksen van Breugel (or Breughel), whose publishing house *De Werelt vol drucx* ['The World full of print'] in Amsterdam was located in an alley named Dirck van Assensteeg. Breugel was active as a publisher between 1610 and 1629 and printed every type of literature, from marriage poems to pamphlets on disasters. He had a preference, however, for literature that supported Dutch Reformed orthodoxy. For example, in the publication *Dry tafelen der Heylighe Schriftuere* [Three tables of the Holy Scripture] (1612), the "Old Godly Teachings" of the Reformed Church were compared to the new, purely human doctrine of the Roman Catholics. In 1610 and 1612 Breugel had published two works of the devout Puritan theologian William Perkins, which had been translated by Vincent Meusevoet.[58] In 1626 Breugel published a eulogy in honor of the late Stadtholder Prince Maurice of Orange, the defender of the orthodox Calvinists, who had died in 1625. This text was authored by "an advocate of the Reformed Church" who was saddened by the end of the fair and successful government of His Princely Excellence.

There is no doubt about whom the anonymous author of *Comfort for the Godly* must have been. On the title page the author is only listed as being an "Advocate of the Truth". But in the body of the text there are two signatures with the name "B[astiaen]. I[ansz]. Krol." The pamphlet is a dialogue composed in rhyme between two characters, one called "Firm Believer" (a Dutch Reformed partisan) and the other "Skeptic" (a sympathizer of the Roman Catholic faith). In some parts a melody is noted, namely the song composed in honor of the popular commander of the Dutch fleet, Jacob van Heemskerck, the heroic survivor of the Nova Zembla expedition of 1596-1597, who died in 1607 during the Battle of Gibraltar against the Spanish. The melody is based on a love ballad entitled "Ick lyd' int hart pijn ongewoon" ["My heart suffers from an unusual pain"] and a religious song entitled "O Heer en goedertieren Godt" ["Oh Lord and merciful God"], which originated from the same period as Krol's pamphlet.[59]

---

[58] Reverend Vincent Meusevoet was most probably the uncle of Reverend Everardus Bogardus; cf. Frijhoff, *Fulfilling God's Mission*, 84-92, and his biography in this volume

[59] The melody of this "contrafact" (a song sung to a known melody) has been identified with the help of Louis P. Grijp at the Meertens Institute of the Royal Netherlands Academy of Arts and Sciences, at Amsterdam.

The pamphlet primarily opposed the Catholics, referred to as "Romanists," "Mother's Folk" or the "Associates of the Anti-Christ." It warns its readers not to believe the Anti-Christ (the Pope) and his supporters. It concludes with an "Encore for the Romanists," composed in the style of a sonnet. The pamphlet can be recited as if someone was just speaking to another person. Its dialogue style, together with the rhyming and the melody, indicate that the author was a layman who was used to memorizing texts and then rewriting them in a cadenced style, then putting them back into the form of a song so they could be easily remembered, and consequently sung in company of others. This was a practice the Dutch were well-known for.[60] That familiarity with oral culture, in combination with literary style and rhetorical technique, is exactly what one might expect from a practical layman like Krol, a strong believer who was concerned about the purity of God's word.

So we should regard Krol as the man behind "Advocate of the Truth." In the course of the dialogue he tried to win the trust of the Skeptic by using spiritual arguments and convincing him of the righteousness of the "True Reformed faith," with the Republic's economic and religious situation looming in the background. In retrospect, the situation for supporters of the Reformed faith was not as glorious as is often believed. It is true that the Reformed were successful in 1619 in having the orthodox doctrine of the Reformed faith accepted at the Synod of Dort as the only "true" one. However, they were less fortunate two years later when the Twelve-Year Truce ended and the war with Catholic Spain resumed. In February 1623 a conspiracy to murder Prince Maurice was uncovered. In October 1622 the city of Bergen op Zoom had been liberated at great cost, but the Spanish still had a significant presence in the rest of the province. In Germany the Catholic league under the command of General Tilly was triumphant in victory after victory, and on August 6, 1623, was successful in wiping out the Protestant army at the Battle of Stadtlohn, which was across from the Republic's astern border near Winterswijk. It was probably against this backdrop during the weeks before his request to the consistory in October 1623 that Krol edited his text so that his fellow believers would have a greater trust in God and be more convinced that the Reformed faith was the only true one and finally would be victorious.

If this analysis is correct, Krol's early years and his relationship with the Reformed faith should be viewed in a new perspective. First,

---

[60] For this process see: Ulrich Bach, "Oral rhetoric in writings for a mixed literate and illiterate audience," *Poetics* 18 (1989): 257-70.

he was not illiterate even when he used a cross mark as a signature. The pamphlet that was published in 1623, edited eight years after his cross-marked signature, indicates that he was a pious and practical man, versed in the Bible, and committed to God's word.[61] But he was also a man who could communicate in the greater context of his community and country, then translate those ideas to people with little or no education. He used a means in which they were most familiar, namely dialogues, rhymes, songs, and poems. This was probably a watered-down version of the kind of poetry being written by members of the local literary societies called "Chambers of Rhetoric."[62] Given the stereotyped literary form of the pamphlet, Krol may have been a member, a supporter, or perhaps even an enthusiastic participant in a Chamber of Rhetoric himself.

But Krol might have also been influenced to write the pamphlet by his Mennonite past, which had the tradition of applying God's word to the events of everyday life. In 1623 the West India Company was expanding rapidly and needed people desperately. In their proclamation appointing a national day of prayer and thanksgiving for the founding of the company, the States General recalled on December 13, 1623, the duty of the company to defend God's honor against the Catholics, and to spread God's word to heathens. That is exactly what one finds in Krol's pamphlet. Krol's ability to adapt to many situations did not prevent him from taking a clear stance on religious matters. Despite his recent conversion from the Mennonite confession around 1623, Krol had become a zealous orthodox and convinced Calvinist. He was an outspoken opponent of the Remonstrants (the more liberal Arminians) and an ardent adversary of Catholicism, both of which he considered a threat. Today there are only two known copies of his pamphlet in existence and no reprint is known, which leads us to believe that it was not widely dispersed.[63] However, the pamphlet was a powerful tool to convince the consistory of his orthodox convictions. At that time Krol's

---

[61] Besides mention of well-known biblical characters such as Joseph, David, Goliath, and Holofernes, the pamphlet also makes explicit references to passages in the Bible: 1 Kings 10:29; 1 Kings 20; John 17:12; and Revelations 1:9; 13:1-10; 18:1-8; 21:8; 22:15.

[62] For the rhyming and poetical practices of the Chambers of Rhetoric see: Willem Frijhoff, "Burgerlijk dichtplezier in 1650?" *Spiegel der Letteren. Tijdschrift voor Nederlandse literatuurgeschiedenis en voor literatuurwetenschap* 43:3 (2001): 248-69; Arjan van Dixhoorn and Susie Speakman Sutch, eds., *The Reach of the Republic of Letters: Literary and Learned Societies in late Medieval and Early Modern Europe,* 2 vols. (Leiden: Brill, 2008).

[63] In the University Libraries of Amsterdam and Leiden (Bibliotheca Thysiana).

personal effort for the sake of the "true faith" was exactly what the West India Company needed and what the consistory sought: a protector of the faith in the threatened homeland and a missionary who would convert heathens abroad. It was this character that made him suitable to be dispatched to a far-away colony intended to shelter orthodox believers.

It is possible that Krol initially wanted to be assigned to Brazil. The "West Indies" was mentioned when he first reported to the consistory. Being dispatched to the West Indies would have meant fighting against the Catholics, the Spanish, and the Portuguese. The :Godless Papists" whom Krol condemned in his pamphlet were the enemy on the borders of the Dutch Republic just as much as they were on the wilderness frontiers in the Americas, especially in the Caribbean and in the South. Because of the adjustments necessitated by illness—the first afflicting the appointee whom Krol then replaced and the second afflicting Krol himself—it was, in all likelihood, only by coincidence that Krol was sent to New Netherland. In the first few years he must have enjoyed working there, especially among so many orthodox believers like himself.

By the time his term expired in 1626, there were not many left of the original group of pious Walloons who had sought refuge in the colony. In the meantime, aspirations for the colony had grown and changed in the direction of agriculture and trade; its leadership did not want development hindered by religious matters. Perhaps that was the reason why Krol resigned from his position as comforter of the sick. But he did remain Reformed, and he may have served as a reader of the Holy Scriptures at the domestic services in isolated settlements along the Hudson River. After his return to the Netherlands he continued to enjoy a reputation as a God-fearing believer. A Reformed colonist who in 1649 anonymously published a pamphlet entitled *Breeden-Raedt* [Broad Advice], addressing the troubles in New Netherland, contrasted the "Eerlijck Commijs Crol" [honest commissioner Krol] with the corrupt secretary of New Netherland, Cornelis van Tienhoven, who cheated Krol out of more than 4,000 guilders.[64]

In 1645 Krol believed it was important to reconcile with the congregation in Amsterdam. Several times he requested that the consistory readmit him to communion. Krol was willing to humble himself before the same consistory that had hired him as a comforter of the sick twenty years earlier. For Krol it must have been high time

---

[64] *Breeden-Raedt aende Vereenichde Nederlandsche Provintien [...] gemaeckt ende gestelt uyt diverse ware en waerachtige memorien, door I.A.G.W.C.* (Antwerpen: Van Duynen, 1649), f. F1 v°.

to exonerate himself of accusations of neglecting church discipline, having weakened faith, and yielding to hollow opportunism. In New Netherland Krol had found his first meaningful task as a Calvinist servant of the church, despite being a layman and not a minister. But he was more observant of practical faith and piety than of orthodox doctrine. In that regard Krol's role as New Netherland's first church servant deserves a more prominent place in the history of the colony that later developed such a deep-rooted piety.

In conclusion, new research on Bastiaen Jansz Krol restores him as a remarkable figure and one of the founding fathers of New Netherland. His astonishing career began with a strong religious drive, which made him fit for pioneering conditions until he fell victim to an internal regime change in 1632. His life course shows the limits and opportunities of lower ranking clerics, but also makes him an excellent representative of the still little-known category of so-called "transit migrants," those who returned to the fatherland.

CHAPTER 2

Jonas Michaëlius (1584–c. 1638): The Making of the First Minister

Jaap Jacobs

As one walks along Fifth Avenue in midtown New York City, it is easy to miss the spire of Marble Collegiate Church amidst the highrises. Despite its limited visibility, Marble and its three sister churches, collectively known as the Collegiate Churches, trace their origin to one of the oldest institutions on Manhattan: the first established congregation of the Dutch Reformed Church, now named the Reformed Church in America.

Marble Church displays its heritage on the tip of the church spire by means of a Dutch *windhaan*, weathervane. Down on Fifth Avenue, other memorials, such as the plaque commemorating the founding of the church in 1628, remind passers-by of the church's history. Interestingly, the text provides only the name of the secular authority at the time, Director Pieter Minuit, without any reference to the religious authority. Although the name of the first minister is omitted from the plaque, the website of Marble Church traces its founding to the arrival of *predikant* Jonas Michaëlius in 1628.[1] One could argue for an earlier

[1] www.marblechurch.org/AboutUs/History/OurOrigin/tabid/86/Default.aspx (accessed May 25, 2010). Marble Church omits the diaeresis mark (¨) on the e in

Picture of Albert Eekhof,
(1884-1933) Church historian
at Leyden University

[Historisch Documentatiecentrum
voor het Nederlands Protestantisme
(1800-heden)
Universiteitsbibliotheek Vrije
Universiteit Amsterdam]

founding date, however, as a religious community holding services was already in existence under comforter of the sick Bastiaen Jansz Krol, four years prior to Michaëlius's arrival and the formal organization of a congregation. The choice for 1628 as the critical moment seems to be a relic from the institutional, i.e. congregational and denominational, focus of previous generations of historians instead of the "religious history" preferred by most historical scholars today. Indeed, it may be more interesting to ask how and why the image of Jonas Michaëlius as founding father of Marble Collegiate Church—and by extension of the Reformed Church in America—was created, considering how little is actually known about him. In the first part of this article, I will aim to outline how the image of Michaëlius was created. Having thus separated the wheat from the chaff, I will in the second part examine Michaëlius as he appears to us from the documentary evidence.

Michaëlius, spelling it Michaelius. As Michaëlius himself in his manuscripts uses the diaeresis mark, I have adopted it as well in this article. The plaque at Marble Collegiate Church is undated, but was affixed in 1900, when Middle Collegiate Church (2nd Avenue, near 7th St.) also put up plaques for Pieter Minuit, the early comforters of the sick, and Jonas Michaëlius. See Edward T. Corwin (trans. and ed.), *Ecclesiastical Records of the State of New York*, 7 vols. (Albany: Lyon, 1901-1916), 1:45, 48, 69, (hereafter cited as *ERNY*. "Tablets to Commemorate the Work of Early Dutch Pastors," *New York Times*, October 27, 1900.

The Search for the First Minister of New Netherland

Michaëlius has not always been considered to be the founder of the Reformed Church in New Netherland. In fact, he is not even mentioned in the first serious history of the colony, E.B. O'Callaghan's *History of New Netherland* of 1846-1848. O'Callaghan designates Everardus Bogardus as "the first clergyman of whom we have any mention in New Netherland."[2] John Romeyn Brodhead, writing with slightly less caution in the first volume of his history of New York State, published in 1853, bestowed on Bogardus the honor of being "the first clergyman at Manhattan."[3] Both O'Callaghan and Brodhead wrote their books on the basis of two specific collections of documents. The first collection, the archives of the government of New Netherland, was then kept at the New York State Capitol and consisted for the most part of council minutes and correspondence, starting in the late 1630s.[4] The other collection, also kept in Albany, consisted of transcripts procured by Brodhead in The Hague and Amsterdam during his sojourn in Europe as agent of the State of New York. The bulk of the material was copied from the archives of the States General.[5] As neither collection contained a single reference to Michaëlius, their conclusions seemed reasonable and valid at the time.

The desire to designate a founder and to attach a year of founding to an existing institution is not in itself surprising and is indicative of the growing historical awareness in the first part of the nineteenth century.[6] By that time the name of Michaëlius had been lost in time.

[2] Edmund B. O'Callaghan, *History of New Netherland, or New York under the Dutch*, 2 vols. (New York: Appleton, 1855), 2:142, n.1.
[3] John Romeyn Brodhead, *History of the State of New York: First Period 1609-1664* (New York, 1853). In the second edition of 1859, Brodhead replaced "the first clergyman" with "who succeeded Michaelius as minister."
[4] O'Callaghan compiled a calendar of these manuscripts, published in 1865: *Calendar of Historical Manuscripts in the Office of the Secretary of State, Albany, N.Y. Part I. Dutch Manuscripts, 1630-1664* (Albany, 1865). This collection is currently housed in the New York State Archives. Large parts of it are published, in the excellent translations of Charles Gehring, by the New Netherland Project. For an overview of sources, see Jaap Jacobs, *New Netherland: A Dutch Colony in Seventeenth-Century America* (Leiden: Brill, 2005), List of Archival Sources, 495-505 and the articles referenced there.
[5] John Romeyn Brodhead, *The Final Report of John Romeyn Brodhead, Agent of the State of New-York, to Procure and Transcribe Documents in Europe, Relative to the Colonial History of said State. Made to the Governor, 12th February, 1845* (Albany: E. Mack, printer to the Senate, 1845).
[6] For a critique of the nationalistic type of history-writing which proclaimed New England to be the foundation of the United States, see Joyce D. Goodfriend, "Present at the Creation: Making the Case for the Dutch Founders of America," *Early American Studies* 7.2 (Fall 2009): 259-69.

The early years of the church had not been recorded in institutional memory or oral tradition. Nor did the local church archives, or what little was left of them, provide any information.[7] Memorials that could have filled the void, like a plaque with the names of former ministers on it, had not survived the migration of the church—via several locations—to its present building on Fifth Avenue, built in 1851-1854. Yet the desire to fill in gaps in the ecclesiastical record was obvious. At the request of Thomas De Witt, then minister of Marble Church and also a vice-president of the New York Historical Society, Brodhead contacted the Classis of Amsterdam during his trip to secure European archives. He received permission to borrow seven bundles of correspondence between the American churches and the Amsterdam Classis, i.e. the original documents, not copies. De Witt later managed to convince his Amsterdam colleagues to transfer ownership of the papers to the General Synod of the Dutch Church in America. The collection, named the Amsterdam Correspondence, is now owned by the Reformed Church in America and is housed in the Gardner A. Sage Library of New Brunswick Theological Seminary. Even these papers would not have made much difference: Michaëlius was not mentioned in them and—unbeknownst to researchers at the time—it was not the Amsterdam Classis but the Amsterdam Consistory that in the early years had assumed responsibility for overseeing colonial churches.[8]

The lack of historical data remained vexing for both Americans and Dutchmen. Reporting on his travels in North America in the 1850s, Derk Buddingh, a Dutchman from Delft, wrote that "the Reformed Dutch Church in America remembers its Dutch descent with grateful love,"[9] but also noted that little knowledge of its earliest days was extant. Without providing any evidence, he put the probable date of founding of the church very early indeed, 1619.[10] Despite his travels to New York,

---

[7] On the earliest archives of the Collegiate Churches, see Francis J. Sypher ed. and trans., *Liber A 1628-1700 of the Collegiate Churches of New York* (Grand Rapids, MI: Eerdmans, 2009).

[8] ERNY 1:11-13. On De Witt, see E.T. Corwin, *A Manual of the Reformed Church in America (formerly Ref. Prot. Dutch Church)* (New York: Board of Publication of the Reformed Church in America, 1902), 421-23. On the classis and the consistory, see Jaap Jacobs, *The Colony of New Netherland: A Dutch Settlement in Seventeenth-Century America* (Ithaca: Cornell University Press, 2009), 145.

[9] D. Buddingh, *De kerk, school en wetenschap in de Vereenigde Staten van Noord-Amerika*. 3 vols. (Utrecht: Kemink & Zoon, 1853), in which *De Hervormde, Hollandsche Kerk in de Vereenigde Staten van Noord-Amerika* (Utrecht: Kemink & Zoon, 1852), v: "de Herv. Hollandsche Kerk in Amerika, zich met dankbare liefde hare Hollandsche afkomst blijft herinneren."

[10] Buddingh, *De Hervormde, Hollandsche Kerk*, 26, very likely based this remark on a footnote in Alexander Gunn, *Memoirs of the Rev. John H. Livingston, D.D.S.T.P. prepared*

where he visited Marble Collegiate Church, Buddingh had no choice but to follow O'Callaghan in designating Bogardus as the first minister.[11] Even so, Bogardus, quarrelsome and inclined to drunkenness, was hardly the exemplary first minister that the nineteenth-century Dutch Reformed Church required in an age of revivals and social reform.[12]

Michaëlius Replaces Bogardus

Bogardus was suddenly ousted as first minister in 1857 when a letter, written by Manhattan dominie Jonas Michaëlius on August 11, 1628, and addressed to dominie Adriaen Jorisz Smout or Smoutius in Amsterdam, came to light in the Netherlands. Its discovery must be credited to J.T. Bodel Nijenhuis.[13] This collector was inspired to

---

in Compliance with a Request of the General Synod of the Reformed Church in North America (New York: Rutgers Press, 1829), 79, which is quoted in David D. Demarest, *History and Characteristics of the Reformed Protestant Dutch Church* (New York: Board of Publication of the Reformed Protestant Dutch Church, 1856), 61.

[11] Buddingh, *De Hervormde, Hollandsche Kerk*, v-vii, 22, 26, 164. On Buddingh, see the *Nieuw Nederlandsch Biografisch Woordenboek*, vol. 1, 510 on www.inghist.nl/retroboeken/nnwb (accessed May 25, 2010), and Wap, "Levensbericht van Derk Buddingh" in *Jaarboek van de Maatschappij der Nederlandse Letterkunde* (1876): 125-34, on www.dbnl.org (accessed 26 May 2010). American writers of this decade, like Buddingh, followed Brodhead and O'Callaghan. See Demarest, *History and Characteristics*, 61 and Thomas DeWitt, *A Discourse Delivered in the North Reformed Dutch Church (Collegiate) in the City of New York, on the last Sabbath in August, 1856* (New York: Board of Publication of the Reformed Protestant Dutch Church, 337 Broadway, 1857), 21.

[12] Firth Haring Fabend, *Zion on the Hudson: Dutch New York and New Jersey in the Age of Revivals* (New Brunswick, NJ: Rutgers University Press, 2000).

[13] Johannes Tiberius Bodel Nijenhuis (1797-1872) was a former director of Leiden publishing house Luchtmans, which he left in 1852 in order to spend the remainder of his life collecting maps, engravings and books, part of which he willed to the Leiden University Library. See *Nieuw Nederlandsch Biografisch Woordenboek*, 10 vols. (Leiden: Sijthoff, 1911-1937), 4:179-80 (hereafter cited as *NNBW*) and W.N. du Rieu, "Levensbericht van Mr. Johannes Tiberius Bodel Nijenhuis," *Jaarboek van de Maatschappij der Nederlandse Letterkunde* (1873), 247-88. Bodel Nijenhuis purchased the letter at the 1833 auction of the collection of Jacobus Koning, a manuscript collector and clerk of the court in Amsterdam. How Koning had acquired the letter is unknown, but the extent of his collection is obvious from the catalogs of the 1828 and 1633 auction: *Catalogus van een aanzienlijke verkooping van Latijnsche, Nederduitsche en Fsransche uitmuntend geconditioneerde boeken en handschriften* (Amsterdam 1828) (Koninklijke Bibliotheek, The Hague: Verzcat 15713) and *Catalogus der letterkundige nalatenschap van wijlen Jacobus Koning ... Tweede deel. Boekwerken enz. waarvan de verkooping zal plaats hebben op maandag, den 14den october 1833 en volgende dagen, des voormiddags ten 10 en des namiddags ten 6 ure, ten overstaan van een bevoegd beambte, ten huize van de wed. C.S. Roos, in Het Huis met de Hoofden, op de Keizersgracht, bij de Heerenstraat, te Amsterdam, onder directie van de makelaars: Jeronimo de Vries, Albertus Brondgeest, Engelbert Michael Engelberts en Cornelis François Roos* (Amsterdam, 1833) (Koninklijke Bibliotheek, The Hague: Verzcat 15714 and Verzcat 13081). The

publish the letter in his possession by contemporary publications on New Netherland—not just American imprints, such as by O'Callaghan and Brodhead, but also Dutch ones, like those by amateur historians H.J. Koenen and O. van Rees.[14] In promulgating the discovery, Bodel Nijenhuis was not just out to correct Brodhead's mistaken identification of Bogardus as the first Dutch clergyman on Manhattan, but he also sought to provide background information on Michaëlius. Finding a "Michaëlis" enrolled at Leiden University on September 9, 1600, Bodel Nijenhuis assumed this to be his man. Similarly, using published lists of Dutch ministers, he identified Michaëlius as the minister of Nibbixwoude and Hem in North Holland and as *predikant* on the West India Company fleet that captured St. Salvador in Brazil in 1624. He furthermore contended that, when this conquest had been abandoned a year later, Michaëlius had proceeded to Fort Elmina in present-day Ghana before traveling back to the Dutch Republic in 1627.[15]

Bodel Nijenhuis's article immediately attracted the attention of Henry Cruse Murphy, who had just arrived as the Resident Minister of the United States to the Netherlands. This was a position with such light official duties that it allowed him ample time to indulge in his main hobby, history. Murphy, Brooklyn-born, had already shown his interest in New Netherland by translating the journal of captain and New Netherland colonist David Pietersz de Vries and two pamphlets on the colony in 1853 and 1854. He later published two letters relating to the Dutch conquest of New Sweden; a volume on New Netherland poetry by Steendam, Selijns, and De Sille; and a book on Henry Hudson. In the meantime he assembled an impressive collection of books and manuscripts on early America and especially New York.[16] Obviously,

---

1628 letter of Michaëlius is lot no. 1180: "Eigenhandige brief van Jonas Michaelis aan den Predikant Smoutius. 1628", purchased by "Luchtmans" for 75 cents. On Jacobus Koning, see *NNBW* 4:849-50.

[14] H.J. Koenen, "Pavonia. Eene bijdrage tot de kennis der voormalige Nederlandsche koloniën," *Bijdragen voor vaderlandsche geschiedenis en oudheidkunde* 5 (1847): 114-32; O. van Rees, *Geschiedenis der Nederlandsche volkplantingen in Noord-Amerika, beschouwd uit het oogpunt der koloniale politiek. Drie voorlezingen, gehouden in de afdeeling koophandel der maatschappij: Felix Meritis, te Amsterdam, op 8, 15 en 22 februarij 1855* (Tiel: H.C.A. Campagne, 1855).

[15] J.T. Bodel Nijenhuis, "Jonas Michaëlius. Eerste predikant der Nederduitsche Hervormde Gemeente op Manhattan of Nieuw-Amsterdam, het latere New-York, in Noord-Amerika," *Kerkhistorisch Archief* 1 (1857): 365-88.

[16] Publications: Henry C. Murphy, *Voyages from Holland to America, A.D. 1632 to 1644. By David Peterson De Vries* (New York 1853); *Vertoogh van Nieu Nederland and Breeden Raedt aende Vereenichde Nederlandsche Provintien. Two rare tracts, printed in 1649-'50. Relating to the administrations of affairs in New Netherland* (New York 1854); "Two Original Letters Relating to the Expedition of Governor Stuyvesant against Fort Casimir, on the Delaware," *The Historical Magazine* 2 (1858): 257-59; *Henry Hudson in Holland* (The

any new find was of importance to him. Within a year Murphy prepared a booklet containing a transcription, translation, and facsimile of Michaëlius's letter. The title is telling: *J. Michaëlius: The First Minister of the Dutch Reformed Church in the United States*.[17] In his preface, Murphy asserted that Michaëlius "may now be called the first minister of the Dutch Reformed Church in the United States," and he added:

> We are now carried back five years earlier in the history of the regular ministration of the Gospel in New-York, and are enabled to add one more to the list of clergymen of the Dutch Reformed Church in America, one who, by his attainments and his holy zeal, as well as the high respect with which he was regarded by his learned brethern [sic] in Holland, is not unworthy to take his place at the head of the roll of that learned and pious body.[18]

In praising Michaëlius so profusely, Murphy may in his enthusiasm over the new discovery well have exceeded the boundaries that the availability of just a single document afforded him. Yet any modern researcher who has discovered previously unknown documents can empathize with his exuberance, if less so with Murphy's brand of ancestor worship.

The publications of 1857 and 1858 firmly established Michaëlius's position.[19] Over the following decades its historical value ensured that

---

Hague: Brothers Giunta, 1859; repr. 1909 and 2009); *Jacob Steendam, Noch Vaster. A Memoir of the First Poet in New Netherland with his Poems Descriptive of the Colony* (The Hague: Giunta D'Albani, 1861); *Anthology of New Netherland or Translations from the early Dutch poets of New York with Memoirs of their Lives* (New York: Bradford Club, 1865; repr. Amsterdam: Israel, 1966); Henry Reed Stiles, *Memoir of Hon. Henry C. Murphy, L.L.D., of Brooklyn, N.Y.* (New York: Trow, 1883); *Catalogue of the Magnificent Library of the Late Hon. Henry C. Murphy, of Brooklyn, Long Island, Consisting almost wholly of Americana or Books Relating to America. The whole to be sold by Auction at the Clinton Hall Sales Rooms on Monday, March 3ᵈ, 1884, and the Following Days. Two sessions daily, at 2.30 o'clock, and 7.30 P.M.* (New York: Geo. A. Leavitt, 1884).

[17] H.C. Murphy, *J. Michaëlius: The First Minister of the Dutch Reformed Church in the United States* (The Hague: Giunta D'Albani, 1858; 2ⁿᵈ ed. Amsterdam: Frederik Muller & Cº, 1883). I have used the 1883 reprint, which is subtitled *Facsimilé of his letter, the only extant, written during the first years of the settlement of New-York. With transscript* [sic], *preface and English translation by the late Hon. Henry C. Murphy*. As Murphy had died in Brooklyn on December 1, 1882, the reprint was most likely intended by Muller as a token of honor to his memory. Murphy's translation was included in two nineteenth-century American publications: E.B. O'Callaghan and B. Fernow (trans. and ed.), *Documents Relative to the Colonial History of the State of New York*, 15 vols. (Albany: Weed, Parsons and Company, 1853-1883), 2:757-80.

[18] Murphy, *Michaëlius*, 3.

[19] The only dissenting voice was that of Mary Louise Booth. In her 1859 book *History of the City of New: from its earliest settlement to the present*, she implicitly questioned the authenticity of the letter. In the main text of chapter two, most likely written

the letter of August 11, 1628, was republished in translation several times, as it remained the only known letter written on Manhattan in the 1620s.[20] That is, until the next Michaëlius document was found. It turned up in the archives of the Van Foreest family, parts of which were auctioned by Amsterdam auctioneer R.W.P. de Vries in November 1902. As the *Nieuws van den Dag* reported, lot 153 was a manuscript letter by the first minister of New York, "a curious letter, very important for the history of the first colonists," addressed to Joannes van Foreest and dated August 8, 1628, thus predating the letter to Smout by only three days. The letter fetched 635 guilders, a considerable amount of money.[21] Its new owner, William Harris Arnold from Nutley, New Jersey, a well-known collector of rare books and manuscripts, allowed Dingman Versteeg, then library clerk and official translator of the Holland Society of New York, to transcribe and translate the letter, resulting in the 1904 publication of his *Manhattan in 1628*.[22]

In his preface Versteeg corrected a few details on Michaëlius's early career in Brazil and West Africa. He was able to show that the minister departed for Brazil with the reinforcement fleet under Jan

---

before Murphy conveyed news of the Michaëlius letter to the United States, she still designated Bogardus as "the first clergyman" (pp. 63-64). In a footnote she acknowledged the letter, "purporting to have been addressed by Jonas Michaëlius" and stated that Murphy was "strongly persuaded" of the letter's authenticity. Yet she remained cautious and pointed out that its provenance was unknown. Later historians, such as Gabriel Poillon Disosway, *The Earliest Churches of New York and its Vicinity* (New York: James G. Gregory, 1865), 15, had no such qualms.

[20] For instance in *Collections of the New-York Historical Society* vol. 13 (1881). There are several later reprints, for an overview see J. Franklin Jameson ed., *Narratives of New Netherland 1609-1664* (New York: Charles Scribner's Sons, 1909; reprint New York: Barnes & Noble Inc., 1967), 120-21 and Kees-Jan Waterman, Jaap Jacobs, and Charles T. Gehring, eds., *Indianenverhalen: De vroegste beschrijvingen van Indianen langs de Hudsonrivier (1609-1680)* (Zutphen: Walburg Pers, 2009), 55-56. The original of the letter is now in the New York Public Library.

[21] *Nieuws van den Dag,* 26 November 1902, 4e blad, p. 13; Jameson, *Narratives of New Netherland,* 121. It was bought by Frederik Muller & Co., who may have been acting as an agent for interested American parties, as the letter subsequently made its way to William Harris Arnold. The letter was later purchased by Henry E. Huntington and is now in the Huntington Library, San Marino, California.

[22] Dingman Versteeg, *Manhattan in 1628 as Described in the Recently Discovered Autograph Letter of Jonas Michaëlius written from the Settlement on the 8th of August of that year and now first published with a Review of the Letter and an Historical Sketch of New Netherland to 1628* (New York: Dodd, Mead and Company, 1904, repr. Salem, MA: Higginson Book Company, s.a.). On Dingman Versteeg, see Peter R. Christoph, 'Introduction,' in Dingman Versteeg trans., Peter R. Christoph, Kenneth Scott, Kenn Styker-Rodda eds., *Kingston Papers. Volume I Kingston Court Records, 1661-1667. New York Historical Manuscripts: Dutch* (Baltimore: Genealogical Publishing Co., 1976), xvi-xvii.

Dircksz Lam of 1625, rather than with the 1624 fleet, for instance. This fleet never arrived in Brazil, as it changed its destination to West Africa after news of the recapture of St. Salvador reached its admiral, Jan Dircksz Lam. Similarly, Versteeg implicitly denounced the supposition that Michaëlius subsequently served at Elmina, as the attack on this Portuguese fort in 1625 failed. The fort was not conquered by the Dutch until a decade later. Versteeg suggested that the minister may have stayed at Fort Nassau on the Guinea coast instead. Acknowledging the scarcity of sources, he put his hope in new discoveries:

> Perhaps there lie buried in obscure and as yet unknown records somewhere in Netherland interesting facts about the Rev. Jonas Michaëlius and also about his son, which research may at some future period bring to light.[23]

New Evidence by Albert Eekhof

Versteeg's wish was partly fulfilled through the research of Albert Eekhof. In his 1926 monograph on Michaëlius,[24] Eekhof introduced another newly-found Michaëlius letter, as well as copies of two letters from Joannes van Foreest written to the minister while in New Netherland.[25] Through excellent research and aided by the greater accessibility of archival sources, Eekhof was able to provide much new information on Michaëlius's early years, especially his background in North Holland and at Leiden University. Eekhof's findings changed Michaëlius's year of birth from 1577 to 1584 and his year of matriculation from 1600 to 1598. It turned out that Michaëlius during his years in Leiden stayed at the Staten College and was specifically recommended by Josias Vibo, the rector of the Latin School in Hoorn. Also, Michaëlius received financial aid for his studies from the city magistrates of Hoorn. These details may flesh out the early part of Michaëlius's biography

---

[23] Versteeg, *Manhattan in 1628*, 23.

[24] A. Eekhof, *Jonas Michaëlius: Founder of the Church in New Netherland: His Life and Work, together with the Facsimile, Transcription and English Translation of an Extensive Unknown Autograph Latin Letter, which He Wrote from Manhattan Island 13 September 1630, Now Published for the First Time by Prof. Dr. A. Eekhof* (Leiden: Sijthoff, 1926). On Eekhof, see J. Lindeboom, "Levensbericht van prof. dr. Albert Eekhof 26 juli 1884-23 maart 1933", *Levensberichten van de Maatschappij der Nederlandsche Letterkunde te Leiden* (1932-1933), 135-45.

[25] These are now in Regionaal Historisch Centrum Alkmaar, archives of the families Van Foreest (1422-1979) and Van Egmond van de Bijenburg (1428-1765), inv. nos. 65 and 71.

but are in themselves hardly remarkable. Like many other young men aspiring to the ministry around 1600, Michaëlius had to rely on patronage to achieve his aim.[26]

Eekhof was also able to find many details on Michaëlius's father, Jan Michielsz., although it must be noted that in his book he glossed over the violent episodes and extolled Michielsz as "a pioneer of liberty" (p. 22). Jan Michielsz was a monk in Flanders who joined the Reformation early on and became a Protestant minister. When the tide turned, he fled to England, only to return with a vengeance in 1568, participating in the murder of Catholic priests in the Flemish Westkwartier. He subsequently became a minister on the fleet of the Sea Beggars and served as messenger between Diederick Sonoy, the leader of the Sea Beggars who organized the war in the Northern Quarter, and William of Orange. In 1582 he was appointed as minister of the Reformed Church in Grootebroeck, where Michaëlius was born two years later. His father made another official trip to England, was a delegate to several synod meetings in North Holland, and died in 1595.[27]

The main focus of Eekhof's book, however, is on New Netherland. While acknowledging the role of Michaëlius in the founding of the church (p. 2), Eekhof devoted much attention on the preceding years, partly based on his own 1910 book on Bastiaen Jansz Krol.[28] Using additional information, Eekhof put "the birth of the Dutch Reformed Church of America" in 1624, when Krol arrived. Yet on the same page he asserted that "the coming of Jonas Michaëlius as a regular minister to Manhattan Island in the year 1628, must be reckoned as the date of founding of the Church in America" (p. 2). Such inconsistencies are minor points amidst what is an impressive work of early twentieth-century scholarship. Eekhof's archival research on Michaëlius was so thorough that it has not been bettered since. At the end of his narrative Eekhof, like Versteeg before him, expressed the hope that "one day or another we may find some small fact or point of contact, perhaps a hint or a document, which shows us the way to enclose the end of [Michaëlius's] career in this world" (p. 78). As this has not yet occurred,

---

[26] In that sense, he is similar to Everardus Bogardus, who also attended Leiden, and Balthasar Stuyvesant, who studied at Franeker. See Frijhoff's contribution on Bogardus in this volume and Jaap Jacobs, "Like Father, Like Son? The Early Years of Petrus Stuyvesant," Joyce D. Goodfriend, ed., *Revisiting New Netherland: Perspectives on Early Dutch America* (Leiden: Brill, 2005), 205-44.

[27] Henk van Nierop, *Het verraad van het Noorderkwartier. Oorlog, terreur en recht in de Nederlandse Opstand* (Amsterdam: Bert Bakker, 1999), 156; *NNBW* 8:1153.

[28] A. Eekhof, *Bastiaen Jansz. Krol, krankenbezoeker, kommies en kommandeur van Nieuw Nederland (1595-1645). Nieuwe gegevens voor de kennis van ons kerkelijk en koloniaal gezag in Noord-Amerika* (Den Haag: Nijhoff, 1910).

our sources are limited to the material that Eekhof amassed in his 1926 volume.[29]

Main Sources for Michaëlius's Life in the New World

For Michaëlius's years in New Netherland—also our main focus here—we therefore can draw upon three of his own letters, two letters addressed to him, and a few other references partly relating to procedures after Michaëlius had returned to *patria*. The two letters by Joannes van Foreest, while interesting in themselves, do not contain much information on life in the young colony, but Michaëlius's own letters do. In particular his two letters written in August 1628, within days of each other, are of importance. The first letter, of August 8 (pp. 107-114), is addressed to Joannes van Foreest, an important man in North Holland. He was member of the city council of Hoorn; became *burgemeester* [burgomaster/mayor] of that city; served on the board of directors of the West India Company; was promoted to the High Council of Holland, Zeeland, and West-Friesland; and, as befits a man of standing, indulged in writing neoclassical poetry.[30] He was Michaëlius's patron in the secular sphere, while the other correspondent, Smout, occupied the same position in the ecclesiastical sphere. Adriaen Jorisz Smout was at that time minister in Amsterdam and a member of the consistory committee that supervised overseas ministers. In his letter of August 11, 1628 (pp. 128-139), Michaëlius asked Smout to convey his greetings to Jacobus Trigland, another minister in Amsterdam. With these affiliations we get a clear idea of Michaëlius's position in the religious spectrum of the 1620s. Both Trigland and Smout were hard-line Counterremonstrants. Trigland had been influential at the Synod of Dordt in 1618/1619, but on the whole was not as fiery as Smout, whose career is quite colorful. He was a firebrand preacher whose intransigent stance towards Arminians set him upon a collision course with secular authorities more than once. In the end his presence turned out to be too much even for the Amsterdam city government, which had him deported in 1630.[31]

---

[29] For the following paragraphs, I have used Eekhof, *Michaëlius*, and Waterman, Jacobs & Gehring, *Indianenverhalen*, except where indicated otherwise. Quotations from the letters are followed by page references to Eekhof's translation, collated against the Dutch original as included in Waterman, Jacobs and Gehring.

[30] Johannes de Laet, *Iaerlyck Verhael van de verrichtingen der Geoctroyeerde West-Indische Compagnie (1644)* (S.P. L'Honore Naber en J.C.M. Warnsinck eds.) 4 vols, ('s-Gravenhage: Nijhoff, 1931-1937), 1:36; *NNBW* 1:880-81.

[31] Karel Bostoen, "Vondel contra Smout. De calvinistische predikant Adriaan Joriszoon Smout in Vondels hekeldichten," *Literatuur* 6 (1989): 199-209; Willem

As might be expected, considering the short time separating them, the two letters overlap in content to a large extent, sometimes so much so that the reader suspects Michaëlius used a copybook. The newly-arrived minister reported on what he considered the long and arduous journey to New Netherland (pp. 107-108, 128),[32] the bad treatment he and his wife received from the skipper (pp. 108, 128-129), and the death of his wife soon after their arrival at Fort Amsterdam (pp. 108-109, 128). He continued in the letter to Van Foreest with a description of Manhattan (pp. 109-111), whereas in writing to Smout he skipped that part. The founding of the church is included in both letters (pp. 111, 129-131), as well as details of the hard life in the budding colony (pp. 109, 135-136) and of the Native Americans (pp. 109-110, 113, 132-135). Both letters included greetings and references to friends, family members, and acquaintances, and it is these that most clearly show the difference in networks. The letter to Van Foreest sheds light on the network of Michaëlius's family in North Holland: his brother; his son Johannes, who stayed in Hoorn and resided at the house of West India Company skipper Jan Jansz Brouwer; Hoorn *predikant* Gregorius Goethals; and some other individuals. The letter to Smout reveals his Amsterdam network, including Smout himself and other Amsterdam ministers.[33] The letters display other differences as well. The tenor of the letter to Van Foreest is slightly more formal and deferential, whereas the letter to Smout has a tone of familiarity in it, suggesting an exchange between equals rather than with a socially superior correspondent.

Frijhoff, *Wegen van Evert Willemsz. Een Hollands weeskind op zoek naar zichzelf, 1607-1647* (Nijmegen: SUN, 1995), 588-89; R.B. Evenhuis, *Ook dat was Amsterdam*, 5 vols. (Amsterdam: Ten Have, 1965-1978), 1:311-14; A.Th. van Deursen, *Bavianen en slijkgeuzen. Kerk en kerkvolk ten tijde van Maurits en Oldenbarnevelt* (orig. 1974; 3rd ed. Franeker: Van Wijnen, 1998), 219, 309, 348.

[32] With just over ten weeks, the voyage was actually average in duration, but the winter weather may have made it unpleasant. See Jacobs, *Colony*, 35-36. Cf. Leendert Jan Joosse, *Geloof in de Nieuwe Wereld: ontmoeting met Afrikanen en Indianen (1600-1700)* (Kampen: Kok, 2008), 233.

[33] In the letter to Van Foreest: Michaëlius's brother (p. 110, 113, 114), *predikanten* Goethals and Theodorus Christiani (p. 111), Hoorn skipper Jan Jansz Brouwer (p. 112), Michaëlius's son Joannes (p. 112), unnamed friends in Leiden (p. 113), Jan Verschuyre (p. 113), and Van Foreest's spouse and his mother (p. 114). In the letter to Smout: WIC-director Godijn (p. 129), members of the deputati ad res Indicas Petri, Sylvius, and Cloppenburgius (p. 138), and Amsterdam minister Trigland (p. 138). On Joannes or Johannes Michaëlius, see A. Eekhof, "De praeceptor-filosoof-dichter Johannes Michaëlius, zoon van den eersten Amerikaanschen predikant (met portret)," *Nederlandsch Archief voor Kerkgeschiedenis* 23 (1930): 81-98 and *NNBW* 9:674-75.

Conditions in New Netherland

Both letters make clear that Michaëlius considered living in the colony to be difficult. Obviously, his wife's death, leaving him with the care of three young children, caused a considerable emotional burden. In addition, he found the supplies meager:

> Food here is scanty and poor. Supplies of butter and milk etc. are difficult to obtain, owing to the large number of people and the small number of cattle and farmers. Everything is expensive [and] to be fed continually from the Fatherland is difficult, expensive, and hazardous (p. 109).

The main fare was "hard stale food, such as men are used to on board ship," such as "beans and gray peas, which are hard enough, barley, stockfish, etc." (pp. 135-136). Michaëlius must have experienced such provisions while traveling to Brazil and West Africa, but it seems his expectation was that once on land things would improve. He blamed it on the mismanagement of both the New Netherland and Amsterdam company officials. The free land promised him in lieu of a free table (i.e. eating with the higher company officials) was meaningless, as the laborers and horses required to till the land were not available. He even blamed the West India Company directors in Amsterdam for deliberately misleading him in this respect (pp. 111, 135), although this may have been unjustified. Despite these difficulties, Michaëlius was enthusiastic about the possibilities of New Netherland in general: the air was healthy, and

> The country produces many kinds of good things, which greatly contribute to the comforts of life: fish, poultry, game in the woods, oysters, tree-fruits, fruits from the earth, medicinal herbs and others of all kinds. But all is as yet uncultivated, and remains in a wild state, as long as no better arrangements are made to bring everything together and people are found, who understand the work and occupy themselves with it (pp. 110, 136).

Both the abundance of nature and the lack of industrious people are well-known topics in descriptions of the New World and can also be found in those written by other new arrivals in New Netherland.[34] Sloth,

---

[34] See for instance Isaac de Rasière (A.J.F. van Laer trans. and ed.), *Documents relating to New Netherland, 1624-1626, in the Henry E. Huntington Library* (San Marino: The Henry E. Huntington Library and Art Gallery, 1924), 206-07; Nicasius de Sille (Haags Gemeentearchief, *archief weeskamer* (402-01), inv.nr. 1413; Arnold J.F. van Laer trans. and ed., "Letters of Nicasius de Sille, 1654," *Proceedings of the New York*

both of newcomers and of the Indians, was ascribed to the perfidious influence of the land that turned people "wild." Bewitched, bothered, and bewildered, newcomers attempted to create order in their minds and often implicitly imposed their preconceived notions when relating their first experiences in the New World to correspondents back in Europe.[35]

When, therefore, Michaëlius, described the colonists as "rather rough and unrestrained" (p. 129), the minister's judgment reflected both class-based prejudice as well an emerging awareness that constant vigilance was required to protect his flock and keep the wildernizing influence of the environment at bay.

Organizing the Church

Michaëlius's main instrument for order was a well-organized church, and he describes its early beginnings at length in his letter to Smout (pp. 129-131). Building upon the foundations laid by Bastiaen Jansz Krol, who spent most of his time upriver at Fort Orange (modern-day Albany) and was thus unable to attend consistory meetings on Manhattan, Michaëlius had thought it best to choose two elders: director Pieter Minuit and his brother-in-law, Jan Huygen, the West India Company's *winckelhouder* [shopkeeper]. Both had experience in ecclesiastical office in Wesel; and in selecting these two men, Michaëlius opted for bridging the French and Dutch-speaking communities of Manhattan.

The next step was forming a congregation. At the first Lord's Supper fifty members participated. Not all those admitted had brought along the required church certificates, but Michaëlius showed himself

---

State Historical Association with the *Quarterly Journal* 18 (1923): 98-108, Willem Kieft (National Archives, Kew, State Papers Foreign, Holland (SP 84), vol. 154, fol. 267-267v (1638)), and Jasper Danckaerts (Brooklyn Historical Society, "Eerste Reis naar Nieuw-Nederland van J. Schilders & P. Vorstman," September 24, 1679; Bartlett Burleigh James and J. Franklin Jameson ed. *Journal of Jasper Danckaerts 1679-1680* (orig., 1913; 2nd ed. New York: Barnes & Noble, Inc., 1941, repr. 1959), 44.

[35] The scholarly literature on these points is too voluminous to attempt a summary here. I have used Anthony Pagden, *The Fall of Natural Man: The American Indian and the Origins of Comparative Ethnology* (Cambridge: Cambridge University Press, 1982), Anthony Pagden, *European Encounters with the New World: From Renaissance to Romanticism* (New Haven: Yale University Press, 1993), Benjamin Schmidt, *Innocence Abroad: The Dutch Imagination and the New World, 1570-1670* (Cambridge: Cambridge University Press, 2001), Michiel van Groesen, "Images of America in the Low Countries until the Seventeenth Century," in Hans Krabbendam, Cornelis A. van Minnen, and Giles Scott-Smith, eds., *Four Centuries of Dutch-American Relations* (Amsterdam: Boom Publishers, 2009), 49-62.

flexible: "one cannot observe strictly all the usual formalities in making a beginning under such circumstances" (p. 130). He was equally adaptable in dealing with the two languages in his congregation. There were too few Walloons to justify weekly services in French, yet at the Lord's Supper Michaëlius delivered a French sermon. As he did not consider himself sufficiently proficient, he wrote these out in full. He was aware that in making such adjustments, he ran the risk of incurring the wrath of the Amsterdam consistory, and in his letter to Smout he therefore submitted himself without hesitation to correction by the Amsterdam consistory (pp. 130-131).

In his choice of elders, Michaëlius had appointed men who also occupied positions of secular authority, thus creating a potentially dangerous situation that might endanger the relations between church and state. The minister was well aware of this and asserted to Smout that he would try and keep within the confines of his calling as much as possible. Completely separating ecclesiastical and civil affairs was difficult, as "many things are mixti generis," and the men on the colonial council were "good people, who are, however, for the most part simple and have little experience in public affairs." Michaëlius was convinced that "political and ecclesiastical persons can greatly assist each other," and he was eager to provide good advice to the secular authorities. Yet it would help, he thought, if the directors would provide those authorities with precise instructions. The same applied to himself, and he specifically asked to be sent the *Acta Synodalia* of Holland and other documents that would help him deal with ecclesiastical difficulties (p. 131).

Contacts with Native Americans

In both letters Michaëlius included sections about Native Americans, but the descriptions show considerable differences. In the letter to Van Foreest, the minister referred to the war between the Mohicans and the Mohawks on the upper reaches of the Hudson River, around Fort Orange. The conflict had left large tracts of land unoccupied and open for settlement by the Dutch (pp. 109-110).[36] In Michaëlius's opinion, the Indians, especially the Mohicans, were treacherous people who had tried to take Fort Orange by surprise. He railed about the "manifold wickedness, devilish tricks, and more than barbarous cruelties of these nations" (p. 110). Yet he showed himself to be ethnologically interested as well. He sent Van Foreest

---

[36] On this war, see William A. Starna and José António Brandão, "From the Mohawk-Mahican War to the Beaver War: Questioning the Pattern," *Ethnohistory* 51 (2004): 725-50.

> two small bones, which the Indian women here wear around their bodies as tassels and ornaments, and of which they are quite proud. These are the small bones of the male parts of beavers, coming with the one end above the scrotum and with the rest along the shaft. It is said here that in the Fatherland, as a curiosity, they are used for the handles of spoons, for the one end is suitable for a little knob and the other end to join the bowl of the spoon to the handle. I have directed my brother to have them thus prepared by the silversmith and then to present them to your Honor, with the request that you be pleased to accept the same, for this once, as a token of friendship and gratitude (p. 113).[37]

In his letter to Smout, Michaëlius focused on other aspects of Native American culture, but was much more eloquent on their perceived perfidy. They are, he asserted,

> entirely savage and wild, estranged of all civil decency, yea, uncouth and blunt as garden stakes, proficient in all wickedness and ungodliness, devilish men, who serve nobody but the Devil, that is, the spirit which in their language they call Menetto, under which title they comprehend everything that is subtle and crafty and beyond human skill and power. They have so much witchcraft, soothsaying, incantations and wicked arts, that they can hardly be held in by any bands or lock. They are as thievish and treacherous as they are tall, and in cruelty they are altogether inhuman, more than barbarous, far exceeding the Africans (p. 132).

In interpreting Michaëlius's assessment, we should realize that the dominie had only been in New Netherland for four months, had arrived during the aftermath of a bloody conflict, and had hardly recovered from the shock of his first encounter with the inhabitants of the New World. Also, he had become painfully aware that proselytization would not be as easy as many of his colleagues in the Dutch Republic believed it to be. His description was at least partly aimed at explaining why he had made little progress. He then proceeded to outline the difficulties of mastering a language far removed from any of the Indo-European languages he was familiar with, like Dutch, Latin, Greek, and French. Michaëlius's solution to prepare the Indians for salvation was to separate the children from the parents so as to educate them in the

---

[37] Versteeg, *Manhattan in 1628*, 75, in translating Michaëlius's letter left out a large part of the sentence "These are the small bones of the male parts of beavers, coming with the one end above the scrotum and with the rest along the shaft," replacing it with a prudish summary: "These small bones are taken from beavers."

Dutch language and in "the fundaments of our Christian religion," similar to what he had suggested when serving in West Africa. He admitted that it would be difficult, as the parents were very fond of their children; but in his view it was the only way (pp. 133-135).[38]

There is no indication that Michaëlius had any success in converting Native Americans to Calvinism. His Latin letter to Van Foreest of September 13, 1630, does not refer to Indians; he instead took aim at Minuit:

> We have a governor, who is most unworthy of his office: a slippery fellow, who under the treacherous mask of honesty is a compound of all iniquity and wickedness. For he is accustomed to the lies, of which he is full, and to the imprecations and most awful execrations; he is not free from fornication, the most cruel oppressor of the innocent and who deems no one worthy of his favour and protection, who is not of the same kidney as he is (p. 68).

Conflict with Minuit

By this time Michaëlius had taken sides in a conflict between director Minuit and secretary Jan van Remunde, as another member of the colonial council attested:

> Now, the director and Jan Romonde are very much embittered against one another. They let the trade slip away and do not exert themselves to increase it either by sloops or otherwise, but are very diligent in bringing exorbitant suits and charges against one another and in neglecting the interests and business of the directors. The minister, Jonas Michielsz, is very energetic here stirring up the fire between them; he ought to be a mediator in God's church and community but he seems to me to be the contrary.[39]

[38] See also Anthony F. Buccini, "Swannekens Ende Wilden : Linguistic Attitudes and Communication Strategies among the Dutch and Indians in New Netherland," Joanna C. Prins, Bettina Brandt, Thimothy Stevens, Thomas F. Shannon, eds., *The Low Countries and the New World(s): Travel, Discovery, Early Relations* (Lanham: University Press of America, 2000), 11-28, Mark Meuwese, "Dutch Calvinism and Native Americans: A Comparative Study of the Motivations for Protestant Conversion among the Tupis in Northeastern Brazil (1630-1654) and the Mohawks in Central New York (1690-1710)," James Muldoon, ed., *The Spiritual Conversion of the Americas* (Gainesville: University Press of Florida, 2004), 118-41, and Lois M. Feister, "Linguistic Communication Between the Dutch and the Indians in New Netherland 1609-1664," *Ethnohistory* 20 (1973): 25-38.

[39] Sijmen Dircksz Pos to Kiliaen van Rensselaer, 16 September 1630, Nederlands Scheepvaartmuseum Amsterdam, Van Rensselaer Bowier Manuscripts, doc. 2 (A.J.F. van Laer, trans. and ed., *Van Rensselaer Bowier Manuscripts, being the letters of Kiliaen*

This echoes Michaëlius's charges against Minuit, but that does not necessarily make those charges true. "Neglecting the affairs of superiors" was a standard accusation in colonial conflicts, and it was a convenient one because only the superiors themselves, residing at a distance of many months of correspondence, could render judgment. Even so, the notarial depositions that Jonas Michaëlius and Jan van Remunde made after their return to Amsterdam indicate that the conflict turned very bitter and split the two hundred to three hundred colonists into opposing camps.[40]

Different interpretations have been put forward in order to explain the conflict between Michaëlius and Minuit. Eekhof, in his 1913 book, describes the conflict and merely remarks that Michaëlius may have advocated the separation of religious and secular spheres but did not practice it. In his 1926 book, a memorial volume for the foundation of the Reformed Church in America, he prudently refrains from passing judgment. Frijhoff is more outspoken and draws parallels with the conflicts between Van Twiller and Bogardus and between Stuyvesant and Backer, pointing to the theocratic strand in the Reformed Church as a common factor in each conflict. The secular and religious authorities claimed to be competent in both spheres. That interpretation makes the conflict in New Netherland an extension of similar conflicts within the Dutch Republic, but it tends to overlook the colonial context. In earlier publications I have put forward the argument that personal incompatibilities between individual ministers and magistrates also played a role. Especially in an isolated colonial setting, where secular and religious authorities were embodied in single individuals without the option of quick consultation with colleagues or superiors, conflicts could quickly get out of hand. Judging from Michaëlius's vehement phrases in his letter of 1630, this applies to his conflict with Minuit as well, as it did in later church-state conflicts in New Netherland.

Yet individual circumstances may also have played a role. In a recent publication Joosse correctly draws our attention to the difficult conditions under which Michaëlius had to work and the lack of support he received from the West India Company. The minister had already expressed his doubts in 1628. If we add to this his belief that the company did not live up to its promises, the fact that he found life in the colony hard, and the difficulties he faced in performing his duties while

---

van Rensselaer, 1630-1643, and other documents relating to the colony of Rensselaerswyck (Albany: University of the State of New York, 1908), 169).

[40] Stadsarchief Amsterdam, notarial archive (5075), inv. nr. 943, not paginated (17 July 1632).

caring for his young children without a wife, we may actually regard it as commendable that he remained in his post for three long years. None of these explanations of the conflict are necessarily mutually exclusive, and it is likely that all played a role. Quoting Michaëlius, "many things are mixti generis" (p. 131).[41]

The conflict with Minuit made it impossible for Michaëlius to continue in New Netherland even if he had wanted to. In the end Minuit, Michaëlius, Van Remunde, and several others were recalled. Minuit left New Netherland on the ship *Eendracht*, which was arrested in the English port of Plymouth on a charge of transgressing the royal patent that allocated North America to the English colonists. Until now it has been unclear whether Michaëlius repatriated on this ship as well. The chronology has made that seem unlikely. It is unknown when the ship left New Netherland, and the first documentary references to its arrest date are from April 1632.[42] Yet the records of the Classis of Amsterdam indicate that Michaëlius appeared before the meeting on March 4, 1632.[43] This incongruity suggests that Michaëlius departed New Netherland on an earlier ship. Yet a recently discovered document provides us with a different time frame, as it puts the time of the arrest of the *Eendracht* in February 1632.[44] This makes it possible that Minuit and Michaëlius both traveled on the *Eendracht*. As the senior West India Company official, Minuit had to remain in Plymouth to represent the company alongside the ship's captain. But Michaëlius had the option to continue his journey to the Dutch Republic on his own, thus grasping the opportunity to gain a critical advantage by presenting his case to his colleagues in classis and the company directors well in advance of Minuit. He may have persuaded the classis, which greeted him with friendship and thanked him for his service, but the directors of the West India Company did not absolve him of his role in the conflict with Minuit. Five years later the Classis of Amsterdam put Michaëlius

---

[41] A. Eekhof, *De hervormde kerk in Noord-Amerika (1624-1664)*, 2 vols. ('s-Gravenhage: Martinus Nijhof, 1913), 1:42-43, 47; Frijhoff, *Wegen*, 585; Willem Frijhoff, *Fullfilling God's Mission: The Two Worlds of Dominie Everardus Bogardus, 1607-1647* (Leiden: Brill, 2007), 351; Jaap Jacobs, *Een zegenrijk gewest. Nieuw-Nederland in de zeventiende eeuw* (Amsterdam: Bert Bakker, 1999), 238-40; Jacobs, *New Netherland*, 274-77; Jacobs, *Colony*, 148-53; Joosse, *Geloof*, 238-40.

[42] Nationaal Archief, The Hague, archive of the States General (1.01.04), *liassen West-Indische Compagnie*, inv.nr. 5753 (5 April 1632; O'Callaghan and Fernow, *Documents Relative*, 1:45.

[43] Stadsarchief Amsterdam, archive of the classis (376), inv.nr. 6, fol. 311 (4 March 1632; Eekhof, *Bastiaen Jansz. Krol*, XXIV).

[44] National Archives, Kew, State Papers Foreign, Holland (SP 84), vol. 144, fol. 190 (18 May 1632).

forward as the prime candidate to succeed Everardus Bogardus, who had indicated that he was "not at all inclined to continue for whatever reason."[45] But the directors finally answered "that if they required him [i.e. Michaëlius], they would summon him. Which greatly displeased the assembly."[46]

And that is the final word on the first minister on Manhattan. He had died by 1645, and, echoing Versteeg and Eekhof, we must conclude that only the discovery of new documents will enable us to find out how he occupied himself between his return from New Netherland and his death. The lack of leads turns any such quest into a search for the proverbial needle in a haystack. Yet I do not exclude the possibility that archival depositories in North Holland, such as the *Westfries Archief* in Hoorn, may yield something. Another possibility is the *Erfgoedcentrum DiEP*, which holds the archives of Dordrecht, where Michaëlius's son Johannes was Latin schoolmaster until his death in 1646.[47] It remains doubtful, however, whether such new finds would substantially change our image of Jonas Michaëlius.

Conclusion

When assessing Michaëlius's importance for New Netherland, we need to distinguish between his own aims and the view of posterity. For the minister, organizing the church was more a means than an aim. As he indicated himself, he was successful in making his congregation grow "in numbers and piety" (p. 68) until the conflict with Minuit got out of hand, causing his return to *patria*. His attempt to be a moral compass to the entire colonial population was also unsuccessful. He may not have made many converts among the Indians, but we may doubt whether he considered that to be a failure. When he returned to the Dutch Republic, he was, I suspect, a disappointed man. Yet his name is better known than that of other New Netherland ministers. He was, after all, the first minister.

---

[45] Jaap Jacobs, "A Troubled Man: Director Wouter van Twiller and the Affairs of New Netherland in 1635," *New York History* 85 (2004): 213-32, esp. 231.
[46] Eekhof, *Michaëlius*, 139-41.
[47] Eekhof, "De praeceptor-filosoof-dichter Johannes Michaëlius."

CHAPTER 3

Everardus Bogardus (1607–1647): A Dutch Mystic in the New World

Willem Frijhoff

An inveterate drunkard, a quarrelsome character unable to control himself, an unfit minister barely tolerated by his flock, and the unruly husband of Anneke Jans, herself a woman of legend, myth, and innumerable descendents: that is the prevailing historical image of the second Reformed minister of New Amsterdam, Dominie Everardus Bogardus. Bogardus surely loved the bottle, his temper was easily inflamed, he was always convinced of the righteousness of his cause, and he did not shy away from heated dispute.[1] He was a strong personality indeed, and a man of extremes. But there are always several ways to look at history and its protagonists. Instead of blaming Bogardus or ridiculing him for his vices, I will try in this article to understand his personality and to discover how the minister charted his own life course to pursue the role to which he felt called in the service of his community.[2]

---

[1] The most recent example of this depreciative image of Bogardus is in the historical novel of Bill Greer, *The Mevrouw Who Saved Manhattan* (New York: Manhattan View Press, 2009), 70, 74-75, 79, 108-09, 186.
[2] This article is a much condensed version of Bogardus's biography in Willem Frijhoff, *Fulfilling God's Mission: The Two Worlds of Dominie Everardus Bogardus, 1607-*

Anonymous portrait, traditionally said to depict Reverend Everardus Bogardus. Hinterglass painting in Senate House, Kingston (NY), early eighteenth century.

[Courtesy of New York State Office of Parks, Recreation and Historic Preservation, Senate House State Historic Site]

An Uncommon Orphan

Everything started when he was fifteen. During the summer of 1622 and the following winter, the small town of Woerden in the province of Holland was buzzing with rumors. A boy called Evert Willemsz (Evert, son of Willem), a native of the town, had been assailed by a sudden illness, physical problems, and a spiritual experience. He claimed to communicate, through an angel, with his heavenly Father. The boy lived at the local orphanage, together with his older brother Pieter and two younger half-brothers. Cornelis, their eldest brother, lived nearby in town; he was probably trained as a tailor, but in 1636 he started a grocery store in the university town of Leiden, the second city of the Dutch Republic. Evert's family name was Bogaert, but as a literate man he only used its Latin form (Everardus) Bogardus at Leiden University, where he matriculated in 1627, and on the island of Manhattan, where he became the minister in 1633.

1647 (Leiden: Brill, 2007), where full references to all the sources and relevant literature is given. On the making of this book and the methodical problems of this biographical narrative: Willem Frijhoff, "The Improbable Biography: Uncommon Sources, a Moving Identity, a Plural Story?" in Volker R. Berghahn and Simone Lässig, eds., *Biography between Structure and Agency: Central European Lives in International Historiography* (Oxford: Berghahn Books, 2008), 215-33.

We know nothing with certainty concerning his parents. Soon after his birth around 1607 Evert lost his natural father, Willem Bogaert, who must have been a craftsman, probably a cabinetmaker. Evert was certainly educated by his stepfather, Muysevoet, who, just as Evert's natural mother, died some years before the onset of the boy's spiritual experience, probably in the plague year of 1617-18. The four younger sons were then put into the town orphanage of Woerden. As the administration of the Woerden orphan chamber makes no mention of any property, the family must have been without means. Without parents, without the help of a local family network, without money or property, and without any formal education (though he was not necessarily illiterate), the boy's chances of climbing the social ladder were virtually non-existent.[3] But Evert had other qualities: he had intelligence and faith.

We know what happened to Evert Willemsz in 1622-23 from two contemporary pamphlets edited by Lucas Zas, the headmaster of the small local grammar school and an eye-witness to the events.[4] In a certain sense, however, the pamphlets' author was Evert himself, for the text consists largely of the messages he wrote down during his spiritual experience, when he was temporarily smitten with deafness and dumbness. At this time he communicated with the people around him via written notes, referred to in the pamphlets as "copies" (*kopije*, i.e., literal transcripts). Every slip of paper contained the questions and answers from the dialogues held between Evert and those who came to converse with him. Other notes contained spiritual messages, which he had written down on impulse, following an angel's appearance or an ecstatic experience. Evert's own version of the summer experience of 1622, written some weeks afterwards in a long hymn, was also included.

In order to understand the first spiritual calling of the later minister, we have to examine what happened to the boy in the spring of 1622. Having completed his elementary education, and while continuing to live in the orphanage, Evert was apprenticed to Master Gijsbert Aelbertsz, a tailor who had a workshop on the river Rhine, a few streets away. The orphanage and the workshop were distinct sites, but they were quite similar in atmosphere. Evert had virtually fulfilled his two-year apprenticeship with this master, whom he loved greatly for his piety

[3] On Dutch society and culture in Bogardus's time: Simon Schama, *The Embarrassment of Riches: An Interpretation of Dutch Culture in the Golden Age* (New York: Alfred A. Knopf, 1987); Willem Frijhoff and Marijke Spies, *1650: Hard-Won Unity* (Assen/ Basingstoke: Van Gorcum/Palgrave Macmillan, 2004); Maarten Prak, *The Dutch Republic in the Seventeenth Century* (Cambridge: Cambridge University Press, 2005).

[4] For a bibliographic description, see Frijhoff, *Fulfilling God's Mission*, 37-38. The quotations that follow are taken from these pamphlets.

and for his readiness to discuss God's Word. It may have been this very companionship that revealed to him his true vocation: to be not a tailor, but a minister of God's Word.

According to the story in the pamphlets, Evert had for some time been seriously ill. He had hardly recovered when other physical symptoms made their appearance. For nine days, from June 21 to 30, 1622, he neither ate nor drank. He even isolated himself from the community of some thirty children in the orphanage. Evert's refusal to attend the common meals was for him the most efficient way to gain the attention of both the orphans and the trustees. The pamphlets show how concerned the matron of the orphanage was about his well-being, and they illustrate her embarrassment over the disarray in the group caused by Evert's dealings with heaven.

This first phase of physical isolation was followed by a second phase, one that lasted throughout the summer for seventy days, from June 30 to September 8. Evert suddenly became both deaf and dumb. He could neither hear nor speak, and he occasionally even lost his sight, "as also for a long time the proper use of his reason."[5] This phase of physical isolation, due to the loss of almost all his senses, suggests a slowly intensifying struggle, preparing Evert for a third, ecstatic phase, which again lasted nine days, from September 8 to 17, 1622. Evert began fasting again; still he could neither hear nor speak. This final phase began with the appearance of an angel of the Lord and ended with a second angelic visitation. This twofold vision points to the true meaning of this episode: communication with heaven. The angel delivered to him a message from the Father (Evert's *heavenly* Father): he had to convert people and warn them to repent and renounce their sins. According to the angel, the heavenly source of the message and the veracity of Evert's encounter with heaven would be proven by his deliverance from the physical disabilities God had visited upon him and by his full recovery from sickness. The angel also conveyed a second message, meant for Evert himself. I shall come back to it.

After the angel's first appearance, Evert went into a kind of trance, a long period of ecstatic writing. For days on end he wrote down his heavenly communications, mostly simple messages of a repetitious nature:

---

[5] *Waerachtige Geschiedenisse / Hoe dat Seker Wees-Kindt binnen Woerden / out ontrent xv. Jaren / tot tweemalen toe vanden Heere met stommigheyd / doofheyd / somtijts oock met Blintheyt besocht / ende van het gebruyck syns verstants berooft zijnde: De sonden bestraffende / ende Gods toorn verkondigende / wonderbaerlijcken door de kracht des Heeren 't selve alles wederomme verkreghen heeft. Op het alder-oprechtste, nae de waerheyd, by een gestelt ende vergaderd door L. Zasium, Rectorem binnen Woerden* (Amsterdam: Marten Iansz. Brandt, 1623), f. A3 v°.

> Spread the word, spread the word, for God is sorely displeased that word of his wondrous works is not spread. Oh spread the word, oh my dear friends, I beg of you, spread the word, for God is displeased that his divine things are not communicated throughout the whole world. Spread the word, then, oh spread the word.[6]

The message was as simple as the outlook on the world of a young tailor's apprentice could be: there are good men and bad; God wants the good to repent; therefore, his word must be spread and the signs read. In the background we may detect a very simplified form of belief in double predestination, as defended by orthodox Calvinism and confirmed in 1618-19 by the Synod of Dort. It resembled the everyday theological discussions at the grassroots level in Woerden, which crop up in documents concerning the confessional struggles of the 1610s and 1620s: the bad are damned and the good are elect, but God will punish even the good if they do not behave as his flock of sanctified believers.

The signs of God's wrath were easy to detect: repeated plagues, famine, and war. This traditional triad was presaged by the famous comet of 1618 ("the rod"). But the most important sign of all was God's wondrous work in his faithful child Evert Willemsz: having first smitten him with sickness and deprived him of the use of his bodily faculties, God would now deliver him at a moment of God's own choosing, announced by an angel. To believe in the truth of Evert's spiritual experience was, therefore, to believe in God's work in his elect. Evert had no doubt about his own election. The affliction God had brought upon him proved it. God afflicts the ones he loves. Evert felt akin to Christ, who too had suffered for his Father but had finally reconciled his will to God's will (Luke 22:42). He was certain that he belonged to the 144,000 elect who would sing the hymn of the Lamb (Rev. 14:1-5, 15:3).

Evert's texts reveal a form of youthful radicalism that meshed well with the rigid positions taken by orthodox Calvinism. He was not naïve, however. He followed the apocalyptic mainstream of orthodoxy but kept his eyes fixed upon his own destiny. He utilized current conventions to achieve personal autonomy. He willingly used church and civil authorities to attain his divine calling, but he refused to become the passive victim of higher powers. Incidentally, Evert's strong language as an adolescent, as we hear it here in his own words, perfectly matches the few wrathful phrases history has preserved from the period of his American ministry.

---

[6] Ibid., f. C3 r°.

Evert's first spiritual experience and the events related to it took place entirely within the confines of the orphan community. But of course his activities drew attention in the town of Woerden, all the more so since the young man had found a promoter in the headmaster of the local grammar school, Master Zas. Lucas Zas had worked as a teacher of Latin and French at Utrecht and nearby Montfoort. He probably taught Evert French, because in New Netherland he was able to understand and probably to speak that language. In addition to publishing the two pamphlets, Zas also wrote a play on parental responsibility for children's education and choice of profession, *The Burgher Household*, published in 1628. This pious play includes a panegyric on the sacred ministry, which may have inspired young Evert's views on his own ecclesiastical calling. Zas was Woerden's independent intellectual, the ideal partner for the independent believer Evert must have been: a convinced Calvinist, but one who always followed his own compass.

Zas came running whenever Evert sent for him; he collected the messages and had them printed. He understood what was happening. Evert had good reason to choose Master Zas; his call to repentance was intended for outsiders, but he had a personal message to share with Zas. On Septermber 17, just before his first redemption from illness, he announced his ambition:

> I hope that God will release me this night so that I may again hear and again speak: I do not know this by myself, but through the Spirit of God, which will enlighten me. [..] If He has the power to inflict things upon me, He also has the power to deliver me again: for do we not read in God's word that He made the deaf hear, the blind see, the crippled walk, the dumb speak [Mathew 11:5; 15:30]? [..] Does He not then have the power to give back two of my five senses? Oh yes, I have had that trust and I still have it. As soon as I have recovered my speech and my hearing, it pleases God and the Spirit of God that I go to school until the time has come for me to do the work through which I shall be blessed. I intend then to become a minister and nothing else. Then you will see what the Spirit of God will work through me. I no longer must sew, once I have finished my clothes; for it pleases God almighty and the Spirit of God that such shall no longer be my work. I must fear the Lord, as the angel of the Lord has commanded me, and this I must do.[7]

Evert's corporal and spiritual experiences, his sickness and his ecstasies, made him aware of his real calling, the sacred ministry. He used the

---

[7] Ibid., f. B2 r°.

impact that the event made on the local community to respond to his calling and to give his life a new direction. However, to be credible, Evert's calling had to be legitimated first by a higher authority. This legitimization, as announced by an angel of the Lord, was to take place through a ritual of redemption.

This first redemption took place nine days after the beginning of Evert's ecstatic experience. Evert himself spoke of his "shedding the old Adam, in order to begin a new life, in all virtue and godliness."[8] He adopted here a characteristic idiom of early pietism, in which illness was closely linked to sin, just as recovery was to conversion from a sinful life, and to the regeneration of the old Adam as a true Christian, instigated by the Holy Ghost. In the almighty God, who caused his rebirth, he recognized his new and only father. The place of his rebirth was the orphanage, where the orphans, the rector, and the matron stood around him. Singing Psalm one hundred together, they helped to bear his spiritual birth pains, as he had predicted in one of his notes. Carried away by the dynamics of the ritual, Evert suddenly found himself singing with them. He had recovered his powers of speech and hearing, and he was now completely restored, reborn as a new Adam. Three days later the magistracy of Woerden, convinced that God himself supported Evert's words, authorized him to leave the tailor's shop and to attend the Latin school at the town's expense without having to earn his own living as a tailor.

In itself, Evert's message was not, of course, sufficient to win the unconditional trust of all the people around him. Evert's spiritual dealings provoked skepticism and resistance. As the boy himself pointed out, critics threatened to beat his deafness and dumbness out of him. In fact, Woerden was not in all respects an average Dutch town. It was profoundly divided and torn apart by three competing confessions. Woerden had been the only Holland town where in 1572 Lutheranism had been officially adopted by the town and church. But it had been superseded by the Arminians after 1586 and by orthodox Calvinism ever since the coup of Prince Maurice in 1618. The Calvinists, a small minority in town, were confronted with two oppositional groups who both claimed political priority and theological superiority. The Calvinists were badly in need of a justification for their own assertions.

Within this religious context, Evert's spiritual experience was bound to be interpreted in a partisan way, as that of a supporter of orthodoxy, the more so as the Woerden orphanage functioned as one of the main agencies of Calvinization. Evert's half-brother, Pieter Muysevoet

---

[8] Ibid., f. A4 v°.

(d. 1650/51), became an orthodox schoolmaster in a nearby village. His elder brother, Cornelis Bogaert (d. 1669), enjoyed the protection of an orthodox Reformed burgomaster at Leiden.

The three brothers must have felt close to a zealous Calvinist minister by the name of Vincent Muysevoet or Meusevoet (1560-1624), who was probably their uncle as a brother of their (step)father. He was the son of a Flemish shoemaker, a convinced Calvinist who had fled in exile to Norwich in England. Back in Holland in 1586, Vincent served first as a minister at Zevenhoven, near Woerden, and then at Schagen, near Alkmaar, where he terrorized the Arminians. Between 1598 and his death in 1624 Meusevoet translated more than thirty Puritan and pietist treatises from English into Dutch, including virtually all writings by the famous Puritan divine William Perkins and several by King James I. He played a leading part in introducing Puritan Pietism in the Netherlands. Small wonder that Evert was familiar with the pietistic idiom and the Puritan doctrine of regeneration. He may well have even read Meusevoet's translation, published in 1599, of Perkins's treatise on the spiritual meaning of sickness and death.

In the second phase of his spiritual experience, Evert's focus was no longer on his own promotion as an agent of God, but on gaining the acceptance of as many social groups as possible for his message. A candidate for adulthood, he had to earn the public, reasoned acknowledgement of his fellow adults. In Woerden many still remained rather skeptical about what had happened to him. It was therefore vital that he finish his task by making his experiences credible to skeptics. The second stage appears, therefore, as more emphatically instrumental in character than the first. Four months after his first regeneration, on the morning of Wednesday, January 18, 1623, Evert awoke with a severe headache. Refusing to eat or drink, he predicted that he would again lose the ability to hear and speak. This did, indeed, occur around noon. This time the loss of his senses lasted only three days. Evert's second experience was more intense and more exhausting, and his message was passed on quickly enough.

One by one Evert called the representatives of the various institutions within his social sphere into a room that had been put at his disposal. Together they legitimized his actions before the whole town. First came the matron, as a representative of the household; then Evert's older brother, as the next of kin and representative of the family; next, the rector of the Latin school, the main representative of literate culture in the town; subsequently, his former employer, the master tailor Gijsbert Aelbertsz; then the ruling mayor, the building contractor Jan Florisz van Wijngaarden; and, finally, in the name of the church council, the two ministers, the more liberal Henricus Alutarius and his orthodox colleague Jacobus Cralingius. The whole community in all its branches, lay and clerical, public and private, paraded symbolically past Evert's chair.

Evert's second redemption was public in nature. It again occurred in the orphanage, though this time Evert announced it well in advance. He made certain that not only the rector but also both ministers were present—three qualified and critical witnesses. When, at a particular moment, he saw the other orphans writing and talking around the hearth fire (it was in the middle of a cold winter), his consciousness was restored. He wrote on a slip of paper that the rector and the ministers should be fetched and then asked everybody present to sing a psalm—a most appropriate one indeed, apparently found by opening the Bible at random: "Out of babes and sucklings hast thou ordained strength" (Psalm 8:2). During the singing Evert successively regained the use of his various senses until he left the state of infancy mentioned in the psalm and sang along with the rector and the ministers as an adult.

For the ministers this was sufficient proof. Evert's authenticity was warranted by the visible reality of God publicly intervening in the life of an individual, an event perceived, and hence sanctioned, by the community present. On the next day, a Sunday, Evert was allowed to read in church, before the whole congregation, the responses of the Heidelberg catechism to Question 35, Lord's Day 14. This, again, was an appropriate text: "What do we call what is received from the Holy Ghost?" Had Evert not repeatedly emphasized that the Holy Ghost was working through him? We may consider this reading as the final rite of passage by which Evert gained official entry into public life. From this point onwards he was empowered to speak in public with adults. However, this confirmation of the change in the orientation of his life resulted in a new round of harsh criticism from the people of Woerden.

We will never know whether he acted intentionally or not, but Evert then played his last trump card. Two nights later his two little brothers who slept in the same bed with him, as well as the other orphans, were awakened by Evert talking aloud in his sleep. Someone went downstairs to fetch the matron. She anxiously woke Evert and asked him whether something was wrong. Evert calmed everyone down and persuaded them to go back to bed. He had hardly fallen asleep himself when he again started speaking out loud, as if he were dreaming. His brother Pieter, five years older than he, obviously understood what Evert was up to. He had a pen, a piece of paper, and a candle ready at hand, and he wrote down Evert's long, rhymed message. Its beginning and end set the tone:

Woe, oh woe, people who live in pride and excess,
Oh, ye people mean and heartless,
Your lives today are so godless. [..]
And so that people know
Through the work of God the Lord
That through me they should repent.[9]

This account of Evert's dream won over the last Calvinist critics to Evert's camp. God himself here legitimized Evert's spiritual experiences and the direction that he wanted to give to his life and to his public mission. The next day the burgomasters called the witnesses, including Evert's brothers, before them, authenticated the story, and ordered the church council to have it published as quickly as possible in Amsterdam by a Calvinist bookseller. And this, indeed, is what happened. The pamphlet was issued by Marten Jansz Brandt, an orthodox printer. It even went into a second printing at Amsterdam and into a new edition by a pietist publisher at Arnhem in the province of Gelderland.

Making Choices

Ten years later Evert's strong personality finally got him what he wanted: a public position as a Reformed minister, in a spirit of obedience to God but also of personal autonomy as a Christian believer. Once again he followed a path of his own choosing. His spiritual experience had brought him the recognition of the Woerden town council. As an exceptional favor to an orphaned boy, he had been admitted to the local grammar school. In June 1626, being nineteen years old, he was authorized to receive music lessons from the new town organist; a year later he left for the higher classes of the Leiden grammar school and matriculated at the University; and in 1629, at age twenty-one, Evert was granted the Woerden scholarship in the States College for Theology at Leiden University. Everybody at Woerden cooperated to make him a regular minister.

Yet, barely a year after having received his scholarship, in June 1630, Evert left the University for Amsterdam, long before completing his study in theology. This presents another mystery. Why should an orphan from a poor social background renounce a position enabling him to achieve the very vocation for which he had fought during the critical years of his identity formation? In the autumn of 1630 he began to work as a comforter of the sick in the service of the West India Company.[10] Comforters of the sick,

---

[9] Ibid., f. E1 v° - E2 r°.
[10] On religion and the West India Company: Willem Frijhoff, "The West India Company and the Reformed Church: Neglect or Concern?" *De Halve Maen* 70.3 (Fall 1997): 59-68.

whose office did not require university training, filled minor ecclesiastical positions in Calvinist communities. Aboard ship they performed some basic community services and functioned as a source of moral authority, representing the spiritual power. The Amsterdam consistory sent him to Fort Nassau at Mouri on the Coast of Guinea (present-day Ghana), a company fortress where he worked in 1631 and 1632, and where he probably also acted as a schoolmaster among young Africans. Actually, this was the usual path to the sacred ministry for so-called *Duytsche clercken* ["Dutch clerics"], younger or older men who wanted to become ministers of the Word but who had no schooling in Latin and were unable to read the ancient languages. As comforters of the sick in company outposts, they were permitted to study the Bible and pious Protestant theologians in preparation for the ministry. This part-time job with enough spare time for study served therefore as a working scholarship.

Though this traditional formula clearly did justice neither to his position as a cleric schooled in Latin nor to his intellectual abilities, Evert used it for achieving autonomy as a minister. In opposition to the learned theology of an academic education, for which his scholarship had been intended, he preferred his own concept of the minister as a field worker schooled in practical piety. His transitional psychosomatic youth experience—the healing of the physical disabilities that God had visited on him—had, indeed, made him exceptionally fit for the spiritual function of a comforter of the sick in what was reputedly the most murderous of all Dutch overseas possessions and a place where at times more than half of the company servants died within a year from the effects of the dreaded Guinea fevers. In fact, Evert's very survival during his Guinea term suggests—his juvenile sickness notwithstanding—that he had no sickly constitution at all. He was a strong man, with an independent spirit and a fierce temper.

An American Ministry

On June 7, 1632, Bogardus presented himself to the church authorities at Amsterdam with excellent testimonials from the colonial authorities. He was examined by the consistory and admitted as a minister of the Word on July 15, 1632. Again, it was not in a parish of his homeland that he chose to achieve his identity as a preacher, but in another overseas colony, in New Netherland.[11] Having recalled home the entire crew of that colony in 1632, the Amsterdam Chamber of

---

[11] On New Netherland: Jaap Jacobs, *The Colony of New Netherland: A Dutch Settlement in Seventeenth-Century America* (Ithaca: Cornell University Press, 2009).

the West India Company badly needed a new preacher. Bogardus was recommended to them by the Reverend Otto Badius, a representative of the orthodox wing of the Amsterdam consistory, and he was ready to depart immediately. At first blush the choice made by the former mystic seems to pose yet another mystery. Why did he refuse to look for a living in the district of his home town, Woerden, which, after all, had invested in his future for many years? In fact, this self-ordained course probably brought him exactly what he was looking for: perfect autonomy, an overseas parish virtually independent from the higher authorities of church and state, and, finally, the liberty to impress, as a minister, his own spiritual stamp on a community within which he could function as the moral leader.

Everardus Bogardus's colonial experience as a Reformed minister lasted from his arrival on Manhattan shore in March 1633 to his death in a shipwreck off Swansea in Wales (Great Britain) fourteen years later, on September 27/28, 1647. But a gradual shift can be noticed. During the first years of his overseas ministry, Dominie Bogardus acted as a faithful servant of his employer, the West Indies Company. His initial flock consisted mainly of company servants, mostly unmarried men hailing from several countries and belonging to various confessions, who served for a limited term prior to their return to Europe. Women and children were scarce, while formal schooling was virtually non-existent until the arrival of schoolmaster Adam Roelants in 1638. Bogardus, like many of those who oversaw political and ecclesiastical affairs in Dutch outposts, saw a pivotal role for the church. Religion was the means to ensure group cohesion and hence was also the instrument of culture and moral education; a moral community was, after all, the best way to guarantee social integration.[12] We also know that Bogardus worked initially for the conversion of Native Americans, and that under his ministry baptized Africans were respected as Christians.[13] In order to make clear his position, minister Bogardus fought, and won, in

[12] Cf. Frijhoff, Willem, "Seventeenth-Century Religion as a Cultural Practice: Reassessing New Netherland's Religious History," in Margriet Bruijn Lacy, Charles Gehring, and Jenneke Oosterhoff, eds., *From De Halve Maen to KLM: 400 Years of Dutch-American Exchange* (Münster: Nodus Publikationen, 2008), 159-74; on the role and place of the Reformed Church under the Dutch dominion: Willem Frijhoff, "Was the Dutch Republic a Calvinist Community? The State, the Confessions, and Culture in the Early Modern Netherlands," in André Holenstein, Thomas Maissen, and Maarten Prak, eds., *The Republican Alternative: The Netherlands and Switzerland Compared* (Amsterdam: Amsterdam University Press, 2008), 99-122.

[13] Frijhoff, *Fulfilling God's Mission*, 524-46; see also Robert J. Swan, *New Amsterdam Gehenna: Segregated Death in New York City, 1630-1801* (Brooklyn: Noir Verite Press, 2006), 178-83.

1634, soon after his arrival, his first battle with the sheriff, Dr. Lubbert Dinclagen, a university-trained jurist of patrician breeding. Whereas the sheriff had to maintain law and order, the minister was, in Bogardus's eyes, the only company agent responsible for defining the colony's moral standards, and he succeeded in imposing his view. Dinclagen was excommunicated and had to return to the fatherland in shame.

On March 28, 1638, a new director arrived, Willem Kieft (1602-1647), another patrician and a former wine merchant in France.[14] At first the cultured Kieft seemed a perfect match for Bogardus, who had fought many quarrels with Kieft's unruly predecessor, Wouter van Twiller. But during Kieft's war against Native Americans, in the early forties, Bogardus's eyes were opened.[15] The atrocities committed on the night of February 25, 1643, when more than eighty Native Americans on the other side of the Hudson River were treacherously and savagely massacred by company soldiers, together with Kieft's cover-up attempt and the way he shifted the blame to others, transformed Bogardus's latent conflict with the director into a permanent feud. For moral reasons Bogardus no longer considered Kieft worthy of governing the colony. The corrupt patrician and the characterless company servant he saw in Kieft was the opposite of the active, experienced, resolute but sensible colonists he chose as his true friends: farmer Cornelis van Vorst, Captain David Pietersz de Vries, and planter Jochem Kuyter.

According to the author of the pamphlet *Breeden-Raedt* [Broad Advice, 1649] Kieft had instituted policies "so antithetical to religion" that Dominie Bogardus had "repeatedly and passionately in his sermons proclaimed God's judgment against the gruesome killings, greed, and other gross excesses."[16] Therefore, Bogardus had immediately prepared

---

[14] Willem Frijhoff, "Neglected networks: Director Willem Kieft (1602-1647) and his Dutch relatives," in Joyce D. Goodfriend, ed., *Revisiting New Netherland: Perspectives on Early Dutch America* (Leiden: Brill, 2005), 147-204.

[15] Some recent interpretations of Kieft's war: Evan Haefeli, "Kieft's war and the cultures of violence in colonial America," in Michael Belleisles, ed., *Lethal Imagination: Violence and Brutality in American History* (New York: New York University Press, 1999), 17-40; Benjamin Schmidt, *Innocence Abroad: The Dutch Imagination and the New World, 1570-1670* (Cambridge: Cambridge University Press, 2001), 249, 276-80; Russell Shorto, *The Island at the Center of the World: The Epic Story of Dutch Manhattan and the Forgotten Colony That Shaped America* (New York: Doubleday, 2004), 112-28, 170-80; Donna Merwick, *The Shame and the Sorrow: Dutch-Amerindian Encounters in New Netherland* (Philadelphia: The University of Pennsylvania Press, 2006), especially 99-179, and "Extortion," *De Halve Maen* 78:3 (2005): 43-48.

[16] *Breeden-Raedt aende Vereenichde Nederlandsche Provintien [...] gemaeckt ende gestelt uyt diverse ware en waerachtige memorien, door I.A.G.W.C.* (Antwerp: Van Duynen, 1649), f. D1 r°; trans. by Henry Murphy: "Broad Advice to the United Netherlands Provinces," in Henry C. Murphy, ed., *Vertoogh van Nieu Nederland, and Breeden Raedt*

the defense of Marijn Adriaensen, a Dutch colonist and a victim of Indian violence. On March 21, 1643 Marijn had tried to kill Kieft with a gun and a saber because he deemed Kieft responsible for his misery. Bogardus thus made himself for some time the moral spokesman of the opposition, a role previously filled by Captain de Vries (who returned home in October 1643) and a little later by Bogardus's friend Adriaen van der Donck, the university-trained lawyer who vigorously defended the rights of the colonists.[17]

Slowly, Bogardus's outlook changed from that of a company employee, with a temporary assignment overseas, to that of a true colonist, firmly established in his new fatherland. A petition by the colonists on October 28, 1644, that he may have drafted, spoke against the arbitrariness of the West India Company. The petitioners called for a regulated society in which justice was administered in an orderly fashion and citizens had the right of appeal. They pled for civil government in villages and towns, for a voice in the governing of the land, and for representatives alongside the director with the right to vote. Bogardus's own point of reference shifted from the company to his congregation. He now assumed his full responsibility as pastor of his flock. He presented its troubles to the highest authorities, in defiance of the director when necessary. The farms were destroyed, he said; no one was sowing seed, crops were rotting in the fields, and there was no money left to support wives and children:

> [We] are sitting here among thousands of wild and barbaric people, with whom no comfort or mercy can be found; we left our dear fatherland, and if God the Lord had not been our comfort, we would have perished in our misery.[18]

Kieft was so deeply offended by Bogardus's frontal attack on his authority that instead of promoting the unity of state and church, as his office and company regulations required, he instituted a complete separation between the two and stopped attending church services altogether. From January 1644 until the arrival of his successor, Petrus

---

aende Vereenichde Nederlandsche Provintien. Two rare tracts, printed in 1649-'50, relating to the administration of affairs in New Netherland (New York: Murphy, 1854), 157.

[17] He is the central character of Shorto, *The Island*. In 1645, Van der Donck married Mary Doughty, the daughter of another minister in the colony, the Presbyterian refugee Francis Doughty (d. after 1665), who was on good terms with Bogardus.

[18] National Achives (The Hague), States General, n° 12564.25 (petition of 28 October 1644); E.B. O'Callaghan and Berthold Fernow (trans. and ed.), *Documents Relative to the Colonial History of the State of New York*, 15 vols. (Albany: Weed, Parsons and Co. 1856-1887),1: 209-13.

Stuyvesant, in May 1647, Kieft "no longer wanted to hear God's Word or partake of the Christian sacraments, making every effort to draw all who depended on him away from the church."[19] In the detailed indictment that Kieft dispatched to Bogardus on January 2, 1616, two different charges were intertwined. One concerned the character and actions of the minister; the other his stand on the affairs of the colony. Kieft's reproaches about the moral aspects of Bogardus's conduct (his immoderate language, his frequent drunkenness) appear to have reached farther back in time than his criticism of the minister's political views.

The real escalation of the conflict came when the war was over and a peace treaty had been signed with Native Americans in August 1645. The minister refused, however, to celebrate the peace in the manner Kieft wanted. A day of thanksgiving was proclaimed for Wednesday, September 6, and the council expressly instructed ministers to choose a suitable text and preach a fitting sermon. Kieft acknowledged that Bogardus "preached a good sermon, but uttered not a single word about the peace, nor did he give thanks to God for the reason we had instituted that day, as the other ministers living within our borders did with great fervor."[20] Bogardus replied: Was there any reason to thank God? The triumphant party should do penance, and such a victory was not his idea of peace. Kieft thus found himself deprived of all sense of triumph.

The immediate cause of Kieft's indictment was Bogardus's Christmas sermon of 1645, in which he had implicitly compared Kieft with a monster. Bogardus had said

> that in Africa, owing to the extreme heat, diverse animals interbreed with others and thus engender many monsters, but here, where the climate is temperate, you do not know (you say) where these monsters of human beings come from; they are the powerful ones, but should have no power, those persons who have many fathers and trust in the arm of the flesh and not in the Lord.[21]

Everyone understood at the time that Bogardus was alluding to Kieft. Thirteen years after his stay on the Gold Coast, images of Africa were still

---

[19] *Breeden-Raedt*, f. C 4v° ('Broad Advice', 155).
[20] *New York Historical manuscripts: Dutch*, A.J.F. van Laer (trans. and ed.), *Council minutes, 1638-1649* (Baltimore: Genealogical Publishing Co., 1974), 4:295 (January 2, 1646).
[21] Ibid., 4:295-96.

vivid in Bogardus's mind. In European eyes, every hybrid was a monster, and the veiled sexual connotations of a hybrid gave his comparison an extra sting.

Now Kieft, too, resorted to heavy ammunition. In the indictment of January 1646 he dredged up all Bogardus's missteps in New Netherland. According to Kieft,

> [you] spread so much verbal abuse during our government that hardly anyone in the whole country was exempt, sparing neither your own wife nor her sister, particularly when you were in good company and enjoying yourself, from time to time even mixing your human passion in the pulpit, associating with the worst criminals in the land, taking their side and defending them, [you] refused to execute orders, to celebrate the sacrament of the Lord's Supper, and even to partake of it.[22]

These reproaches were followed by a series of concrete examples, but the indictment is actually as interesting for what it does not contain as for what it does. There was not a word about the war itself or the treatment of the Indians, only about the aftermath and the effects on the congregation. Kieft reproached Bogardus for his bold and public partisanship: as a minister it was his duty to support the director, and both of them should have stood above the factions. In Bogardus's view, however, this claim was absurd: the director had turned himself into a faction.

Kieft dragged a good many people into his feud with the minister. During the sermon people outside the church intentionally made as much noise as possible, playing ninepins, stomping, dancing, singing, jumping, "and all other frivolous exercises" in order to make it difficult for those inside to hear.[23] Church members who came to the fort to celebrate the Lord's Supper were mocked by the soldiers, and during the introductory sermon Kieft more than once ordered a drum to be beaten or a canon fired. When Bogardus then asked to have the drumming done a little farther away from the church, the director replied that the drummer had to give a roll at the spot where the director had ordered him to stand. Besides irritating to churchgoers, the noise must have been especially offensive to Bogardus, for as a thinly disguised form of "kettle music," or charivari, it implied an attack on his honor. When another communion service was approaching, the director told his

---

[22] Ibid., 4:291-92.
[23] *Breeden-Raedt*, f. D 1r° ("Broad Advice," 155-56).

loyal followers, "Only one and a half men and horse's head will show up, eventually they will all follow us and the whole crowd will stay outside."[24]

To understand what was at stake in this quarrel between two major representatives of the European population, we have to realize that New Netherland was changing. The crisis in the fur trade made intensive colonization for the cultivation of tobacco and Indian corn more attractive. As colonists established themselves for longer periods of time, the community's identity itself was transformed. Dominie Bogardus's own life offers the best example. In 1638 he married a Lutheran immigrant from Norway, Annetgen (or Anneke) Jans (c. 1605-1663), the widow of the recently deceased Scandinavian colonist Roelof Jansz.[25] Evert added four sons to her five surviving children. Until then he had assisted other people in their financial needs, including his brother Cornelis, with a loan for the start of a grocery shop at Leiden. Now he needed his income for his growing family.

Since Bogardus no longer had vested interests in his European homeland, it is striking to see how his mental horizon changed within a few years, and how this led him to redefine his personal identity, both socially and with regard to the way he perceived himself. From a Dutch preacher accountable to the West India Company, the Reverend Bogardus developed into a pioneer colonist whose prime responsibility was to the local community. He adopted as his own the positions and problems of the settlers, and he focused fully on the need for new forms of social integration. The church remained his major instrument, but he used its rituals, in particular, Holy Communion, to shape the new community. Committed to defining the moral standards of the colony, his perspective changed from that of a European guarding the interests of his homeland, to a North American with the welfare of his colony and his community at heart. He advocated a harmonious society marked by cultural diversity and comprised of European settlers, enslaved and free blacks, and Native Americans. In fact, he functioned as the colony's moral conscience.

---

[24] Ibid.
[25] The story of Anneke Jans and the myths woven around her person in the 19th and 20th centuries, concerning the property of the so-called Anneke Jans Farm on Manhattan, is a narrative in itself. See Frijhoff, *Fulfilling God's Mission*, 571-91; and Willem Frijhoff, "Emblematic myths: Anneke's fortune, Bogardus's farewell, and Kieft's son," in Laura Cruz and Willem Frijhoff, eds., *Myth in History, History in Myth: Proceeedings of the Third International Conference of the Society for Netherlandic History (New York: June 5-6, 2006)* (Leiden: Brill, 2009), 117-46.

Because the colonists had to share their new identity with other ethnic groups on the new continent, conversion offered an apposite language for the integration of all cultural groups into one single colonial society. In the first half of the seventeenth century the Europeans of New Netherland still formed a minority in a mainly Native American world. Since the second quarter of the century, African slaves had come in small numbers to Manhattan, some of whom were emancipated after years of labor. Slavery did not yet have the massive character it acquired once the trade triangle between Africa, the Americas, and Europe was scaled up. Nor was slavery as yet legitimated by the new Christian ideology of the black race as the cursed descendants of Noah's son Ham (Gen. 9:18-27). In fact, many slaves came from former Portuguese possessions in Africa and had been Christianized before being enslaved.[26] They had adapted the ritualized religion of Portuguese Catholics in various ways to their native religious practices, traditions, and beliefs. However, since African Americans and Native Americans were basically considered uncivilized heathens, their integration required education in the religion of the Word. Minister Bogardus baptized African Americans in significant numbers. He was presumably unaware that many of them did not fully understand the Protestant rejection of rituals as superstition. Both African and Native Americans considered ritual as the true form of religion. But the message was clear: the church on the new continent had to function as an agent of integration.

A Life's Harvest

How ought one assess the harvest of this rather short but full, restless, and busy life? Beginning already with Kieft's indictment and continuing until the present, Bogardus's biographers have exclusively linked his two major vices—his wrathful nature and his excessive drinking—to his supposedly unpleasant demeanor and personal failures. Consequently, in most historical narratives of New Netherland Bogardus has almost been retroactively disqualified as a Christian

---

[26] This is not the place to assess the debate between the tenants of the Creolization thesis and more Afro-centric interpretations of Black American culture and religion in America. Cf. Ira Berlin and Leslie M. Harris, eds., *Slavery in New York* (New York: New Press, 2005); Linda M. Heywood and John K. Thornton, *Central Africans, Atlantic Creoles, and the Foundation of the Americas, 1585-1660* (New York: Cambridge University Press, 2007); id., "Intercultural relations between Europeans and Blacks in New Netherland," in Hans Krabbendam, Cornelis A. van Minnen, and Giles Scott-Smith, eds., *Four Centuries of Dutch-American Relations* 1609-2009 (Albany: SUNY Press, 2009), 192-203.

pastor. His continuous anger seems at first glance to have been an instance of uncontrolled emotion; the minister ranted and raved and accused his opponents of everything imaginable just to get his way. But it would be naïve to take either Kieft or Bogardus literally. Just as the director was not the African monster to which Bogardus compared him in the pulpit, the minister was not the drunkard and quarrel monger that Kieft portrayed in his indictment. The language of both men was rooted in both rhetoric and strategy. When Kieft accused Bogardus of outbursts of rage, he used an age-old tactic: he dismissed the minister's criticism of the functioning of the colony by presenting it as a problem of personal psychology.

Was Bogardus really as out of control as Kieft depicted him? Caution is necessary. According to the pamphlet *Broad Advice*, written by a supporter of Bogardus, he unleashed passion and wrath only when it was genuinely necessary, but he then pulled out all the stops, and they were numerous and expressive. Bogardus must have been a star of the pulpit! In the events of 1622-23 young Evert had already shown himself to be a masterful champion of his own interests in the public arena. By carefully dosing his expressions of emotion he managed to secure for himself maximum support among the various strata of Woerden society. This brings us to an alternative assessment: rage and wrath were for Bogardus a legitimate instrument of his mission because they were well-defined standard elements in the pietistic and Puritan emotional regime. Wrath was expressly allowed because it helped preserve the proper relation between the interests of God and of man. Where God had to be served, every measure was enlarged to his dimension. Evert's wrath took its cue from the degree of divine intervention and was proportional to the punishment at hand. For Bogardus a cardinal *sin* thus became, in the right context, a cardinal *virtue*.

Secondly, how ought we to understand his excessive drinking in a colony where drunkenness was endemic? Much of the alcohol consumption was certainly a form of what the anthropologist Mary Douglas has called "constructive drinking," i.e., a rite of aggregation, a symbolic form of fraternizing, and an effective means of fostering community formation. The sources show that in New Netherland every opportunity was seized for community-wide drinking festivities. But drunkenness in some circumstances, or in some persons, was considered a sin of immoderation that betrayed a lack of self-control. On this point we find a clear inconsistency in Bogardus's personality. His commitment to orderly religion and controlled behavior clashed with his love for the bottle.

Actually, his reputation for intemperance was something he shared with many Dutch ministers, including some of considerable prominence in the world of Reformed orthodoxy. Yet, drunkenness can also have a second, positive connotation. People are said to be drunk with joy or even to be drunk with the Spirit. It is a metaphor for euphoria, for rapture, for ecstasy. Evert Willemsz never recovered the ecstatic experience he had on the threshold of adulthood, at a prophetic moment in local church history, in the religious ferment of Woerden. Was his drunkenness twenty years later, at a time of mounting conflict, strife, and responsibility, an unconscious substitute for that sense of mystical transport? Was he seeking to recover some of the euphoria that had changed his life in the winter of 1622-23? Given Bogardus's difficulties with his own passions, aggravated by his drinking habits, it is not surprising that his opponents soon came to view his constant potential for explosive anger, both from the pulpit and in the community, as unworkable, no matter how legitimate his references to God. He could have tempered his message, but his personality was ill-suited to such temperance. It was all or nothing.

By way of conclusion I want to draw attention to a thematic thread running through Evert Willemsz's entire life, namely his pietism, in its practical manifestation. Pietism, the *praxis pietatis*, is perhaps the strongest thread that unites the adult Bogardus with young Evert Willemsz and, more generally, the colony of New Netherland with his fatherland. We find it in his uncle Meusevoet, in the ministers of Woerden, and in his Amsterdam publisher. It was pivotal to Evert's perception of his relationship with God, his task in the world, and the reality around him. But it also explains a great deal about the minister's actions in New Netherland, his sense of self, and his understanding of his calling. Ultimately, what mattered in his image of the ideal colony was not a type of civil authority; nor was it the legal status, ethnic group, skin color, or even religious denomination of its inhabitants. Bogardus's highest priority was a God-fearing life, the sanctification of the individual. And the Reformed Church was the community best suited to nurture this ideal because of its position as the dominant church in the world of the Dutch Golden Age.

Bogardus took the local community seriously, perhaps even more seriously than the ecclesiastical precepts to which he was bound. This explains his struggle over taking communion. It is conceivable that the Reformed Church, given its special political status in the Dutch commonwealth, was for Bogardus more a precondition for a personal conversion and a sanctified society than a means of salvation in itself. There is an intriguing consistency in the way he distanced himself already in Woerden from ecclesiastical pretensions, opted out of academic theology in Leiden to study further on his own in a subordinate capacity in Africa, and, finally, remained loyal to the classis while nevertheless going his own way on Manhattan Island. This gave him the necessary leeway to shape church discipline in accordance with his own ideas and ideals. Even after he was ordained to the ministry, he never renounced his independent tendencies. When director Kieft plunged New Netherland into the war with the Indians, Bogardus was the right person to take him on: indomitable, headstrong, eloquent, but also gripped by ideals that could not be compromised, and, as God's elect, never doubting that he was right.

Placing his conflict with Kieft and his attitude towards blacks in this perspective suddenly brings to light not only the close mental ties that still existed between Old and New Netherland, but also the potential power of pietism as a binding agent for the colonists in the Dutch New World, across boundaries of religious and ethnic differences. Although Evert had grown up in a good Calvinist environment, he strikes us neither in his youth nor during his ministry as a dogmatic quibbler. When he emphasized discipline, or a life pleasing to God, he did so in terms comprehensible to all Christians and as a servant and guardian of public godliness, in the name of the West India Company and not as the leader of a Reformed faction. In this light it is not surprising to find Calvinist pietism flourishing a good half century later in the colony, which had in the meantime come under English rule.

During Bogardus's years in New Netherland, this model for piety grew at the same time that the Reformed Church was clericalizing. Young Evert himself developed from an underprivileged and recalcitrant layman into the Reverend Bogardus, a driven leader of a congregation and a pillar of society. His youthful pietism metamorphosed into orthodox fire-and-brimstone sermons—still full of fervor and biblical inspiration and without respect to person, but increasingly entangled in the contradictions that came with the unavoidable compromise between personal convictions, social position, and group interests. That was his personal tragedy.

In a sigh to his Rensselaerswijck colleague Johannes Megapolensis in the summer of 1646 he hinted at his weariness with life and preoccupation with death.[27] Death came for him soon indeed,

---

[27] Megapolensis to Classis Amsterdam, August 15, 1648: New Brunswick Theological Seminary, Gardner A. Sage Library, Amsterdam Correspondence, box I, n° 3 (quoted in Frijhoff, *Fulfilling God's Mission*, 519).

unexpectedly, at age forty, far away from home. In August 1647 Kieft set sail for *patria* aboard the *Princess Amelia*, together with Bogardus. Both wanted to justify their policy and attitude in front of the West India Company and the States General. Moreover, Bogardus wanted to recover unpaid salary from the company and must have planned a visit to his elder brother at Leiden, whose grocery shop he had helped to set up a decade before. As they arrived near the English coast on September 27, 1647, a drunken steersman maneuvered the ship into the wrong channel. Towards midnight it was wrecked on the rock mass of the Mumbles near Swansea, off the coast of Wales. Both Kieft and Bogardus disappeared in the waves.

STABILIZERS

Laying the Foundations of the Church
in the Late Seventeenth Century

CHAPTER 4

Gideon Schaats (1607–1694): Old World Dominie in a New World Setting

Firth Haring Fabend

When Dominie Gideon Schaats (also spelled Schaets) arrived in the patroonship of Rensselaerswijck in the summer of 1652 to minister to the acting director Jan Baptist van Rensselaer and his settlers, he was already a middle-aged man of forty-five years with the career of schoolmaster behind him.[1] Rensselaerswijck, on the east shore of the Hudson, with neighboring Fort Orange, on the west shore, was in 1652 the only population center of any magnitude in New Netherland other than New Amsterdam. The population of this upper Hudson community that year has been estimated at about three hundred, as compared to New Amsterdam with an estimated population of one thousand.

The Dutch West India Company, which had control of the colony of New Netherland, gave patroonships to rich Dutchmen willing to settle the land with fifty families within four years. Rensselaerswijck

[1] He traveled from the Netherlands aboard the *Gelderse Blom*. Jaap Jacobs, "The Shipping and Trade from the Dutch Republic to New Netherland, 1609-1675" (on line at www.olivetree.com) reveals that the *Gelderse Blom* was the only ship arriving from the Netherlands in 1652, and it arrived in New Amsterdam "before August 20, 1652."

First Reformed Church of Albany, New York, demolished in 1806. The church in the image was built in 1715 around the 1656 structure, which was later removed through the windows and doors of the new building. The same hour-glass-shaped pulpit that Schaats used in the original blockhouse church of 1656 is still in use, as is the voorlezer's semicircular pulpit, in what is now called First Church in Albany.
[Original at the New York State Library, Albany.]

eventually, but not in Schaats's lifetime, comprised a million acres on both sides of the upper Hudson River in today's Columbia and Albany counties. Bestowed on Amsterdam jewelry merchant and company director Kiliaen van Rensselaer, Rensselaerswijck was the only successful one of a number of the company's patroonships.

Family and Education

Gideon Schaats was born in 1607 in Leerdam, a town northeast of Dordrecht in today's province of South Holland.[2] He came from a family of Reformed ministers, but he did not enter the ministry himself until after a long tenure as a schoolmaster.[3] Whether this was because he

---
[2] Leerdam had been since 1551 a sovereign possession of the family of Orange-Nassau through the marriage of William the Silent with Anna van Egmond. Therefore, any records pertaining to Gideon or his family would be in the Domain Council of the Nassauche Domein Raad in the National Archives in The Hague, not in the Royal Archives as one would suppose. Personal communication with Royal Archives, November 2, 2009.

[3] Fred A. van Lieburg, *Repertorium van Nederlandse hervormde predikanten tot 1816*, 2 vols. (Dordrecht: Van Lieburg, 1996), 1:217.

lacked the funds for a university education, or because he was genuinely interested in a teaching career, or whether his wife, herself a teacher, influenced his decisions, is a matter of speculation.

At age nineteen in 1626, finished for the time being with his education, Gideon took a position as tutor to the children of the Count of Treslong, also known as Buren, an infantry captain at The Hague. Captain Treslong was subsequently promoted to military governor of the fortress at Brielle. Gideon accompanied the Treslong family to Brielle, where he met the children's governess, Agnetie Reyniers, whom he married in 1634 when he was twenty-seven and she was about twenty-four.[4] For the next eighteen years, until he emigrated to New Netherland in 1652, Gideon was a schoolmaster first at Brielle and then at Beesd, a town just east of Leerdam in the county and Classis of Buren in what is today South Holland. In Beesd, population twenty-four hundred, he opened his own school, perhaps with the assistance of his wife, the former governess.

On the side, "for some time" he began to study "sacred theology," with the permission of the Classis of Amsterdam.[5] As Gideon was described as a "Voetian" by a contemporary observer, one might expect or at least hope that his teacher was Gisbertus Voetius, the eminent theologian at Utrecht University, especially since Beesd is not far from Utrecht. But Gideon Schaats is not among those mentioned in a list of Utrecht matriculants published in 1886.[6] It is more likely that Gideon did not have a university education but studied either with his minister father, who lived until 1659, or perhaps with the Reverend Justus Wilhelmus Molenis, the minister of the Beesd church from 1643 to

---

[4] John T. Palmer and J. Michael Skaates, "The Schaets (Skaats, Skaates, Skates) Family in the Netherlands (1400-1652) and in America (1652-1983)" (Hancock, MI: J.M. Skaates Associates, Inc., 1983), 9.

[5] E. T. Corwin, trans. and ed., *The Ecclesiastical Records of the State of New York*, 7 vols. (Albany, 1901-1916), 1:253. Hereafter *ERNY*. Evidence of Gideon's membership in the Beesd church occurs in a group of papers held at the Streekarchief Geldermalsen. There is no reference number. They are listed under "Gereformeerde Gemeente Beesd." Microfiche copies are held at the Central Bureau of Genealogy in The Hague, described in the CBG Catalog as Benoemingen ouderlingen diakenen ca.1640-1683; kerkeraadshandelingen 1643, 1671, 1681; L 1644; 1687; T. 1684-1685, D. z.j. enz. Thanks to Terry Haslan-Jones for this information. According to the Regional Archief Rivierenland, personal communication, November 2, 2009, this school was not a Latin School. It was simply a small village school.

[6] *Album studiosorum Academiae Rheno-Trajectinae MDCXXXVI-MDCCCLXXXVI: accedunt nomina curatorum et professorum per eadem secula* (Utrecht: Beijers en Van Boekhoven, 1886). The Utrechts Archief confirms this information and adds that the name of Gideon Schaats is not found in the *lidmatenregister* of the Reformed Church in the city of Utrecht. Correspondence of August 4, 2009.

1652, or both. Another possibility is Petrus Ceporinus, the *predicant* of the Beesd church from 1621 until his death in Beesd in 1642.

Schaats was identified in 1647 as a *schoolmeester* and *defent propon,* which means he "exhorted" as a ministerial hopeful. In 1649 he was described as one who *mag examen doen* (or "may do his examination"), and in 1650 as *praeparatorie geexamineert* ("having been preparatorily examined").[7]

On June 28, 1649, with two years of study under his belt, Schaats appeared before the Classis of Amsterdam "with [a] very good testimonial" from the Classis of Buren to ask permission to go to the East Indies as a *sieckentrooster* or comforter of the sick. Johan de Niet has written that *sieckentroosters* usually had no academic education. "They went through an exam before being admitted, but the requirements were not high." But, De Niet goes on, "their [published] writings show a considerable knowledge of and interest in ... theological discourse. It is a proof of the possibilities of learning outside the regular schools and institutions."[8]

Perhaps because the Classis of Amsterdam noticed that it would be possible for Gideon to rise in the ministry with only a little more education, it recommended him "provisionally" for the ministry. "[I]nasmuch as he had for some time exercised himself in *proponeren*" (exercises preparatory to the ministry), the classis urged him to take his preparatory examination at the next session of the Synod of South Holland to make this recommendation a reality.[9]

The classis may possibly have had the pulpit of the patroonship of Rensselaerswijck in mind for Gideon, for Rensselaerswijck in the summer of 1649 was on the brink of losing its minister, Johannes Megapolensis, who had accepted a call to the church in New Amsterdam. Even so, it was three years before Schaats satisfied the requirements of the Synod of South Holland and accepted, on April 15, 1652, a call to Rensselaerswijck.[10]

Because he had not had a formal university education, Schaats was known as a "Dutch clerk" or *Duytsche clerk*. Those answering to this description were not required to know ancient languages to

---

[7] Historische Naamindex Rivierenland, Historische Kring West Betuwe. I thank again Terry Haslan-Jones for this new information and Earl William Kennedy and Dirk Mouw for help in understanding it.

[8] ERNY, 1:253, 308; Johan de Niet, "Confessional Care of Souls and Pietist Comfort in the Dutch Republic," in Fred van Lieburg, ed., *Confessionalism and Pietism: Religious Reform in Early Modern Europe and North America* (Mainz: Von Zabern, 2006), 203.

[9] ERNY, 1:253, 308.

[10] ERNY, 1:309.

become full-fledged ministers in the church.[11] The process of accepting these particular candidates for the ministry involved the local classis obtaining the approval of the Provincial Synod, an examination, and "according to their proficiency," a course of private exercises, "after which they shall be dealt with as shall be judged most conducive to edification."

A month after his call, on May 6, 1652, Gideon Schaats, "candidate in Sacred Theology," was introduced by its Deputies on Indian (i.e., colonial) Affairs to the classis, which had previously given him permission to accept the call. He presented his credentials and gave a short sermon on Matthew 11:28 ("Come unto me, all ye who labor and are heavy laden, and I will give you rest"), which so pleased his hearers that he was allowed to proceed immediately to his final examination. After his successful examination, the president of the classis ordained him to the ministry of God with the laying on of hands.[12] Three months later he was in Rensselaerswijck with his wife and children, sons Bartholomeus and Reynier and daughter Anna.

Life in Rensselaerswijck

Gideon's contract with the patroon required him to "use all Christian zeal . . . to bring up both the Heathen [i.e., the Indians] and their children in the Christian religion," to teach the Heidelberg Catechism, to instruct the people in the Holy Scriptures, to "pay attention to the office of Schoolmaster," to teach the confirmation class, and to do "everything fitting and becoming a public, honest and Holy Teacher." His annual salary was 800 guilders, which was increased to 1,300 guilders by 1655.[13]

What was it like for him in the frontier community on the upper Hudson? Five years into his pastorate, as his second contract with the patroon was coming to an end, Schaats described life in Rensselaerswijck. So far it had not been easy. In a letter to a colleague, dated June 27, 1657, he referred to the "indiscreet walk of many [in Rensselaerswijck]. There are many hearers but not much saving fruit." His congregation numbered about one hundred thirty full communing members, of whom he had received about thirty over his five-year tenure.

[11] Willem Frijhoff, *Fulfilling God's Mission: The Two Worlds of Domine Everardus Bogardus, 1607-1647* (Leiden: Brill, 2007), 326-332; "1619 Rules of Church Government," printed in E. T. Corwin, *A Digest of Constitutional and Synodical Legislation of the Reformed Church in America* (New York: Chauncey Holt, 1906), xvi.

[12] *ERNY*, 1:309.

[13] Contract, *ERNY*, 1:309-11; Notarial Archives, Stadsarchief, Amsterdam, inv. no. 1100, fol. 23v and 26.

There were sometimes between three hundred and four hundred at church, he reported, and if all attended there might be six hundred, "but the taverns and villainous houses have many visitors" and the people liked to gamble and drink. He described himself as having been "deceived by certain ones . . . on account of their inconsistent walk" and had been obliged to suspend these offenders from the Lord's Table. "The people are rather reckless and refrain from communion for the slightest reason."[14]

"The work here is very hard for one minister," he continued, for he had no prelector (*voorlezer*) and had to fulfill the duties of that office as well as his own. (The *voorlezer's* duties usually included teaching school, which had also been mentioned in Schaats's contract, but it is not clear in the records whether he taught school or not. Two schoolteachers are mentioned in the local records, so he may not have had to take on this function.) Moreover, he went on, everything was more expensive upriver than in Manhattan and "four times as dear as in the Fatherland," a clear indication that he needed a larger salary than he was receiving. Further, his wife seems to have been ailing, for he referred to her as not having "succumbed yet," and he longed to take his three children back to *patria*. "Here they learn nothing but rudeness, instead of useful things. This journey is desirable especially for my sons," he added, "each of whom is now fit to undertake something to his liking."[15] After five years in Rensselaerswijck he was still holding services in the back room of the patroon's house and himself lived with his family in a building built as a poorhouse. But things were about to change; the extension of his ministry to include Beverwijck solved his financial problem and gave him a proper edifice to conduct his worship services when a "pretty" church, as he described it, was built for him.

In 1652 Director General Petrus Stuyvesant had created a court at Beverwijck, a humming little town across the Hudson River from Rensselaerswijck, and at the conclusion of Schaats's contract with the patroon Stuyvesant had informed the West India Company that Gideon Schaats had been called to Beverwijck, with half of his salary of 100 guilders per month to be paid by the patroon, for the church was intended to serve both communities. In Beverwijck the community built a "handsome parsonage" and a proper church, which also served as a blockhouse, or place where the people could take refuge in case of attack, in the center of the village.[16]

[14] *ERNY*, 1:382-86.
[15] *ERNY*, 1:384.
[16] *ERNY*, 1:395.

Beverwijck in 1657 was a place much in need of a minister's moral guidance and direction. The Fort Orange court minutes for the years 1652-1664 reveal that the citizens of Beverwijck went to court on a wide range of issues: to sue for wages and debts, to pay fines for unlawful tapping, fighting, stealing cheese, abusive language, slander, and contempt of court; to settle disputes over guns, knife wounds, breached promises, and violated ordinances; and to pay fines for serving liquor on the Sabbath, for selling brandy to "savages," for not enclosing gardens, for not buildings on lots, for sleeping with a woman when not married to her, and for shooting a dog. A wife beater came to the court's attention, as did a runaway boy, a missing tub of butter, the composer of "notorious lampoons" (a man with a curious penchant for nicknaming houses in ways that offended the house owners), and an illegitimate child.[17]

Unfortunately, Schaats's daughter Anna also produced an illegitimate child, to the great shame and dishonor of Gideon and his wife. The boy child was born in 1663. As if this were not scandal enough, the father was Arent van Curler, a married man, a nephew of the patroon, and the prominent founder of Schenectady. Somehow, Schaats weathered this cruel storm, the unsavory details of which were soon relayed to everyone from Petrus Stuyvesant and his council to the directors of the West India Company in Amsterdam to their High Mightinesses in the Classis of Amsterdam and throughout the general populace of New Netherland. One can speculate that for Schaats it must have been a time for what Gisbertus Voetius had called "spiritual desertion," when the Christian believer experiences the fear that he has been deserted or abandoned by God.[18] Nevertheless, he did not disown his daughter, and it says reams for Schaats's character that he stood up for her in public when she and he were verbally attacked by the scandalized consistory and community.

In 1667, three years after the English takeover of New Netherland, he wrote another letter to the Classis of Amsterdam, charging the English for cutting his annual salary by 200 guilders. Although people were leaving the area in droves, he wrote, "I do not intend to leave, although I must remain a penniless tramp in prison; for I have not the means to get away. Nevertheless, with the help of God, it is my hope to come over to *patria*, accompanied by my sons, who here can only

---

[17] Charles T. Gehring, trans. and ed., *Fort Orange Court Minutes, 1652-1660* (Syracuse, NY: Syracuse University Press, 1990), passim.

[18] *ERNY*, 1:534, 542-43, 546-47; and M. Eugene Osterhaven, ed., *Spiritual Desertion* (Grand Rapids, MI: Eerdmans, 2003), 11-23, 26-53.

come to grief; and as for the rest of my family, I hope the Lord will grant us relief." By this time, as Gideon's wife had died, "the rest of his family" would have meant sons Bartholomeus and Reynier, daughter Anna, now married, his illegitimate grandson Benoni, and his daughter Alida.[19]

Over the years, among Schaats's many concerns as dominie were the poor in the communities he served. The deacons' accounts tell their story. The same year that Schaats and his family arrived in Rensselaerswijck, 1652, Director General Stuyvesant and his council provided a lot to the deaconry for the use of the poor, whose numbers would increase dramatically when the fur trade declined in the mid-1650s. Historian Janny Venema has estimated that 20 percent of the community needed help to survive in the years 1653 to 664. By 1657, when the fur trade was a shadow of its former self, the number of the poor increased from two receiving alms in 1653 to twenty-six in 1660. Church and state worked together to provide relief, and, as the head of the church in the community and overseer of the deacons, who had responsibility for collecting funds and disbursing them, Dominie Schaats would have been intimately familiar with the problems and privations of his flock. This is especially true since he lived in the poorhouse, where alms were distributed and where his wife may have been involved in record-keeping. Venema states that Schaats and the consistory together examined the deacons' records every year, and she speculates that "the *matres* or 'mother' Schaets kept the count of who received what, and handed the information over to the deacon-bookkeeper."[20] This is a brief summary of what is known of Schaats's history, but what do we know of his beliefs? How did he fit into the theological controversies of the day? Was he a pietist, or was he of the orthodox school?

Religious Controversy

In 1679 the Labadist Jasper Dankaerts, fresh from the fraught religious atmosphere in the Netherlands, and in the thick of his own

---

[19] ERNY, 1:587. Arent van Curler's wife had also died, and so had Arent himself, on August 26,1665. In his will he made Anna his heir, "if there was anything left and this for the benefit of her little son Benoni." In Dutch: *"haer soontien Benoni:B,"* the B standing for bastard. A. J. F. Van Laer, *Minutes of the Court of Albany, Rensslaerswijck, and Schenectady, 1668-1685*, 3 vols. (Albany, NY: University of the State of New York, 1926-1932), 3:7.

[20] Janny Venema, *Beverwijck: A Dutch Village on the American Frontier, 1652-1664* (Hilversum: Verloren, 2004), 328-29, 334, 422 n. 96.

controversy as a follower of the radical Jean de Labadie, described Gideon Schaats, whom he heard preach in New York on September 24, as "it appears, a Voetian." At this same time Dankaerts also declared the ministerial candidate Petrus Tesschenmaecker to be a Voetian and labeled Schaats's colleagues Wilhelmus van Nieuwenhuysen, Casparus van Zuuren, and Laurentius van Gaasbeeck as Coccieans. The legacy of Voetius and Cocceius, according to Jonathan Israel, "infused Dutch Reformed theology, politics and culture down to the middle of the 18th century." It seems that Dankaerts, off the boat only one day before he met Schaats, Van Nieuwenhuysen, Van Zuuren, and Van Gaasbeeck in New York, was quick to see these theologians' influence in the men of the cloth he encountered on American soil.[21] But as there is no evidence that Gideon Schaats studied under Voetius at Utrecht (as Corwin suggests Tesschenmaecker may have done). It is more likely that in Schaats's case Dankaerts was using the term Voetian to mean Schaats's moral mindset, pietist values, attention to living the godly life most fully, and literal reading of the Bible.

In 1634, the year that Gideon married in Brielle, the government had set up a so-called "illustrious school" in nearby Utrecht and in other cities to prepare young men for university. That year, Gisbert Voet, now calling himself the Latinized Gisbertus Voetius in keeping with his new status, bade farewell to his congregation in his home town of Heusden (near Leerdam, Beesd, and Buren, three towns associated with Gideon Schaats) and repaired to Utrecht. Two years later, in 1636, Utrecht University was formally founded, and Voetius became its "doyen," to use Jonathan Israel's term.[22]

In describing Schaats and Tesschenmaecker as Voetians, Dankaerts could have meant to draw attention to, among other characteristics of Voetius, his philosophy of biblical interpretation, which was well known in his day and is amply illustrated by his objection to Copernicus's hypothesis that the earth moved around the sun, a subject of intense debate in the seventeenth century.[23]

Such new ideas called Holy Scripture into question, for Voetius found the basis for his belief about the relationship between sun and

---

[21] B. B. James and J. Franklin Jameson, ed., *Journal of Jasper Dankaerts, 1679-1680* (New York: Charles Scribner, 1913), 44-45; Charles E. Corwin, *A Manual of the Reformed Church in America, 1628-1922*, 5th ed. (New York: Reformed Church in America, 1922), 522, 525. Hereafter, *Manual*. The same information occurs in Corwin's father's 1902 edition of the *Manual*.

[22] Jonathan Israel, *The Dutch Republic: Its Rise, Greatness, and Fall, 1477-1806* (Oxford: Clarendon Press, 1995), 664, 573-75.

[23] J. A. Van Ruler, *The Crisis of Causality: Voetius and Descartes on God, Nature, and Change* (Leiden: Brill, 1995), 18.

earth in a literal reading of Psalms, Ecclesiastes, and Joshua. "And the sun stood still, and the moon stayed, until the people had avenged themselves upon their enemies" (Joshua 10:13). His opponents in the heliocentric school maintained that "either that the Bible spoke metaphorically . . . or the Bible was not relevant for answering non-religious questions." But Voetius countered that the Copernicans, for the sake of their hypotheses, violated Holy Writ. "The true interpretation," he wrote, is a literal one. Everything in history happened just as the Bible said it had.[24]

Other characteristics of Voetius that Dankaerts would have had in mind in describing Schaats and Tesschenmaecker as Voetians are Voetius's famous intolerance for Catholics, Lutherans, Jews, and Arminians—that is, anyone who was not ardent for the pure doctrines of the Reformed Church. Voetius may have been painted with too broad a brush in this respect, however, for Willem Frijhoff has noted that in the Dutch Golden Age dissident cults could be tolerated, "provided that they placed themselves in the same spiritual fraternity with orthodoxy" and did not threaten the socio-Christian order. Even Voetius, he continues, "put up with certain differences of opinion."[25] As we will see in a moment, Schaats, though intolerant of Lutherans and Episcopalians, was also ambivalent about them and could and did tolerate and even accept them when it was to his advantage to do so.

Dankaerts would also have meant as Voetian the theologian's insistence on strict Sabbath observance (in vivid contrast to Cocceius, who considered the fourth commandment as optional) and his desire for the continuing reform of life style and morals, as well as urging the ongoing reform of the Reformed Church itself. (Even today the Reformed Church considers itself "the Reformed Church always reforming.") As Israel has written, "The Voetians were the Calvinist orthodox who rejected liberal tendencies in theology, as well as Cartesianism in science and philosophy, and championed rigorous enforcement of anti-Catholic legislation." The Voetians were also devoted to the so-called Further Reformation, the movement that they had pursued to lead society to be more godly in lifestyle. Or as the Reverend Dr. M. Eugene Osterhaven put it in his introduction to *Spiritual Desertion*, an important Voetian devotional text, the Further Reformation "was an attempt to make the daily living of Christians conform to their

---

[24] Ibid., 12-15.
[25] Willem Frijhoff, "Religious Toleration in the United Provinces: From 'Case' to 'Model,'" in R. Po-chia Hsia and Henk van Nierop, eds., *Religious Toleration in the Dutch Golden Age* (Cambridge: Cambridge University Press, 2004), 28.

profession of faith [and was] dedicated to the deepening of spiritual life in post-Reformation Europe."[26]

Although Schaats did not prepare for the ministry under Voetius himself, a look at three aspects of his career suggests a Voetian influence: his censoriousness, his attitude toward Lutherans, and his conflict with the Anglican-ordained Dominie Nicolaes van Rensselaer.

A Voetian Influence

First, we know from his reports to the Classis of Amsterdam that Schaats was strict in matters of behavior and banned those with an "inconsistent walk" from the communion table. To be critical of bad behavior was hardly unusual for a Reformed minister in the seventeenth century, but particularity in behavior was much more frequently associated with the Voetians than with the Cocceians at the time of the Further Reformation. In 1681, after a serious illness, and perhaps sensing that his life was ending, Schaats preached on the Second Letter of Peter, 1:12-15, where Peter, aware that "the putting off of my body will be soon," reminds his hearers of the right way to live after he is gone: "supplement your faith with virtue, and virtue with knowledge, and knowledge with self-control, and self-control with steadfastness, and steadfastness with godliness, and godliness with brotherly affection, and brotherly affection with love." It could have been advice straight from the pens and pulpits of the leaders of the Further Reformation.[27]

Second, Schaats's response to the repeated requests by Lutherans for a minister of their own persuasion recalls Voetius's fierce rejection of all theological and doctrinal opposition. Like the renowned theologian, Schaats did not tolerate deviation from Reformed doctrine, as illustrated by his reaction to the Lutherans' attempts to have their own pastor in New Netherland. Even though there were some contentious points of dissimilarity, Lutheran doctrine was not radically different from Reformed doctrine (although Schaats and like-thinkers would have disagreed). Nevertheless, public worship by Lutherans was proscribed in New Netherland, where only the Reformed Church could have a public presence.

Schaats was firmly of the opinion that Lutherans were free to worship in private in both places, but not openly, much less with a Lutheran minister to guide them. Yet by 1653, one year after Schaats arrived in Rensselaerswijck, one hundred fifty Lutheran families in

---

[26] Israel, *Dutch Republic*, 662-63; and Osterhaven, ed., *Spiritual Desertion*, 11.
[27] ERNY, 2:768.

New Netherland were "longing and thirsting" for their own pastor, and Schaats must have been able to empathize with such a thirst. A Lutheran minister arrived in 1657 to serve them, at which point Dominies Megapolensis and Drisius in New Amsterdam wrote to the Burgomasters and Schepens in Amsterdam to say "[I]t is evidently their intention, if they obtain a foothold in this place, to extend themselves ... to other parts of this province. In our opinion this must ... [injure] the policy of the government as well as of the Reformed Religion unless it be successfully opposed." Petrus Stuyvesant and his council ordered the Lutheran minister away, and he went into hiding, finally leaving the colony in July 1659.[28]

Religion and politics went hand in hand in the seventeenth century. Ministers in New Netherland and later in New York were ever vigilant as to the political fortunes of the government, and Schaats was no exception, as his communications with the Classis of Amsterdam reveal. By that year, 1659, from seventy to eighty Lutheran families could be counted in Schaats's upriver domain. To allow them to worship openly was, Schaats and the Reformed establishment feared, to bring disorder and disharmony to the fragile society that was New Netherland. On September 22, 1660, Schaats took it upon himself to write to the Classis of Amsterdam, "partly on the advice of the Brethren at New Amsterdam" (i.e., Megapolensis and Drisius) to inform it that the Lutherans were raising funds for the salary of yet another Lutheran preacher in New Netherland. "They say, or pretend, that this has been allowed to them by the gentlemen of the West India Company," he wrote. But if a Lutheran preacher should come, he warned, "it would create a great schism among us here ... because there are several Lutherans here, who are members of our church ... who are gradually being led to us. Some of these are on the point of becoming members." He begged the classis to "protect Christ's sheep against the wolves and foxes, and catch also the young foxes, that they may not injure the vineyard of the Lord—the vines which are still very young and tender in this country, and especially in this place" (i.e., Beverwijck).[29] It is clear that, far from despising these fellow Christians, Dominie Schaats hoped to win them over to his own church.

It took the classis more than a year to reply to this letter because it wanted to consult the directors of the West India Company as to

---

[28] A. J. F. Van Laer, *The Lutheran Church in New York, 1649-1742* (New York, 1946), 24-25; and *ERNY*, 1:385, 386-88.

[29] *ERNY*, 1: 515-16. While more militant than some, Schaats was quite typical in his view of religion and society for a European of his era—even for many Cocceians.

whether they had consented to allowing the Lutherans to institute public religious gatherings or to introduce a pastor in New Netherland. But when they did answer, they assured Gideon Schaats that neither they nor Petrus Stuyvesant, "a staunch lover and defender of the true Reformed religion, would . . . endure the existence of the Lutherans. . . . The pretended consent was not given [by the company] . . . nor will [the Lutherans] ever obtain such permission," they declared.[30] And they never did, until the English took over in 1664.

Third, Schaats had the same xenophobic reaction in 1675 to the foisting by English Governor Edmund Andros of an eccentric Episcopalian priest upon the Albany pulpit as his colleague, and again religion and politics were bedfellows. (Or "palmed off upon the pulpit, rather than called to it in a legal way," as his colleague Dominie Wilhelmus van Nieuwenhuysen huffed in his own indignant letter to Amsterdam.)[31] Though he was a Dutchman with the iconic name of Nicolaes van Rensselaer and was a son of the original patroon, Kiliaen, this priest had been ordained by the laying on of English Episcopalian hands and thus was not acceptable to Schaats or to any other Reformed Dutch minister in the former New Netherland, whether Voetian or Cocceian. Nor was he acceptable to Jacob Leisler, wealthy merchant of New Netherland, who in 1689, in the aftermath of the Glorious Revolution in England, was to become the temporary governor of New York. In the case of Nicolaes van Rensselaer, Leisler went to court to accuse him of unorthodox views unacceptable in a Reformed pulpit. Schaats, of course, approved and gave testimony in support of Leisler's views.

On September 7, 1675, Schaats wrote again to the Classis of Amsterdam to complain of the "disorderly preaching" of his annoying colleague. The whole community, he said, was disturbed by the situation. Maria van Rensselaer wrote in November of that year, "May the Lord preserve us and soon settle the sad dissensions which prevail here in God's church and which have arisen between our brother [Nicolaes] and Domine Schaets." But dissension ruled until Van Rensselaer agreed to "conduct himself in his service according to the Constitution of the

---

[30] ERNY, 1:482-83. The Lutherans had to wait for their next preacher until the English takeover in 1664. On December 15, 1664, they appealed to Royal Governor Richard Nicholls, who the very next day gave his consent for them "to freely and publicly exercise their religion according to their conscience." The long-suffering Lutherans did not actually receive a preacher until 1669, and he lasted only a year, as he "does not behave himself or live as a pastor should. He is very fond of wine and brandy and knows how to curse and swear." Van Laer, *Lutheran Church*, 73, 76-77.

[31] ERNY, 1:515-16.

Reformed Church of Holland" and swear allegiance to the Church.[32] As for Voetius in the Netherlands, only the true and undiluted Reformed religion as set forth in the Synod of Dort in 1619 was acceptable to Schaats and other Reformed ministers in the former Dutch colony on the Hudson. Once Van Rensselaer toed the line by agreeing to conform to Reformed formularies and confessions, both ministers affirmed to the court that "they are willing to be reconciled with all their hearts."[33]

Finally, whether of Voetian or Cocceian persuasion, Dominies Schaats, Van Nieuwenhuysen, Van Gaasbeeck, and Van Zuuren were extremely careful to remember their vows to be faithful to the church rules as set down at the Synod of Dort in 1619. In a case that has a most ironic twist, these four ministers, against the rules, gathered in the form of a classis in New York in 1679 to ordain Petrus Tesschenmaecker, who had been called to minister to the Reformed Church in New Castle, Delaware. Gideon Schaats was president of this ad hoc classis. After the fact, at length and in great detail, they explained to the Classis of Amsterdam why it had been necessary for them to take this unprecedented action, and they were no doubt much relieved when the classis approved of it, after the fact. But the irony is, if the Classis of Amsterdam had gone a step further and encouraged this American classis not to disband but to continue as a body qualified to license and ordain ministerial candidates on American soil, history may have taken a different turn. The entire long furor over having a classis in America equal in powers to the Classis of Amsterdam, which erupted in the eighteenth century and continued for decades, with many political repercussions in the American Revolution, might have been avoided. Instead, it divided the church into bitter Coetus and Conferentie factions that were not healed until the Plan of Union in 1772, and then only temporarily as the war began to reignite the old conflicts.[34]

Demise

In 1682, when Schaats was seventy-five, his consistory seconded his earlier request to the Classis of Amsterdam for a pastor to help him, "for on account of his extreme age and feebleness, [he] can scarcely be heard any more; yet the congregation is daily increasing." But his feebleness was fleeting, for when help arrived the following year in the

---

[32] ERNY, 1:676-77; *The Correspondence of Maria van Rensselaer, 1669-1689* (Albany, NY: University of the State of New York, 1935), 16.
[33] ERNY, 1:678, 681; David William Voorhees, ed., *Papers of Jacob Leisler*, forthcoming, Document 216, 307.
[34] *Manual*, 1922 edition, 522-28.

person of Dominie Godfriedus Dellius, a surprised Dellius wrote to the classis that his aged colleague had gone to New York to enter into a second marriage.[35]

Seven years later, a widower again, Dominie Gideon Schaats, now eighty years old, was "failing fast," in the words of his consistory. Still, he lived another seven years, dying at age eighty-seven in 1694. He was buried under the floor of the church he had served for thirty-eight years.[36]

Though he had wanted to return to *patria* in 1667, he never realized this wish. He stayed in Beverwijck, now Albany, until his death.

---

[35] *ERNY*, 2:883.
[36] Through the three children who survived him to have children of their own, Gideon Schaats has many descendants alive today. See Palmer and Skaates, "The Schaets... Family."

CHAPTER 5

Henricus Selijns (1636–1701): Churchman with a Steady Hand

Jos van der Linde

"Of all the ministers who have worked in New Netherland, [Henricus Selijns] appears to me to have had the broadest knowledge and the greatest influence. Higher even than Johannes Megapolensis I believe I may place him when I convey the total impression that I have gained from his letters and notes."[1]

Almost one hundred years after church historian Albert Eekhof wrote these words, it is hard to take issue with his assessment, especially if one extends the period under review to the end of the seventeenth century. From 1689 to the mid 1690s the Dutch Reformed Church in North America went through a period of severe crisis. Without Selijns at the helm, this article argues, its survival would have been unlikely.

Selijns's formative years and ministerial posts in Breuckelen and Waverveen prepared him well for the huge challenges in New York. He

---

[1] A. Eekhof, *De Hervormde Kerk in Noord-Amerika (1624-1664)*, 2 vols. (The Hague: Nijhoff, 1913) 1:205-06; the translation is mine. I am most grateful to David Voorhees and Jaap Jacobs for helping me keep a watchful eye on Selijns over the years; to Jan Bos for providing access to the vast resources of the Koninklijke Bibliotheek; and to all three for their friendship and expertise.

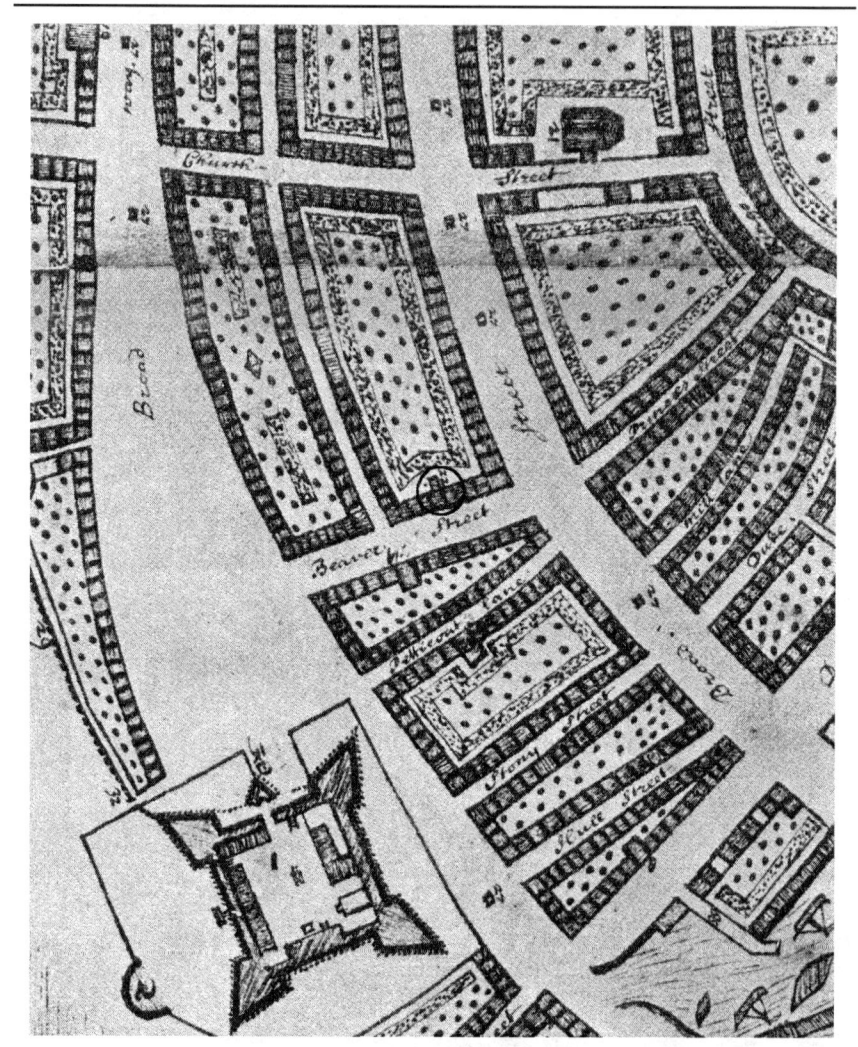

Map of Henricus Selijns's (marked with circle) house and surrounding streets

realized the paramount importance of promoting and maintaining peace and harmony within the Reformed community. He recognized the lasting destabilizing effect of discord and confrontation. He came to appreciate that conditions in the New World were different from those in the home country and that, consequently, a significant degree of tolerance and compromise was inevitable. At the same time he was acutely aware and protective of the Reformed Church's legal rights and developed a keen sense for when and where to draw the line. He fine-tuned his communication skills, verbal and written, and learned to interact comfortably with ecclesiastical, secular, and military authorities. His experiences in Breuckelen and Waverveen were instrumental in shaping Selijns's steady leadership.[2]

Amsterdam, Utrecht, Leiden

Although several aspects of young Selijns's life remain obscure, it is clear that he had a strong middle class background that allowed him to receive a solid education. He and the churches he served would greatly benefit from this firm foundation. Henricus (Hendrick) Selijns was baptized in the Oude Kerk (Old Church) in Amsterdam on March 23, 1636, the son of Jan Hendricksz. Selijns, a merchant, and Agneta Webber. Henricus was the couple's third child. Daughters Anna and Janneke had been born in 1634 and 1635, respectively. In 1641, when Henricus was five years of age, a third sister, Susanna, was born. Henricus may have known a half-brother, Daniel, born in 1629 from an earlier marriage of his father to Janneke de Marees. Four other children from Jan's earlier marriage had already died by 1641.[3] Aside from Henricus, Susanna was the only other sibling who we know with certainty reached adulthood.[4]

Little is known about Selijns's early childhood in the family home on Warmoes Straat [street]. He probably attended one of Amsterdam's Latin schools, then was enrolled at the renowned Athenaeum Illustre for several years in a propaedeutic program preparing him for university-

---

[2] For earlier overviews of Selijns's life, see E. T. Corwin, ed., *A Manual of the Reformed Church in America, 1628-1902* (4th ed.; New York: Board of Publication of the Reformed Church in America, 1902), 732-40; A. Eekhof, "Selijns (Henricus)," in: P.C. Molhuysen a.o., eds., *Nieuw Nederlandsch Biografisch Woordenboek*, 10 vols. (Leiden: Sijthoff, 1911-1937) 3:1160-66; A.P.G. Jos van der Linde, "Henricus Selijns (1636-1701): Dominee, dichter en historicus in Nieuw-Nederland en de Republiek," in J.F. Heijbroek, A. Lammers and A.P.G. Jos van der Linde, eds., *Geen schepsel wordt vergeten: liber amicorum voor Jan Willem Schulte Nordholt ter gelegenheid van zijn vijfenzestigste verjaardag* (Amsterdam/Zutphen: Trouw/Terra, 1985), 37-60; David William Voorhees, "Henricus Selijns," in: John A. Garraty and Mark C. Carnes, eds., *American National Biography* (New York: Oxford University Press, 1999) 19:625-26.

[3] Frans C.M. Gouverneur, "Dutch Origins of Some Early Settlers and Allied Families, Part 7: Selijns, Specht," *New Netherland Connections* 9 (2004): 89-104; 14 (2009): 67-70; John Reynolds Totten, "Editorial Comment on William J. Hoffman's Selijns Family Notes," *The New York Genealogical and Biographical Record* 63 (1932): 119-30. A portrait of Selijns with his brother "when they were children" is mentioned in the last will and testament of Selijns's second wife, Margaretha de Riemer, 1712; William S. Pelletreau, ed., *Abstracts of Wills on File in the Surrogate's Office, City of New York*. 2 vols. (New York: The New-York Historical Society, 1893-1894), 2:115-16.

[4] In the course of his life Selijns dedicated several poems to Susanna, among other occasions on her 28th and 30th birthdays; Henricus Selyns, Book of Manuscript Poems, New-York Historical Society (hereafter cited as NYHS, Selyns Poems).

level education. Founded and supervised by city magistrates, the school had a liberal reputation reflective of their generally tolerant attitude toward people's religious convictions. All instruction at the Athenaeum was in Latin. Teaching methods included private lessons at teachers' homes and the *disputatio,* a proposition or thesis defended by the student in a session open to the public. In addition to strengthening argumentative ability, disputations helped students develop their rhetorical skills.[5] These theses were often published ahead of the public event, and at least nine authored by Selijns have been preserved, all supervised by Arnoldus Senguerdius, presumably his primary teacher and mentor.[6] Senguerdius taught all areas of what was referred to as philosophy at the time: physics, metaphysics, logic, ethics, politics, and history.[7]

In September 1654, at eighteen years of age, Selijns matriculated at the University of Utrecht to study theology.[8] It was the next logical step on his way to a career in the Reformed Church. Direct involvement in the church had been common among members of the Selijns family and their in-laws for generations, ever since Amsterdam became a Protestant-controlled city in 1578. Selijns's own father served as deacon or elder numerous times over a period of four decades.[9]

Details of this important period in Selijns's formative years are sketchy. The theology department at the University of Utrecht was dominated by forceful defender and fierce guardian of Reformed orthodoxy, Gisbertus Voetius, assisted by like-minded professors Meinardus Schotanus, Carolus de Maets, and Andreas Essenius. Selijns must have studied with Voetius on many occasions, yet only one

---

[5] On the Athenaeum Illustre, see Dirk van Miert, *Humanism in an Age of Science: The Amsterdam Athenaeum in the Golden Age, 1632-1704* (Leiden: Brill, 2009); the *disputatio* is discussed on pp. 149-160.

[6] In the absence of student lists, the disputations preserved in libraries in Amsterdam, Paris, and Philadelphia are the only tangible proof of Selijns's enrollment at the Athenaeum in 1653 and 1654. Ibid., 5-7, 11-13, 387; Paul Dibon, *La Philosphie Néerlandaise au Siècle d'Or. Tome I: L'Enseignement Philosophique dans les Universités à l'Époque Précartésienne (1575-1650)* (Paris, etc.: Elsevier, 1954), 244.

[7] Senguerdius was a graduate from the Universities of Leiden and Franeker and had taught at the University of Utrecht before his appointment at the Athenaeum Illustre in 1648. He was married to Cornelia Webber, sister of Selijns's mother; van Miert, *Humanism,* 70-73; Totten, "Editorial Comment," 121.

[8] *Album Studiosorum Academiae Rheno-Traiectinae 1636-1886* (Utrecht: J.L. Beijers and J. van Boekhoven, 1886), 43 (hereafter cited as *ASART*).

[9] Jonathan Israel, *The Dutch Republic: Its Rise, Greatness, and Fall, 1477-1806* (Oxford: Clarendon Press, 1995), 192-93; Louis P. De Boer, "Selyns-Kock-Webber and Other Family Relations," *The New York Genealogical and Biographical Record* 57 (1926): 365-68.

concrete example of their direct interaction has to date been identified in the archival record: a *disputatio* defended in July 1656.[10]

What we do know with certainty about Selijns's years in Utrecht is that he met his future wife there, Machtelt Specht. They may have made their first acquaintance through Machtelt's older brother Philippus, another theology student, who matriculated five months after Selijns did. Their father, Herman Specht, ran a bookstore on Teeling Straat [street]. There were four other siblings. Machtelt, the second surviving child, had been baptized in the Dom Church on December 20, 1635.[11] On the occasion of her twentieth birthday in December 1655, Selijns wrote a long poem in praise of her virtue and modesty, a composition that to this day has not lost any of its freshness, tenderness, and elegance.[12] Henricus made no secret of his intentions, presenting her with a copy of Jacob Cats's best seller *Houwelijck* (Matrimony), in which he had written a dedication in verse urging her to take its content to heart.[13] Almost seven more years would pass before they were married.

In March 1657, around his twenty-first birthday, Selijns was admitted to the University of Leiden.[14] The reasons why he transferred from Utrecht, where he had lived for several years, are unclear. Had he gotten into personal trouble of some sort? At the university had he become exasperated with Voetius's iron grip on curriculum content and faculty appointments in the theology department (which did not loosen until years later)? Was he attracted by the more open educational environment in Leiden, where Cartesian ideas had begun to make major inroads? The Leiden faculty included "Voetian" theologian Johannes Hoornbeek, who had come from Utrecht a few years earlier, but he was outnumbered by celebrated professors Johannes Cocceius and Abraham Heidanus, proponents of the concept that the Bible text is complex and should not always be taken literally.[15] Or had Selijns in

[10] Andreas J. Beck, "Gisbertus Voetius (1589-1676): Sein Theologieverständnis und seine Gotteslehre" (Ph.D. diss., University of Utrecht, 2007), 451. See also J.A Cramer, *De Theologische Faculteit te Utrecht ten tijde van Voetius* (Utrecht: Kemink en Zoon, 1932), 9-20.

[11] Gouverneur, "Selijns, Specht," 96-99; *ASART*, 45.

[12] van der Linde, "Henricus Selijns," 53-55. Much of Selijns's fine verse is lost in Henry C. Murphy's translation: *Anthology of New Netherland, or: Translations from the Early Dutch Poets of New York with Memoirs of Their Lives* (Amsterdam: N. Israel, 1966) (originally published in New York, 1865), 148-53.

[13] J. Cats, *Houwelyck. Dat is de gansche gelegentheyt des echten staets,* (Middelburg: J.P. van de Venne, 1625), and reprinted many times; van der Linde, "Henricus Selijns," 55.

[14] *Album Studiosorum Academiae Lugduno-Batavae 1575-1875* (The Hague: Nijhoff, 1875), 456.

[15] Willem Otterspeer, *Groepsportret met Dame. Vol. 1: Het bolwerk van de vrijheid: De Leidse universiteit, 1575-1672* (Amsterdam: Bert Bakker, 2000), 380-82.

fact completed his program in Utrecht and moved to Leiden to broaden his intellectual horizons for the ministry he was seeking, possibly in a colonial setting overseas?

Less than half a year into his enrollment in Leiden, Selijns contacted the Classis of Amsterdam of the Dutch Reformed Church in September 1657 and asked to be examined for licensure as a minister. He passed the examination the following month and was admitted to the "public sermons" with the title of *proponent*, which allowed him to preach but not to administer sacraments.[16] His whereabouts during the next two years are largely unknown. He may have continued his studies in Leiden and spent time with Machtelt in Utrecht. He is likely to have stayed with his parents for a while, as the archival record shows he honed his skills as a preacher in churches around Amsterdam.[17]

Breuckelen in New Netherland

In the fall of 1659 the Classis of Amsterdam received a request from the directors of the Dutch West India Company for a minister to be appointed to Breuckelen in New Netherland. Breuckelen (now Brooklyn) was one of several rural villages founded by Dutch and English settlers over the previous twenty-five years on western Long Island. The other Dutch settlements included Nieuw Amersfoort (Flatlands), Midwout (Flatbush), Nieuw Utrecht (New Utrecht), and Boswijck (Bushwick). Their spiritual needs were tended to by Dominie Johannes Theodorus Polhemius, who inadvertently had arrived in New Netherland in 1654 as a refugee from Brazil after the West India Company had lost that colony to the Portuguese. Polhemius was approaching the age of sixty and had difficulty covering the large geographical area entrusted to his care. The people of Breuckelen, on their part, complained about Polhemius's infrequent visits, the long distance to Midwout where they usually went to church, and the 300 guilders they had to contribute annually to the salary of a minister whose sermons they found to be brief and of little substance. It was their petition to have a minister of their own that Director General Petrus Stuyvesant and his council had approved and forwarded to the company directors in Amsterdam.[18]

---

[16] Eekhof, "Selijns," 1161; Gerald F. De Jong, "The Founding of the Dutch Reformed Church on Long Island," *de Halve Maen* 54.2 (Summer 1979): 12.

[17] Hugh Hastings and Edward T. Corwin, eds., *Ecclesiastical Records, State of New York*, 7 vols. (Albany: James B. Lyon, 1901-1916), 1:472 (hereafter cited as *ERNY*).

[18] E.B. O'Callaghan and B. Fernow, eds., *Documents Relative to the Colonial History of the State of New-York*, 15 vols. (Albany: Weed, Parsons and Company, 1853-87), 14:380-82 (hereafter cited as *DRCHSNY*); *ERNY* 1:462-63; Eekhof, *Hervormde Kerk*, 1:205.

The Classis of Amsterdam delegated the matter to the *deputati ad causas Indicas*, its permanent executive committee handling all church-related affairs in the colonies. The *deputati* assisted the classis in its most important task of selecting and appointing new ministers. It corresponded with ministers, consistories, and congregants abroad and acted in close cooperation with the boards of directors of the Dutch East India and West India companies.[19] Six candidates were identified for the ministerial post in Breuckelen. The deputies narrowed the field to three, and after listening to each of them preach, unanimously selected Selijns. On February 16, 1660, after a trial sermon and final examination, the classis admitted Selijns to the ministry with great acclaim and issued a letter of call appointing him to Breuckelen. Another minister for New Netherland, Hermanus Blom, was ordained that same day. His destination was Wiltwijck on the Esopus River (present-day Kingston, New York). The West India Company directors gave their approval the following month.[20]

Later that spring Selijns and Blom crossed the Atlantic aboard *de Vergulde Bever* (Golden Beaver). Its cargo included iron, tools, and ammunition, as well as little books of psalms, prayers, and verse for distribution among the various congregations. At the insistence of the company directors, and against the wishes of the classis, they also brought along copies of an old form for baptism. The old form lacked certain language found in the newer form then in use in *patria* (the fatherland), which Lutheran settlers in the colonies found unacceptable. Both ministers had indicated that they did not object to using the older form. In conformity with their letters of call requiring them to look after God's flock "on water and on land," Selijns and Blom assumed their ministerial duties immediately after putting out to sea. They took turns holding services on Sundays and holidays. On weekdays they led morning and evening prayers and concluded with the singing of a psalm. After an uneventful crossing they reached New Amsterdam on June 11 of 1660.[21]

For an excellent discussion of the early vicissitudes of the Dutch Reformed Church on Long Island, see DeJong, "Founding."

[19] The committee was also referred to as *deputati ad res Indicas, deputati ad res maritimas* or *deputati ad res externas*; Eekhof, *Hervormde Kerk* 1:8-9; *ERNY* 1:19-20; Jaap Jacobs, *New Netherland: A Dutch Colony in Seventeenth-Century America* (Leiden: Brill, 2005), 266-67.

[20] Eekhof, *Hervormde Kerk*, 1:207; *ERNY* 1:466-68. On the roles played by religious and secular authorities in the selection of a new minister, both in the colony and in *patria*, see also Jacobs, *New Netherland*, 270-71.

[21] Eekhof, *Hervormde Kerk*, 1:211-12; 2:25-34; *DRCHSNY* 14:461, 467.

Local ministers Johannes Megapolensis and Samuel Drisius were probably among the dignitaries welcoming him to the New World. Director General Petrus Stuyvesant, however, was away at Esopus trying to negotiate an end to the hostilities between colonists and Indians that had caused widespread destruction and claimed many lives. Selijns and Blom followed him there and farther north to Fort Orange (now Albany) to present their credentials. It was Stuyvesant's intention to formally install Selijns in Breuckelen, but almost three months went by before he found an opportunity. Selijns spent most of that time in New Amsterdam, where he incurred expenses for room and board. Since his compensation as a minister had not yet gone into effect, he turned to the director general and his council for help. They granted him one beaver skin for every week he had been without salary. In the meantime a more serious financial problem had arisen. Selijns had been promised an annual salary of 1,200 guilders, but in late August the Breuckelen congregation advised Stuyvesant they would only be able to compensate their new minister with 300 guilders' worth of grain as well as a suitable residence. When Stuyvesant's efforts to extract more from them failed, he promised he would contribute 250 guilders of his own, provided that Selijns preach every Sunday evening in the chapel at the director general's *bouwerij* (farm) north of New Amsterdam on Manhattan. Selijns had given sermons in Wiltwijck, Fort Orange, and New Amsterdam, and the young minister must have made a very favorable impression on Stuyvesant to receive such an honorable appointment.[22]

On September 5, 1660, Selijns finally took the ferry from Manhattan to Long Island and was installed by Stuyvesant's deputies— Marten Kregier, *burgemeester* of New Amsterdam, and Nicasius de Sille, a member of his council. Selijns gave a full account in a letter to the Amsterdam classis four weeks later: "In Breuckelen I found 1 elder, 2 deacons, 24 members, 31 families, and 134 persons." Preparations for a minister's residence were under way. A granary functioned as a temporary place of worship, and construction of a church building was to start in the winter. Selijns's audience during his Sunday morning services in Breuckelen included people from surrounding villages and hamlets. His sermons on Sunday evening at Stuyvesant's bowery, which he described as "the place for recreation and pleasure in Manhattan," had begun to draw people from New Amsterdam, a feat quite remarkable as that town was already being served by ministers Megapolensis and

---

[22] Eekhof, *Hervormde Kerk,* 1:212-14; *DRCHSNY* 13: 155, 158, 186-87; 14:479.

Drisius. Separate mention was made of "40 negroes," most of them probably slaves working on Stuyvesant's farm.[23]

On the day following his installation Selijns began making entries in a volume of blank pages that he had brought with him from Holland or acquired in New Netherland. The Breuckelen church book has survived and is testimony to the minister's talent for organization, his clarity of writing, his fine penmanship, and his drive to create and preserve a historical record for posterity.[24] Selijns not only maintained lists of baptisms, marriages, and members, but also kept a running account of the deacons' revenues and expenditures, meticulously recording every financial transaction. For the benefit of the poor the deaconry leased a handful of cows to members of the congregation. The proceeds were tracked in a separate cow-lease section of the church book.

In yet another section, called *protocol of the consistory*, Selijns recorded noteworthy events. The *protocol* offers a detailed chronicle of life in Breuckelen during Selijns's tenure there and of his calming presence as mediator and peacekeeper—tasks he undertook with great diligence and a keen sense of fairness. One particular incident troubled him more than others in that it threatened to unsettle the delicate separation of ecclesiastical and secular authority. In April 1662 Selijns and an elder visited one Gerrit Dirckz. Croesen, who had been widely rumored to have stolen some fruit trees, and advised him not to partake of the Lord's Supper pending further investigation. Croesen, furious with Selijns, proceded to have the minister served with a court citation the next Saturday. This in turn upset the minister, who adamantly supported the Reformed Church's position that no church-related matter should be subjected to the authority of a secular court. It was clear, moreover, that Croesen deliberately wanted his anger to be felt by the entire congregation, and being cited in the Breuckelen court jeopardized the minister's ability to officiate at the Lord's Supper. After consulting with his colleague Megapolensis in New Amsterdam, Selijns required Croesen to appear before the Breuckelen consistory, and Croesen's suspension from the Lord's Supper was confirmed. The consistory wrote a letter to the court officials requesting that

---

[23] Eekhof, *Hervormde Kerk*, 1:214-17; *ERNY* 1:487-89; A.P.G. Jos van der Linde, transl. and ed., *Old First Dutch Reformed Church of Brooklyn, New York: First Book of Records, 1660-1752* (Baltimore: Genealogical Publishing Co., 1983), 226-29 (hereafter cited as *OFDRCB*).

[24] The original manuscript volume is in the Gardner A. Sage Library in New Brunswick, NJ. For a complete translation, see *OFDRCB*.

they thoroughly investigate Croesen's alleged larceny and annul the minister's citation. They should abstain from any such citations in the future, the letter argued, in matters of dispute among church members, especially those involving a minister or consistory.[25]

Selijns's ministry in Breuckelen bore ample fruit; church membership quadrupled between 1660 and 1664. Before long Selijns felt the strain of preaching in two places and leading the singing in an as yet improvised sanctuary with poor acoustics. A call went out across New Netherland for a reader and precentor who would also serve as schoolmaster for the rapidly expanding group of children. After a careful search Carel de Beauvois, a teacher in New Amsterdam, was appointed in July 1661.[26] During the winter months, when short days and hazardous travel conditions held Selijns back from his weekly preaching assignment at the bowery on Manhattan, he devoted extra energy to catechetic instruction and confirmation classes. A list of young catechumens from November 1662 shows no fewer than thirty-eight names.[27] Among the black population, however, pastoral success was limited. Selijns joined other ministers in refusing on principle to baptize Negro children, not only for "lack of knowledge and faith," but also because in his opinion their parents' primary motivation was "freeing their children from material slavery without pursuing piety and Christian virtues." Intensive catechizing among those children looked promising but had little effect on the adults, "who do not understand."[28]

The only wedding ceremony in the Breuckelen church not conducted by Selijns himself took place on July 25, 1662. Dominie Megapolensis came over from Manhattan that day to marry Selijns and his beloved Machtelt.[29] There is no earlier record of Machtelt's presence in the New World, and it is unclear when she crossed the Atlantic. Four months after the wedding the couple became guardians of Laurens Haff, the first of several orphans placed with families in Breuckelen by the deaconry. Laurens was about thirteen years of age. According to the custody contract, he was to live in the Selijns residence and serve the minister for six years. Selijns on his part committed to feeding and clothing him and during the winter season, sending him to school or teaching him himself.[30] The following spring Machtelt gave birth to the

---

[25] OFDRCB, 36-47. See also Jacobs, *New Netherland,* 287-88.
[26] Ibid., 18-25.
[27] Ibid., 54-57.
[28] Selijns to the Classis of Amsterdam, June 9, 1664, OFDRCB, 228-31; ERNY 1:547-50.
[29] OFDRCB, 212.
[30] Ibid., 56-59.

couple's first child, Agneta. Listed among the witnesses at the baptism, administered by Megapolensis in New Amsterdam on July 1, 1663, were Selijns's parents. They must have been represented by proxy because they were living in Amsterdam at the time.[31]

Citing concern about his parents' advancing years, Selijns notified the Classis of Amsterdam in June 1664 that he would not extend his four-year contract.[32] Uncertainty about his pay, a perennial problem among Reformed ministers in the New World, may have contributed to his decision to return to *patria*. Moreover, he must have been all too aware of the increasing vulnerability of the colony to English encroachment, especially on Long Island. Stuyvesant and his council accepted the minister's resignation in mid-July, and Selijns spent the next couple of weeks preparing the Breuckelen congregation for life without a minister of their own. Megapolensis and Drisius promised to administer the sacrament of the Lord's Supper on appropriate occasions. On Sundays schoolmaster and precentor Carel de Beauvois would lead the congregation in prayers and psalms and read from a book of sermons. He would, for the time being, be allowed to live in the minister's residence. No mention was made of the elderly Polhemius, who again was to become the only active Dutch minister on western Long Island. After placing orphan Laurens with another family, Selijns boarded the same *Vergulde Bever* that had carried him westward four years earlier.[33] He probably was still at sea when Stuyvesant surrendered New Netherland to an English flotilla on September 6. Selijns had built a great reputation on both Long Island and Manhattan, and his absence was deeply felt. Drisius lamented, "We could have wished that domine Selijns had longer continued with us, both on account of his diligence and success in preaching and catechizing, and of his humble and edifying life. By this he has attracted a great many people, and even some of the Negroes, so that many are sorry for his departure."[34]

Waverveen

When Selijns reported to the Classis of Amsterdam at the end of September, he received similar praise. The classis thanked him for his excellent and loyal service and promised to recommend him highly to congregations in need of a minister.[35] Almost two years went by before

[31] Gouverneur, "Selijns, Specht," 95.
[32] *OFDRCB*, 228-31; *ERNY* 1:547-50.
[33] *DRCHSNY* 14:550-51; *OFDRCB*, 88-97, 198-201.
[34] Drisius to the Classis of Amsterdam, August 5, 1664, *ERNY* 1:554.
[35] *ERNY* 1:562.

he was called to service in Waverveen, a rural community near the boundary between the provinces of Holland and Utrecht, surrounded by wide stretches of peat bogs. Had Selijns prolonged the wait by passing up on earlier, less desirable opportunities? Or were vacancies scarce and was he very fortunate to find his new benefice centrally located between Amsterdam, Utrecht, and Leiden, the towns where he had spent most of his life and where many of his relatives, friends, and acquaintances lived?[36] The Waverveen congregation numbered one hundred fourteen members at the time, thirty-eight men and seventy-six women. Chosen by the male members by a wide margin from a group of four candidates, Selijns was formally appointed by the Amsterdam classis on September 26, 1666.[37]

Selijns was horrified to find Waverveen's church records, the oldest of which dated back to the 1590s, in a state of utter chaos and neglect. Prompted by the same zeal for preserving the historical record that had driven him in Breuckelen, he set to work and labored for two and a half months organizing the archives. Gaps in the congregation's historical documentation were filled with information from records at the Amsterdam classis and other institutions. When he had finished, Selijns presented the consistory with a large folio volume with chronological lists of ministers, deacons, elders, and members, as well as baptisms and marriages. Some of the sections opened with a title page decorated with calligraphy in Selijns's own hand.[38] A *protocol* of consistory minutes included a detailed account of the origins and development of the Reformation in Waverveen.[39] The finances of the deaconry, too, were thoroughly examined and put in order. The framework was now in place for the kind of diligent record keeping

---

[36] Waverveen was a manorial domain. Another explanation why Selijns pursued an appointment there is that perhaps he had ties with the family owning it. Further research is needed. I am indebted to Fred van Lieburg (private correspondence, February 2011).

[37] A. Eekhof, "De Noord-Amerikaanse predikant Henricus Selijns in de Gemeente Waverveen (1666-1682)," *Nederlandsch Archief voor Kerkgeschiedenis*. New Series 12 (1916): 97-157 (hereafter cited as Eekhof, "Waverveen"), 102; ERNY 1:581-82. On Selijns in Waverveen, see also A. Bloed, *Waverveen door de eeuwen heen: Grepen uit de Hervormde geschiedenis* (Waverveen: Hervormde Kerkvoogdij, 1987), 56-87 (hereafter cited as Bloed, *Waverveen*); J.F. van Rooijen, "Henricus Selijns (1636-1701): predikant in Waverveen," in S. Boerdam et al, eds., *Van Angstel tot Kromme Mijdrecht: Levensbeschrijvingen van bekende en onbekende mensen uit Abcoude, Baambrugge en De Ronde Venen* (Utrecht: SPOU, 2001), 161-65.

[38] Eekhof, "Waverveen," 103-104; van der Linde, "Henricus Selijns," 46-47. The church book is still being preserved at the parsonage in Waverveen.

[39] Eekhof, "Waverveen," 105-28.

Selijns considered essential. An important new section of the church book documented the placement of poor deaconry-dependent boys and girls in church members' homes. Selijns's concern for the well-being and future development of these children is evident from the stipulation, appearing in all boarding contracts, that they be sent to school for two to three months each year.[40]

As he had done in Breuckelen, Selijns kept a detailed chronicle of noteworthy events. The *protocol* section of the church book offers numerous instances of the exemplary pastoral care he provided for the Waverveen congregation as well as his vigilance against attempts to infringe on the Reformed community's rights. Of particular note is a sequence of events in 1671 when the local *schout* (law enforcement officer) and *schepens* (municipal court members) made the claim that they, rather than the consistory, should manage the proceeds of a special collection, taken up during Sunday services for the maintenance of the church, parsonage, and school. This so-called *tweede sackie* (second offertory bag) had been instituted by the consistory in 1634. Mindful that the *schout* was not Reformed and that three of the five *schepens* were "papists," Selijns was suspicious of their motives. Both parties argued their case before the *Rekenkamer* (Chamber of Accounts) of the Province of Holland in the Hague, which ruled in favor of the consistory.[41] Wariness about the influence of Roman Catholicism is a recurrent theme in the *protocol*. In 1668 Selijns had one Geertie Everts van der Sluys summoned and reprimanded before the consistory for having remarried in the "papist" church. After professing genuine remorse and pledging to have any children baptized in the Reformed church, she was reconfirmed as a member and admitted to the Lord's Supper.[42]

The Waverveen church book also reveals details about Selijns's own family life. When his wife Machtelt was accepted as a member of the congregation, she was recorded as having transferred from Gorkum, a town on the Waal River some twenty miles south of Utrecht. This is the only known reference to the couple's whereabouts during the first two years following their return to *patria*. It is not known how long they had lived in Gorkum before moving to Waverveen. An entry with a postscript in the baptismal register reveals the tragically brief experiences of Selijns and his wife as parents. On October 13, 1669, Selijns's father Jan and Machtelt's younger sister Cornelia were witnesses at the baptism of Agneta Cornelia. The choice of name for their second daughter indicates

---

[40] Ibid., 129-32.
[41] Ibid., 132-35.
[42] Ibid., 136-37.

that their firstborn, Agneta, had already died. The couple would soon be childless again; with his own hand Selijns recorded January 12, 1670, as the date of the baby's untimely death.[43]

Tragedy on a larger scale struck the village community as a whole in 1672. An international alliance of France, England, Münster, and Cologne declared war on the Dutch Republic, and a large French army invaded the southern provinces. Waverveen was overrun by some four hundred troops. Selijns wrote a gripping eyewitness account of the attack, which took place in November. Most of the houses went up in flames, and there were dozens of casualties. Miraculously, the church, parsonage, and school were saved. Waverveners began an exodus to surrounding villages and towns, many of them fleeing to Amsterdam, which proved safe behind a wide barrier of deliberately flooded fields. Selijns kept in touch with his scattered flock as best he could and arranged a couple of gatherings in the nearby hamlet of De Nes. Regular church services in Waverveen did not resume until July 1673.[44] The war with France dragged on for five more years, and in 1675 Selijns was away for six months on a special assignment as army chaplain. It appears that he spent at least part of that time at Fort Steenbergen in the south. Waverveen was served by substitute ministers during his absence.[45]

Army chaplain assignments were usually given to ministers from major towns. The fact that the Classis of Amsterdam selected the pastor of a rather insignificant village such as Waverveen from a large pool of potential candidates is yet another indication of Selijns's extraordinary qualities. In every location he served he established a reputation as an excellent preacher. He was a master of the word, not only in the pulpit but also in his letters and poems.[46]

Selijns was a prolific poet, and he appears to have written more verse in Waverveen than at any other stage in his life. Like many well educated people of his day, he exchanged poems with friends and acquaintances on festive occasions such as a birthday, a marriage, a graduation, or a new job. His earliest surviving poems were contributed to the published disputations of fellow students at the Athenaeum

---

[43] Ibid., 128-29, 137; Gouverneur, "Selijns, Specht," 95.
[44] Eekhof, "Waverveen," 140-145; van der Linde, "Henricus Selijns," 38, 52-53. See also Bloed, *Waverveen*, 70-84; J.G.J. van Booma, "Tragedie in Waverveen: Ooggetuigeverslag van de Franse overval op Waverveen in 1672," *Jaarboek Oud-Utrecht 1979*, 113-28.
[45] Eekhof, "Waverveen," 145-148; *ERNY* 1:672, 676, 682.
[46] On Selijns's poetry, see Murphy, *Anthology*, 13-17, 77-183; Ellis Lawrence Raesly, *Portrait of New Netherland* (New York: Columbia University Press, 1945), 309-29; van der Linde, "Henricus Selijns."

Illustre and the University of Utrecht in the 1650s. They were among the very few of Selijns's poems that appeared in print in his lifetime.[47] That he nevertheless was widely known for his poetic ability suggests that the number of people receiving poems from him must have been significant. Many of these poems are known to us only because Selijns copied them into a pocket-sized notebook that he had with him throughout his life. The notebook has been preserved,[48] and it contains some two hundred poems, the majority of them in Dutch, a few in Latin, and one in Greek. An analysis of events commemorated in the poems shows that Selijns must have started writing in the notebook no later than 1659 and that he was still adding entries in 1685.

More than a quarter of the poems are epitaphs, not only for close friends and relatives but also for people of local, national, and international stature such as ministers, theologians, statesmen, and military commanders. Other events commemorated in verse range from the French occupation in 1672 and the subsequent murder of Grand Pensionary Johan de Witt to little incidents in everyday life. A peat cutter's improbable good fortune of finding a pouch with gold coins in the mud; the failure of a local supplier to deliver wine; the sudden death of the minister's cat (whose task of catching mice, ironically, was cut short after it ate a poisoned mouse)—Selijns found inspiration everywhere. His brilliant play with words, synonyms, names, rhyme, and rhythm is impossible to reproduce in translation.[49] Also on full display in Selijns's poetry are his urge to moralize, his sense of humor, and his grasp of human emotion and behavior at various stages in people's lives. He composed moving tributes to his wife Machtelt, mother Agneta, sister Susanna, sisters-in-law Anna and Cornelia, and other relatives, varying in length from a handful of lines to several pages. They provide invaluable insights into his private life and personality.

---

[47] Selijns's best known poem, a tribute to Puritan minister Cotton Mather in Boston on the opening pages of Mather's *Magnalia Christi Americana* (London: Thomas Parkhurst, 1702), did not appear in print until after Selijns's death. For a full transcript of the original Latin text and an English translation, see Corwin, *Manual*, 735-40.

[48] NYHS, Selyns Poems.

[49] The intricate *Bruijdlofs-Toorts* that Selijns wrote on the occasion of his friend Aegidius Luyck's marriage to Judith van Isendoorn in New Amsterdam in 1663 measured 104 lines and has been called a masterpiece; Frans R.E. Blom, "Of Wedding and War: Henricus Selyns' *Bridal Torch* (1663), Analysis, Edition, and Translation of the Dutch Poem," in Margriet Bruijn Lacy, Charles Gehring, Jenneke Oosterhoff, eds., *From De Halve Maen to KLM: 400 Years of Dutch-American Exchange* (Münster: Nodus Publikationen, 2008), 185-200.

New York

Ever since his return to *patria* in the summer of 1664, Selijns had kept abreast of developments overseas. No sooner had he received his appointment in Waverveen than he traveled to Amsterdam to take up his seat in the classis. Through the *deputati ad causas Indicas* of the classis, he had access to news from territories under the supervision of the Dutch East India and West India companies. He also gave his colleagues advice, drawing on his own experience in the New World.[50] The colonists on their part had not forgotten about him. When early in 1670 Johannes Megapolensis died and the pastoral care in New York was left to Drisius, who suffered from memory loss, and to the elderly Polhemius on Long Island, the Amsterdam classis was urged repeatedly to send Selijns. He could not be persuaded to leave Waverveen, however, not even after the English governor, Francis Lovelace, had guaranteed him a decent salary and a free residence. The vacancy was finally filled in March 1671 with the appointment of Wilhelmus van Nieuwenhuysen, who had been examined by Selijns on behalf of the classis.[51]

A second major push was made by Breuckelen and the other predominantly Dutch communities on western Long Island after the death of Polhemius in 1677. The Classis of Amsterdam spoke out in favor of his going, but when the consistory of Waverveen put up a major fight, Selijns decided to stay.[52] Van Nieuwenhuysen's death four years later prompted yet another attempt. The consistory of New York wrote to the Amsterdam classis, "We remember Domine Henricus Selijns. His faithful services, his pious life, his peculiar zeal, his amiable conversation, his pleasing and ready speech left a deep impression upon many hearts."[53] Months of indecision followed, but in December 1681 Selijns finally consented. In the presence of witnesses representing the congregation in New York, notary Jacob Lansman in Amsterdam drew up a contract guaranteeing Selijns an annual salary of 1,000 guilders effective the date of his departure from Holland; financial support for his wife upon his death, even if that were to occur en route to their new destination; free passage; a free residence with free fuel; and other benefits.[54] Selijns signed, then fell victim to hesitation again. It was only

---

[50] Eekhof, "Waverveen," 148; *ERNY* 1:582-83, 603.
[51] Eekhof, "Waverveen," 148-50; *ERNY* 1:607-608, 610-11, 615-17.
[52] Eekhof, "Waverveen," 150-51; *ERNY* 1:692-93.
[53] New York consistory to the Classis of Amsterdam, February 25, 1681, *ERNY* 2:759-62.
[54] Gemeente-Archief Amsterdam, Notarieel Archief, 4702 (Nots. Jacob Lansman), fol. 123, December 10, 1681; Francis J. Sypher, Jr., ed. & transl., *Liber A, 1628-1700, of the Collegiate Churches of New York* (Grand Rapids, MI: Eerdmans, 2009), 60-65; *ERNY* 2:797-99.

in mid-March that he gave the Classis of Amsterdam definitive assurance that he had accepted the call overseas. On April 19 he delivered his final Sunday sermon in Waverveen and bade farewell to the consistory.[55] After a stop in Dover on the southeast coast of England, where he preached to the Dutch community, Selijns and his wife embarked on their third transatlantic crossing. Lack of favorable winds slowed them down, and they spent twelve weeks on the high seas before reaching New York on August 6, 1682.[56]

Thus began the final phase of Selijns's long career. His ministry in New York over the next nineteen years was eventful and at times tumultuous, yet not without major accomplishments. It is presented here in broad outline, with emphasis on developments that most affected him personally and on his ability to serve his flock.[57]

Selijns arrived not a moment too soon, as New York's large congregation had been without a minister of its own for the past eighteen months. Only three other Dutch ministers were active in the province at this time: Johannes Weeksteen in Esopus (Kingston), the elderly Gideon Schaats in Albany, and Casparus van Zuuren on Long Island. In October Selijns wrote the first of what would become a long series of informative letters to the Classis of Amsterdam.[58] He reported that the congregation numbered approximately six hundred members. Selijns preached three times a week and on Sunday evenings held a catechetical class for children that was "filled to overflowing." He would also officiate in Bergen in East Jersey three times a year and in Harlem once a year. The church building within the confines of the old fort at the tip of Manhattan had become too small and dilapidated, and the construction of a new edifice was being considered. English residents

---

[55] According to Eekhof, Selijns had admitted 85 new members, baptized 211 children, and married 70 couples during his twelve-year tenure in Waverveen; Eekhof, "Waverveen," 156.

[56] Eekhof, "Waverveen," 153-156; *ERNY* 2:785, 803, 805-06, 811, 828, 836.

[57] For comprehensive studies of this period, see Thomas J. Archdeacon, *New York City, 1664-1710: Conquest and Change* (Ithaca: Cornell University Press, 1976); Robert C. Ritchie, *The Duke's Province: A Study of New York Politics and Society, 1664-1691* (Chapel Hill: University of North Carolina Press, 1977); Joyce D. Goodfriend, *Before the Melting Pot: Society and Culture in Colonial New York City, 1664-1730* (Princeton: Princeton University Press, 1992); Randall H. Balmer, *A Perfect Babel of Confusion: Dutch Religion and English Culture in the Middle Colonies* (New York: Oxford University Press, 1989).

[58] From 1682 to 1700, Selijns sent the classis an average of one extensive letter per year, usually in the fall. While in Breuckelen, he had written the classis only twice, at the beginning and end of his tenure there in 1660 and 1664, respectively. The original letters are now in the Gardner A. Sage Library in New Brunswick, NJ.

also used the church for worship, although as yet without a minister of their own. Other active worship groups in New York included Lutherans, Quakers, Jews, and Labadists,[59] but no overt "Papists," Selijns expressed concern about the situation at New Castle along the Delaware, where large numbers of Quakers were arriving at a very inopportune moment. Dominie Petrus Tesschenmaecker had just left, and the congregation was considering calling Jacobus Koelman, a Labadist, from *patria*. Selijns urged the classis not to allow this to happen.[60]

The inadequacy of the old church building in New York, the need for more ministers to serve the growing population, the uncertain position of the Reformed Church under English rule, and the proliferation of ever more dissenters and sects were recurring themes in Selijns's letters through most of the 1680s. At the same time he was usually able to give the classis a positive assessment of his pastoral work. Membership, attendance, and participation in catechization classes were all on the rise. In the summer of 1683 he was delighted to welcome Godefridus Dellius, who had been appointed in Albany to assist Schaats. Tesschenmaecker moved from New Castle to Staten Island, but no new minister would arrive from *patria* for the next three years.[61] When Van Zuuren left Long Island in May 1685 and Jacob Tellner, a German Quaker, began disrupting services in Breuckelen and Midwout, Selijns complained bitterly about the perceived inaction on the part of the Amsterdam classis. He added: "I lived in Abraham's bosom at Waverveen but am sorrowful to live here among so many wild beasts and bulls of Bashan."[62] His anxiety was to subside soon. The vacancy on Long Island was filled by Rudolphus van Varick in July 1686, and references to subversive religious groups became less frequent. Two years later Selijns reported that Tellner and his Quakers had moved to Pennsylvania and that the number of Labadists in New York had dwindled to a dozen at most.[63]

In the summer of 1686 the total number of church members living on Manhattan was 566.[64] The exact figure is known, as Selijns

---

[59] French minister and prolific author Jean de Labadie was a radical pietist who favored separating from the Dutch Reformed Church rather than submitting to its authority; Balmer, *Perfect Babel,* 22-23.
[60] Selijns to the Classis of Amsterdam, October 28, 1682, *ERNY* 2:827-34.
[61] Selijns to the Classis of Amsterdam, October 31, 1683, *ERNY* 2:865-69.
[62] Selijns to the Classis of Amsterdam, September 20, 1685, *ERNY* 2: 906-09.
[63] Selijns to the Classis of Amsterdam, October 10, 1688, *ERNY* 2:957-59.
[64] This calls into question the earlier number of "approximately 600" that Selijns reported to the classis shortly after his arrival in 1682. That initial estimate was probably too high.

had written their names in a little notebook he carried with him during family visits.[65] To facilitate his walks around town, he had arranged the members' names by street, and within each street by family. Selijns's own residence, a handsome three-story brick house the congregation had built for him upon his arrival, was listed as situated on Bever Straat (Beaver Street). He lived there alone at this time, as Machtelt had died in February.[66] He did not remain a widower for long. On October 20, 1686, he married Margaretha de Riemer, widow of Cornelis Steenwijck, who had made a fortune as a merchant, had served as mayor of New York, and had been influential in the church as an elder. Margaretha, who was forty-six years old, had been married to Steenwijck for twenty-six years and had borne him seven children, all of whom had died before reaching adulthood.[67] "[The Lord] has given me a wife not only well endowed with worldly goods, but one still more endowed with all spiritual graces," Selijns exulted.[68] As a member of the Dutch Reformed clergy, he already enjoyed a privileged position within colonial society, and his marriage to Margaretha instantly promoted him to the ranks of the ruling elite.

With wealth and status came worldly responsibilities and concerns. As co-owners of a cargo ship trading between New York and Amsterdam, Selijns and his wife became involved in a financial dispute with the other owners and were sued in the Admiralty Court.[69] Legal proceedings also complicated the formal transfer of ownership of the Manor of Fordham from the Steenwijck estate to the Reformed Church. The bequest had been arranged by Cornelis Steenwijck shortly before his death in November 1684, but claims laid on the property by the neighboring town of Westchester prevented the church from assuming ownership. Matters did not improve when Selijns married the executrix of Steenwijck's will. A clumsy effort in 1688 to force the issue

---

[65] The original "pocket book" is in the archives of the Collegiate Churches of New York in Manhattan. The names of 140 non-members also found their way in Selijns's notes. Children's names were not included, merely their number by street for a total of 698. See Tunis G. Bergen a.o., eds., *Records of Domine Henricus Selyns of New York, 1686-7* (New York: The Holland Society of New York, 1916).

[66] Selijns referred to her passing away "seven months ago" in a letter to the Classis of Amsterdam, September 20, 1686; *ERNY* 2:936.

[67] Frans C.M. Gouverneur, "The De Riemer Family," *New Netherland Connections* 7 (2002): 80-81; idem, "Dutch Origins of Some Early Settlers and Allied Families, Part 1: Steenwijck, Godtschalck, Maurits (Sluiswachter), ten Broecke (Paludanus), van Nieuwenhuijsen," *New Netherland Connections* 8 (2003): 32-33.

[68] Selijns to the Classis of Amsterdam, October 10, 1688, *ERNY* 2:957.

[69] Peter R. Christoph, ed., *The Dongan Papers, 1683-1688*, 2 vols. (Syracuse, NY: Syracuse University Press, 1993, 1996), 1:226-43.

and drive Westchester residents off the property caused a riot and failed to change the status quo.[70] Despite the setback, Selijns wrote an upbeat letter to the Classis of Amsterdam describing the church as *"in pristino statu."* Dominie Tesschenmaecker was moving from Staten Island to Schenectady. The French Protestants were doing well, accepting new refugees from Europe on a daily basis. Selijns looked forward to welcoming Sir Edmund Andros, governor of the newly created Dominion of New England and New York, who had been governor of New York, was a member of the Church of England, and spoke Dutch and French.[71]

Survival of the Reformed Church

Within months of this rosy assessment, Andros would be living in a jail cell in Boston. Like many of his contemporaries, Selijns appeared entirely unprepared for the upheavals that were about to convulse colonial society. The Glorious Revolution in England created a power vacuum overseas that allowed existing problems to intensify and long-simmering tensions to break out into the open. Leisler's Rebellion in New York had economic, social, ethnic, and religious undercurrents as well as deep roots in factional strife in the Dutch Republic.[72] Jacob Leisler, a wealthy merchant, prominent church member, and proponent of a popular pietist movement that had been spreading among the Reformed congregations, seized military power in July-August 1689 and effectively remained in charge until his arrest nineteen months later. He enjoyed widespread support among the lower classes, especially the majority of Dutch colonists, whose fortunes had not improved under English rule and who had become increasingly frustrated with worsening economic conditions and the gradual anglicization of society on many fronts. Leisler claimed to be acting on behalf of William III, the new king, but this was disputed by his opponents. These were essentially the ruling elite in positions of economic and political power in the late 1680s, which in the eyes of many included the Dutch clergy. From the outset Selijns and some of the other Dutch ministers

---

[70] *ERNY* 2:888-90, 960; *Liber A,* 96-101, 160-65, 172-73; Harry C.W. Melick, "The Fordham "Ryott" of July 16, 1688," *New-York Historical Society Quarterly Bulletin* 36 (1952): 210-20.

[71] Selijns to the Classis of Amsterdam, October 10, 1688, *ERNY* 2:957-59.

[72] Balmer, *Perfect Babel,* 28-50; idem, "Traitors and Papists: The Religious Dimensions of Leisler's Rebellion," *New York History* 70 (1989): 341-72; David William Voorhees, "The Dutch Roots of Colonial New York's Factional Politics," in: Martha Dickinson Shattuck, ed., *Explorers, Fortunes & Love Letters: A Window on New Netherland* (Albany, NY: New Netherland Institute / Mount Ida Press, 2009), 129-47.

preached against Leisler, and he reacted with an iron hand. The partisan nature of many documents in the archival record, often created years later, makes it difficult to distinguish fact from fiction. There appears to be consensus that Leisler was very abusive, openly scolding and threatening Selijns during church services. Selijns's residence was searched and his correspondence intercepted. Van Varick was dragged from his house on Long Island and thrown into jail. Dellius fled from Albany to New England. Adding to the general sense of chaos and insecurity was a horrific midnight attack by French and Indian soldiers on Schenectady in February 1690. Sixty people were killed, including Dominie Tesschenmaecker.[73]

When royal troops from England took control in March 1691, Leisler and dozens of his closest associates were imprisoned. His opponents, freed from jail, were returned to positions of power, and the outcome of the ensuing trial for high treason was never in doubt. Selijns had openly rejoiced at the turn of events and joined others in advocating severe punishment. Leisler and Jacob Milborne, his son-in-law and chief henchman, were sentenced to death. It was Selijns who was sent to the prisoners to advise them of their fate and who, two days later, stood by them at the gallows in the pouring rain.[74] Leisler and Milborne had remained popular figures among large sections of the population, and their execution appalled many. Leislerian versus anti-Leislerian partisanship intensified and dominated New York society and politics for decades to come. Anger with the Dutch clergy was widespread. Selijns and others were vilified, church attendance plummeted, revenues declined, and the payment of ministers' salaries fell behind. In a letter to the Classis of Amsterdam in October 1692, their first in "two or three years," Selijns, Van Varick, and Dellius presented a gloomy picture. "[The churches of] Bergen, Hackensack, Staten Island and Harlem have deserted us, yielding to the power of evil. They say they can live well enough without ministers or sacraments."

And yet, in the midst of the misery, the ministers were able to report in the very same letter that a new stone church edifice was being constructed (on Garden Street). It was hoped that it would attract many new worshippers who in the past had been reluctant to come to the church in the fort.[75] The classis advised the ministers to stay calm

[73] Thomas E. Burke, Jr., *Mohawk Frontier: The Dutch Community of Schenectady, New York, 1661-1710* (Ithaca: Cornell University Press, 1991), 103-108.
[74] John Romeyn Brodhead, *History of the State of New York*. 2 vols. (New York: Harper & Brothers, 1853, 1871) 2:647-48.
[75] Selijns, Van Varick, and Dellius to the Classis of Amsterdam, October 12, 1692, *ERNY* 2:1041-45.

and forgiving, and two years later the situation had much improved. "The troubles are, no doubt, diminishing," Selijns wrote. Attendance at church services was on the increase and his pay was better, although he had given up on the idea of ever receiving his back wages. With the exception of the towers, the new church building was finished. The congregation in Bergen had welcomed him back, and Hackensack had a minister of its own again, albeit a Koelmanite,[76] Guiliam Bertholf. Unfortunately, Van Varick had died and the Long Island communities were having trouble agreeing on a new candidate.[77]

On multiple occasions after his return to the New World, Selijns had been made aware of the Reformed Church's vulnerable legal position, exposed as it was to prevailing political winds. A Charter of Liberties and Privileges, guaranteeing freedom of religion in the colony, had been passed by the General Assembly in New York in October 1683, only to be vetoed by the Committee of Trade and Plantations in Whitehall in March 1685.[78] With every change of governor and every shift of power among rival political factions in the colony or in England, the church's situation could change. Recent questions and complications regarding the legal ownership of church properties, such as the Manor of Fordham and the new church building, were another incentive for Selijns to seek a change in status. In the spring of 1695, sensing a favorable political climate, Selijns and prominent church members formed a committee to pursue the matter. A petition to become a corporation was submitted to Governor Benjamin Fletcher in December; and on May 11, 1696, King William III issued the charter.[79] It was Selijns's crowning achievement. In a letter to the Classis of Amsterdam he elaborated on the charter's significance:

> My Consistory and I have for a long time labored, and taken much trouble to secure certain privileges for our Reformed Church here. These we have at length obtained in a very satisfactory instrument, which is also confirmed with the King's seal. It is entitled "THE CHARTER OF THE REFORMED PROTESTANT

[76] Follower of pietist Jacobus Koelman, minister in Sluis in the province of Zeeland.
[77] Classis of Amsterdam to Selijns, Van Varick, and Dellius, April 20, 1693, *ERNY* 2:1054-57; Selijns to the Classis of Amsterdam, November 14, 1694, *ERNY* 2:1106-09. Between the summer of 1689 and the end of 1694, Selijns was underpaid almost 2,000 Dutch guilders. In 1691 and 1692, his average pay every three months fell more than 100 guilders short of the 250 guilders guaranteed in his contract; *Liber A*, 206-09.
[78] Balmer, *Perfect Babel*, 29.
[79] *ERNY* 2:1116-17, 1127-28 (erroneously dated June 1695), 1136-1165; *Liber A*, 210-11, 216-19, 18-49.

DUTCH CHURCH IN THE CITY OF NEW YORK, GRANTED A. D. 1696." Its contents are in respect to the power of calling one or more ministers; of choosing elders, deacons, chorister, sexton, etc.; and of keeping Dutch schools, all in conformity to the Church-Order of the Synod of Dort, Anno, 1619; also, the right to possess a church, a parsonage and other church property as our own, and to hold them in our corporate capacity, without alienation. Also the right to receive legacies of either real or personal property, and other donations, for the benefit of the church, etc. This is a circumstance which promises much advantage to God's church, and quiets the formerly existing uneasiness.[80]

A similar charter was granted to the English Trinity Church a year later, and Selijns attended the installation of its minister, William Vesey.[81]

In the same letter in which he described the charter, Selijns complimented the classis on the appointment of two excellent new ministers, Johannes Nucella in Kingston and Wilhelmus Lupardus in Long Island. Along with Dellius in Albany, Bertholf in New Jersey, and himself in New York, the group was complete, in his view. He was beginning to feel his advancing years, however. Eager for help with the pastoral care of more than six hundred fifty members, Selijns and several other members of the consistory asked the classis in 1697 to call a second minister to New York. The majority of the selection committee, among whom Selijns must have had the most influential voice, chose Hieronymus Verdieren, minister in Bruinisse in the Province of Zeeland. Others protested that they had not been consulted, that due process had been ignored, and that the choice of Verdieren ought to be annulled. The ensuing feud among prominent church members between Leislerians and anti-Leislerians dominated the correspondence with the classis for almost two years.[82] Although a minority in the conflict, the Leislerians undoubtedly felt emboldened by the rehabilitation of Leisler and Milborne, whose death sentences had been reversed by Parliament in 1695 and whose mortal remains were laid to rest, with great pomp, in the Garden Street church in October 1698. Pressured by both parties in the congregation and anxious to preserve the peace, the church masters had felt that they could not consent to the request for reburial, but neither should they hinder it.[83] In *patria*, meanwhile, Verdieren had

---

[80] Selijns to the Classis of Amsterdam, September 30, 1696, *ERNY* 2:1171-72.
[81] *ERNY* 2:1136-65.
[82] Ibid., 1189-1213, 1228-33.
[83] Ibid., 1242, 1261.

withdrawn his candidacy. It was not until May 1699 that the classis appointed Gualtherus Du Bois—young, talented, and an "enemy to all partiality." The classis expressed confidence in his ability to heal the scarred congregation.[84]

Du Bois was to serve the Reformed Church in New York for half a century, and his presence and energy greatly alleviated the burdens of office for Selijns. Despite their age difference of thirty-five years, they got along well. Selijns gradually yielded center stage to his younger colleague but continued his pastoral activities. He had become particularly pleased with the results of his work among children. In September 1698, in the midst of the controversy about the appointment of a second minister to New York, he sent the Classis of Amsterdam the names of forty-four boys and twenty-one girls who had learned to recite, in public and without error, "psalms, hymns, and prayers in rhyme." Although fewer in number, the girls had learned almost as many psalms as the boys had. Referring to a recent church service, Selijns wrote: "After my prayer and address, our regular Sunday prayer, which is made before the sermon, was recited without any mistake, and with energy and manly confidence, by Marijcken Popinga, a child of five years. It was then repeated, not without tears, by my church members."[85]

In the twilight of his career Selijns was careful to reserve enough time for the completion of an ambitious project: the preservation of all baptismal, marriage, and membership records of the congregation. As before in Waverveen, Selijns must have found the church records in New York to be in poor condition when he arrived there in 1682. Sensing their historical significance, he copied them, and it is only in his fine handwriting that they have survived.[86] Selijns also made an extensive compilation of "Synodical and Ecclesiastical Decrees, Resolutions, Usages, and Privileges for the benefit of the Dutch Churches and especially here at New York in America, in use from time to time, and still being used," essentially a documentary history of the church during his tenure in New York.[87] The whereabouts of a similar compilation that he made of records relating to the early years of the Reformed Church in New Netherland are unknown.[88]

---

[84] Classis of Amsterdam to New York consistory, May 1699, *ERNY* 2:1304-05.
[85] Selijns to the Classis of Amsterdam, September 14, 1698, *ERNY* 2:1233-40.
[86] The earliest records are dated 1639. Although Selijns did not arrive in New York until 1682, all records from 1639 to 1682 are in his handwriting.
[87] Published in full in 2009; see *Liber A*. The original manuscript Liber A is in the archives of the Collegiate Churches of New York in Manhattan.
[88] This manuscript, "Nieuw-Amsterdamsche Kerkelijke Zaken," was sold at auction in Amsterdam to an unknown buyer in 1859 or 1860; Eekhof, "Selijns," 1165.

Selijns's hand had lost some of its steadiness when on November 13, 1700, "sick in body but by the grace of God of perfect memory," he wrote his last will and testament. He distributed 5,000 guilders among relatives and friends on both sides of the Atlantic and left the remainder of his estate with Margaretha, whom he appointed as sole executrix.[89] His final entry in the church book dates from June 28, 1701, when he officiated at a wedding. He died on July 19 and was buried three days later in the church "in front of the baptistry."[90]

Conclusion

Selijns's ministry is one of the best documented among the colonial clergy. He had a strong hand in the preservation of his own records and, more importantly, of the continuity of the Reformed Church in North America. He would have scored well on any test of the attributes necessary for success. Whatever he embarked upon throughout his career, he pursued with great care, due diligence, and a strong sense of duty. His record keeping, his letters, the contracts he drew up to hire a teacher or church master—all of it was done in an exemplary, thorough way and reveals his respect for accountability and clarity. With utmost dedication and commitment he heeded the church's call to look after the spiritual well-being of its flock and spread the gospel. He did so in times of peace as well as of turmoil, and in any setting: in church, during house visitations, on board ship, and with the army in the field. His effectiveness in resolving conflicts among congregants is well documented. So is the high priority he gave to the edification and education of children and orphans, girls as well as boys, even in such rural environments as Breuckelen and Waverveen. By all accounts he was an exceptionally gifted preacher, well educated and erudite, an artist with words who also must have been formidable in debate.

Historians assess Selijns's lasting legacy primarily on the basis of his tenure in New York from 1682 until his death, but it was far from inevitable that he serve in this role. Even after he had committed himself by contract, he was reluctant to go back to the New World in 1681-1682. Surely, he had the experience and skills that were needed

---

[89] Pelletreau, *Abstracts of Wills*, 2:6-7. Selijns's manuscript will is preserved at the New-York Historical Society.

[90] Historians have disagreed whether Selijns died in July or September but Margaretha recorded the date in her family Bible: William J. Hoffman, "The De Riemer Family Bible Record," *The New York Genealogical and Biographical Record* 63 (1932): 285-89. See also: "Burials in the Village of Bergen in New Jersey Beginning 1666," in: *Year Book of the Holland Society of New York* 1915, 31.

to succeed on a prominent stage such as New York. He had lived and worked in urban as well as rural settings. He had studied with both Voetius and Cocceius, was familiar with a wide spectrum of Calvinist theology, and without a doubt adhered to liberal Cocceian principles that he knew would serve him well in the increasingly diverse religious and social landscape along the Hudson. Yet, he may have felt anxious about the proliferation of new religious groups and the future of the Reformed Church under English rule. When he signed the contract in December 1681, he made a point of asserting that his primary reasons for going to New York were his love of the congregation there and his desire to spread the gospel truth to its farthest regions.[91] It would take another three months for these considerations to prevail.

Once in New York, Selijns proved to be the energetic and successful shepherd that the Reformed community had hoped for, both within the congregation and in the church's external relations. He moved confidently in powerful circles, corresponded in various languages with people of stature on both sides of the Atlantic,[92] and affirmed his position as a member of the establishment when he married into the influential Steenwijck-de Riemer family. Although a man of the world, aware of a constantly changing political landscape, Selijns could not foresee the fervor and ferocity of the Leisler Rebellion. While some ministers initially may have felt hesitation as to which side to choose in the conflict, the Reformed clergy's official position was never in doubt. The modest privileges they had gained for the church through years of careful maneuvering with the English authorities were in serious jeopardy. Selijns really did not have a choice: the future of the church could not be laid into the hands of rebels with questionable claims of authority.

Selijns and his colleagues paid a heavy price for denouncing the rebellion and supporting the execution of the two main perpetrators. Internal discord continued to plague the Dutch Reformed community. Yet already by 1696 it was clear that the worst of the crisis was over and that the church would survive. A new church edifice and a royal charter were proof of Selijns's extraordinary stewardship. The Classis of Amsterdam relied on his services for several more years. The complexity of the situation had frequently bewildered them, and they had come to appreciate the full extent of his contributions. Unquestionably,

---

[91] *ERNY* 2:799; *Liber A,* 64-65.
[92] Most famously, Cotton Mather in Boston. The correspondence between Selijns and Mather is lost.

Selijns had been the right man at the right time. In Henry Murphy's eloquent words: "As a minister, he possessed in an eminent degree that rare combination of faculties which unites the zeal of the preacher for the salvation of souls, with the prudence of the presbyter for the temporalities of his church."[93]

---

[93] Murphy, *Anthology*, 80.

CHAPTER 6

Petrus Tesschenmaecker, c. 1642–1690: Atlantic Preacher and Adventurer[1]

Dirk Mouw

Dominie Petrus Tesschenmaecker might at first blush seem to be an unlikely subject for a biography. He has heretofore been remembered solely for the last years of his life, which he spent as a minister—notwithstanding the fact that he was, in all likelihood, a mediocre preacher. Moreover, for most of that brief clerical career—barely a decade—he served in two remote Dutch outposts in British North America: New Castle, Delaware, and Schenectady, New York. It is surprising, in light of this, that vocational and avocational historians have invested more ink in him than in most pre-revolutionary Dutch ministers. Most of these historians have focused on the unusual circumstances surrounding his ordination to the ministry or the gruesome attack that ended his life. These aspects of his life make for compelling prose, but they are hardly the only interesting or instructive features of his life.

The narrative of Tesschenmaecker's adulthood (we know almost nothing of his youth) falls neatly into three acts, each of which offers

[1] I am grateful to my fellow editors, Hans Krabbendam and Leon van den Broeke for carefully reading drafts of this essay and offering many useful comments.

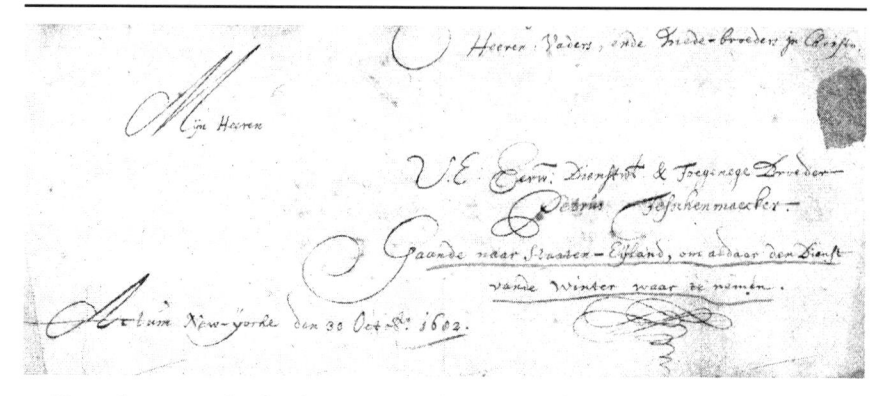

Tesschenmaecker's signature at the close of a letter he wrote to the Classis of Amsterdam on October 30, 1682. The line below his signature reads: "Going to Staten Island to attend to winter services there."
[Amsterdam Correspondence, Archives of the Reformed Church in America, New Brunswick, NJ]

a window on different aspects of Tesschenmaecker the person and the world in which he lived. In the first act we are introduced to a well-educated, well-traveled, multilingual young man who aspired to be a Dutch Reformed minister and evidently reveled in the porosity of the cultural and political boundaries of Reformed Europe. In the second act—spanning barely a year—we find Tesschenmaecker, having evidently abandoned his aspirations to enter the ministry (though not his *wanderlust*), putting his education, skills and wealth to work in the service of the territorial expansionism of the Dutch political and commercial empire. Here he was introduced for the first time to the hazards of colonial life in an age of bloody contests among European powers. In the final act—spanning roughly a decade—we find Tesschenmaecker, having escaped disaster with little more than his life, reviving his erstwhile aspirations, and putting his education and talents to work for an empire of a different sort, the Dutch ecclesiastical empire of the seventeenth century. This empire extended farther than the territorial empire, including outposts in some British colonies in North America. Through Tesschenmaecker's transition from refugee from one vanquished Dutch colony to clergyman in another vanquished Dutch colony, we can learn something of the relationships of the Dutch churches of British North America to other outposts on the periphery of the Dutch ecclesiastical empire as well as to its center in Amsterdam. It is also in this act that we gain some insight into the intense eagerness of communities in these North American colonies to have a dominie of their own, even a dominie of modest gifts (though, as we shall see, the colonists were not uniformly or completely without standards).

Early Life and Preparation for the Ministry

Petrus Tesschenmaecker's youth remains mysterious. Despite extensive research in registers of congregations of various linguistic and theological flavors throughout the province of Utrecht—likely his place of birth—I have been unable to find any document created before 1662 with his name on it. Thus, we do not know from which branch of the Tesschenmaecker family our subject sprang; but among the many Tesschenmaecker lines in the Netherlands and Germany, as well as in Dutch East Indies' territories, one finds a fair number of Reformed theologians and clergy. Despite the scarcity of records, however, we have tantalizing clues of an interesting youth. A 1664 letter described him as "a young man who has traveled" to "many" places, perhaps even points in central Europe. By that date the young Tesschenmaecker was also offering to conduct worship in any of four languages (though, lamentably, we do not know how he learned them).[2]

Tesschenmaecker almost certainly matriculated at the University of Groningen as a student of philology on April 2, 1662—probably when he was about twenty years old. The matriculation record indicates that he was from the province of Utrecht, which is corroborated by a later account. In mid-July 1663 he passed his preliminary examination before the Classis of Rhenen, in the province of Utrecht, and received the title of "proponent"—authorized to deliver sermons (though not to administer sacraments) and eligible for a call to a Dutch Reformed congregation. Upon receipt of such a call he could be ordained to the ministry, pending success in another examination.[3] Shortly after

[2] Dutch congregation of Mortlake to London Dutch Church Consistory, 27 February 1664, in Jan Hendrik Hessels, ed., *Ecclesiae Londino-Batavae Archivum*, 3 vols. (Cambridge: Typis Academiae Sumptibus Ecclesiae Londino-Batavae, 1887-1897), 3:2502-03. My translation.

[3] See selected Groningen matriculations in E. T. Corwin, *A Manual of the Reformed Church in America (Formerly Ref. Prot. Dutch Church), 1628-1902*, 4th ed. (New York: Board of Publication of the Reformed Church in America, 1902), 783. On the quality of and difficulties interpreting matriculation *alba*, see Willem Frijhoff, *La société néerlandaise et ses gradués, 1575-1814: une recherche sérielle sur le statut des intellectuels* (Amsterdam: Academic Publishers Associated, 1981), esp. 33-40, 80-81. For the corroborative report, Jasper Danckaerts and Peter Sluyter, *Journal of Jasper Danckaerts, 1679-1680*, ed. Bartlett Burleigh James and J. Franklin Jameson (New York: Scribner's, 1913), 45. For Tesschenmaecker's promotion, see Classis of Rhenen, 16-17 July 1663, NHK Classis (Rhenen-) Wijk; Acta Classis Rheno Wicanoe, 1656-1676 (Acc. 24-3, Inv. 3), Utrecht Archive. I am grateful to Fred van Lieburg for his assistance in locating this.

Tesschenmaecker passed his preliminary examination, the Reverend Gisbertus Voetius, the highly influential theology professor at Utrecht, reported that the norm for a proponent was to wait three to eight years for a call to a Dutch pulpit. If true, Tesschenmaecker's experience was atypical. He received no such call—at least not one he chose to accept— in the fifteen years after he passed his examination in Rhenen.[4]

It is evident, however, that Tesschenmaecker sought a call, exhibiting his gifts widely. By early 1664, less than six months after he was promoted to the status of proponent, Tesschenmaecker had made his way to a Dutch Reformed congregation in Mortlake, near London. His sojourn there might have gone unrecorded—like so much of his life—but for a marriage ceremony he performed (illegally) and for the ire he drew from the Dutch consistory of London, both for preaching in English in a Dutch church and for saying things in sermons and prayers that appeared to be critical of the British religio-political establishment. Such behavior, the consistory asserted, "could have disastrous results for all of the foreign churches in the country." Members of the Mortlake congregation defended him, writing that he had proposed to lead worship in four languages; only two of his sermons had been in English, and he had stopped preaching in that language when apprised of the dangers it presented. Above all, he had not disparaged the British. Indeed, the congregation could

> not do otherwise than to provide a good testimonial for such a worthy instrument of the Lord, because we have found him to be a very zealous and devoutly peaceful [*godtsalich vreedtsaem*] servant of the Lord, throughout his sojourn among and contacts with us.

Perhaps Tesschenmaecker's behavior, from the perspective of the Dutch in London, improved; perhaps the consistory's displeasure inspired him to move on. In any event, there were no more letters from London or Mortlake weddings recorded.[5]

---

[4] Voetius, *Politica ecclesiastica* (Amsterdam: 1663-1676), 3:233, paraphrased in Peter T. van Rooden, *Religieuze regimes: Over godsdienst en maatschappij in Nederland, 1570-1990* (Amsterdam: Bert Bakker, 1996), 58.

[5] A couple was married in Mortlake, "door D. petrús Tessemackerús proponent," February 26, 1664, "Trouw Doop- en Begrafenis Boek, 1602-1874," Dutch Reformed Church, Austin Friars, City of London (M.S. 7382), Guildhall Library, London, (microfilm) Salt Lake City: Genealogical Society, 1965; London Dutch Church Consistory to [Petrus] Tessemaker, February 10, 1664; Willem Rushout to Cæsar Calendrin, February 12, 1664; members of Mortlake Dutch congregation to London Dutch Church Consistory, February 27, 1664, in Hessels, ed., *Ecclesiae*, 3:2501-03. My translation. Here and elsewhere, dates are adjusted to the "new style."

By September of the following year Tesschenmaecker had settled down in the Hague, where he would remain for more than a decade. At least at the beginning of his time there he continued to hope for a call; by the autumn of 1666 he was even considering serving in a distant Dutch colony. Deputies of the Classis of Amsterdam, however, rejected his application to be "recommended" for a colonial pulpit because he did not have a letter (less than one year old) demonstrating that he was a member in good standing of a Dutch Reformed congregation. From later reports it is nevertheless clear that he was well known to both the Dutch and English congregations of the Hague. It is also likely that he was well known to the German Reformed people of the city.[6]

The English church at the Hague had a long history by the time of Tesschenmaecker's involvement. In earlier years William Ames, John Paget, and John Burgess had preached there; and (the arch-Anglican) Archbishop Laud had expended considerable energies over many years trying to quash its Puritan and non-conformist tendencies. By the mid-1660s, however, it was of a more moderate Reformed stripe, pulled by Congregationalist, Presbyterian, and Anglican forces on one side and a Dutch Reformed establishment—distrustful of both congregationalism and anything "Romish"—on the other. In the 1620s the congregation also began sharing its sanctuary and pooling resources with the city's German Reformed congregation.[7]

[6] Classis of Amsterdam, deputies [for colonial churches], 25 October 1666, in E. T. Corwin and Hugh Hastings, eds., *Ecclesiastical Records: State of New York*, 7 vols. (Albany: James B. Lyon, 1901-1916), 1:584. (Hereafter cited as *ERNY*). By the fall of 1665 he served as a witness to a notarial act there: Notary M. Beeckman, September 14, 1665, Notarial Acts, 1650-1700 (Inv. 490, f. 262), Gemeente Archief, the Hague, (microfilm) Hague: Gemeentearchief, 1989. For a later report, see Gideon Schaats, Wilhelmus van Nieuwenhuysen, Casparus van Zuuren, and Laurentius van Gaasbeeck to Classis of Amsterdam, [October] 1679, in *ERNY* 1:732. The editor has assigned a November date to this undated letter; it was clearly sent under cover of the October 25, 1679, letter by Van Gaasbeeck. See translations in *ERNY* 1:727-33.

[7] Keith L. Sprunger, "Archbishop Laud's Campaign against Puritanism at the Hague," *Church History* 44 (1975): 308-20; Sprunger, *The Learned Doctor William Ames: Dutch Backgrounds of English and American Puritanism* (Urbana: University of Illinois Press, 1972), 35; Sprunger, *Dutch Puritanism: A History of English and Scottish Churches of the Netherlands in the Sixteenth and Seventeenth Centuries*, Studies in the History of Christian Thought, no. 31 (Leiden: Brill, 1982), esp. 417-22; Jacob de Riemer, *Beschrijving van 's Graven-Hage. . . .*, 2 vols. in 3 parts (Delft: Reinier Boitet, 1730-39), 413-15; Rosemary van Wengen-Shute, "The English Church in The Hague during William and Mary's Time," in P. G. Hoftijzer and C. C. Barfoot, eds., *Fabrics and Fabrications: The Myth and Making of William and Mary*, DQR Studies in Literature (Atlanta: Rodopi, 1990), 41-58; Frederik Oudschans Dentz, *History of the English Church at the Hague, 1586-1929; together with a Short Account of the Family Tinne, a Member of which, John Abraham Tinne, Founded the Present Church Building* (Delft, the Netherlands: W. D. Meinema, 1929), 15-25, 27-29.

It is likely that Tesschenmaecker served this church in some capacity, probably leading worship in both English and German. Notarial documents confirm that he associated with people who had English, German, and Dutch names. An association with the English congregation would explain the fact that Tesschenmaecker does not appear in classical records there: the relationship of the English church with Dutch ecclesiastical assemblies was not particularly close (but closer when the congregation had needed help against Laud). Thus Tesschenmaecker would not have needed approval from the classis to serve as a proponent among the English and Germans.[8]

Tesschenmaecker's closest associate in the Hague—undoubtedly his friend—was the Reverend John Price, "Apricius," as he styled himself, the minister of the English church. The two men appeared together as notarial witnesses, and Tesschenmaecker was a witness at the baptism of Price's daughter. Like Tesschenmaecker, Price crossed political and cultural borders early and easily. The son of an English minister in Amsterdam, he had crossed the Atlantic as a young man to the Dutch colony in Brazil. There in 1644 he had appeared before a gathering of the two Brazilian Dutch Reformed classes, requesting examination to become a proponent in the Dutch church under article eight of church order (meaning he had no university degree). Apparently successful, Price—perhaps around the time of the 1654 Dutch capitulation of Brazil—relocated to the Caribbean. In 1661 he accepted a call from the English church of the Hague. He was, like Tesschenmaecker, multilingual; in addition to his English lineage, his Dutch birth, and his Latinate self-appellation, Price also presented one of his sons for baptism in the German Reformed Church at the Hague.[9]

---

[8] See the notarial act cited in note 321 as well as Notary Zacherias van der Heyden, September 6, 1674, Notarial Acts 1666-1682 (Inv. 782, p. 598); Notary Casper Bovetius, August 30, 1675, Notarial Acts, 1666-1688 (Inv. 788, p. 152); Notary Alexander Ennis, October 23, 1675, Notarial Acts, 1658-1663 (Inv. 427, p. 215) Gemeente Archief, the Hague, (microfilm) Hague: Gemeentearchief, 1989. I have not been able to find his name anywhere in the records of the Hague Classis: "Registers van de handelingen van de classis 's-Gravenhage," 1636 April 21- 1676 February 10 (Acc. 3.18.62.02, Inv. 3), National Archive, the Hague; nor in the Hague congregational records, though these are incomplete, "Acta Consistorialia," 1673-1701, (Acc. 0203-01, Inv. 4), Gemeentearchief, the Hague.
Tesschenmaecker does not appear to have held official office in the English congregation. See, Marinus Godefridus Wildeman, ed., *The Eldest Church Book of the English Congregation in the Hague, Holland* (The Hague: De Wapenheraut, 1906).

[9] See 1674 notarial act in note 323; baptismal records, 11 July and (n.d.) August 1672, in Wildeman, ed., *Eldest Church Book*, 73; article 4, Recife, 18-26 July 1644, "Acta van de gemeene t'samenkomste, bestaende uijt beyde de Classes," in Classis of Brazil, "Classicale Acta," in J. A. Grothe, ed., *Archief voor de geschiedenis der oude Hollandsche*

Orange on the Oyapok

Two errors have heretofore obscured the next chapter in the Tesschenmaecker's life: the first was a slip of the pen by an eighteenth-century correspondent that has deprived scholars of an important clue about Tesschenmaecker's whereabouts prior to his arrival in New York. The second was an erroneous translation that concealed evidence that could have brought his role in the English church at the Hague and his activities in the late 1670s into clearer focus. Researchers have thus far relied on translations of a few sentences in letters written in New York for information about Tesschenmaecker's life before 1678. One critical phrase—as it was translated and published—states that prior to his arrival in North America, Tesschenmaecker had "accompanied the fleet destined for Guyana, under Director N. Price, and had previously been a preacher of the English church at the Hague." Dominie Casparus van Zuuren's mistake as he penned the letter has left scholars perplexed because histories of Dutch maritime exploits contain no mention of the "Director N. Price" of whom Van Zuuren wrote. They do, however, mention a John Price who led an expedition to Guiana; Van Zuuren had the director's initial wrong. Centuries later, a translator compounded the minister's error by misaligning subject and verb. It was not Tesschenmaecker who "had previously been a preacher of the English Reformed Church at the Hague." It was John Price, the man known both to church historians (as a minister) and to maritime historians (as leader of a campaign to establish a Dutch outpost in South America). In defense of the translator, the erroneous rendition seems far more plausible than the truth. Tesschenmaecker had not, in fact, been a preacher in the English church at the Hague. Rather, he had accompanied an English minister who left his Hague pulpit to lead a Dutch effort to found a colony in French Guiana.[10]

By late 1674 Price had become interested in—perhaps obsessed with—founding a Dutch colony near the Oyapok River in Guiana, a region hotly contested among European empires. The Dutch West India Company had lost both Brazil and New Netherland in recent decades and was at war with France. Price succeeded in gaining official support for planting a colony there under the supervision of the States of Holland

---

zending, 6 vols. (Utrecht, The Netherlands: Van Bentum, 1885), 2:312-13. See also, Philip Christiaan Molhuysen et al., *Nieuw Nederlandsch biografisch woordenboek*, 10 vols. (Leiden: Sijthoff, 1911-37), 7:1023-25.

[10] The translation is in Schaats *et al* to the Classis of Amsterdam, [October] 1679, in *ERNY* 1:731. The manuscript is in Amsterdam Correspondence, Archives of the Reformed Church in America, New Brunswick, NJ.

and the Admiralty of Amsterdam, with the immediate direction of a council of five men, to be chosen from among would-be colonists by the admiralty. Price and his associates attempted to drum up support by publishing pamphlets, cobbled from travel accounts, portraying the region as edenic: blessed with "perpetual summer," valuable minerals, and "fat, exquisite fish," tastier than any in Europe. Colonists would be greeted by "very obliging" natives. With the anticipated profits, the "support of our State" and "God's protection," colonists would surely "sit, as if under a fig tree, in rest and peace." The effort would not, of course, result in material gain alone; it would also establish "the Church of Jesus Christ in those wild regions, pure in [its] teaching and conduct, to turn the blind heathens from the darkness to the light."[11]

Price was chosen to be the governor of the colony, and Tesschenmaecker was appointed as secretary of the Council of Justice. "Principal" colonists had to make significant financial investments in the expedition. Each was to recruit twelve servants and purchase a year's provisions, two horses, eight cows, sixty sheep, and some goats and pigs. By one conservative estimate, each principal had to invest more than 2,500 guilders—a remarkable sum. Thus, despite the fact that Tesschenmaecker had been a candidate for the ministry for more than a decade—without a call from a congregation and the consequent salary—he was not without financial means. And yet, while Petrus seems therefore to have come from a monied branch of the Tesschenmaecker family, the expedition was apparently another occasion for him to be reminded that his inheritance had not included the skills necessary to be an attractive candidate for the ministry—even for a "pulpit" in a fledgling colony across the Atlantic. Among the principal colonists were three Tesschenmaeckers (presumably somehow related); and Wernerus Tesschenmaecker, not Petrus, was appointed dominie.[12]

Recruitment for the expedition to Guiana fell short of expectations. Plans were scaled back dramatically and delayed. Finally, in December 1676, a convoy set sail, although vessels carrying some provisions and ammunition remained in frozen water at Amsterdam. On February 2, 1677, land was sighted. The start was not auspicious. The expedition had arrived during the rainy season, and it founded the

---

[11] *Pertinente beschrijvinge van Guiana. . . . .*, (Amsterdam: Jan Claesz. ten Hoorn, 1676), esp. 1st pagination 4, 2nd pag. 4, 10-13, 17, 33, 38, 42-43; M. G. de Boer, "Een Nederlandsche nederzetting aan de Oyapock," *Tijdschrift voor Geschiedenis, Land- en Volkenkunde* 14 (1899): 327. My translations.

[12] *Pertinente*, 1st pag. 5-12, 2nd pag. 48; *Verloren arbeyt; ofte, klaar en kortbondigh vertoogh van de colonie in de lantstreke Guiana. . . .*, (Amsterdam: Pieter Timmers, [1680]), 9-10.

settlement they named "Orange" in a particularly marshy and humid spot. Livestock wandered off or died; supplies rotted. As many as one in five colonists perished. A bitter dispute arose among survivors over actions taken by the director. Tesschenmaeckers were found on both sides, but Petrus sided with his friend Price.[13]

Among the soldiers and servants recruited for the expedition had been a number of French deserters, some of whom (as conditions worsened) tried to escape north to Cayenne, a French outpost. France and the Netherlands—each supported by a shifting array of alliances with other European powers—had been at war since Louis XIV's invasion of the Netherlands in 1672, the so-called "year of disasters" in the Netherlands. By the late 1670s France and its allies had lost much of their early advantage and most of their territorial gains in the Low Countries, but violent clashes continued in Europe and on the other side of the Atlantic. Cayenne had, itself, just withstood a Dutch naval attack. When deserters from Orange reached Cayenne with reports of the new Dutch colony and its sorry state, scores of Frenchmen responded quickly. Orange was caught unprepared. Price was alone in resisting the French and was soon mortally wounded, crying, as he fell, "Vive Orange." Orange had survived for only about six months. Most of the colonists were rounded up and taken first to Cayenne and later to Martinique, where principals were billeted and servants put to work, not to regain their freedom until the Peace of Nijmegen in the summer of 1678.

The records are silent about Tesschenmaecker's activities from the fall of Orange to his appearance in the Middle Colonies the following spring. Since most fellow adventurers were at that point still held by the French, it is evident that Tesschenmaecker had eluded his would-be captors. He probably made his way to the Dutch colony of Suriname and from there to the Delaware and Hudson valleys. Judging from Tesschenmaecker's habits before and after his adventure at Orange, he probably supported himself *en route* by preaching in various languages.[14]

---

[13] De Boer, "Een Nederlandsche nederzitting," 328-34; *Verloren arbeyt*, 1-3, 14-15. Another account of the journey and first days in Guiana is in Lucy Hotz, "A Young Lady's Diary of Adventure in 1677: Journal of Elizabeth van der Woude," *The Blue Peter* 9 (1929): 611-18, published in extended form in Kim Isolde Muller, *Elisabeth van der Woude: memorije van 't geen bij mijn tijt is voorgevallen, met het opzienbarende verslag van haar reis naar de Wilde Kust, 1676-1677*, ed. Darja de Wever (Amsterdam: Terra Incognita, 2001).

[14] De Boer, "Een Nederlandsche nederzitting," 337-42; Jan Jacob Hartsinck, *Beschrijving van Guiana, of de wilde kust....*, 2 vols. (Amsterdam: Gerrit Tielenburg, 1770), 935-42; *Verloren arbeyt*, 49-60; Pieter Marinus Netscher, *Geschiedenis van de koloniën Essequebo,*

Arrival and Ordination in North America

Almost immediately upon arrival in the Mid-Atlantic, Tesschenmaecker went to New Castle, on the Delaware, at the invitation of a congregation that wanted a bilingual minister. Initially, things went well for Tesschenmaecker at New Castle. Within weeks the local court ordered that locations be chosen for a parsonage and a church. Within a year he was performing his duties "so well that that church, to the general gratification of everybody there," wanted to call him as its minister. The congregation petitioned dominies in the region for Tesschenmaecker's ordination, thus setting the stage for the event for which he would be most often remembered.[15]

Tesschenmaecker was, of course, ordained in New York to the Dutch Reformed ministry, the first so promoted in North America. That fact is widely acknowledged, but when we carefully examine the records that report the ordination and when we understand it in the context of events elsewhere in the Dutch ecclesiastical empire, we see that its importance has been exaggerated by scholars. It was not a watershed event within the realm of church history, nor was it a paradigmatic example of the oppression of the Dutch church by overbearing English colonial officials in New York.

Casparus van Zuuren, minister on Long Island, noted in congregational records that on September 10, 1679, all four Dutch ministers in the colony were asked to meet to discuss the request from New Castle. Three of them arrived in New York City at month's end. The men did not act immediately, which suggests they may not have uniformly favored Tesschenmaecker's promotion to the ministry or had qualms about the means proposed to effect it. They also noted that some of their "church-members made not a few difficulties about" the proposal. A contemporary, on the other hand, believed the ministers hesitated because Tesschenmaecker was a Voetian and "the other ministers were all Cocceians."[16]

Demerary en Berbice. . . . ('S Gravenhage: Martinus Nijhof for Provinciaal Utrechts Genootschap van Kunsten en Wetenschappen, 1888), 364-66. See also Synod of Enkhuizen, 1678 in Grothe, ed., *Archief*, 1:82. For the Franco-Dutch War, see Jonathan Israel, *The Dutch Republic: Its Rise, Greatness, and Fall, 1477-1806*, (New York: Oxford University Press, 1995), 796-829.

15   Tesschenmaecker to Classis of Amsterdam, October 30,1682; New Castle Consistory to Classis, September 25, 1682, in *ERNY* II:834-36; court order, December 3,1678 in Louise B. Heite, "New Castle Under the Duke of York: A Stable Community," (M.A. Thesis, University of Delaware, 1978), 79.

16   [Van Zuuren,] "Minutes regarding what took place at the calling and ordination of Domine Petrus Tesschenmaker as Pastor of the Congregation of New Castle, etc. on the South River," September 10-c. October 15, in David William Voorhees,

More recently, scholars have explained the ministers' actions in various ways, ranging from a dutiful yielding to an oppressive governor, to an expression of an ecclesiastically independent spirit. For its time, however, Tesschenmaecker's ordination was hardly unusual in the Dutch world, and it certainly did not make the Dutch Reformed Church in British North America "practically independent of the fatherland."[17]

It was not mere coincidence that the governor issued an order to the ministers on the same day they convened, though it is unclear whether the dominies had scheduled their meeting to coincide with the governor's return to the city (from an official trip) or whether Dutch parties had advised the governor about the timing of his order. Furthermore, scrutiny of the records regarding Governor Andros's involvement demonstrates that it was orchestrated by both Dutch and English actors, perhaps including one or more of the dominies. It was certainly not the intervention of a meddlesome governor with sinister intent. By September 24—nearly a week before the ministers met to consider the matter—Tesschenmaecker was certain that a gubernatorial order would ensure the success of the bid for his ordination. It was no accident, then, that Van Zuuren wrote that the governor "had conceded [*geconzedeerd*] a letter of authorization" for Tesschenmaecker's ordination. Andros was clearly making this concession to some Dutch party or parties. The clerk of the council meeting was even coached on how to word the act properly for a Dutch Reformed audience. He struck out wording pressing them to "admitte" Tesschenmaecker, for example, replacing it with a request that the dominies "ordain" him. Upon receipt of the document, the ministers, "after some debate back and forth, voted to proceed with the promotion." Whether the governor and council had provided the ministers with the cover they felt they needed, or tipped the wavering toward consent, the concession worked. Even in his own notes, Van Zuuren wrote that they agreed "particularly" because of the "request and desire" of the governor.[18]

---

ed., *Records of the Reformed Protestant Dutch Church of Flatbush, Kings County, New York*, (New York: Holland Society of New York, 1998), 94-95; Schaats *et al* to Classis of Amsterdam, [October 1679], in *ERNY* 1:730-31; Danckaerts and Sluyter, September 24, 1679, in *Journal*, 45.

[17] Randall H. Balmer, *A Perfect Babel of Confusion: Dutch Religion and English Culture in the Middle Colonies*, Religion in America Series (New York: Oxford University Press, 1989), 22; John Fiske, *The Dutch and Quaker Colonies in America*, 2 vols. (Boston: Houghton Mifflin, 1899), 2:85.

[18] Danckaerts and Sluyter, September 24, 1679, in *Journal*, 45; [Van Zuuren,] "Minutes," in Voorhees, ed., *Flatbush Records*, 94-95; council minutes, September 30, 1679, in Peter R. Christoph and Florence A. Christoph, eds., *The Andros Papers: Files*

The ministers reconvened on October 9 to examine and ordain Tesschenmaecker. Van Zuuren noted that Tesschenmaecker had "good knowledge and understanding" of theology. The dominie deviated from standard language, however, when he described Tesschenmaecker's examination sermon. Usually such records encoded evaluations with words about the assembly's "great," "complete" or "adequate" satisfaction. Van Zuuren instead wrote that the group was "fairly [*tamelijk*]" satisfied with Tesschenmaecker's sermon; he had passed, but with less than a resounding endorsement.[19]

Tesschenmaecker's ordination was not a particularly important milestone in the history of colonial Dutch churches, nor was it an act of defiance against the mother church—though defiance and declarations of independence were hardly unknown within the wider Dutch world. The congregations of Dutch Brazil in the 1630s and 1640s had formed themselves into a classis, then into two classes and even a synod, ordaining men to the ministry in those assemblies. All of this had been seen as rebellious activity by the Classis of Amsterdam. Similar behavior in the East Indies (in what is now Indonesia) also irked the classis and the Synod of North Holland. Three of the ministers who ordained Tesschenmaecker had themselves been ordained in Amsterdam during the 1670s, years of heightened frustration over East Indian ordinations.[20]

Evidence of the four ministers' solid grasp of activity in Asia and how events there were perceived in Amsterdam can be seen in the way they proceeded and how they then explained their actions to the classis. There were a number of aspects of East Indian affairs that particularly displeased Amsterdam: it was a lone consistory in Batavia (now Jakarta) that was promoting men to the status of candidate, and then candidates to the ministry. Some of the men so promoted were, in Amsterdam's view, grossly underqualified; and—worst of all—"the Brothers" in the East Indian church "continue to talk" in general terms about the "rights" of colonial churches so to act. In New York, however, the four ministers, each with an elder, gathered "in the form of a classis," electing officers and an examiner, thus substantially conforming to Dutch church order

---

of the Provincial Secretary of New York during the Administration of Governor Sir Edmund Andros, 1674-1680, 3 vols., New York Historical Manuscripts Series (New York: Syracuse University Press, 1989-91), 3:144.

[19] [Van Zuuren,] "Minutes," in Voorhees, ed., *Flatbush Records*, 95-96.

[20] For examples, see "Aantekeningen uit de acta der provinciale synoden van Noord-Holland," in Grothe, ed., *Archief*, 1:1-85; Frans Leonard Schalkwijk, *The Reformed Church in Dutch Brazil (1630-1654)* (Zoetermeer, The Netherlands: Boekencentrum, 1998), esp. 82-94, 129-132; Classis of Amsterdam, March 16, 1671, March 15, 1677, March 7, 1678, in ERNY 1:617, 693, 708.

and practice. That body examined and ordained a man who was well qualified—one with a university degree who had passed his preliminary examination before a classis of the mother church. In explaining their actions to Amsterdam, the ministers were not obsequious, nor did they write "anxiously," as one scholar has asserted. Neither, however, did they write of inherent rights, but rather of duties dictated by circumstances, asking the classis to look upon their proceedings with a "benevolent disposition," to approve their actions, and to "pardon" them if they had departed from church order.[21]

The response from Amsterdam, which had known far greater irregularities elsewhere in the world, was certainly not "chary." The subcommittee that usually corresponded with colonial congregations did read the letter to the full classis before answering. The classis, however, directed the subcommittee to inform the colonial ministers that it was "pleased to be satisfied with their labors in this particular instance" and encouraged them to maintain both "good order" and "correspondence" with Amsterdam.[22]

A subsequent statement from Henricus Selijns, known for defending Reformed orthodoxy, demonstrates both that he also knew about the transgressions of Dutch churches in Asia and was determined that the North American congregations would remain on a more orderly and conservative course. Faced with a request from a nearby congregation asking for the promotion of a grain merchant who he considered to be a radical separatist, Selijns refused to cooperate, writing:

> we remembered the struggles of the city of Batavia, and those of Ceylon, in their efforts to make licentiates out of Comforters of the Sick, and Ministers out of Licentiates, and especially that it would lean toward the Independents of New England, and therefore I refused to second it, and spoke against it.[23]

In the middle of the eighteenth century many would come to see the benefits of colonial ordinations, but not during Tesschenmaecker's lifetime. Ultimately, his ordination was not a particularly noteworthy event in the history of the Dutch colonial church, except, perhaps, in

---

[21] For the report of the classis, see Synod of North Holland at Hoorn, 1677, in "Aantekeningen," 81; my translation; [Van Zuuren,] "Minutes," in Voorhees, ed., *Flatbush Records*, 97-98; Schaats *et al* to Classis of Amsterdam, [October] 1679, in *ERNY* 1:730-33.

[22] Balmer, *Perfect Babel*, 22; Classis of Amsterdam, January 29, 1680, in *ERNY* 1:737.

[23] Henricus Selijns to Classis of Amsterdam, September 30, 1685, in *ERNY* 1:908.

that it had been achieved by the collaboration of Dutch colonists with English officials pursuing the best interests of a Dutch congregation.

New Castle

New Castle already had a complicated history by the time Tesschenmaecker arrived, and its population reflected that history. Once known as New Amstel, the community had been—over the course of twenty-seven years—under the direction of the Dutch West India Company (three times), of Sweden, of the City of Amsterdam, and of the British (twice). From among its diverse population, Tesschenmaecker drew about one hundred sixty Dutch- and English-speaking worshippers, probably (at least at first) in and around an aging wooden structure converted from house to sanctuary. Though Tesschenmaecker was well received in New Castle in 1678, his popularity in that community was already in decline at the time of his ordination. Anglophonic hearers reneged on pledges to contribute to his salary within months of his arrival. Tesschenmaecker won lawsuits against two of the English for nonpayment, though he only sued estates, not the living. His success among English congregants was undoubtedly impaired by the activities of an Anglican minister, then drumming up support (and financial pledges) for Anglican worship. In so doing the Anglican probably heightened ethnic tensions in the community and drew English support away from Tesschenmaecker.[24]

Within two years of his ordination, the New Castle Dutch, too, began to sour on Tesschenmaecker. To Tesschenmaecker the issue was inadequate remuneration. In seventeenth-century North America, Dutch ministers were seldom paid in hard currency; often in pelts, wampum, or grain. This led to frequent disagreements, particularly when payer and payee differed about the value of the payment. Tesschenmaecker was paid in tobacco in New Castle, a commodity he believed was overvalued by his church and undervalued by the few willing to buy or trade for it. The congregation believed that Tesschenmaecker only wanted an excuse to find a more lucrative call. The difficulties, becoming known to his colleagues in New York in 1681, worsened in 1682. During that year

---

[24] Jean E. Bankert, *A History of New Castle Presbyterian Church* ([New Castle]: [New Castle Presbyterian Church], 1989), 1-3; Schaats *et al* to Classis of Amsterdam, [October] 1679; Tesschenmaecker to Classis, October 30,1682, in *ERNY* 1:730-33, 834; court records, May 3-4,1679, March 2-3, April 5-8, 1680, in *Records of the Court of New Castle on Delaware, 1676-1681*, 2 vols. (Lancaster, PA: Wickersham Printing Co. for the Colonial Society of Pennsylvania, 1904), B:321, 390, 478; J. Thomas Scharf, *History of Delaware, 1609-1888*, 2 vols. (Philadelphia: L. J. Richards, 1888), 2:874-75.

Tesschenmaecker began making frequent trips to communities in New Jersey, Staten Island, and Manhattan, and he even traveled to Boston while he continued to cooperate with his colleagues' futile attempts at reconciliation.

As with his difficulties with English worshippers, the difficulties Tesschenmaecker encountered with the Dutch in New Castle were likely driven by more than finances. Two visitors from the Netherlands, who were particularly robust Dutch pietists, Jasper Danckaerts and Peter Sluijter, spent time in New Castle in 1679 and 1680. They were openly critical of Tesschenmaecker and found sympathetic ears in the congregation. Their presence and activities likely weakened support for Tesschenmaecker, and their influence in New Castle may have endured. Indeed, in 1682 Jacobus Koelman—a man so closely associated with radical Dutch pietism that his name became an adjective for the strain he promulgated—explored the possibility of settling in the area with hundreds of followers. It is impossible to determine whether the theological orientation of the congregation was shifting or whether Tesschenmaecker had turned out to be less robust in his pietism than congregants had hoped. Whatever the case, the congregation's eagerness to embrace Koelman suggests that Tesschenmaecker's problems had little to do with the price of tobacco in New Castle.[25]

Staten Island and Schenectady

With the help of the New York City consistory, Tesschenmaecker finally received a formal release from his obligations to the now openly hostile congregation on the Delaware, and he left for Staten Island in late summer 1682. At first he planned only to winter there, but about a year later he accepted a call. When he settled there he was already known to church members. He had undoubtedly visited the area earlier and, given the diverse population of the island, had probably already preached there in Dutch, English, and, perhaps, French. Evidently he planned to establish himself, registering a cattle mark and acquiring eighty acres of land. There is no indication that Tesschenmaecker was

---

[25] Van Zuuren to Classis of Amsterdam, October 30, 1681, October 1682; New Castle Consistory to Classis, September 25, 1682; Selijns to Classis, October 28, November 1; Tesschenmaecker to Classis, October 30, 1682, in *ERNY* 2:795, 838-39, 823-24, 830-32, 834-36. See also Albert Eekhof, "Jacobus Koelman, zijn verblijf in Amerstdam en zijn beroep naar Noord Amerika II," *Nederlands archief voor kerkgeschiedenis* 11 (1914): 13-40; Evan Haefeli, "The Pennsylvania Difference: Religious Diversity on the Delaware before 1683," *Early American Studies* 1 (2003): 53-56.

unhappy on Staten Island, nor that the Staten Islanders were unhappy with him. Nevertheless, within a few years, he resolved to leave.[26]

The Dutch Reformed congregation in Schenectady had been courting Tesschenmaecker almost from the moment he left New Castle in 1682. They had sent letters, dispatched commissioners to New York City, and probably even constructed a parsonage. He finally succumbed to their advances in 1686. Tesschenmaecker had spent about three years as minister in New Castle and little more on Staten Island, and his tenure in Schenectady would be of similar duration. Though few records of Schenectady survive from the 1680s, there is no evidence of discord between Tesschenmaecker and his Schenectady flock; financial records show that the church prospered significantly during his pastorate. Indeed, much of his final year was occupied with weighty matters in Kingston, working with ministers and elders of other congregations to adjudicate a scandal surrounding another Dutch Reformed minister, Laurentius van den Bosch.[27]

Tesschenmaecker's leadership role in the Van den Bosch affair and with the Schenectady church came to an abrupt end on February 8, 1690. Tradition has it that the community was blanketed with

---

[26] Why Tesschenmaecker accepted the call to Schenectady in 1686 is not known. Schenectady had likely improved the terms of its offer more than once over time, but ministers accepted and rejected calls based on a variety of spiritual and material considerations.

Evidence regarding his formal dismission from New Castle is incomplete. It appears, however, that he did ultimately receive a non-penal dismission from the congregation, though—as was generally the case in the Middle Colonies—formal classical approval of that dismission was never sought or required.

Tesschenmaecker to Classis of Amsterdam, October 30,1682; Selijns to Classis, October 31,1683, in *ERNY* 2:384-36, 867-68; Henry Delevan Frost, "The Church on Staten Island," in *Tercentenary Studies, 1928, Reformed Church in America: A Record of Beginnings*, ed. William H. S. Demarest ([New York]: General Synod of the Reformed Church in America, 1928), 83-84. No contemporary records of the French congregations on Staten Island survive, but a Staten Island historian dates a French congregation to about the time of Tesschenmaecker's departure, and at that time a French Reformed minister complained about a Dutch-Walloon minister insinuating himself into Francophonic congregations on Staten Island. A careful Reformed Church historian likewise believed that Tesschenmaecker preached for at least one such congregation. See Charles William Leng and William Thompson Davis, *Staten Island and its People, a History, 1609-1929*, 5 vols. (New York: Lewis Historical Publishing Company, 1930-33), 1:433; Corwin, *Manual*, 1012. Tesschenmaecker may have owned land on the island as early as 1680. See Leng and Davis, *Staten Island*, I:124-25.

[27] Selijns to Classis of Amsterdam, October 31, 1683; to Gisbertus Oostrum September 20, 1685; Rudolphus van Varick to Classis, September 9, 1686, in *ERNY* 2:867-68, 908-09, 922; "Minutes, Accounts, Baptisms, 1683-1728," First Reformed Church, Schenectady, NY; Van den Bosch papers, New York Historical Society, New York, N.Y.

Artist's rendition of Schenectady as it was shortly before the French attack in which Tesschenmaecker died
[Painting by L. F. Tantillo]

deep snow and rent by weeks of discord surrounding the New York manifestation of the Glorious Revolution (Tesschenmaecker sided with Jacob Leisler). Residents may have been less than alert to danger for other reasons as well; one undocumented version of events indicates that some members of the community had been engaged in merrymaking that evening, in celebration of Tesschenmaecker's betrothal to "a buxom young widow." Whether or not that was so, Tesschenmaecker, whose arrival in New York was a consequence of a contest between the Dutch and the French, died that night in Schenectady because of hostilities between the French and the British. Tensions over fur and Native American alliances had simmered for years, and Schenectady was a strategic—and exposed—outpost. England's declaration of war against France opened an opportunity for a French attempt to remove obstacles in North America, including those in the upper Hudson valley. Sometimes called an "Indian attack," the assault on Schenectady was executed by a group that at the outset had already been majority French and from which many Amerindians had subsequently defected. Orders had been given to spare Tesschenmaecker—a potentially valuable source of intelligence—but he was not identified before "4 or 5 french had murderd ye Minister." Various graphic reports survive about his fate: that he was shot "throu ye leggs, & then hewd wth. there Swords," that his "head was split open (by a tomahawk) and his body burned up to the shoulders," and that "his head put upon a pole was carried in triumph to Canada." Though these barbarities appear to be mutually exclusive, it is evident that Tesschenmaecker's death was a violent one.[28]

Dominie Tesschenmaecker and the Dutch Churches of British North America

Tesschenmaecker's story suggests a man with an appetite for both adventure and material success. Unless his taste for the exciting and exotic was voracious, it had probably been sated by February 1690. By that time he had also achieved some material success. He had invested tremendous sums in the Guiana expedition, escaping with only his life. He had left his first pastorate, as he himself had put it, "destitute and disheartened." In his final years, however, he was earning about 500 guilders annually, plus—in keeping with common practice in the region—significant in-kind remuneration. The salary was only about half of that commanded by some of his colleagues down-river and in the towns of Holland. Few dominies could be enticed to cross the Atlantic for so little. Tesschenmaecker did not, however, have to be lured across an ocean; and he was, moreover, single and thus had fewer expenses than a married minister—for which reason many congregations specifically sought young, unmarried ministers. With few obligations and a salary that, while on the low side for a minister, was nevertheless better than the incomes of many of his neighbors, Tesschenmaecker prospered. Early in his Schenectady tenure he was seeking the return of two escaped slaves. Even if he owned no more, he likely ranked among village elite. And at his death, he still owned land both in New Castle and on Staten Island.[29]

---

[28] William Elliot Griffis, *The Story of New Netherland: The Dutch in America* (New York: Houghton Mifflin Company, 1909), 207-208; Voorhees, "The 'fervent Zeale' of Jacob Leisler," *William and Mary Quarterly*, 51 (1994): 466; Thomas E. Burke, Jr., *Mohawk Frontier: The Dutch Community of Schenectady, New York, 1661-1710* (Ithaca, NY: Cornell University Press, 1991), 68-108. Quotes about Tesschenmaecker's fate are from Peter Schuyler et al, report, March 3, 1690, in Lawrence H. Leder, ed., *The Livingston Indian Records, 1666-1723* (Gettysburg: Pennsylvania Historical Association, 1956), 159; New York City Consistory to Classis of Amsterdam, October 21,1698 in "Documents Relating to the Administration of Leisler," in *Collections of the New-York Historical Society*, Publication Fund Series, vol. I (New York: New York Historical Society, 1868), 403; Selijns to Classis of Amsterdam, September 14,1690, in *ERNY* 2:1007.

[29] Tesschenmaecker to Classis of Amsterdam, October 30,1682; Selijns to Classis, October 31,1683; Van Zuuren to Classis, October 30, 1678; Classis to Long Island consistories, April 2, 1680, in *ERNY* 2:834, 867-68, 1:714, 741; Van Varick to Esopus Consistory, November 30, 1689, Van den Bosch papers; Wildeman, ed., *Eldest Church Book*, 73; Israel, *The Dutch Republic*, 353; de Denonville to Dongan, June 5, 1686, in E. B. O'Callaghan, et al, ed., *Documents Relative to the Colonial History of the State*

Tesschenmaecker also desired professional success. On this count the evidence is mixed. The very fact that he remained a proponent in the Old World for more than a dozen years without receiving a call—or at least an attractive call—suggests that he may not have been a great preacher. The opinions of Danckaerts and Sluijter, who had heard him preach in New Castle, corroborate this assessment: they had "never heard worse preaching." When that congregation's affections cooled, attempts to reconcile shepherd and flock failed because the consistory, canvassing the congregation, found "no desire" to have him back. Indeed, the other colonial ministers had only been "fairly" satisfied with his examination sermon.[30]

Yet the Dutch in Mortlake, in Great Britain, had written glowingly about Tesschenmaecker. People in the Esopus, Schenectady, Staten Island, and northern New Jersey (perhaps also in the Hague) sought him out and welcomed him into their pulpits. As we shall see, it is likely that to some extent the theological orientations or stylistic preferences dominant in these communities predisposed them to be receptive to Tesschenmaecker. Perhaps, however, communities like Mortlake and Schenectady, though thousands of miles apart, had another important commonality. Danckaerts and Sluijter had been amazed at the New Castle congregation's eagerness to hear Tesschenmaecker's sermons, concluding that "in these spiritually, as well as physically, waste places, there is nevertheless a craving of the people to accept anything that bears even the name of food, in order to content rather than satisfy themselves therewith." Laying aside the theological agenda embedded in that statement, the writer was observing the paucity of Dutch clergy

---

of New York, 15 vols. (Albany: Weed, Parsons and Co., 1856-1887), 3:458; *Calendar of N.Y. Colonial Manuscripts, Indorsed Land Papers; in the Office of the Secretary of State of New York, 1643-1803*, (Albany: Weed, Parsons & Co., 1864), 30; Jonathan Pearson, *A History of the Schenectady Patent in the Dutch and English Times: Being Contributions toward a History of the Lower Mohawk Valley*, ed. Junius Wilson MacMurray (Albany, NY: J. Munsell's Sons, 1883), 339; patent, November 20, 1679, in *Original Land Titles in Delaware: Commonly Known as the Duke of York Record, Being an Authorized Transcript from the Official Archives of the State of Delaware, and Comprising the Letters Patent, Permits, Commissions, Surveys, Plats and Confirmations by the Duke of York and Other High Officials, from 1646 to 1679*, (Wilmington, DE: General Assembly of the State of Delaware, 1903), 186; New Castle Court, minute, May 3-4, 1679, in *Records of the Court of New Castle*, B:321. He was still among the taxables in the constablery of New Castle in 1687, see Scharf, *Delaware*, 1:154. For post-massacre slavery statistics in Schenectady, see Susan Jane Staffa, *Schenectady Genesis: How a Dutch Colonial Village Became an American City, ca. 1661-1800* (Fleischmanns, NY: Purple Mountain Press, 2004), vol. 1, *The Colonial Crucible, ca. 1661-1774*: 96.

[30] Danckaerts and Sluyter, December 17, 1679, in *Journal*, 138; Selijns to Classis of Amsterdam, October 28 and November 1, 1682, in *ERNY* 2:830-32.

in the colonies. When Tesschenmaecker preached in Bergen (Jersey City), for example, he was augmenting Bergen's meager access to clergy. It was visited only three times per year by a minister from across the river, even though the "considerable congregation" was "abundantly able to support a minister." In Bergen, as elsewhere in British North America, it was, simply "not easy to obtain one." If Tesschenmaecker was, in fact, a mediocre preacher, he was still eagerly sought out by colonists who strongly preferred a poor preacher to no preacher at all.[31]

But Tesschenmaecker's warm reception in places like Staten Island and Schenectady also tell us about the theological orientation of these communities. Tesschenmaecker himself was almost certainly a moderate Dutch pietist. When he was a young man the Dutch in Mortlake had described Tesschenmaecker as "very zealous," also noting that he had lamented the fact that their blessings in the political realm had not resulted in "more reformation and purification from their sins [*beter gereformeert ende gesuyvert en was van hare sonden*]." These are strong indications that Tesschenmaecker was influenced by some strain of Dutch Reformed pietism. Danckaerts and Sluijter—themselves representatives of a particularly robust form thereof—wrote that Tesschenmaecker was a Voetian. They could have meant a number of things, but the statement is a strong indicator of at least a moderate pietism. This conclusion is further supported by their observation that Tesschenmaecker, though by their strict standards "a perfect worldling," had nevertheless sought to "effect" a "reform" in New Castle. They bemoaned the fact that he seemed to lack the "grace therefor."[32]

More clues appear from his correspondence and relationships in North America. When reports surfaced that Koelman was planning to relocate to North America with a multitude of followers, Tesschenmaecker's colleagues saw great peril. Tesschenmaecker, however, reported the information without comment, despite the fact that during his time in the Hague the churches had been repeatedly warned about the plans and activities of this dangerous schismatic. Tesschenmaecker apparently feared Dutch Reformed pietists little, even those who pushed or exceeded the limits of Dutch ecclesiological and theological orthodoxy. Equally evident, however, is the support and collegiality he found among his colleagues in America who were near the opposite end of the theological spectrum. They examined

---

[31] Danckaerts and Sluyter, October 28 and December 17, 1679, in *Journal*, 83-84, 138.
[32] Mortlake Dutch congregation to London Dutch Church Consistory, February 27,1664, in Hessels, ed., *Ecclesiae*, 3:2502-03 (my translation); Danckaerts and Sluyter, September 24 and December 17,1679, in *Journal*, 45, 138.

and ordained him, defended him, and entrusted him with weighty ecclesiastical matters. Had Tesschenmaecker been strongly influenced by one of the more robust strains of Dutch pietism, he would not have been received by his colleagues with that level of trust and cordiality.[33]

That Tesschenmaecker achieved a measure of success in British North America is in part attributable to the pervasiveness of Dutch pietism among the colonial Dutch laity. His brief tenure in New Castle is particularly instructive in this regard. It is likely that Tesschenmaecker's moderate pietism was initially appealing to the majority of that congregation. Interest waned, however, when Danckaerts and Sluijter, representatives of a heartier strain of pietism, visited and proselytized in the community. A trajectory in New Castle toward a more vigorous pietism is further suggested by that congregation's subsequent negotiations with Koelman. Tesschenmaecker was received warmly in places like Staten Island and Schenectady because congregants there shared his pietist bent; his successors in those pulpits included notable pietists such as Guillam Bertholf and Bernardus Freeman.[34]

Tesschenmaecker's linguistic skills also contributed to the degree of success he achieved in North America. The ability to lead worship in more than one language was, not surprisingly, a valuable skill in the Dutch ecclesiastical empire. Broader assemblies in the Netherlands had long maintained that the language of worship should be appropriate to the congregation; orthodoxy did not touch upon the language of worship, only on its content and form. In Tesschenmaecker's lifetime the Dutch of British North America shared this view. His linguistic abilities made it possible for Dutch Reformed laypeople in places like New Castle and the Esopus to secure essential financial support from Anglophones. Students of the Dutch in British North America well know that in the eighteenth century (and beyond), bitter disputes erupted over the language of worship. Yet, so long as the Dutch Reformed Church in New York and New Jersey remained, as one of Tesschenmaecker's contemporaries wrote, "on a better footing" than the Anglophonic churches, no one quibbled about a dominie delivering a sermon in English. Indeed, Dutch laypeople continued for years to reach out (or

[33] See, for instance, Selijns to Classis of Amsterdam, October 28 and November 1, 1682; Tesschenmaecker to Classis, October 30,1682; New York City Consistory to Classis, October 30, 1683; Van Zuuren to Classis [n.d.] October 1682, in *ERNY* 2:831-33, 835-36, 837, 838-39. See also Hague "Acta Consistorialia," 1673-1701.

[34] For the changed attitudes of some of Tesschenmaecker's erstwhile advocates in New Castle, see Danckaerts and Sluyter, May 25,1680, in *Journal*, 233-34. See also Eekhof, "Koelman," 13-40. Another scholar has come to similar conclusions; Haefeli, "Pennsylvania," 53-56.

hold out) their hands to Anglophones, just as Tesschenmaecker had done in both Europe and North America.[35]

Conclusion

A twentieth-century church historian had it right. Tesschenmaecker has captured the attention and imagination of many chiefly for "his tragic death" and for being "the first minister in the denomination to have been ordained" in North America.[36] While these events have made for compelling narratives, they do not set Tesschenmaecker apart as an extraordinary figure. Indeed, it is the very fact that the "dramatic" events in his life were not particularly unusual that makes Tesschenmaecker's story instructive and offers a useful perspective on the Dutch empire, British North America, and the Atlantic world.

Tesschenmaecker was, in a number of ways, a typical colonist in seventeenth-century North America. He did not simply pull up stakes in some European village where his family had lived for generations and immediately establish himself in a colonial community where descendents would cherish stories about him as their clan patriarch. Quite the contrary, North America was but one in a series of Tesschenmaecker's destinations. He was highly mobile before he crossed the Atlantic, mixing with people of many nations and tongues in Europe before doing the same in South and North America. He was also just one of many multilingual Dutch colonists and preachers at points around the globe—and not an exceptionally gifted one. Moreover, Tesschenmaecker was hardly unusual in receiving ordination on a shore distant from his homeland. And, in point of fact, he was just one of many Europeans who sought adventure and wealth in distant places. He was also one of many who died far from their homeland, victims of contests between colonial powers.

Petrus Tesschenmaecker was indisputably an Atlantic citizen—having lived and worked in the Netherlands, England, South America, and three Mid-Atlantic colonies (and perhaps even ascending one or two Boston pulpits). Throughout his adult life he surrounded himself with

---

[35] For examples, see Synod of North Holland at Hoorn, August 20 et seq. 1679; Classis of Amsterdam, January 5,1660, in *ERNY* 1:77, 462. For examples of efforts to supply religious publications and worship in various languages in Brazil, "Classicale Acta," especially, October 16,1636 (215-16), April 20, 1640 (274-75), November 21, 1640 (287-88), October 17, 1641 (307-09), July 18 et. seq. 1644 (319).

[36] John J. Birch, *The Pioneering Church of the Mohawk Valley (De Baanbrekende Kerk van de Mohawk Vallei)* (Schenectady, NY: Consistory of the First Reformed Church of Schenectady, NY, 1955), 24.

people—especially Reformed people—of various tongues and nations. Unsuccessful as a young man in his bid to become a dominie, he invested his skills and wealth in a venture that also failed. Almost by accident he found himself in North America. Though materially destitute, he was still in possession of a university degree and the status of a proponent in the Dutch Reformed Church. Reviving his earlier ambitions, he finally—with the help of Dutch colonists and a British governor—received ordination. It was in New York where Tesschenmaecker, a moderate Dutch pietist with modest gifts, found himself a sought-after commodity and, shortly before his death, achieved a degree of material and professional success. Ironically, Tesschenmaecker found that success in a remote corner of a British colony in a community that was—of all of those he had inhabited throughout his adult life—the most homogeneously Dutch.

DIVERSIFIERS

Clerical Triumphs and Tragedies in the Seventeenth Century

CHAPTER 7

Rudolphus van Varick (1645-1694): Mild, Mobile, and Mistreated Pastor

Leon van den Broeke

Introduction

The Reformed Church in the Dutch Republic was spiritually rich with respect to its human capital: there were many aspiring pastors, even more than there were vacant congregations.[1] Not all of the aspirants were willing to leave the Republic and to serve the Dutch Reformed Church in distant places. Some, however, saw this as an appealing alternative to the tight labor market at home; and for many, especially those who were young and single, the prospect of seeing more of the world was attractive. They chose to live and work outside the Republic, even though for some this meant they would not have a pulpit and a church of their own. Or they, especially when they were young and single, enjoyed the prospect of seeing more of the world.

One of these young, unmarried, and ambitious pastors was Rudolphus van Varick (1645-1694).[2] His story is of a young pastor ready to face the world, but it also reveals that the Dutch Reformed

---

[1] I thank Bill Kennedy, Hans Krabbendam, Dirk Mouw, and David Voorhees for their comments and help.
[2] Despite several spellings I will use the name Van Varick.

Tombstone (Cunera Church Rhenen) and handwriting
(October 13, 1693)
of van Varick
[pictures by author]

Church abroad was young and vulnerable. Van Varick is an example of a Dutch Reformed minister with strong ambitions to serve a colonial congregation—who ostensibly enjoyed a measure of success early in his career—but whose mission later faltered because he found himself drawn into a political and ecclesiastical hornets' nest (on Long Island, where he was, in his own words, *"Pastor ecclesiae Belgicae in Insula Longa"*) ["pastor of the Dutch church on Long Island].[3] Subsequently, he could no longer meet the expectations of his congregants. In what seems to have been an effort to escape the ecclesiastical problems on Long Island, Van Varick in 1692 requested a transfer from the Classis of Amsterdam (which oversaw the Dutch colonial congregations, consistories, and ministers in the New World, although the inhabitants had become British subjects in 1664) to another church elsewhere in the Dutch empire. He began the letter, written jointly with colleagues Godefridus Dellius, Jr.,[4] of Albany and Henricus Selijns[5] of New York City, "There are more congregations without a pastor, in Curaçao, Surinam and [Dutch] East-Indies."[6] The classis never transferred Van Varick. He remained a minister on Long Island, but he had become a broken man as a result of his experience with the crisis that was Leisler's Rebellion; he died at the age of forty-nine. Of his twenty-two-year ministerial career he had spent eight years in the New World. This was the last phase of a career in which he had served as a naval chaplain, as a minister in Malacca (a state in present-day Malaysia and a part of the Dutch East Indies), and as a minister in Hem in the Dutch Republic.

Training, Selection, and International Career

Van Varick was born in Rhenen, a garrison city and also a center of the tobacco trade along the banks of the Nederrijn, in the Province

---

[3] Rudolphus described himself as 'Pastor ecclesiae Belgicae in Insula Longa' in his address to William and Mary on May 19, 1690; Address of New York Merchants and Ministers to the King and Queen; Hugh Hastings, *Ecclesiastical Records, State of New York*, 7 vols. (Albany: J. B. Lyon, 1901-1916), 2:997-98.

[4] Godefridus Dellius jr. (1651-1738), pastor Albany 1683-1699; F. A. Van Lieburg, *Profeten en hun vaderland. De geografische herkomst van de gereformeerde predikanten in Nederland van 1572 tot 1816* (Zoetermeer: Boekencentrum: 1996) Bijlage 1: *Repertorium van Nederlandse hervormde predikanten tot 1816*. Bijlage 2: *Repertorium van Nederlandse hervormde gemeenten tot 1816*, 47.

[5] Henricus Selijns (1636-1701), pastor Breukelen/Brooklyn 1660-1664, Waverveen 1666-1682, New York 1682; R. L. Gasero, ed., *Historical Directory of the Reformed Church in America 1628-1800* (Grand Rapids, MI: Eerdmans, 1992), 356. See also Jos van der Linde's biography on Henricus Selijns.

[6] New Brunswick Theological Seminary, Sage Library, Amsterdam Correspondence (hereafter cited as SLAC), Letter Van Varick to the Classis of Amsterdam, October 12, 1692.

of Utrech.[7] He was baptized as Roelof or Rollef[8]—together with his twin sister Neeltjen[9]—on April 4, 1645, in the Cunera Church. The twins were among six children born to Neeltje Voncken van Doornik and Jan van Varick (†1690), who was a baker, city treasurer, member of the city council, and supervisor of a hospital.[10] Jacob Roeloffs van Varick was their grandfather, a master bricklayer/builder who was married to Anthonia Hendricxdr. Jacob was buried in the Cunera church. The Van Varicks belonged to the middle-class citizens of the city of Rhenen.

Roelof entered his studies in 1666 at the age of twenty-one at the University of Utrecht, where Gisbertus Voetius was the leading theologian.[11] In that same year Roelof made profession of faith, becoming a member of the Utrecht congregation, and Latinized his name to Rudolphus. The records do not show when he graduated, but in 1670 he requested both the Classis of Rhenen and the Classis of Utrecht to recommend him to congregations without a pastor. Both classes consented after listening to his sermons. Like other students, Van Varick sought a call to a congregation, a precondition for being ordained to the ministry. In those days there were more pastoral aspirants than vacant congregations in the Netherlands. Thus, to improve his chances, he even expressed a willingness to serve outside the Republic. On April 6, 1671, he asked the Classis of Amsterdam to designate him as "recommended" for service in overseas congregations, exhibiting a testimonial from the pastor of the Dutch Reformed Church of Rhenen, Johannes Cupius. By January of the following year Van Varick was among a group of four candidates from which the classis was to select two for ministry in the East Indies. Van Varick was not, however, chosen.[12]

Naval Chaplain

Nevertheless, Van Varick was persistent. He wanted to enter the ministry but probably understood that the most he could hope for in

---

[7] His name is not recorded in C. L. van Groningen, P. H. D. Leupen and E. R. M. Taverne, *Rhenen: 750 jaar stad* (Utrecht: Matrijs, 2008); Aleid W. van de Bunt, *Wageningen/Rhenen* (Baarn: Het Wereldvenster, 1969); W. van Iterson, *De stad Rhenen: De resultaten van een rechtshistorisch onderzoek* (Assen: Van Gorcum, 1960).

[8] Utrechts Archief, Archives of the Dutch Reformed Church of Rhenen, Baptismal Register 1641-1657.

[9] Or Neeltgen.

[10] Gasthuismeester.

[11] *Album Studiosorum Academiae Rheno-Traiectinae MDCXXXVI-MDCCCLXXXVI* (Ultraiecti: Van Boekhoven, 1886), 60. Gisbertus Voetius (1589-1676), pastor in Vlijmen and Engelen 1611; Heusden 1617; professor Utrecht 1634; D. Nauta, "Gisbertus Voetius," *Biografisch Lexicon voor de Geschiedenis van het Nederlandse Protestantisme* (Kampen: Kok, 1978) 2: 443-449. (hereafter cited as BLGNP).

[12] The other one was Petrus de Lange.

the Republic was a pulpit with a meager salary in a small village. He resolved to go abroad and see something of the world. Did he opt for this type of ministry because there was a surplus of pastors, or was he lured by the prospect of service in a distant land? Probably both reasons motivated the young candidate. Van Varick saw more opportunities abroad and seemed eager to go. His persistence was rewarded, and a year later he was successful. In March 1672 he returned to the Classis of Utrecht[13] and handed over a letter from the Amsterdam Admiralty asking the classis to attest to his fitness to serve as a chaplain on the ship of Lt. Admiral Willem Joseph Baron van G[h]ent (1626-1672). The classis examined him the next day and listened to him preach on Timothy 2:11-12.[14] Both the classis and the deputies of the provincial synod voted unanimously to admit him, and he was ordained.

Van Varick was by then almost twenty-seven years old.[15] The so-called "year of disasters" (1672) had already begun in the Republic. England had declared war on the Netherlands in March,[16] and France followed twelve days later. In May the bishop of Münster and the sovereign of Keulen joined them. On June 7, in the Battle at Solebay, Van G[h]ent was wounded and died. Although the British lost more men, the Dutch lost more ships. As Van Varick served in the squadron of Van G[h]ent, he must have been on or near the *Dolfijn* [Dolphin], Van G[h]ent's flagship. We know nothing of his experience during that battle, although we do know that the death of van G[h]ent brought an early end to Van Varick's commission. He returned to the Netherlands—though only briefly—having received an introduction to the perils of the maritime ministry.

Malacca

The next thing we know of Van Varick is that on September 11, 1673, he sailed from the isle of Texel in the Netherlands. From an undated letter from Batavia, which was discussed at the meeting of the Deputies for Indies' Affairs of the Classis of Amsterdam on March 26, 1675, it appears that he arrived in Batavia on May 12, 1674, aboard the ship *De Zijp* (meaning most probably "the Channel" or "the Spring").[17]

---

[13] Utrechts Archief, Archives Classis of Utrecht (hereafter cited as ACU), inv. nr. 5, March, 5-6, 1672.
[14] The clerk did not write down whether the sermon was on 1 or 2 Timothy. Since he was still a candidate, he did not preach a sermon but he delivered an exhortation.
[15] ACU, inv. nr. 5, March 5-6, 1672.
[16] A.Th. van Deursen, *De last van veel geluk: De geschiedenis van Nederland 1555-1702* (Amsterdam: Bert Bakker, 2005).
[17] J.R. Bruijn, F.S. Gaastra, and I. Schöffer, eds., *Dutch-Asiatic shipping in the 17th and 18th centuries*. Rijks Geschiedkundige Publicatiën Grote Serie vols. 165, 166, 167 (Den

Van Varick was commissioned to accompany Commissioner Andries Bogaert to Djanbi on the East Coast of Sumatra.[18] Afterwards he was sent to Malacca, which the Dutch had conquered from the Portuguese in 1641. In 1665 the city had 3,817 inhabitants and the surrounding region had more than ten thousand. The Dutch Reformed Church of Malacca had, in addition to Van Varick, a second pastor, Hubertus Leydekker.[19] Since it was necessary for one of them to be able to speak Portuguese, Leydekker must have learned the language, but it is possible that Van Varick did so as well. Rudolphus may have met Margrieta Visboom (1649-1695), his future wife, through Leydekker. Margrieta was the niece of Abraham Burgers, Leydekker's brother-in-law, a merchant and storekeeper there. The congregation had eighty adult members in 1660.[20]

Van Varick served this congregation for three years. The records do not reveal much about his work or his ministerial style, but he is mentioned as "a man of sound scholarship and an uplifting nature."[21] In its meeting of October 10, 1677, the consistory encouraged him to repatriate for health reasons, though the specific illness remains unknown. He was praised as "our esteemed fellow" and for being "in his

---

Haag: Rijks Geschiedkundige Publicatiën, 1979-1987), 166:180-81; Stadsarchief Amsterdam (Municipal Archives of Amsterdam), Acta Deputati ad Res Indicas (Acts Deputies for Indies' Affairs) of the Classis of Amsterdam (hereafter cited as SACDCA), March 26, 1675.

[18] May 21 through October 11, 1674; M. Veeris, *Oud en nieuw Oost-Indien: vervattende een naaukeurige ... verhandelinge van Nederlands mogentheyd in die gewesten, benevens eene ... beschryvinge der Moluccos, Amboina, Banda, Timor, en Solor, Java, en alle de eylanden onder dezelve landbestieringen behoorende ...; alles zeer naaukeurig, in opzigt van de landen, steden ..., zeden der volken, boomen, gewasschen, land- en zeë-dieren, met alle het wereldlyke en kerkelyke, van d'oudste tyden af tot nu toe aldaar voorgevallen, beschreven. Zaaken van den Godsdienst op het Eiland Java*, 4ᵉ dl. 2ᵉ st. (Dordrecht/Amsterdam: Van Braam/Onder de Linden, 1726), 65.

[19] SACDCA, November 12, 1675. Leydekker was pastor in Malacca 1672-1682; J. P. de Bie en J. Loosjes, *Biographisch Woordenboek van Protestantsche Godgeleerden in Nederland*. 5 vols. ('s Gravenhage: Nijhoff, 1919-1949), 5: 772; F. Nagtglas, ed., *Levensberichten van Zeeuwen. Zijnde een vervolg op P. de La Rue, Geletterd, staatkundig en heldhaftig Zeeland*. 2 vols, (Middelburg: n.p., 1893), 2: 65; C.A.L. van Troostenburg de Bruyn, *Biografisch woordenboek van Oost-Indische predikanten* (Nijmegen: Milborn, 1893), 257-258. Troostenburg mentions the fact that Lucas Bosch ab Osch (1645-1723) worked for less than a month in Malacca. He arrived on January 5, 1675 in Batavia and was in the same year a month (or less) in Malacca; Van Lieburg, *Repertorium*, 1:31; Troostenburg, *Woordenboek*, 44.

[20] G.J. Schutte, "Een handelskerk: Malakka," G. J. Schutte, ed., *Het Indisch Sion: De Gereformeerde kerk onder de Verenigde Oost-Indische Compagnie* (Hilversum: Verloren, 2002), 219-24.

[21] Den Haag, Nationaal Archief (National Archives, hereafter cited as NA), 1.11.01.01, inv. nr. 1674, Consistory Dutch Reformed Church Malacca, September 30, 1674.

life edifying, in his contact peaceful and friendly, [and] in his ministry serious."[22] From this it is evident that Van Varick was well received as a minister in Malacca.

Marriage

Margrieta Visboom, Rudolphus's bride, was the daughter of Dirck Jansz. Visboom and Grietje Jans Burgers, who had died in 1664 and 1667. Margrieta's uncle cared for her until she married either Jacob Hustaert or Egbert van Duijns. In either event, it is clear that she had been married at least once by the time she met Rudolphus and that she moved in the upper echelons of Malaccan society.[23] Unfortunately, there is no information about the date and place of their marriage, and it is therefore unclear whether they were married before or after they left for Hem.[24] The timing of the birth of their first child, Cornelia Hesther, does not help to solve the mystery; her baptism on October 20, 1680, was sixteen months after Van Varick's installation in Hem.

Marrying this wealthy widow certainly improved Van Varick's standard of living and social status. From the "Inventory of estate of

---

[22] Ibid., October 10, 1677.
[23] There is uncertainty about Margrieta's first husband: was it the wealthy Jacob Hustaert or Egbert van Duijns? Jacob Hustaert (1619-1675) was baptized in Amsterdam as Jacques, son of P(i)eter Hustaert and Elisabet de Moucheron. Until this moment I am not completely convinced that Margrieta was married to Van Duijns as the art historian Marybeth DeFilippis stated at her exhibition "New York Between East and West: The World of Margrieta van Varick. Hustaert," widower of Geertrudyt Christiaens, had been tradesman and governor of Ternate, Ambon, Coromandel and Ceylon. As no marital records can be found that are legible, we remain uncertain about the dates and the places of Margrieta's marriages. If it had been Egbert, then she was already a widow on September 14, 1677; NA, 1.11.01.01, inv. nr. 1674, Consistory Malacca, September 14, 1677. On that day a man by the name of A. Steven asked the consistory to dismiss the widow Van Duijns. Her late husband had stood surety for a payment that Stevens owed the deacons. The consistory agreed to do so. If Van Duijns was Margrieta's first husband, what happened to Elbert and Magdalena, his children? Elbert was baptized on September 20, 1663, and Magdalena on December 10, 1666. Did Margrieta take them to Hem? The ecclesiastical records do not show their names. Hoorn, Westfries Archief (hereafter cited as WFA), Archives of the Dutch Reformed Church of Hem, inv. nr. 2.
[24] C. L. van Otterlo and Ph. J. van Daal, *Historische Reeks Rhenen. II Rhenense Geslachten* (Zeist/Rhenen 1990), 10-12; Conversation on January 26/27, 2010 with Ph. J. van Daal; Marybeth De Filippis, "Margrieta," in Deborah Krohn and Peter N. Miller, eds., *Dutch New York Between East & West: The World of Margrieta van Varick* (New York/New Heaven/London: Bard Graduate Center/The New-York Historical Society/Yale University Press, 2009), 41-53, especially 52 n31; W. Wijnaendts van Resandt, *De Gezaghebbers der Oost-Indische Compagnie op hare Buiten-Comptoiren in Azië* (Amsterdam: Liebaert, 1944), 61; *De Nederlandsche Leeuw* 65 (1948): 133-37; 66 (1949): 189; 71 (1954):187; 77 (1961):113-14.

Margaret van Varick, widow of D°. Rudolphus Van Varick" it appears that Margrieta had numerous pieces of furniture, china, jewels, books, and many more fine and precious possessions.[25] The couple apparently shipped their possession to the Republic to decorate their Hem parsonage. Real estate transactions show that in 1686 Rudolphus gained some money as he sold property in and outside of Rhenen—among others a house at the Market Place.[26] But by then he had already moved from Asia to the Republic and from the Republic westward, across the Atlantic Ocean to the New World. But first he returned to the Old World.

Hem as Haven

The acts of the Provincial Synod North-Holland of August 1678 reveal that Van Varick requested to be admitted as *recommandatus*. That meant that the synod would recommend him to congregations without a pastor, just as eight years earlier when he asked classis for the same designation. The famous classical scholar and poet (psalm versifier) Roldanus of Enkhuijzen installed him as pastor of Hem on June 18, 1679.[27] Why did Van Varick choose such a small, obscure village? In the opinion of this author he had no alternative, due to the continued surplus of pastors in the Dutch Republic.[28] Hem was undoubtedly not Van Varick's first choice, but—after almost two years of seeking a call—the Dutch Reformed Church of Hem finally offered an opportunity for him to have a pulpit of his own, to start a family, and to recover from his health problems. For Margrieta, Hem also served as a haven after the death of her first husband and new marriage, as well as an opportunity to start a family of her own. For Rudolphus the new start in small and insignificant Hem was quite a change after living the city of Rhenen in Utrecht during his theological studies and at Mallaca far from the fatherland.

The oldest mention of Hem dates from 1312.[29] Hem was granted a charter on February 2, 1414.[30] Earl Willem VI of Holland gave Hem

[25] Krohn and Miller, *Dutch New York*, 342-63.
[26] UA, Register van Transfers of Rhenen. Catalogue Juridical Archives, n°. 516.
[27] Joh. Roldanus (±1619-1688), pastor in Enkhuizen since 1647; *BLGNP* I, 293; Joh. Roldanus, *De CL psalmen Davids, mitsgaders eenige andere gedichten ende lofsangen die men ook gewoon is in de Gereformeerde Kerken te singen, uyt de oorspronckelijke text, volgens den oversettinge des Bibels* (Enkuizen: Jan Dircksz Kuyper voor Hendrik van Straalen, 1685).
[28] Van Lieburg, *Profeten*.
[29] M. S. Pols, *Westfriesche stadrechten*, 2 vols. ('s Gravenhage: Nijhoff, 1885/1888).
[30] J. C. M. Cox, *Repertorium van de stadsrechten in Nederland* (Den Haag: VNG Uitgeverij, 2005), 133.

and the nearby village, Venhuizen, the privilege of being the *"Stede Hem"* [townships of Hem]. This meant the union of the twin villages as one jurisdiction, although they remained independent.[31] In 1630 Hem had 159 houses, and it took two hours to reach the town of Enkhuizen.[32] When the Van Varicks arrived in 1679, Hem had just recovered from the flood of 1675. Hem's connections to the wider world were almost exclusively limited to voyages made by its sailors and fishermen to Scandinavia. The St. Lucas church in which Van Varick preached had been built in the mid-fourteenth century, on top of the foundations of a tenth-century church.[33] The Reformed church of Hem had its first Reformed minister in 1573, Sibrandus Vomelius, and Van Varick became the fifteenth minister of this church.[34] One of his predecessors was the sixth pastor of Hem, Jonas Jansz. Michaëlius (1614-1624), who had subsequently become the first minister of New Amsterdam. Like Van Varick, Michaëlius is more often remembered for his service in North America than for his ministry in Hem.

While Hem seemed to be a remote corner for the Van Varicks, they enjoyed, early on, the company of Margrieta's sister Sara, who lived in Hem before she married Rudolphus's brother Jan. They received their marriage license on May 9, 1680,[35] and Rudolphus officiated at their wedding. They must have subsequently moved to Rhenen, Jan's residence, because their children were baptized there.[36] The family appears to have been close; indeed, it seems likely that Sara prepared the way in Hem for the couple.

The strong connection between Rudolphus and Margrieta and Jan and Sara van Varick deepened when Jan and Sara followed Rudolphus and his family to the New World. On July 1, 1687, they became members of the New York congregation. Their presence was an important point of continuity in Rudolphus's and Margrieta's new life. In fact, the children of Margrieta's late sister Dieuwertje and brother-in-law Abraham Davits also left the Republic and joined them, as did Van Varick's old friend, Samuel Meinerts, a glove maker from Utrecht, together with his wife Annichje Tenhage. Meinerts practiced the same profession in New York as he had in Utrecht. It was Meinerts to whom

---

[31] Cox, *Repertorium*, 33.
[32] A. J. van der Aa, *Aardrijkskundig woordenboek der Nederlanden*, 13 vols. (Gorinchem: J. Noorduyn, 1844), 5:410.
[33] J. Goesinnen, "Een stukje historie rond de verdwenen kerk van Hem," *West-Frieslands Oud en Nieuw* 45 (Hoorn: West-Friesland BV, 1978), 61-65.
[34] Van Lieburg, *Repertorium* 2, col. 143.
[35] http://www.genealogiezuidoostutrecht.org (checked on January 30, 2010).
[36] Jacobus (June 15, 1681), Margariet (June 13, 1683) and Cornelis (August 9, 1685).

Van Varick, years earlier, had given power of attorney in order to collect wages due him for his service as a naval chaplain.[37]

In addition to her sister's children, Margrieta's and Rudolphus's family grew. Not counting the accretions to their household from her sister's children, the couple had five children of their own. After the birth of Cornelia Hester (1680) and Johanna (1682) in Hem,[38] three more children were born in America: Marinus, Rudolphus, Jr., and Cornelia.[39] Marinus was probably born in 1686 on the ship to the New World and died in 1719. Rudolphus, Jr., was born about 1690, and another baby probably in 1693. As the first Cornelia had died, the newborn was also named Cornelia. The Van Varicks' daughters did particularly well. This (second) Cornelia married Barent de Kleyn on August 18, 1711, and after his death she married the famous goldsmith Peter van Dyck (1684-1750) on July 22, 1715. They had eleven children, among others a son who carried the name Rudolphus. Cornelia died in 1734. Johanna married Elbert Willett on May 13, 1701, in the Dutch Reformed Church of New York.[40] One of their grandchildren was Marinus Willett, mayor of New York City from 1807 to 1808.[41] He was named after his great-uncle Marinus van Varick. One of his and Margaret Bancker's four children became a minister, but not in the Dutch Reformed Church.

Long Island

The minutes of the consistory of the Dutch Reformed Church of Hem from 1679 to 1686 record Van Varick's installation and the names of new elders, deacons, and members, but contain no further details.[42] Perhaps nothing of note happened; in any case, Van Varick did not choose to keep records.

Whatever his motivation may have been, he presented himself in November 1685 to the Classis of Amsterdam to be recommended as pastor for New Netherland and was subsequently called.[43] Again he used

[37] UA, Notarial Acts of the City of Utrecht, inv. nr. U89 A1, aktenr. 31, April 9, 1672; UA, Notarial Acts of the City of Utrecht, inv. nr. U110 A1, aktenr. 109, November 27, 1683.

[38] Cornelia Hester was baptized on October 20, 1680. Johanna was baptized on December 20, 1682; WFA, DTB Hem 1637-1699, inv. nr. 2.

[39] Ruth Piwonka, "Margrieta Van Varick in the West: Inventory of a Life," Krohn and Miller, *Dutch New York*, 114 n15. WFA, Baptism Book 1637-1699, inv. nr. 2. The mother is called 'Grietje'. At the first baptism a sister of Grietje, Dieuwertje, was witness.

[40] Krohn and Miller, *Dutch New York*, xxi, 106, 212, 283, 307-25.

[41] Ibid., 330-31.

[42] WFA, Minutes of the Consistory of the Dutch Reformed Church of Hem 1653-1691, inv. nr. 2.

[43] SACDCA, November 12, 1685.

the strategy of requesting to be admitted as *recommandatus*. Apparently he and Margrieta were up for another international adventure and were ready to leave Hem after seven years. Perhaps it was not their aim to improve their situation in the Republic by finding a church in a bigger, more important and more prestigious town. Or, perhaps they had tried, but were not successful. We do, however, have one hint regarding their choice of a congregation on the other side of the Atlantic: one of Margrieta's maternal aunts, Sara Burgers, had sailed to New York with her husband Laurens Carstenszen in 1661.[44]

The Classis of Amsterdam left it to him to choose from among the pastorless congregations in the New World. The classis probably did so because it lacked a full understanding of the conditions there and could not adequately assess where Van Varick would be most helpful. Besides, there were more congregations than ministers. Yet, a letter of March 12, 1686, reveals that Van Varick was called to the congregations in Kings County on Long Island (Breukelen, New Amersfort, Utrecht, and Midwout).

Does the fact that the Van Varicks left Hem so quickly mean that they were eager to leave the Republic? The records do not contain any evidence of an emergency that would have prompted the Van Varicks to leave in a hurry. Unfortunately, neither the minutes of the consistory of the Dutch Reformed Church of Hem nor the acts of the Classis of Enkhuizen and the Classis of Amsterdam can help us to understand why the Van Varicks left so soon after the call from the church in the New World. We have to note that most probably Margrieta was great with child when she left Hem. Was Van Varick experiencing problems in the Dutch Reformed Church of Hem? Was Hem a too small world for him and his worldly wife? And/or was he at last completely recovered from his illness and feeling ready to start a new adventure?

The children of Margrieta's late sister Dieuwertje probably also set sail for the New World in March 1686. Margrieta's and Sara's sisters Engeltje and Aeltje made a long visit in 1688. The daughter of Dieuwertje, Maritje Abrahams, married Nicolas van Tienhoven on December 26, 1686, in Midwout/Flatbush,[45] with Rudolphus officiating.

By March of 1686 the Deputies for Indies' Affairs had already granted Rudolphus a dismissal from both the Dutch Reformed Church

---

[44] Krohn and Miller, *Dutch New York*, xviii and 51.
[45] David W. Voorhees, ed. and transl., *Records of the Reformed Protestant Dutch Church of Flatbush, Kings County, New York 1, 1677-1720* (New York: The Holland Society of New York, 1998), 256-57.

of Hem and the Classis of Enkhuizen.[46] In its meeting of April 1, 1686, the classis noted that Van Varick's dismissal and the call from *Nieuw Nederland* had already been executed and that he had already left.[47] The acts do not reveal whether the classical delegates or the deputies were unpleasantly surprised that things had not gone by the book.[48] Perhaps they were glad that the church in the New World would receive another Dutch Reformed minister.

Many authors have written that Van Varick started his ministry on Long Island in 1685, but this is incorrect. Only Corwin and Voorhees correctly give 1686 as the year in which Van Varick became pastor there.[49] Upon arrival in the beginning of July, after a three-month journey, he was asked to become pastor in Albany, but he thought it would be better to stay on Long Island, most probably because on Long Island he would receive a higher salary (900 guilders) and a new/renovated parsonage with free fire wood—and that his ministry was more needed on Long Island.[50]

The family lived in the parsonage in Midwout, where Peter Stuyvesant had established a Dutch Reformed Church in 1654. This village was comparable to Hem, with four hundred to five hundred inhabitants and was in an agricultural area.[51] Specialized craftsmen, such as wheelwrights, millers, and blacksmiths had come to live and work in Flatbush since about 1680, and in 1685 the English established Flatbush as the county seat of Kings County.

Dominie Petrus Tesschenmaecker,[52] the minister at Staten Island, had moved to Schenectady, so Van Varick preached and administered the Lord's Supper at Staten Island four times a year.[53] He also had the care of the congregation at Hackensack and took turns supplying the

---

[46] Stadsarchief Amsterdam (Municipal Archives of Amsterdam), Acta Classis Amsterdam (Acts Classis of Amsterdam), (hereafter cited as SAACA), March 12, 1686.
[47] SAACA, April 1, 1686.
[48] According to reformed church polity it should have been the consistory and the classis who were supposed to grant the dismissals.
[49] Corwin, *Manual*, 871-72; David W. Voorhees, "Flatbush in the Time of the Van Varicks," Krohn and Miller, *Dutch New York*, 83-96.
[50] SACDCA, September 9, 1686.
[51] A.J. van der Aa, *Aardrijkskundig Woordenboek der Nederlanden* (Gorinchem: Noorduijn, 1851) 5:410; Voorhees, "Flatbush," 84-86.
[52] Petrus Tesschenmaecker (ca. 1642-1690), pastor Kingston NY 1678, New Amstel DE, Staten Island NY & Bergen NJ 1679-1682, First Schenectady NY 1682-1690, Hackensack NJ 1686-1687; Gasero, *Historical Records*, 392. See also Dirk Mouw's article on Tesschenmaecker.
[53] SLAC, Letter Van Varick to the Amsterdam Classis, September 9, 1686.

South River (New Amstel/New Castle) congregation in Delaware.[54] That meant that Van Varick was not only a local pastor but also traveled to other places to serve congregations there.

From Peace to Civil War

Van Varick had an ecumenical spirit. He was willing to cooperate with people of other denominations, but the Leisler Rebellion thwarted his efforts. He wrote in 1688 to the Classis of Amsterdam that he lived in peace with his congregation.[55] He told the classis about the calm ecclesiastical conditions before the rebellion: there were eight English pastors—Episcopalians, Presbyterians, and Independents—and they all lived in peace with each other. The French congregation grew daily with people who arrived from Europe and the Caribbean. He had had three peaceful years there and had a constructive relationship with his colleague and friend Henricus Selijns, pastor at New York,[56] who also enjoyed a life that suited his ecumenical and irenic spirit.

Like Gideon Schaats, Petrus Tesschenmaecker, and Henricus Selijns, Van Varick became a mediator in the conflict involving a Kingston pastor, Laurentius van den Bosch.[57] What started as a controversy in a congregation whose minister was surrounded by allegations of drunkenness, sexual harassment, and spousal abuse, developed into an ecclesiastical problem: how should the church in the New World deal with the immorality of one of its ministers? To make matters even worse, Leisler's Rebellion also became a factor. Van den Bosch was suspended by his consistory, but the quarrels and recriminations continued. Rumors about Van den Bosch spread throughout the colony and threatened the standing of the church, but the incident also challenged the power of ecclesiastical authorities. Because of the uncertainties caused by Leisler's Rebellion, no legal proceedings were taken against the wayward minister.

Several pastors at different stages tried to bring about reconciliation. Despite the joint efforts of church leaders Schaats, Selijns, Tesschenmaecker, Van Varick, and elders in their own (and Van den Bosch's) congregations, they could not—either by themselves or together—resolve the case. Because his resignation was not according to Reformed Church polity, Van den Bosch's resignation revealed the vulnerability of the young colonial church and its pastors. Van den Bosch should have addressed himself to the Classis of Amsterdam because no

---

[54] SLAC, Letter Van Varick to the Amsterdam Classis, September 30, 1688.
[55] SLAC, Letter Van Varick to the Amsterdam Classis, September 30 1688.
[56] SLAC, Letter Selijns to the Classis of Amsterdam, September 20, 1686.
[57] See also Evan Haefeli's biography on Van den Bosch.

minister, once ordained for a lifetime, was allowed to withdraw himself from the office (Art. 12 of the *1619 Dortian Church Order*).[58]

Selijns appears to have been chief among the clerical mediators in the Van den Bosch affair, but Van Varick played a role as well, and his words reveal much about his character. Van den Bosch quoted Selijns in his August 6, 1689, letter as having described Van Varick as "an irenic man and mild." The correspondence surrounding the Van den Bosch case suggests that Selijns was right. Van Varick received copies of much of the correspondence between his colleagues and Van den Bosch. On August 16, 1689, Van Varick wrote that although he had received several letters regarding this case, he had not answered them because he was uncertain how to proceed. He wrote Van den Bosch that his letter " is written with a very harsh pen" and " do you not have yet, reverend, enough enemies?" Rather than simply taking note of the rumors and insinuations swirling about his fellow minister, Van Varick stated them as fact, imploring Van den Bosch to turn away from such sinful behavior. He also warned Van den Bosch about blaming and accusing Selijns. Above all, "my father" wrote Van Varick, "be neither too proud, nor too confident about your case." Despite the very different roles and approaches of Selijns and Van Varick in the Van den Bosch affair, it is evident that their esteem and affection for each other only grew. The fact that Selijns's last will, dated November 13, 1700, bequeathed the amount of 200 guilders to Rudolphus Van Varick, Jr., and his siblings can be seen as evidence of their warm and lasting relationship.[59]

Van Varick welcomed Lutherans and Roman Catholics as members of his congregation. The classis rejoiced about this and expressed the hope on August 22, 1689, "that all these churches (the congregations on Long Island) under your ministry may also increase; and not only in numbers, but also in faith and in the power of true godliness." On November 30, 1689, however, Van Varick wrote the classis that he longed for a meeting with colleagues regarding the newly dangerous times. The Leisler's Rebellion, 1689-1691, had begun to disrupt the peace.[60]

---

[58] Selijns to Van den Bosch, quoted in Van den Bosch to Selijns, August 6, 1689; Van Varick to Van den Bosch, August, 16 1689, "Letters about Dominie Vandenbosch, 1689," Frederick Ashton de Peyster mss., Box 2 #8, New-York Historical Society, New York, NY.

[59] Abstracts of Unrecorded Wills, 11, prior to 1790, 6-7; http:/archiver.rootsweb.ancestry.com/th/read/Dutch-Colonies/1998-11/0911089627

[60] David W. Voorhees, "Dutch Political Identity in English New York," Hans Krabbendam, Cornelis A. van Minnen and Giles Scott-Smith, eds., *Four Centuries of Dutch-American Relations 1609-2009* (Albany/Amsterdam: State University of New York Press/Boom, 2009), 132-42.

The rebellion cannot be understood apart from the Dutch political and theological context. When William III invaded England as Prince of Orange, he replaced the Roman Catholic king, James III. As a result of this "Glorious Revolution," rebellions erupted in the Middle Colonies and mobs replaced the king's appointees with others. Just as in the Dutch Republic, factionalism arose in the colonies between adherents of the *Raadpensionaris*—the principal representative of the town regents—on the one hand and the Organists, the supporters of the *Stadhouder*—or provisional military commander-in-chief—on the other. The first group aligned with Leiden theologian Johannes Coccejus, who stood for a covenantal theology with less stringent approaches to matters such as biblical hermeneutics and moral codes. The principal theological representative of the other group was Gisbertus Voetius, professor at Utrecht University, where Rudolphus had studied. Voetius emphasized scholastic theology and a pietistic Christian life. Dellius, Selijns, and Van Varick opposed this pietistic movement, being more in favor of a Coccejan approach.

Jacob Leisler (1640-1691) was a prominent merchant, a large landholder, and a political ideologue. Yet, he was an Orangist and an exponent of late-seventeenth-century Reformed orthodoxy.[61] Born into a prominent German Calvinist family, Leisler was a zealous defender and promoter of Calvinist orthodoxy and pietist theology on colonial soil. He assumed the role of governor of New York from 1689 to 1691. As he took over the New York government, he led the revolt against British officials and other pro-English inhabitants, seizing Fort James on Manhattan Island in order to hold it for the new governor, whom he expected would be appointed by the new king. Leisler's administration resulted in two distinct factions, comparable to the supporters of the Regent and the Organists in the Netherlands and the Whigs and the Tories in England. Some scholars are of the opinion that the rebellion was a forerunner of the American Revolution. The rebellion was not only about politics but had economic, social, cultural, and religious dimensions as well, leading to a bitter struggle between the factions. When King William III appointed the royal governor, Henry Sloughter, for the colony, Leisler refused to cede authority to Mayor Richard Ingoldsby. Leisler and his son-in-law were tried for treason and executed on May 16, 1691.

Initially, Van Varick supported Leisler, and things would have gone much differently for him if had he continued to do so. He would

---

[61] http://www.nyu.edu/leisler

have received the support of the majority of his congregation as well as that of Leisler himself. One must be careful, however, when practicing counterfactual history. If Van Varick had continued to support Leisler, he would have found himself in a great deal of trouble in the aftermath of the rebellion. In any event, Van Varick did come to oppose Leisler, warning Leislerians against unjust wrath and violence. Was that not something pastors were supposed to do?

Ecclesiastical Journey

In June 1690 Van Varick took advantage of an opportunity to fulfill an agreement to preach along the Delaware River, traveling to Philadelphia and on to New Castle. According to his letter to the Classis of Amsterdam of September 30, 1688, Van Varick and Selijns had begun taking turns serving the Reformed people on the Delaware.[62] On his way to Philadelphia he came across a man by the name of Captain Israel, who asked him to become a Lutheran pastor. He also traveled through a Dutch village near Philadelphia with forty-four families—twenty-eight Quaker and sixteen Reformed. The Lutherans, Mennonites, Roman Catholics—and everyone who opposed the Quakers—were meeting together that Sunday to hear an Amsterdam Mennonite, Dirck Keyser, read a sermon. By this time Van Varick believed the Quakers had infected some simple minds of his flock.[63] During his trip to the Delaware, however, he found hospitality in Jacob Tellner's house. Telner and Van Varick, who had been opponents earlier, had become friends.[64] A few months after his arrival in the New World Van Varick had written to the Classis of Amsterdam that Telner had Van Varick preach three times and administer the Lord's Supper at New Castle, where there was a small congregation of Dutch, Swedish, and Finnish people.[65]

When Van Varick returned in the late summer of 1690, his life would never be the same. Indeed, by the time of his return, a transformation was well underway in his community, one wrought by Leisler's Rebellion and as baffling to historians as it seems to have been to Van Varick himself. The pietist schoolmaster Johannes van

---

[62] SLAC, Letter Van Varick to the Amsterdam Classis, April, 9 1693.
[63] SLAC, Letter Van Varick to the Classis of Amsterdam, September 9, 1686.
[64] A. Eekhof, *De Hervormde Kerk in Noord-Amerika, 1624-1664*, 2 vols. ('s Gravenhage: Nijhoff, 1913), 2:88-89; W. I. Hull, *William Penn and the Dutch Quaker Migration to Pennsylvania*, (Swarthmore: Swarthmore College, 1935), 239-53.
[65] http:/www.hanoverchurch.org [based on the work of James L. Latchum; July 30, 2009].

Eeckelen[66] and colonel Gerardus Beekman accused him of high treason. They were part of a group that dragged him out of his house and threw him into prison. Van Eeckelen had been appointed as schoolmaster in Flatbush on October 1, 1682, and had begun teaching on May 1, 1683.[67] He had already worked there for four years when Van Varick arrived. In fact he was more than a schoolmaster. He was a *voorlezer* (church reader), a position that also included the duties of song leader and sexton.[68] His predecessors, Jan Gerritsz. van Markken (1681-1681) and Jan Thibaud (1681-1682), had worked as *voorlezers* for a short time. Van Markken had been discharged for various misdeeds. Among other things he had slandered Van Varick's predecessor, Casparus van Zuuren, who had been pastor from 1677 to 1685.[69] Thibaud had been charged with drunkenness and with molesting several women in Flatbush.[70] It was not unusual for *voorlezers* to experience difficulties with their congregations; conflict with ministers was particularly common, and *voorlezers* did have a special and important role in congregations. Although Van Eeckelen had already worked for four years with Van Varick, it was not until 1690, during the Leisler's Rebellion, that their relationship soured. In 1691 the consistory dismissed the Leislerian Van Eeckelen because he had mistreated Van Varick, then appointed Johannes Schenck in his place. Van Eeckelen fought back and won the support of the majority of the town. In 1694 he once again became schoolmaster, but in 1699 he again lost that position to Schenck. These events demonstrate that Leisler's Rebellion had divided the town, the congregation, and the consistory in complex but profound ways that even manifested themselves in ostensibly contradictory decisions about *voorlezers* and schoolmasters. The situation in the congregation of Flatbush had become complicated, especially for Van Varick.

After being arrested, treated with cruelty, and dragged out of his house, Van Varick was put into prison for five months and deposed from his ministerial functions. He was also fined eighty pounds. Selijns tried to make bail for him but was not allowed to do so. The records do

---

[66] E. Nooter, *Between Heaven and Earth: Church and Society in Pre-Revolutionary Flatbush, Long Island* (Amsterdam: n.p. 1994); W. H. Kilpatrick, *The Dutch Schools of New Netherland and Colonial New York* (Washington: Government Printing Office, 1912); J. M. Murrin, "English Rights as Ethnic Aggression: The English Conquest, the Charter of Liberties of 1683, and Leisler's Rebellion in New York," in W. Pencak and C. E. Wright, eds., *Authority and Resistance in Early New York* (New York: Historical Society of New York, 1988), 56-94.
[67] Voorhees, *Records*, 127, 134, 240, 368 and 453.
[68] Ibid., 126-30.
[69] Ibid., 101-15.
[70] Ibid., 67, 71-79, 84-89, 117-26.

not tell why Rudolphus or Margrieta did not or could not pay this. Was it because Margrieta had already fled, or that they did not have enough money by that time? Van Varick's cell did not have closed windows, as did the cells of the others, and was not underground. He was not tied up and shared his imprisonment with a French captain, from whom he learned French.

According to Van Varick, the accusations against him had arisen because he had warned his neighbor, elder Beekman, to stop doing vicious things to decent citizens.[71] According to the less sympathetic reports of his opponents, there was more going on.[72] They said that Van Varick had accused Leisler in a sermon of being "a usurper of the office." Apparently at first Van Varick had been pro-Leisler. Did he identify with the pietistic Leisler? Van Varick had, after all, studied under Gisbertus Voetius at the University of Utrecht. At some point he must have changed his mind. A man with Van Varick's irenic spirit must have detested the way Leisler's Rebellion had developed and the way people had expressed their rage. He was suspected of "conspiring to seize the fort in New York," whereupon he was arrested and released upon his submission to Leisler. Later on, according to these unsympathetic sources, he stated that he had favored the execution of Leisler, had delivered intolerable sermons against him, and had even cherished animosity toward him until his dying day.

Van Varick's greatest fear was being murdered while in prison, but he did not reveal who he feared in this respect. He had already lost everything, but now he also feared for his life. Margrieta fled with everything she had because she was constantly threatened with being robbed. Their inventory reveals that they possessed many luxurious articles and therefore had a lot to lose. They also owned the sixth part of a sloop, the *Flying Fish*. Additionally, Margrieta had a shop on Long Island to augment her husband's salary. The wealth suggested by their luxurious possessions notwithstanding, they felt that this step was necessary because a substantial part of Rudolphus's salary went unpaid. By opening a shop, Margrieta tried to close the budgetary gap.

---

[71] Gerardus Beekman (1653-1723); Voorhees, *Records*; Krohn and Miller, *Dutch New York*, 213-15.

[72] Henry R. Stiles, *A History of the City of Brooklyn* 1 (Brooklyn: 1867). Facsimile reprint (Bowie: Heritage Books, 1993), 169 footnote 149 and 169 especially footnote 1 on 169; E. B. O'Callaghan, ed., *Documents relative to the Colonial History of the State of New-York*, procured in Holland, England and France by J. R. Broadhead (Albany: Weed, Parsons and Company, 1854), vol. 2, 431 and 432; Nooter, *Between*, 62 n173; Murrin, "English Rights," 56-94.

Selijns wrote the Classis of Amsterdam in September 1690 that he and Van Varick suffered from the hostility of Leisler's adherents due to the rebellion.[73] The esteem they had earlier enjoyed in their congregations had evaporated. They—especially Van Varick—had suffered emotionally and spiritually in their church life and faith. Together with Dellius of Albany they wrote a letter to the Classis of Amsterdam in October 1692.[74] They described what they had endured during the rebellion, detailing in particular everything Van Varick had gone through. Their complaints and pleas were numerous. Noteworthy among them was Van Varick's plea to be transferred elsewhere "because here one cannot live." A half year later he wrote the classis that he needed "safe accommodation."[75] In so writing, Van Varick was not only referring to the strained relations between himself and members of his congregation, but also to the impact the rebellion had had on his income.[76] Although it was not uncommon in those days in the New World for pastors not to receive the salary that had been promised them when they were called, in this specific situation it had everything to do with the Leisler's Rebellion. Many dissatisfied churchgoers withheld the sums they had pledged toward his salary. Even the British magistrate, Governor Fletcher, stepped in to help by requiring Van Varick to report the names of those who had left the congregation, thus frightening people into paying his salary. At this time only one quarter of the church members were attending services. This number subsequently doubled, but many still wanted nothing to do with their minister.[77] The congregations on Staten Island and Hackensack no longer invited him into their pulpits. Only in Bergen did he remain welcome; he preached there on June 11, 1692.[78]

The final years of Van Varick's life were generally unhappy, yet he did have a few reasons for optimism. After his release the court ordered the arrears of salary due him by his congregation to be compelled if necessary.[79] He was a free man, but the imprisonment and the attitude of some of his congregants had hurt him, and he carried this bad

[73] SLAC, Letter Selijns to the Amsterdam Classis, September 14, 1690.
[74] SLAC, Letter Selijns, Dellius and Van Varick to the Amsterdam Classis, October 12, 1692.
[75] SLAC, Letter Van Varick to the Amsterdam Classis, April 9, 1693.
[76] In 1688: 995 guilders and 5 stuivers, in 1690 523 guilders and 18 stuivers, in 1693 747 guilders and 16 stuivers; Krohn and Miller, *Dutch New York*, 204-05.
[77] Benjamin Fletcher (1640-1703) was governor of New York from 1692-1697.
[78] D. Versteeg and T. E. Vermilye jr., ed. and translation, *Bergen Records: Records of the Reformed Protestant Dutch Church of Bergen in New Jersey 1666 to 1788* (facsimile print; Bowie: Heritage Books, 1997), 67.
[79] Council Minutes 6 55; 2; Stiles, *History*, 169; Corwin, *Manual*, 1879, 531.

experience with him until his death. Although the letter of October 1693 shows that Van Varick suffered very much, he also wrote that his family was in good health.[80] The Classis of Amsterdam discussed his letter three months later[81] and expressed its happiness that Van Varick was no longer imprisoned. A half year later[82] the classis responded to his request by instructing the deputies to keep him in mind when looking for candidates to fill vacant colonial pulpits. According to Selijns, an effort had been made to have Van Varick become the new pastor in Esopus.[83] Selijns mentioned that "they" made an attempt, but he does not reveal who "they" were. Perhaps they were Selijns, the governor, and/or the consistory of New York. In any case, the effort was not successful, and Van Varick stayed on Long Island. On April 9, 1693, Van Varick wrote that the love among the members of the congregation and between him and the congregation was diminished because of the change in government.[84]

Death

The situation in Van Varick's congregation in the autumn of 1693 was not good. Many members no longer attended church services,[85] and the pastor was deprived of part of his salary (300 pounds). Although the members were no longer as hostile as they once had been, the relationship between the congregation and Van Varick would never be the same as before. In his letter of October 7, 1694, Dellius had to inform the Classis of Amsterdam that Rudolphus van Varick had died on September 24.[86] He was buried three days later.[87] Dellius was right when he concluded that Van Varick had not found any peace in his congregation during his last four years of life. According to Bertholf's letter of May 15, 1695, to the Classis of Walcheren, hardly anyone was

[80] SLAC, Letter Rudolphus Van Varick to a friend, October 13, 1693.
[81] SACDCA, July 27, 1693.
[82] SACDCA, April 6, 1693.
[83] "Sy hadden getracht syn E[erwaarde, LvdB] te verplaetsen ind[e] Esopus, denkende, dat syn gemeinte doort schryven vanden Governeur meest tot ruste gebracht zyn gewerden;" SACDCA, Acts Deputies for Indies' Affairs, inv. nr. 158, Extract letter Selijns to the Classis of Amsterdam, December, 30, 1692.
[84] SLAC, Letter Van Varick to the Classis of Amsterdam, April 9, 1693.
[85] SLAC, Letter Van Varick to the Classis of Amsterdam, October 13, 1693.
[86] SLAC, Letter Dellius to the Classis of Amsterdam, October 1 or 7, 1694. W. J. van Varik was wrong by writing August as the month in which Rudolphus died; W. J. van Varik, "Nog eens het geslacht van Vari(c)k," *De Nederlandsche Leeuw* 71 (1954): 187.
[87] SLAC, Letter Selijns to the Classis of Amsterdam, November 14, 1694.

in tears regarding "the pastor of Long Island."[88] Bertholf did not even mention the name of the deceased. Five members of the congregation of the Dutch Reformed Church of New York wrote four years after the death of Van Varick that he had been "much affected to Cap. J. L. (Jacob Leisler's) execution and made intolerable sermons and died without the least reconciliation."[89] It is striking that the funeral and burial took place not on Long Island, but in Manhattan. Among those who attended the funeral were Governor Fletcher and the governor's council. A committee from the churches in King's County, Long Island (Amersfort, Breuckelen, Midwout, and New Utrecht) wrote the Classis of Amsterdam on May 7, 1695, that God "in his wise providence" had taken Van Varick and that "our church is thus deprived of his faithful service."[90] Almost a year after his death Van Varick was commemorated in a meeting of the Classis of Amsterdam. In its eyes he had been a pastor "in the fear of the Lord."[91]

Conclusion

It was not feelings of homesickness that prompted Rudolphus Van Varick to ask the Amsterdam Classis in 1692 to be transferred from Long Island; otherwise he would have asked for a one-way ticket to the Dutch Republic. Besides, the middle colonies were not his first foreign residence. Van Varick was not only minister of the Word; he was a minister of the world. He was eager to travel and serve the Lord in distant places outside the Republic. Neither the battle at Solebay nor his illness and repatriation diminished his longing to see more of the world. To achieve that end, he repeatedly used the strategy of seeking the status of *recommandatus* from ecclesiastical assemblies. It was this strategy and Van Varick's wanderlust that took him to Long Island, where he put his international experience to use. He had been naval chaplain, pastor in the Dutch East Indies, and pastor at Hem, in the Province of North Holland. Rudolphus must have enjoyed a luxurious and peaceful life together with Margrieta in Malacca (if they were married there), in Hem, and later on in Flatbush. Margrieta's

---

[88] Middelburg, Zeeuws Archief, Classis of Walcheren, East (sic!) Indies Correspondence, inv. nr. 68, Letter Classis of Walcheren to Guillam Bertholf, May 15, 1695.
[89] *Documents Relative to the Colonial History of the State of New York*, 4, 219. Those five men were Johannes Van Giesen, David Provoost Jr., Johannes De Peyster, Jacobus Goelet, and Albartus Ringo.
[90] SLAC, Letter of the committee of the churches in King's County, Long Island, to the Classis of Amsterdam, May 7, 1695.
[91] SAACA, September 5, 1695.

"inventory" presents an impressive list of possessions, including many items that were expensive and precious. As a minister, he must have enjoyed his preaching, pastoral, and teaching duties more than he liked tasks associated with ecclesiastical administration. Yet, he remained a dedicated traveler between the East and West. Hem appears to have been a haven, an extended layover between East and West, chosen most probably for health reasons and the opportunity to start a family in a tranquil setting. On Long Island Rudolphus and Margrieta continued their way of life, albeit under different circumstances.

Their happiness and peace lasted only three years, however. Although he had international experience, Van Varick was not prepared for the problems he faced on Long Island during Leisler's Rebellion. He appears to have fallen victim to an alignment of political and ecclesiastical tensions and was unable to cultivate a diplomatic style of leadership and ecclesiastical administration. One is left to wonder whether Van Varick was merely the victim of an unfortunate alignment of political and ecclesiastical tensions in the New World or whether tragedy came to him because he maneuvered himself naïvely within that hornet's nest. Indeed, Van Varick's actions during the rebellion are both revealing and puzzling. At first he supported Jacob Leisler, but later on—due to his fears about the way the uprising was developing, as well as through the influence of his colleague Selijns—Van Varick changed his mind. Thus, Van Varick, who had been a student of Voetius, later turned against the Voetius-minded Leislerians, instead siding with the anti-Leislerians who were supporters of the more liberal Coccejus. The crisis exposed not only Van Varick's vulnerability, but also the vulnerability of the church, the society, and the political system.

Near the end of his life he asked the Classis of Amsterdam to transfer him. To be sure, that request shows that Van Varick hoped to flee and get away from the problems on Long Island, but it also demonstrates that he was willing to serve the Lord in another distant church, far away from the Republic. Van Varick was not, however, successful, and he died in the autumn of 1694 at the age of forty-nine. Did he never fully recover from the severe impact of Leisler's Rebellion on his health, as he wrote? Or had his health remained fragile since his time in the Dutch East Indies? It seems clear, in any event, that he was unable to cope with the effects of Leisler's Rebellion on his ecclesiastical work and on his private life. Yet, we would be misjudging him if we viewed him only as a casualty of the rebellion or as a pastor who maneuvered himself into trouble. He was more than a victim and a naïve pastor. He was also the single and promising young naval chaplain and a pastor in the Dutch

East Indies who sailed to ports around the world. Similarly, when examining his role in the Van den Bosch case, it would be easy merely to call him ineffective. It should be noted, however, that a satisfactory resolution to the problems created by that Kingston pastor eluded his colleagues as well, both individually and collectively. Moreover, Van Varick's letters demonstrate that although he was an irenic and mild man, he did not hesitate to take a stand against Van den Bosch and dared to confront and warn him.

It is nevertheless a fact that his personal and pastoral legacies are dominated and overshadowed by the effects of the troublesome years of the Leisler's Rebellion. The earthly tranquility that Van Varick, as a peace-loving, ecumenical, and dedicated traveler, had sought and at the beginning of his Long Island years had enjoyed, was disrupted. This "Pastor ecclesiae Belgicae" made a number of adventurous moves in his life, and his story shows that in so doing he was taking serious risks.

CHAPTER 8

Guiliam Bertholf (1656-1726): Irenic Dutch Pietiest in New Jersey and New York

Earl Wm. Kennedy

Dominie Guiliam Bertholf, the first resident Dutch Reformed minister in New Jersey, served the twin congregations of Acquackanonk (Passaic) and Hackensack from 1694 to 1724. He also founded or supplied many churches in northern New Jersey and southeastern New York, in addition to being a reputed forerunner of the Great Awakening among the Dutch Reformed there. Bertholf's New Jersey ministry began in controversy, however, because New York's Reformed ministers regarded him as an unqualified interloper and his pietism as divisive; but his tireless, irenic labors eventually overcame the initial prejudice against him.[1]

---

[1] Thanks to Leon van den Broeke, Firth Fabend, Russell Gasero, the late Howard Hageman, Willem op 't Hof, Leo Hollestelle, Hans Krabbendam, Fred van Lieburg, Dirk Mouw, Huib Plankeel, and Huib Uil for assistance with this article. The most recent overall treatment of Bertholf is Firth Haring Fabend, "Bertholf, Guiliam," in *American National Biography* (New York, Oxford University Press, 1999), 2:693-94; also note the George Olin Zabriskie file (1976), based on J. Grooten's research in Middelburg on Bertholf, at Gardner Sage Library, New Brunswick Theological Seminary.

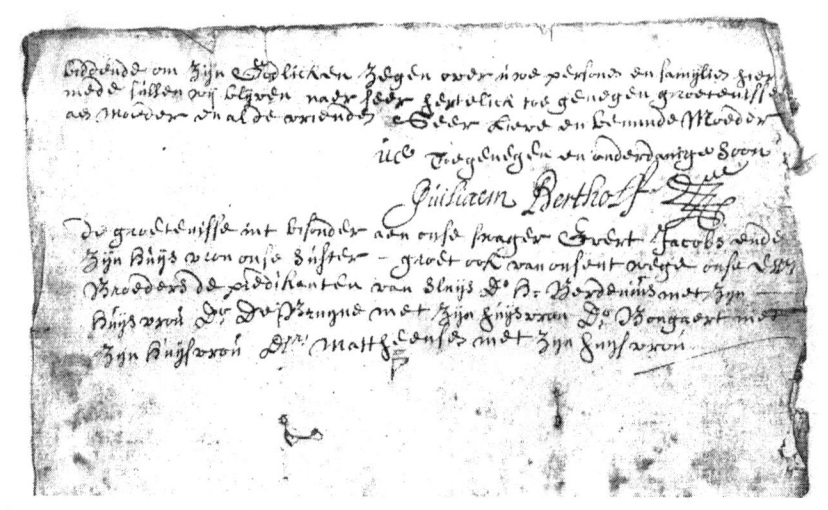

Signature of Guiliam Bertholf.
[picture by author]

Pietist Formation

Bertholf was born in Sluis, in Zeelandic Flanders (*Zeeuws Vlaanderen*), a garrison town and defensive bulwark near the coast on the southern edge of the Protestant Dutch Republic, bordering the Spanish Netherlands (now Belgium). The town's predominantly Reformed character was reinforced during the seventeenth century by Flemish, Walloon, and French refugees.

Around 1672, when Bertholf was a teenager, Louis XIV's armies threatened the northern Netherlands, including Sluis, which experienced then a religious revival.[2] During the mid-1600s the town had a series of Reformed pastors promoting the *Nadere Reformatie* ("Further Reformation," sometimes called Dutch pietism). These pastors included Jodocus van Lodenstein (1650-1652) and Jacobus Koelman (1662-1675), both students of the Utrecht professor Gisbertus Voetius, a champion of the Synod of Dort as well as of the *Nadere Reformatie*. Pietism was indebted to British Puritanism and was characterized by religious seriousness, emphasis on conversion, holy living, church discipline, and "conventicles" for Bible study, prayer, and

---

[2] A. Eekhof, "Jacobus Koelman te Sluis en de 'Nadere reformatie' in Zeeland," *Nederlandsch Archief voor Kerkgeschiedenis* 14 (1918): 201-09.

testimony. It aimed to deepen and apply the Reformation in the daily lives of ordinary church members and in the larger society as well.[3]

This intense piety was sometimes viewed by the Reformed establishment as disruptive and divisive, as in the case of the followers of Jean de Labadie, a Walloon Reformed pastor in Middelburg, Zeeland, until 1669, when he was deposed and the "Labadists" seceded from the "impure" Dutch Reformed Church. The presence of a few of them in the New World shortly before Bertholf's arrival made New York's clergy more apprehensive about religious enthusiasts, although Koelman repudiated both Labadism and separatism.

Jacobus Koelman (1631-1695) was the most educated, prolific, and confrontational of Sluis's pietist co-pastors during Bertholf's youth. Koelman's reforms included impassioned preaching of repentance, rigorous congregational oversight, protest against public sins, "prophetic" criticism of the policy and lifestyle of the authorities, pleas for keeping Sunday holy, and abolishing various nonbiblical "papist remnants," e.g., observing Christmas, Easter, and Pentecost. By 1673 Koelman started omitting the Dort-appointed prayers and formulas for the sacraments in public worship, substituting his own explanations and free prayers. Therefore the civil rulers forbade him in 1674 to preach or administer the sacraments. Because he refused to cease all religious activities, including conventicles (secret meetings for worship not sanctioned by law), he was banned in 1675 from Sluis and the Generality Lands (border areas directly ruled by the States General in the Hague).[4]

Koelman moved to Amsterdam, where he conducted (forbidden) conventicles from 1676 to 1691. Among his adversaries in the Classis of Amsterdam was its clerk, the Reverend Henricus Selijns (1636-1701), earlier a minister in New Netherland, who would return in 1682 to what had become New York.[5] There he would clash with

[3] Joel Beeke, *Assurance of Faith: Calvin, English Puritanism, and the Dutch Second Reformation* (New York: Peter Lang, 1991), 383-401; James Tanis, *Dutch Calvinistic Pietism in the Middle Colonies: A Study in the Life of Theodorus Jacobus Frelinghuysen* (The Hague: Nijhoff, 1967), 1-8, 44-46. F. A. van Lieburg, *Levens van vromen: gereformeerd piëtisme in de achttiende eeuw* (Kampen: De Groot Goudriaan, 1991), 179-87; W. J. op 't Hof, "De Nadere Reformatie in Zeeland . . . ," in A. Wiggers, ed., *Rond de kerk in Zeeland* (Delft: Eburon, 1991), 37-82.

[4] D. Nauta, "Labadie, Jean de," and "Koelman, Jacobus," in *Biografisch lexicon voor de geschiedenis van het Nederlandse protestantisme* (Kampen: Kok, 1983, 1988), 2:293-97, and 3:212-19.

[5] A. P. G. Jos van der Linde, eds., "Henricus Selijns (1636-1701), Dominee, dichter en historicus in Nieuw-Nederland en de Republiek," in J. F. Heijbroek, A. Lammers, and A. P. G. Jos van der Linde, *Geen schepsel wordt vergeten. Liber amicorum voor Jan*

Bertholf, whom he understandably took to be a "Koelmanist," since Bertholf came from Sluis, shared some of Koelman's views, and sought ordination "irregularly." Bertholf, however, might conceivably have also been influenced by David Montanus (c.1630-1687), the longest serving (1656-1687) and ablest of Koelman's colleagues at Sluis, whose pietism, less radical than Koelman's, escaped the authorities' ire.[6]

Guiliam Bertholf was baptized February 20, 1656, in Sluis's St. Jan's Church, the seventh of eleven children of Crijn Bertholf, a barrel-maker and master wine-seller, with roots in Sluis, and Sara Guiliamse van Coperen, daughter of a magistrate's officer in Rotterdam, where they married and Crijn learned the cooper's trade.[7]

Guiliam Bertholf probably received his primary education from his mother's sister's husband, Regaert van de Vijver, who moved from Rotterdam to Sluis in 1661. The instruction included not only reading, etc., but the Lord's Prayer, Apostles' Creed, Ten Commandments, Heidelberg Catechism, and the Psalter, thereby reinforcing the preaching and family devotions to which Guiliam was exposed in the religiously charged atmosphere of Sluis. This education was evidently sufficient for him to become a schoolmaster in rural New Jersey.[8]

Willem Schulte Nordholt (Amsterdam/Zuthpen: Trouw/Terra, 1985), 37-60; A. Eekhof, "Jacobus Koelman, zijn verblijf in Amsterdam en zijn beroep naar Noord-Amerika, II," *Nederlandsch Archief voor Kerkgeschiedenis* 11 (1914/1915):19n.

[6] Montanus was pastor at Sluis for all of Bertholf's life there, whereas Koelman served that church for only thirteen of those twenty-eight years. A. Ros, "David Montanus. Stichelijke dichter tussen Renaissance en Nadere Reformatie," in *Nadere Reformatie en literatuur, Documentatieblad Nadere Reformatie* 19.1 (1995):37-40, 58; Op't Hof, "De Nadere Reformatie in Zeeland," 11.

[7] David Cole, *History of the Reformed Church of Tappan, N. Y.* (New York: Stettiner, Lambert & Co., 1894), 8-9. Cole, once the main (albeit flawed) source for Bertholf, is still valuable because he used the Sluis church registers, destroyed in World War II. Email information W. J. op 't Hof to author, February 8 and Marc 3, 2009. For the paternal ancestry of Bertholf and more details about his father, see Zabriskie Bertholf file (note 1 above). Rotterdam Reformed Church baptisms, marriages, and burials, and Rotterdam notarial archive. www.gemeentearchief.rotterdam.nl/content/index.php?option=com_content&task=view&id=14&Itemid=56. The Van Coperens could have been of French extraction, as the name Guiliam (a Dutch variant of "Guillaume") suggests. "Van Coperen" may derive from "le Copen," in Sanghen, south of Calais, and have originally been "Van Cop[p]ehem" or "Van Copehen"; Email information Huib J. Plankeel to author, February 8, 2010. Guiliam Bertholf's first and last names were variously spelled in the records, but he signed "Guiliaem Bertholf."

[8] Rotterdam Reformed Church marriages. www.gemeentearchief.rotterdam.nl/content/index.php?option=com_content&task=view&id=14&Itemid=56; Reformed Church members, Sluis, 1658-1700, inv. 337.1, no. 147, Zeeland Archives, Middelburg. http://www.grijsbaard.nl/Sluis/LidmatenSluis3.html; email information Huib Uil (based on Sluis Reformed Church records, from doctoral

Crijn Bertholf participated in community and church affairs (as militia officer and as deacon) and prospered modestly, living at the harbor (suitable for his business); but in 1675 he was drowned at sea off nearby Cadzand, leaving the family in debt.[9] A year later, Guiliam, at the early age of twenty, married Martijntje Hendriks.[10] She had then been a communicant member of the Sluis congregation for over a year, whereas Guiliam became this in 1677, just before their first child's baptism.[11]

The couple remained in Sluis for eight years, during which time their first three children were baptized (five others would be born in New Jersey). Guiliam bought a bakery in 1679, his mother died in 1682, and he served as a deacon for a two-year term ending December 1683.[12] On May 7, 1684, the consistory gave the Bertholfs letters of transfer "to New Netherland"; two days later they sold their house in Sluis to Guiliam's older sister.[13] They may well have set sail the same month.

Move to the New World

The main reason for the Bertholfs' move may have been that Guiliam thought that he could more easily employ his gifts, as a layman aspiring to church work, in the needy hinterland in America than in Sluis; possibly he already knew people in New Jersey.

In any case, several factors—particularly the personal and theological links between the region of his birth and that of his ministry—provide some context, if not precedent, for the Bertholfs' transplantation. In 1682 Koelman himself was called to pastor the Dutch in New Castle, Delaware. He had hoped to go there with about two hundred fifty of his followers, but, partly through the pressure of the New York Reformed authorities, including Selijns, he did not

---

studies on Zeeland schoolmasters, 1576-1806) to author, January 18, 2010; "Schoolreglement 1655 (Generaliteitslanden)." http://de-wit.net/bronnen/histo/schoolreglement_generaliteit_1655.htm.

[9] Op't Hof research in the notarial archive, etc., at the Zeeland Archives; Grooten research in Zabriskie Bertholf file.

[10] There is little evidence for the surname Vermeulen, commonly assigned to her; her origin remains uncertain. Cole, *Tappan*, 9-10, 14 calls her "Vermeulen," but no known primary Dutch or colonial source gives her a surname; a Jan Cornelis Vermeulen witnessed her first child's baptism.

[11] Reformed Church members, Sluis, 1658-1700.

[12] Cole, *Tappan*, 14; Grooten research; Reformed Church consistory minutes, Sluis, inv. 7 (1681-1688), December 2, 1681, and December 2,1683. Bertholf's New York adversaries would assign him his father's occupation of cooper.

[13] Reformed Church departing members, 1664-1741, Sluis, inv. no 7; Grooten research.

accept the call.[14] Also, in 1683, New Castle got a teacher, namely, Isaac Seloivre, a cartwright, schoolmaster, and *voorzanger* (song leader) of Schoondijke, eight miles from Sluis.[15] Furthermore, the April 1683 firsthand testimony of Anthonij Crespel, who, after two decades in America, visited Groede, also in western Zeelandic Flanders, may have encouraged further emigration.[16]

When the Bertholfs arrived in New York City in the summer of 1684, they undoubtedly heard the Reverend Henricus Selijns preach and also met him, perhaps benefiting from his hospitality and advice. Supporting this supposition is Selijns's complaint, in a 1685 letter to the Classis of Amsterdam, that, besides the vexing presence of Labadists and Quakers,

> certain troubles are arising in other of the neighboring churches. Certain men came over last year [1684] with certificates from Sluis in Flanders, and from Middelburg and Groede, in Zeeland. They were only tailors or shoemakers or cobblers, yet they endeavored to be promoted in this place or in that to lay reader or schoolteacher. Some of them were assisted by me because of their great zeal; but how is it possible to agree with most of them? They speak against the church, public prayers, and the liturgy of the church. They say, "We are Coelmanists, catechize, have private exercises and special prayers"; and almost say, that the public prayers are apocryphal [spurious]. True orthodox people are grieved at these things.[17]

Doubtless, Selijns had Bertholf (although neither tailor, shoemaker, nor cobbler) foremost in mind here.[18] Moreover, it appears that Bertholf, because of his "great zeal," had been somehow "assisted"

---

[14] Henricus Selijns to Classis of Amsterdam [CA], October 28, 1682, Hugh Hastings and Edward T. Corwin, eds., *Ecclesiastical Records, State of New York*, 7 vols. (Albany: Lyon, 1901-1916), 2:831-33 (hereafter cited as *ERNY*; Eekhof, "Koelman in Amsterdam," 16-24.

[15] Huib J. Plankeel, "I. Généalogie établie en 2004," in Rik Sohier, "Sohier." http://sohier.free.fr/riknl.htm (accessed March 15, 2010); email information H. Uil to author, January 25, 2010.

[16] Email information Plankeel to author, January 27, 2010. The Huguenot Crespel's many American descendants include two Reformed Church pastors (Crispell).

[17] Selijns to CA, September 20, 1685, *ERNY*, 2:907. In 1679 and 1680 two Labadist missionaries visited the area where Bertholf would settle and met Dominie Tesschenmaecker. William Nelson, *History of Bergen and Passaic Counties, New Jersey...* (Philadelphia: Everts & Peck, 1882), 388.

[18] The Bertholfs' letters of transfer were the only ones to North America issued by the Sluis church in these years. Reformed Church departing members, 1664-1741, Sluis. Further evidence of Selijns's anxiety then about the Koelmanist intrusion

by Selijns, who also requested the classis to send him "extracts . . . concerning schoolmasters and lay readers in order that churches and schools in this country may be regulated and conducted according to the formulas of the churches and schools in the fatherland."[19] Is it possible that Selijns, making the best of a bad situation, provided literature even to "Coelmanists" like Bertholf, whom he felt obliged, reluctantly, to guide as a schoolmaster and lay reader, seeing the need in Acquackanonk (and Hackensack), where the Bertholfs would settle? In any event, Guiliam's "official" designation as teacher and lay reader probably awaited the organization of a congregation there in 1686.

Preparation for the Ministry

The Bertholfs, within a month or two of arriving, were likely in East Jersey, possibly already getting acquainted with the pastorally neglected Acquackanonk folk. On October 6, 1684, Guiliam and Martijntje were received as members of the vacant Bergen (now Jersey City) Reformed Church, across the Hudson River from Manhattan and perhaps a day's walk from Acquackanonk. Selijns doubtless presided at the consistory meeting receiving the Bertholfs, since, as the nearest Reformed minister, he visited Bergen periodically to preach, administer the sacraments, and perform other pastoral duties.[20] Additional contacts between the Bertholfs and Selijns would have been when their children were baptized in Bergen (1686 and 1692) and in New York City (1688).[21]

The fact that the three male witnesses at these three baptisms had been among the fourteen original Acquackanonk land purchasers in 1684 implies that the Bertholfs were settled there within a year and a half of their landing.[22] Furthermore, the March 1693 petition

---

into Dutch America—certainly exacerbated by his encounter with Bertholf—is that in the fall of 1685, just after penning his complaint to the Classis of Amsterdam, Selijns felt compelled to set down in his church record book numerous extracts from the minutes of the civil and ecclesiastical actions taken against Koelman in the Netherlands between 1674 and 1683; Francis J. Sypher, Jr., ed. and transl., *Liber A 1628-1700 of the Collegiate Churches of New York*, (Grand Rapids MI: Eerdmans, 2009), 106-23.

[19] Selijns to CA, September 20, 1685, *ERNY*, 2:908: Eekhof, "Koelman in Amsterdam," 23-24.
[20] Cole, *Tappan*, 10; *The Reformed Protestant Dutch Church of Bergen [Jersey City], New Jersey, 1666-1788*, vol. 3 (Bowie, MD: Heritage Books, Inc., [1915] 1997), 65; Selijns to CA, October 28, 1682, *ERNY*, 2:829.
[21] Cole, *Tappan*, 14; Holland Society of New York, *The Reformed Protestant Dutch Church of Bergen [Jersey City], New Jersey, 1666-1788*, vol. 1 (Bowie, MD: Heritage Books, Inc., [1913] 1997), 31, 37.
[22] John Whitehead, *The Passaic Valley, New Jersey*... (New York: New Jersey Genealogical Company, 1901), 260-61.

of Acquackanonk and Hackensack requesting Bertholf's ordination declares that "Mr." (*Meester*, meaning [school]master) Guiliam Bertholf had been serving them for "about seven years" as *voorlezer* (lay reader of ministers' sermons). This means that he taught school and led worship (commonly linked activities) beginning in 1686.[23] The 1693 petition asserted that he had been catechizing, doing "exercises"[24] (i.e., probably exhorting in a conventicle, not preaching his own sermons), and that he was a *voorzanger*. Selijns, as noted, complained that the invading "Coelmanists" may already (1685) have been engaged in such semi-pastoral activities.

The Reverend Petrus Tesschenmaecker, a probable pietist, very likely appointed Bertholf to these functions (he was never an elder) in 1686, when he organized the congregation of Hackensack and presumably that of Acquackanonk, possibly en route from his previous pastorate on Staten Island to his new charge in Schenectady. Utrecht-educated (like Koelman) and New York-ordained (somewhat irregularly), he ministered at New Castle until 1682, after which Koelman was called.[25]

From April 1690 to September 1691 Bertholf's gifts for "ministry" were further affirmed by a stint as part-time visiting *voorlezer* at the Nieuw Haerlem (New Harlem) church on Manhattan,[26] at which time he may also have more fully realized that he himself should seek ordination to help remedy the dearth of preaching and the sacraments in most Dutch congregations, a situation exacerbated by the disaffection of some of them from the few Reformed ministers then available. This estrangement was occasioned largely by the Leisler "troubles" of 1689 to 1691, when Jacob Leisler led an uprising in the New York City area (there being no English governor after the Catholic King James II was

---

[23] He was also called "Mr." when he witnessed a Bergen baptism early in 1687. Holland Society, *Bergen*, 1:32.

[24] Probably leading expository studies of biblical texts in a conventicle, not preaching his own sermons.

[25] *Records of the Reformed Dutch Churches of Hackensack and Schraalenburgh*... (New York: Holland Society of New York, 1891), 1-2, 290. There are no Hackensack and Acquackanonk consistory minutes for the Bertholf years. Tesschenmaecker is sometimes said to have begun his Schenectady ministry in 1682, but *ERNY* 2:882, 909, 922, 944, 947, 957, shows it was 1686. See Dirk Mouw's chapter on Tesschenmaecker.

[26] It is unclear how Bertholf's presence in Harlem fits with his "seven" years' pre-1693 New Jersey work. Probably the Bertholfs did not move there, but Guiliam exhorted in Harlem periodically, sometimes staying to teach school. Reportedly, he served there from April 24, 1690 to September 13, 1691; James Riker, *Harlem (The City of New York): Its Origins and Early Annals*... (New York: printed for the author, 1881), 458.

deposed) and governed for over a year, avowedly to keep the Catholics out of power until the governor of the Stadtholder King William III arrived. The well-intentioned Leisler was executed for rebellion. Much of the economic, civil, and religious establishment, including Selijns, opposed Leisler, who was supported, among others, by many of the Dutch farmers.[27] These included at least some of Bertholf's parishioners in Harlem and New Jersey, and, reportedly, Bertholf himself, which doubtless further alienated Selijns.

Thus, in October 1692 the Reverends Henricus Selijns, Rudolphus van Varick, and Godefridus Dellius complained to the Classis of Amsterdam that, besides *voorzangers* and schoolmasters "performing ministerial duties" (e.g., Bertholf?), the dominies' congregations were decimated, their salaries in arrears, and "the churches of Bergen, Hackensack, Staten Island, and Harlem have deserted us . . . . They say that they can live well enough without ministers or sacraments."[28] The Leisler troubles suspended observance of the Lord's Supper at Harlem for several years (including Bertholf's),[29] as well as at Hackensack and Acquackanonk. This could have prompted Bertholf's New Jersey people, during the following spring (1693), to request his ordination—perhaps at his suggestion.

Dominie Van Varick of Long Island wrote the Classis of Amsterdam in April 1693 that he had formerly "preached twice a year on Staten Island and at Hackensack, and also administered the Lord's Supper," but because of the Leisler troubles

[27] Recently the Leisler rebellion has been reinterpreted as rooted in local elite family rivalries and as a New World extension of theological-political quarrels in the Netherlands between Orangist-Voetian pietists (like Leisler) and anti-Orangist (*Staatspartij*) Cocceian "traditionalists" (like Selijns). Selijns presumably studied under the anti-Voetian Johannes Cocceius at Leiden University, whereas Bertholf had a Voetian heritage. David William Voorhees, "Family and Faction: The Dutch Roots of Colonial New York's Factional Politics," in Martha Dickinson Shattuck, eds. *Explorers, Fortunes, and Love Letters: A Window on New Netherlands* (Albany: New Netherland Institute, Mount Ida Press, 2009), 129-47; David William Voorhees, "'All Authority Turned Upside Downe': The Ideological Origins of Leislerian Political Thought," in Hermann Wellenreuther, ed., *Jacob Leisler's Atlantic World in the Later Seventeenth Century...* (Berlin: Lit Verlag Dr. W. Hopf, 2009), 89-118. A possible complicating factor with part of this picture is that Selijns studied at Utrecht before he went to Leiden. Louk Lapikás, "Fragment Genealogie Specht" (version 1.1, Muiden, 2009), at www.nikhef.nl/~louk/SPECHT/generation2.html.

[28] Selijns, (Van) Varick, and Dellius to CA, October 12, 1692, *ERNY*, 1043. Nevertheless, infants continued to be baptized, at least at Bergen (presumably by Selijns): 12 in 1691, 21 in 1692, 8 in 1693. Bertholf had not been able to administer the sacraments as a layman, but, in February 1694, immediately upon returning from ordination, he baptized three infants in Bergen. Holland Society, *Bergen*, 1:36-40.

[29] Riker, *Harlem*, 458.

they do not ask me any more. I hear now... that there is a onetime cooper from Sluys ... [Bertholf] who is also schoolmaster and *voorzanger* there [Hackensack]. He is a man well known to me,[30] of courageous and bold spirit, a Coelmanist by profession. He strongly urged on the revolting party recently. They [his congregation] chose him for about one fourth of our usual salary, to be their teacher, and he is about to take ship at the first opportunity, to be ordained by some Classis, perhaps that of Zeeland, or Sluys. If he succeed, there will soon more of his kind follow."[31]

Writing to the classis two months later, Van Varick offered similar warnings about Bertholf, "a man of very restless spirit," of a "schismatic humor," who would cause unrest and trouble. Van Varick and his colleagues "earnestly wish that these things may be prevented."[32]

Ordination in Zeeland

Bertholf's ordination to the ministry could not be stopped. A petition—really a letter of call—dated March 14, 1693, and signed by fifty-seven men, including two elders and two deacons, was sent by "the congregation" [singular] of Acquackanonk and Hackensack, stating that they had enjoyed for about seven years the ministry of a *voorlezer*, "in accordance with the church order of the Dutch Reformed churches, to the edification and complete satisfaction of the congregation, [and] having grown to almost 60 families, and it taking a three-day trip to Bergen to partake of the Lord's Supper under the ministry of the Rev. Henricus Selijns—therefore, because of this great difficulty we wish to have a shepherd here in our congregation to administer both the sacraments and the Word." Moreover, their *voorlezer*, Bertholf, "is qualified to become a *Duijtsche Clark* [Dutch cleric][33] and to fill the

[30] Van Varick must have met Bertholf when ministering semi-annually at Hackensack, e.g., when he baptized infants in 1689. *Records Hackensack*, 74.
[31] (Van) Varick to CA, April 9, 1693, *ERNY*, 1051; Eekhof, "Koelman in Amsterdam," 25. Van Varick's reference is to Bertholf's future "salary" as "teacher" (pastor); "courageous and bold" (*moedighe en wrevelighe*) is my revision of the *ERNY* translation ("courageous but stubborn").
[32] (Van) Varick to CA, June 27, 1693, *ERNY*, 2:1067.
[33] "Dutch clerics" were ministerial candidates who were so named because they were monolingual, not having the linguistic, liberal arts, and theological education (Latin school and university) normally required for ordination, but who possessed "singular gifts" to offset these deficiencies. Bertholf took the Dutch cleric route "just in time," since the last known such ordination was in 1695. Fred van Lieburg, "Preachers Between Inspiration and Instruction: Dutch Reformed Ministers

shepherd's role in this congregation—and at her request is resolved to go to Europe to obtain proper qualification." So they recommend him "so that Christ's Kingdom may be expanded in this farthest region of the world." He lived "an exemplary life" and had done "catechizing and exercises and great service for the youth and the uninstructed." The petition had no specific address, except to the "honorable" (men) of an unnamed ordaining body (classis), that it might "judge his doctrine, gifts, and abilities." The petitioners hope that Bertholf would return to them joyfully with the "authorization of a lawful call."[34]

Bertholf probably crossed the Atlantic with this document by the summer and went to Sluis to see family and friends, find a willing classis, and perhaps prepare for his examination. The minutes of the regular monthly session of the Classis of Walcheren, held at Middelburg September 2, 1693, announce that "Guiljam Bertholf, presently *voorlezer* in the congregation of two villages in Nieuw Nederland, having handed over a certain letter signed by many members of this congregation, who request to have him permitted to be ordained as their shepherd and teacher, it is resolved to deal with him about this tomorrow."[35] After Bertholf appeared the following day, the classis decided to examine his gifts and competence in two weeks, "in view of the zealous passion and attachment of this church to his person, and not wishing to hinder this."[36] Classis's desire to cooperate is obvious, although it was normal for ordination examinations to be conducted at special classical sessions.

Accordingly, the classis met again, on September 16, 1693, at Middelburg, when Bertholf "gave such satisfaction in his trial sermon on Matthew 11:28" ["Come unto me all you who are weary and heavy laden, and I will give you rest."] that "he was admitted to the examination, in which he also gave such satisfaction of his abilities that the meeting granted the request of the church of Acquackanonk and Hackensack to ordain him as pastor and teacher—and the call of the congregation to him is approved." After a sermon by the president, "the

---

Without Academic Education (Sixteenth-Eighteenth Centuries)," *Dutch Review of Church History* 83 (2003):166-67, 172-80; Willem Frijhoff, *Fulfilling God's Mission: The Two Worlds of Dominie Everardus Borardus, 1607-1647* (Leiden: Brill, 2007), 83, 326-28.

[34] Archive of the Classis Walcheren, inv. 25, no. 1210, Zeeland Archives (my translation); George Olin Zabriskie, "Residents of North-Eastern New Jersey in 1694," *New York Genealogical and Biographical Record* 108 (July 1977): 157-58; Randall H. Balmer, *A Perfect Babel of Confusion: Dutch Religion and English Culture in the Middle Colonies* (New York: Oxford University Press, 1989), 66-67.

[35] Minutes, Classis of Walcheren (CW), September 2, 1693, Article 9, Zeeland Archives; cf. *ERNY*, 2:1072.

[36] Minutes, CW, September 3, 1693, Article 5; cf. *ERNY*, 2:1073.

brother was ordained by laying on of hands," then accepted and signed the formulas of unity.[37]

Understandably, Bertholf had avoided the anti-Koelmanist Classis of Amsterdam, which oversaw the New York Dutch Reformed ministers, who were biased against him. Whether it concerned the rebel Leisler or the upstart Bertholf, the Classis of Amsterdam stood for law and order, for unity and peace.

Return to New York

About a month after Bertholf returned to his flock in East Jersey, he penned an epistle to his "very dear and beloved Mother," namely, his home church in Sluis, dated Acquackanonk, March 23, 1694. He contrasted his warm reception on returning to New Jersey with the "hatred and slander" of those (the New York clergy) who had written trying to prevent his ordination and who subsequently asserted that "only two or three ministers of Walcheren" favorable to him had examined and ordained him, and that they would not recognize him until ordered to do so by Amsterdam. But it was sufficient for Bertholf that his flock and God recognized him, and he was thankful that the Spirit had enabled him to preach to the satisfaction of many, "even of those belonging to their congregation, which embitters them the more toward us."[38]

Bertholf next recounted his futile effort to pacify Selijns by visiting him in New York City just after his return.[39] When Selijns read the ordination certificate that Bertholf showed him, he inquired as to the answer Walcheren had given to Selijns's letter, which had been seen

---

[37] Minutes, CW, September 16, 1693, Article 2; cf. *ERNY*, 2:1073. Bertholf signed the Reformed standards less than two months before the classis added to them the "Five Articles of Walcheren," rejecting various deviations from orthodoxy by three Reformed ministers; Bertholf doubtless heard some of this discussion. Minutes, CW, September 3 and November 5, 1693; Cornelis van den Broeke, *Een geschiedenis van de classis. Classicale typen tussen idee en werkelijkheid (1571-2004)* (Kampen: Kok, 2005), 89.

[38] This evidently refers to Bertholf's preaching (and baptizing) in Selijns's flock at Bergen the day after he arrived back in America, as well as to members of Selijns's (and perhaps Van Varick's) congregations going to hear Bertholf in Acquackenonk and Hackensack. See the end of this letter and Selijns's November 14, 1694, letter below.

[39] The Rev. Daniël Beukelaer, then pastor in Middelburg, was a Utrecht graduate and friend of Koelman, but, like Selijns, an Amsterdammer; the two had been examined together for ordination by the Classis of Amsterdam. F. A. van Lieburg, "Jacobus Koelman (1631-1695): jeugd en studietijd," in T. Brienen et al., eds., *Figuren en thema's van de Nadere Reformatie*, 2 vols. (Kampen: Uitgeverij De Groot Goudriaan, [1990] 2006), 2:61-62

there by Bertholf.[40] Bertholf replied that the classis "had found more convincing reasons" in his congregation's petition than in Selijns's letter, "and that this was the answer that the classis had given to his letter, namely, this [ordination] certificate, . . . upon which he became very angry and did not speak for a time." Bertholf urged Selijns not to be angry, since that would defeat the purpose of Bertholf's visit, which was to show him respect "and for the peace of his own congregation." Moreover, Bertholf warned Selijns not to continue on the path of opposition. The result of the encounter was that Selijns and his colleagues would write the Classis of Amsterdam for guidance, while Bertholf countered that "we would recognize the Classis of Amsterdam as our brothers, but that we would not know them as masters. And even if it were to be that the reverend classis should forbid us (which we said not to believe), that we nevertheless would wait until prohibited by the reverend Classis of Walcheren."[41]

Bertholf then explained to "Mother" Sluis that he had set forth the foregoing clearly in this letter, should his letter to classis be delayed, and suggested that one of the Sluis brethren show it to the classis.[42]

The rest of the letter recounted Bertholf's activities in England and arrival in America. He spent several weeks in England trying to find passage home—and presumably honing his skills in English. The voyage itself was "speedy," taking two months from Dover to New York, where he arrived Saturday afternoon, February 24, 1694. The very next day he preached twice in Bergen, returning to New York City on Monday to pick up his luggage and (evidently) to meet Selijns. Selijns was predictably displeased with Bertholf's activity at Bergen, which was usually supplied by himself. Bertholf reported that "There were many people in Bergen to hear us, [they] having come from New

---

[40] Selijns's letter was not found in the CW minutes; moreover, no letter from him opposing Bertholf's impending ordination is found in the CA minutes in *ERNY*.
[41] Selijns's disapproval of Bertholf may partly have had to do with his own multi-step, by-the-book experience in the Classis of Amsterdam, 1657-1660, of examination, ordination, and call to New Netherland. Jaap Jacobs, *New Netherland: A Dutch Colony in Seventeenth-Century America* (Leiden: Brill, 2005), 270-71. Moreover, Selijns, who identified with the New York establishment and was to obtain a charter from the English for the Reformed Protestant Dutch Church in New York in 1696, would naturally discourage disturbers of the status quo like Bertholf or Leisler. Other probable factors (listed in no particular order) militating against Selijns's acceptance of Bertholf included: class, status, education, scholarship, sophistication, manners, dress, wealth, age, experience, birthplace, theological orientation, ecclesiology, polity, *praxis pietatis*, and personality.
[42] Bertholf's letter to the Classis of Walcheren did not reach its destination, but this one to "Mother" Sluis did and was preserved by the classis; Minutes, CW, inv. 8, 5 August 1694, Article 5, and inv. 9, September 1, 1694, Article 5.

York and from Long Island or Nassau Island, who returned with great contentment. And [we] have again and again people from New York and thereabouts under our preaching, who come six to seven miles to hear us, some out of curiosity, others to their edification, but the Lord alone must have the glory, whom it pleases to use the least of all his servants for his service." The epistle ends with suitable piety, greetings, and the signature of "Your affectionate and submissive Son, Guiliaem Bertholf."[43] In the Hackensack church register Bertholf commemorated his return: "On Feb. 24 1694—Arrived here from Zeeland, Guiliaem Bertholf, with a legal classical authorization, to be preacher, pastor, and instructor of Acquiggenonck and Ackinsack, and has been received by the congregation with great affection." The Lord's Supper was first celebrated with the congregation in May, but already on March 18 the voting members of both places met at Acquackenonk to each choose an elder and two deacons.[44]

Opposition from Colleagues

Meanwhile, word had reached Amsterdam, where the classical minutes in May 1694 note, "Touching foreign churches, special mention is made of one Guilielmus Bartolt [sic], who is a cooper. He is also a Koelmanist, sent out by the churches of Zeeland to the New Netherland churches, against the recommendation of the North Holland Synod, and the Classis of Amsterdam. This was received for information."[45]

The two surviving Reformed dominies in New York were particularly unhappy that their efforts to block Bertholf's ordination had failed. Godefridus Dellius of Albany wrote the Classis of Amsterdam in October 1694 that "Bartholts [sic], . . . without being legally qualified, [had] performed ministerial duties." Dellius, in upstate New York, may not have known Bertholf personally and depended on Selijns and Van Varick for information about him. Dellius repeated some of the usual charges against Bertholf, particularly his supposed offenses against church polity. He also fretted that the reputations of religion, church, and ministry would suffer. Dellius could not fathom why the Classis

---

[43] CW, inv. 68, no. 33 (East [sic] Indies correspondence; my translation). To my knowledge, this remarkable document has heretofore escaped scholarly notice.
[44] Cole, *Tappan*, 12; *Records Hackensack*, 1-2, 290; Nelson, *History*, 388.
[45] Minutes, CA, May 3, 1694, Article 9 (my translation), Gemeentearchief Amsterdam, inv. 379, no. 8, p. 199; ERNY, 1100. The source of this information is not stated, the recommendations of the synod and classis were not found, and the Selijns-Van Varick letter to CA of November 20, 1693, says nothing about Bertholf; ERNY, 2:1089-90.

of Walcheren had ordained Bertholf, ignoring the protests of the New York dominies. He believed it would be very hard to accept Bertholf as a colleague, but Selijns and he would submit to Amsterdam's counsel.[46]

Over a month later Selijns also wrote the classis—on the back side of Dellius's letter—of his displeasure. He reported that the Albany and New York church leaders had been unable to gather to discuss recognizing Bertholf's ordination. Thus, Selijns had "remained quiet," recommending to Bertholf that he "be satisfied and contented with the churches of Acquackanonk and Hackensack . . . and continue his work begun there, in the fear of the Lord. Meanwhile, however," wrote Selijns, "he has preached at Bergen, which is a church under my charge. He asserts that he is authorized to do this because it lies between New York and Acquackanonk; and his letter of call reads 'To preach on water and on land and by the way.' But Bergen remains faithful, and has requested me to continue my services there."[47] Bertholf, however, "moves about and preaches everywhere. He praises the Classis of Walcheren, which qualifies ministers at slight cost to them. He also says that he sought his ordination there, rather than in Amsterdam, because one half of your Rev. Body are not regenerated preachers."

Thus Bertholf's chief faults, according to Selijns, were that he preached outside his own bailiwick (on Selijns's turf), was ordained by Walcheren, and was judgmental. Selijns went on to note that a member of the classis had written him already a year before, in November 1693, informing him that it (presumably during the preceding summer) had referred the matter of Bertholf to the Synod of North Holland, which in turn urged the Classis of Walcheren not to ordain him. Selijns reported that some Amsterdam letters had not reached him, so that he needed copies and advice. "In the meantime we will remain quiet, and whatever directions may be given [by the classis] shall be observed. Nevertheless, it is a sad circumstance that your Reverences have been rejected, and that we are placed under a Classis in Zeeland! for in case of disagreement, he would appeal to the Classis of Walcheren, and we to the Classis of Amsterdam for a decision."[48]

[46] Dellius to CA, October 7, 1694; *ERNY*, 2:1105-06; Eekhof, "Koelman in Amsterdam," 25. Bertholf's name is regularly misspelled by his opponents; Selijns finally gets it right in 1696 (below).

[47] Although Van Varick said that Bergen had not desired the sacraments, it appears that Selijns continued to administer them there during and after the Leisler troubles; see note 28 above. Selijns's tone here (fall 1694) concerning Bertholf seems slightly milder than that of Dellius, who knew Bertholf less well.

[48] Selijns to CA, November 14, 1694; *ERNY*, 1106-1108; Eekhof, "Koelman in Amsterdam," 25-26. Rather than Amsterdam's letters being lost (and thus needing to be copied), as Selijns supposed, they were likely never written, witness the classis's

Selijns therefore appeared resigned to a *fait accompli,* because there was no national synod to adjudicate between the rival claims of the two classes. Moreover, the Classis of Amsterdam was responsible to the Synod of North Holland, whereas the Classis of Walcheren was under no higher judicatory, the Synod of Zeeland having last met in 1638. Given this situation and the never fully uncontested authority of the Classis of Amsterdam over the churches in the New World, Bertholf's choice of Walcheren instead of Amsterdam may have been unusual but not clearly unlawful.[49]

The next surviving correspondence of Bertholf, written May 15, 1695, from Hackensack to the Classis of Walcheren, testifies of Selijns's growing acceptance of his New Jersey colleague.[50] In the letter Bertholf wondered why he had not heard from the classis, reported that about thirty persons had been added to his flock in the previous year, and that he had organized a church at Tappan (near the New York border).[51] "The opposition of the brothers preachers here seems to be markedly decreasing, since by God's grace they find nothing to reprove in our person or ministry. One of them [Van Varick] has died . . . . There was little or no sadness about this in these churches of Long Island. The aforementioned churches . . . immediately called me to be their preacher in place of the deceased. But, although there are four churches and we could have more than double the salary there, yet I declined the call because I know that this congregation of Hackensack and Acquackanonk is not capable to get a preacher like me to come to replace me and those of Long Island have sufficient means to get one from the fatherland." Yet he agreed to administer the sacraments on Long Island, either on Sunday or on a weekday, his own congregation permitting, just as he had done at Breukelen (Brooklyn), Nieuw Utrecht (in Brooklyn now), and Staten Island. In summary, "our ministry at present is almost too heavy for us. But unless the Lord had in an extraordinary manner supported us by his Holy Spirit, we would have

---

procrastination between May and September 1694 in answering the New Yorkers' complaints. *ERNY,* 2:1100-01, 1104.

[49] The reluctance of Amsterdam to reply to New York's objections to Bertholf may support this view. Van den Broeke, *Een geschiedenis van de classis,* 88-90, 116; Jacobs, *New Netherland,* 264-72, describes the Classis of Amsterdam's authority up to 1664; email information Dirk Mouw to author, October 8, 2009.

[50] Trans-Atlantic postal service was unreliable. Apparently three previous communications to the Classis of Walcheren had failed to reach their destination—two from Bertholf and one from his congregation. He was evidently unaware of the loss of his earlier letters when he wrote his third report to classis in May 1695.

[51] Bertholf visited the Tappan church until 1725 to administer the sacraments and preach, usually quarterly. Cole, *Tappan,* 13-17.

gone under. Praise the Lord."[52] In sum, Bertholf's energetic and irenic ministry was flourishing (he provided statistics for each place) and was encountering less clerical opposition. Perhaps, most impressively, he declined significant financial gain, choosing instead to remain with the flock that had given him his start and that he would serve the rest of his life.

In its October 1695 response to Bertholf's optimistic May report, the Classis of Walcheren commended his work and criticized his ministry's opponents. It praised his loving decision to stay with his congregation rather than accept the Long Island call, urged him to seek peace, prayed for him, and gave some news. The classis instructed him, however, to henceforth write to it in the name of his consistory—and also to report the form of government of his churches. There is thus some concern that Bertholf should adhere to church order (note the New York dominies' worries).[53]

No subsequent letters between Walcheren and Bertholf have been found. The classical minutes, however, reported in June 1697, and again in March 1699, that a letter from him was read aloud, with good news of his ministry in America ("these heathen regions"), and asking that the clerk should reply, thanking and encouraging him. His second letter had been composed ten months previous to its reading in classis! The once living relationship was becoming a distant memory. Bertholf was now basically on his own in New Jersey, without any active classical oversight, although still belonging (in his and others' eyes) to the Classis of Walcheren (see below).[54]

Maturity

After 1695 relatively little is heard of Guiliam Bertholf's doings, although he lived and ministered for another three decades. The gulf between him and Selijns apparently narrowed quickly. In a 1696 letter to the Classis of Amsterdam, Selijns simply names him without comment on a list of the five Dutch Reformed ministers in the colony.[55] Bertholf's activities over the years are recorded occasionally in the *Ecclesiastical Records of the State of New York,* as well as in the extant registers of the many churches that he visited, administering the sacraments, marrying couples, and receiving members. Both Dellius and Selijns were soon

---

[52] CW, inv. 68, no. 32 (East [sic] Indies correspondence; my translation); Minutes, CW, October 6, 1695, Article 3, summarizes the contents of Bertholf's letter.
[53] Minutes, CW, October 20, 1695, Article 4; CW, inv. 26, no. 1242 (my translation).
[54] Minutes, CW, inv. 9, June 13, 1697, Article 3; March 19, 1699, Article 5.
[55] Selijns to CA, September 30, 1696, *ERNY*, 2:1171, 1187.

gone, the former in 1699 (by returning to the Netherlands) and the latter in 1701 (by death), making Bertholf the senior pastor among the colonial Dutch. New ministers came, e.g., Selijns's young successor Gualtherus du Bois, who in 1706, in a letter to the Classis of Amsterdam, described Bertholf as "a very honorable and pious man," who was "much inclined" to participate in a proposed informal fraternal gathering of all the Dutch ministers in the colony, even though he belonged to the Classis of Walcheren. Du Bois also reported that Bertholf had asked his advice about installing the difficult pietist, Bernardus Freeman, at New Utrecht.[56] Thus, Bertholf, thoroughly "rehabilitated" by age fifty, was no longer an outsider, and Amsterdam and Walcheren were, in a sense, reconciled in colonial America.

Then, in 1721, Bertholf and Freeman composed a short endorsement prefacing three sermons published by the newly-arrived pietist, the Reverend Theodorus Jacobus Frelinghuysen of Raritan. These messages were intended to display Frelinghuysen's orthodoxy to those who had attacked him as schismatic and unReformed.[57] Bertholf and Freeman were themselves soon queried about their support of Frelinghuysen, who claimed to be able to distinguish the regenerate from the unregenerate in his congregation, barring the latter from the Lord's Supper. This claim was denied from within his flock and also by the New York City's pastors, whose own regeneration he also may have questioned. Bertholf, however, had already (in 1720) urged Frelinghuysen "to refrain in his services at Raritan from these strange proceedings," since he should know that his flock there was "very feeble in respect to spiritual things, and that there was danger that . . . [he], by his harsh conduct, should change the people into Quakers, or Atheists, or Suicides, or Pharisees."[58]

Finally, although Bertholf is reputed to have been not only a forerunner of Frelinghuysen (and thus of the Great Awakening), but his kindred spirit and good friend, both having begun their ministries

---

[56] Gualtherus du Bois to CA, May 23, 1706, *ERNY*, 3:1649, 1655.

[57] Recommendation of Frelinghuysen's sermons by Freeman and Bertholf, *ERNY*, 3:2179-2180. Bertholf had organized the Raritan church in 1699 and supplied it at least twice annually. Tanis, *Pietism*, 45. Joel R. Beeke, ed., *Forerunner of the Great Awakening: Sermons by Theodorus Jacobus Frelinghuysen (1691-1747)* (Grand Rapids, MI: Eerdmans, 2000), xvii-xix, 1-64.

[58] Joseph Anthony Loux, Jr., trans. and ed., *Boel's Complaint against Frelinghuisen* (Rensselaer, NY: Hamilton Printing Company, 1979), 4-5, 32; *ERNY*, 4:2319. In addition, Bertholf differed with Frelinghuysen over the latter's support of and relationship with his zealous young protégé, Jacobus Schuurman. Loux, *Complaint*, 33, 148; Balmer, *Babel*, 109-113. Freeman later referred to charges of immorality against Schuurman as old wives' tales; Tanis, *Pietism*, 50

as anti-establishment Dutch pietists with Voetian roots.[59] It should also be noted, however, that one of Frelinghuysen's Raritan critics testified in 1723 that Bertholf, after hearing Frelinghuysen preach, was asked what he thought of the latter's teachings when he said in a prayer that he was certain that some people who were present had "set grins and snares" against him. Bertholf reportedly replied reluctantly: "They say that he is a Koelmanist, but he is not. He rather appears to be a Labadist. I should even dare to say that he *is one*; else how could he be so harsh as to say this about his hearers. He must have intended *me*. Before I leave Raritan, I shall speak to him about it."[60]

Clearly Bertholf in old age was much less divisive than Selijns had feared him to be three decades earlier. Bertholf might even be said to have become part of the "establishment," especially if he thought that the youthful firebrand Frelinghuysen had gone beyond Koelmanism into Labadism.[61] This does not seem to be the Bertholf whom Selijns in 1694 claimed had questioned whether half the Classis of Amsterdam were regenerate. Age and experience evidently mellowed Bertholf, although his opponents may have exaggerated his initial views, and perhaps he had also absorbed at Sluis some of David Montanus's milder Dutch pietism.

Bertholf's active ministry ended in 1724, as recorded by the Acquackanonk consistory on March 23: "It has pleased the Almighty to afflict our reverend, godly and well learned pastor and teacher, Dominie Guilliam Bertholf, who for more than thirty years has faithfully proclaimed the Gospel, in his advanced age in such a manner that it is acknowledged that he can no longer continue in his office as preacher." Therefore a successor would be called from the Netherlands and Bertholf would be given something like a pension from Acquackanonk (and presumably also from Hackensack). His death was not recorded. He was mentioned as baptizing a child at Tappan in 1725, and he and his wife deeded land to their son in February 1726. Guiliam Bertholf may have reached three score and ten years. Martijntje likely survived him.[62]

In conclusion, the traditional picture of Guiliam Bertholf as the initially controversial but ultimately vindicated "apostle of New

---

[59] Tanis, *Pietism*, 44-45.
[60] But another person who heard the sermon said that Bertholf told Frelinghuysen, as he descended from the pulpit, "I thank you for your edifying sermon." Loux, *Complaint*, 179.
[61] Frelinghuysen denied being a Labadist but not a Koelmanist. Tanis, *Pietism*, 143.
[62] Cole, *Tappan*, 12-13, 15; *ERNY*, 3:2215-16.

Jersey" remains intact. Nevertheless, his reputation as a forerunner of Frelinghuysen and the Great Awakening needs revision.[63]

---

[63] Space limitations necessitate omitting the story of Bertholf's many descendants (some famous), as well as a consideration of all the churches he began or supplied. Suffice it to say that he "was responsible for organizing congregations and establishing churches in communities in what are now Somerset, Hudson, Bergen, and Passaic counties in New Jersey, and Rockland and Westchester counties in New York." Fabend, "Bertholf," 693. Another close student of the subject notes that "he became the founder of almost every early Dutch church in New Jersey.... The Sleepy Hollow church at Tarrytown and the churches at Tappan, the Ponds, Pompton Plains, Totowa, Second River, Bergen, Staten Island, Three Mile Run, Six Mile Run, New Brunswick and Raritan all proudly claim Guiliam Bertholf as their pastor." Adrian C. Leiby, *The United Churches of Schraalenburgh and Hackensack, New Jersey, 1686-1822* (River Edge, NJ: Bergen County Historical Society, 1976), 50. To Bertholf's itinerations may be added, as mentioned previously, Harlem, Brooklyn, and Nieuw Utrecht, as well as Flatbush (now in Brooklyn) and probably others. David William Voorhees, trans. and ed., *Records of The Reformed Protestant Dutch Church of Flatbush..*, vol. 2, *Midwood Deacons' Accounts 1654-1709* (New York: Holland Society of New York, 2009), 299.

CHAPTER 9

Laurentius van den Bosch (c. 1660?–1696): Scandalous Founder

Evan Haefeli

Laurent van den Bosch is a little known but colorful figure in the history of Colonial America. A Walloon without clear family ties in Europe or America, he played an important—albeit not always edifying—role in the Huguenot, Dutch Reformed, and Anglican churches in North America. His obscurity reminds us of the importance of family in creating and preserving knowledge about individuals from seventeenth century America. At the same time his inability to establish a stable family life is consonant with the little that we know of his personality. He was bold enough to take on a pioneering role in the Huguenot and Dutch Reformed Churches in America, but he lacked a talent for building community. Valued as a minister in a time and place where they were scarce, Van den Bosch could have been remembered as a founding figure. Instead, he brought controversies that tested the integrity of his fledgling congregations. His scandals challenged the way colonial churches related to their ministers, for, unlike many of the churchmen who came to colonial America, he was unwilling to behave according to local community norms or to cooperate with local religious authorities. Nonetheless, his services were in such demand that he was

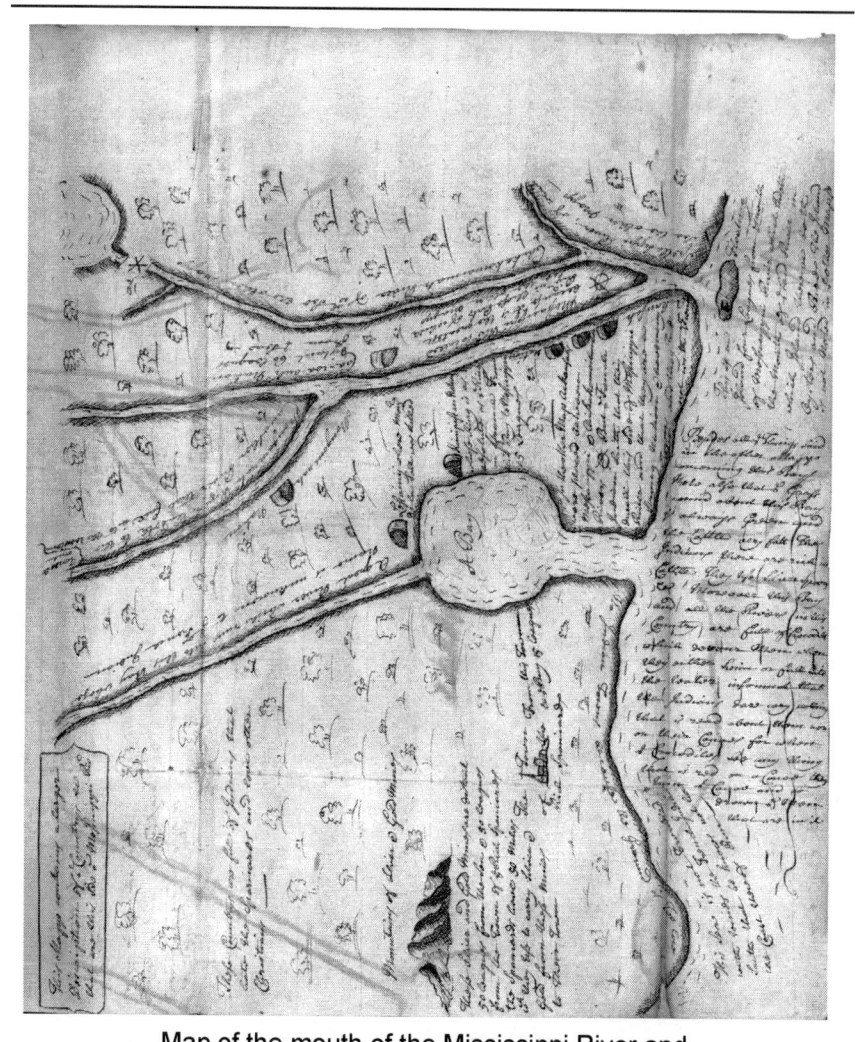

Map of the mouth of the Mississippi River and
the Gulf Coast to its west.
[Newberry Library: Edward E. Ayer Manuscript Map Collection and the
Edward E. Ayer Manuscript Collection Vault drawer Ayer MS 339 map 1]

able to move from one community to another, revealing how permeable the distinctions between Huguenot, Dutch Reformed, and Anglican churches could be in the years before they built institutions.

Biographical treatments of Van den Bosch have been sketchy. His extraordinarily peripatetic existence made him rather elusive, even to his contemporaries. In the twenty-five years for which we have documentary evidence about him (1679 to 1694) he moved through two European countries (the United Provinces of the Netherlands and England), two Dutch provinces (Holland and Gelderland), and four American colonies (South Carolina, Massachusetts, New York, and Maryland). His life has hitherto been relegated to a handful of (occasionally perplexed) asides; indeed, the fullest treatment is in a brief 1926 essay on the French Church in Boston.[1] Until recently his time in Boston has drawn the most attention, but recent research has uncovered his subsequent career in New York's Dutch Reformed Church as well as tracing him back to the Walloon community in the Netherlands.

The Netherlands

While we do not know exactly where or when he was born, he was undoubtedly a Walloon—a member of the French-speaking refugee community from the Southern Netherlands—and not a Huguenot, or Protestant, from France, as was once thought.[2] Yet the boundaries between the groups could blur, as they did in New Paltz, New York.[3] Indeed, Van den Bosch is a personal case study in the possibilities and limits of Huguenot-Walloon cooperation in the 1680s, not to mention that of the Dutch and English. Educated, good at languages (growing up bilingual—French and Dutch—and learning English as an adult), and Protestant but not doctrinaire, he brought out the cosmopolitan possibilities of early colonial life.

Van den Bosch first enters the historical record in Holland. On April 19, 1679, Leiden's Walloon Synod reimbursed him a sum of money. The following year he must have been in Gelderland, for on

---

[1] Percival Merritt, "The French Protestant Church in Boston," *Publications of the Colonial Society of Massachusetts* (Boston: The Colonial Society of Massachusetts, 1926), 26:323-29. Other biographical sketches can be found in Charles W. Baird, *History of the Huguenot Emigration to America*, 2 vols. (New York: Dodd, Mead and Co, 1885), 2:224-26; Jon Butler, *The Huguenots in America: A Refugee People in New World Society* (Cambridge, MA: Harvard University Press, 1983), 64-65; Bertrand van Ruymbeke, *From New Babylon to Eden: The Huguenots and their Migration to Colonial South Carolina* (Columbia: University of South Carolina Press, 2006), 117.

[2] Baird, *Huguenot Emigration*, 2:224 suggests Van den Bosch was a Dutchified version of "Du Bois." But as Merritt, "French Protestant Church," 323 notes, he used only some variant of Van den Bosch: "his name appears also as Lawrence Vandebost, Laurent Van den Bosck, Laurence Vandenbosk, Lambertus van der Bosch, Laurence van den Bosch, Vandenbosch, and Vanden Bosch." On the distinction between Walloons and Huguenots see Bertrand van Ruymbeke, "The Walloon and Huguenot Elements in New Netherland and Seventeenth-Century New York: Identity, History, and Memory," in Joyce D. Goodfriend, ed., *Revisiting New Netherland: Perspectives on Early Dutch America* (Leiden: Brill, 2005), 41-54.

[3] Eric J. Roth, "'where ye walleons dwell': Rethinking the Ethnic Identity of the Huguenots of New Paltz and Ulster County, New York," *New York History* 89:4 (2008): 346-73.

May 4, 1682, the Walloon Synod of Nijmegen noted that he had been a candidate (*proposans*) there for about two years. At his request the synod wrote a testament to his good character, for he had decided to go to England "or elsewhere" in search of employment. He had impressed the Walloon churchmen with his good conduct and zeal for the service of the church, and he seemed to be giving all the signs that he would one day be a "worthy instrument in the hand of God to serve his church with great success."[4]

Why would he leave the Netherlands for America? Van den Bosch was probably influenced by pamphlets promoting Huguenot settlement in the Carolina colony. Once the repression of Protestantism in France increased in 1679, the Carolina proprietors began targeting Huguenots as likely immigrants to their under-populated colony. They had agents working in the Netherlands to recruit Huguenots, and in France to print and distribute materials. From 1679 to 1686 eight different French-language promotional pamphlets appeared in Rotterdam and The Hague as well as in London and Geneva. The first contingent of Huguenots sailed for Carolina in 1679, and more soon followed.[5] Van den Bosch must have been aware of this and saw an opportunity. The complete absence in all available sources of any reference to family or friends suggests that he was a young man more or less on his own. Rootless and autonomous, he was prime material for emigration.

Carolina

Like the roughly three hundred fifty adult Huguenots who eventually migrated to Carolina, Van den Bosch made the transition to America through England, where he had arrived by July of 1682 at the latest.[6] On August 1, 1682, the bishop of London, Henry Compton, formally ordained him, as he would other Huguenot ministers serving in English territories.[7] Not yet able to preach in English, Van den Bosch was ordained to serve the Huguenots.[8] Eight days later he received

---

[4] Guillaume H.M. Posthumus Meyjes and Hans Bots with Johanna Roelevink, eds., *Livre des Actes des Eglises Wallonnes aux Pays-Bas, 1601-1697* (Den Haag: Instituut voor Nederlandse Geschiedenis, 2005), 839, 869-70.
[5] Van Ruymbeke, *From New Babylon to Eden*, 35-40.
[6] Ibid., 71.
[7] Merritt, "First French Church," 324: "'Primo die Augusti 1682, Laurentius Van den Bosck Flandriae Natione in Sacros Diaconatus et presbyteratus Ordines fuit admissus,' Ordination Book, 1675-1809, in Bishop of London's Registry, Doctor's Common."
[8] Van den Bosch mentions his inability to preach in English in his July 4, 1685 letter to the Bishop of London CO 1/58, No. 4 British National Archives.

two pounds sterling and "a quarto edition of a Geneva Bible" from the Nonconformist Threadneedle Street Church.[9] Then he sailed for Carolina.

It is entirely possible that, if only for a few weeks, Laurentius van den Bosch was the first French-speaking Protestant minister in British America. He was without a doubt the first minister of the Huguenot church in Charleston. Though records are few, it seems likely that he arrived in the fall of 1682. The only other French Protestant minister who might have been in North America at that time was Pierre Daillé. Formerly a professor at the Huguenot academy of Saumur, Daillé "forsook France on account of persecution," as noted by Henricus Selijns, the dominie of New York. Daillé probably arrived some time between November 1682 and early January 1683. The first evidence is from January 22, 1683, when he helped set up the church at New Paltz.[10] If Van den Bosch had departed in August after receiving his Bible, he could have been in Carolina by September or October 1682, giving him at least a few weeks head start to Daillé. A respected figure, Daillé played an important foundational role among the Huguenot congregations in New York and Massachusetts.[11] Van den Bosch would not.

Van den Bosch's time in Carolina was brief, barely two years, and remains largely obscure. Although he served as the first minister to the new Huguenot church in Charleston, his pioneering role has been forgotten. As a Walloon with an Anglican ordination, he had little in common with the still fairly small community of French and Swiss refugees (about fifty-six individuals). He claimed that material difficulties forced him to leave. In a 1685 letter Van den Bosch complained that the Huguenots could not contribute to his subsistence, leaving him in a "miserable condition." However, the fact that the one recorded religious act on record for the time of his pastorship was the baptism of a Huguenot baby, Jacob Thibou, by an English minister (presumably a Dissenter) leads one to think that he was not Calvinist enough for his congregation. Van den Bosch left for Boston in late 1684 or early 1685, arriving by March 1685. That April hundreds of Huguenots began to arrive in Carolina, including the reliably Calvinist Florent-Philippe

---

[9] Records of the French Church, ms. 7, "Livres des Actes, 1679-1692" (August 9, 1682), French Protestant Church Library, London, cited in Van Ruymbeke, *From New Babylon to Eden*, 309 n139.

[10] Selijns mentions Daillé in May and October 1683 but not in his October 1682 letter, Baird, *Huguenot Emigration*, 2:397 and Edward T. Corwin, ed., *Ecclesiastical Records of the: State of New York*, 7 vols., (Albany: Lyon, 1901-16) 2:866 (hereafter cited as *ERNY*).

[11] For Daillé, see Merritt, "French Church," 337–43.

Trouillart, Van den Bosch's replacement. Trouillart would go down in history as the church's founding minister. Van den Bosch had missed his first great rendezvous with destiny.[12]

Boston

The Huguenot presence in North America was still very small in the spring of 1685. Communities existed in Carolina, Massachusetts, and New York (where there was also a Walloon community at New Paltz). Van den Bosch was probably aware of Daillé's presence in New York. Having given up on Carolina, he aimed for the fledgling Huguenot community in Massachusetts.

Van den Bosch is remembered as the first minister of Boston's Huguenot church.[13] But once again, he made no lasting contribution. Boston's Huguenot community was smaller than Charleston's, consisting of a handful of "French Protestants" (twelve men, women, and children, to be precise) who had arrived in 1682. New England had not made the effort to recruit Huguenots the way Carolina had, and not until 1686 would a significant number arrive. In July 1685 Van den Bosch wrote that he was attempting "to assemble a French Church" but it would be difficult, given the "weakness and small numbers of French" present. There may have been a few Huguenots other than the refugees from 1682, but not enough to establish a thriving church.[14]

But Boston would remember Van den Bosch. His notoriety came less from his role in the Huguenot Church than from his attempt to foster the Church of England. Shortly after his arrival he performed some marriages and baptisms according to the Anglican rites in the privacy of a colonist's home. Marriage in seventeenth century Massachusetts was a civil affair, and baptism was a matter for the established Congregational Church. Van den Bosch was flouting both the religious and secular authorities of Massachusetts. Taken before the County Court on April 9, 1685, he promised to cease. But in his July 4 letter to the bishop of London (written in French) he lamented that his inability to preach in English prevented him from organizing an Anglican congregation. Nonetheless, he was determined to promote Anglicanism in New England, claiming he would not return to London unless compelled to by dire necessity.

---

[12] Laurent van den Bosck [sic] to the Bishop of London, July 4, 1685 CO 1/58, No. 4 British National Archives; Van Ruymbeke, *From New Babylon to Eden*, 72-74, 109, 117-19.

[13] Though some doubt he deserves this credit, see "Ezekiel Carré and the French Church in Boston," *Proceedings of the Massachusetts Historical Society* 52 (1918):122-24.

[14] On the Huguenot community in Boston, see Baird, *Huguenot Emigration*, 2:195-200.

In addition to a pledge of undying loyalty and a request for support to the cause of the Church of England in Boston, Van den Bosch's letter to Compton is the first source to reveal his personality. He complained of his suffering at the hands of the "Independants de Boston." Simply for performing his duties as an Anglican minister and marrying those who were members of the church and baptizing others who wished to join it, he was subject to all the "outrages imaginable, excepting prison, whipping, and banishment, with which they have threatened me nonetheless." The "cause of all this disorder" was "Mr. Mather and Mr. Moody, Independent ministers, with their followers." Van den Bosch maintained that he always resisted them without ever giving way to them in anything. "But since I am alone against so many people, who have the power in hand here, and who continually threaten me," he needed the bishop of London's protection.[15]

At the beginning of September Van den Bosch was caught performing another illegal marriage in a private home. By September 23 Samuel Sewall noted in his famous diary that Van den Bosch had fled to New York. The man Van den Bosch had married was Giles Sylvester, son of Nathaniel Sylvester, lord of the manor of Shelter Island, New York. Giles probably carried Van den Bosch out of Boston and into New York.[16]

Though in Boston for as little as seven or eight months, he had angered the local authorities. Increase Mather would later refer to him as a "Debauched Priest" who had baptized "a noted whore or two of his acquaintance" and performed private marriages without public announcements, calling him "a nusance & Bane to all humane society." The government Van den Bosch experienced as persecutory, Mather claimed was "so tender" that it only made "some Orall Rebukes" that nonetheless scared the "guilty knave" away. Mather remembered Van den Bosch as a man who would "Drink, Sweare, Fornicate, practice and preach up (the honest games of) Cards, Dice," and more. He should have "had more Witt [a reference to the murdered Dutch politician Johan de Witt] than to Cross the Ocean for a dwelling in so Cold a Country." His scornful portrayal of Van den Bosch, however accurate, was designed to drive home the point that until 1689 there had been no serious Church of England presence in New England.[17]

[15] Van den Bosch to Bishop of London, July 4, 1685.
[16] This was the reasoning of the great New England genealogist James Savage, *A Genealogical Dictionary of the First Settlers of New England, showing three generations of those who came before May, 1692, on the basis of the Farmer's Register*, 4 vols. (Boston, 1860-1862) 4:99, 364.
[17] Quotes from "The Present State of New English Affairs, 1689" reprinted in William H. Whitmore, ed. *The Andros Tracts: Being a collection of pamphlets and official papers issued*

Once again, Van den Bosch was just barely out of step with the times. If he had been able to preach to the English and had arrived just a little later, he could have been considered the first Anglican minister in Boston. By 1686 Massachusetts was incorporated into the Dominion of New England. When an English Anglican minister then arrived in Boston, he was protected by the dominion's liberty of conscience clause. In 1687 the new governor of the dominion, Edmund Andros, even supported the efforts of the Anglican community to worship publicly.[18] Or Van den Bosch could have served as the Huguenot minister, because by 1686 enough Huguenot refugees were arriving to build a strong congregation. Somehow, being at the right place at the right time was out of character for Van den Bosch. Operating on his own in the years before the great Huguenot migration and the founding of the Anglican Society for the Propagation of the Gospel, Van den Bosch was a pioneer without resources or allies. There was little support for his talents, and less for his background, in the colonial English and Huguenot communities. But only after exhausting his options there did he move on to the place that most resembled where he originally came from—the multi-ethnic yet still heavily Dutch colony of New York.

New York

New York was the last remaining place in North America with a French-speaking Protestant community for Van den Bosch to serve. He arrived by mid-September 1685, a distinct turning point in the Huguenot immigration to America. Van den Bosch, unwittingly, would be able to benefit from it, at least temporarily. The Edict of Nantes would not be formally revoked until October 22, 1685, but, sensing the difficulty of their situation, hundreds of Huguenots began moving to America in the months leading up to it. Whereas in Carolina and Boston there had barely been enough Huguenots to form a church, by the time Van den Bosch arrived in New York he would find enough to sustain him even with another Huguenot minister around.

Van den Bosch was not exactly welcomed with open arms by New York's Huguenots; his actions in Boston had threatened to ruin the reputation of the fledgling Huguenot community in America. In May and July 1686 the other Huguenot minister in New York, Pierre Daillé,

---

during the period between the overthrow of the Andros government and the establishment of the second charter of Massachusetts, 2 vols. (New York: B. Franklin, 1967), 2:36-37.

[18] On the Anglican Church and the Dominion of New England, see Viola Barnes, *The Dominion of New England: A Study in British Colonial Policy* (New Haven: Yale University Press, 1923), 47-70, 122-73.

wrote to Increase Mather apologizing for Van den Bosch's conduct, imploring him not to hold the one man's actions against the entire French congregation in Boston. "I beg you, most celebrated sir, that the annoyance occasioned by Mr. Vanderbosch may not be the occasion of your favoring less the French who are now in your city, and who shall betake themselves thither." He added "you are justly hostile to him, because he acted badly to your State and Church." Daillé sought to keep the Huguenot churches on good terms with the Congregational churches rather than pull them into the Church of England. This undoubtedly contributed to the rift that soon emerged between the two men in New York.[19]

Van den Bosch did not give up his Anglican activism once in New York. In July 1686 Daillé complained that Van den Bosch "acts perversely in everything." Against the will of the consistory he had tried to persuade New York's Huguenot community to admit a man named Deschamps, a resident of Boston and someone who "excited certain tumults in our church, which had previously been peaceful." In addition to "many other matters," Van den Bosch was causing something of a split with the nascent New York Huguenot Church. He "snatched away to himself two parts of our Church (which reside in the country)." The Huguenot Church, founded by Daillé only four years earlier, had until Van den Bosch's arrival been "intimately joined together, and, so to speak, one heart and one soul." Now it "went off into distinct parts."[20] Daillé gives no specifics, but it seems likely that once again Van den Bosch was offering a less than perfectly Calvinist form of religion to the Huguenots, as had likely been the case in Charleston and Boston. This was an issue that would cause divisions in the colonial Huguenot churches into the eighteenth century, and he seems to have had the support of at least some of the Huguenot laity.

Who supported Van den Bosch in New York? Not, apparently, the Walloons. In 1685-86 there were three French-speaking Protestant communities in New York, divided into two churches. One church was at New Paltz in Ulster County, where a small Walloon community had been gathered into a church by Daillé in January 1683. Too small and poor to support its own minister, New Paltz would not get a resident

---

[19] H. Haley Thomas, ed., *The Diary of Samuel Sewall, 1674-1725,* 2 vols. (New York: Farrar, Straus and Giroux, 1973), 1:78-79n; 2:1114 mistakenly has him as ministering 1685-1686; Merritt, "French Church," 325; Daillé to Increase Mather, May 2, 1686 and July, 1686, in Baird, *Huguenot Emigration,* 2: 398-400; Butler, *Huguenots,* 64-65 and Van Ruymbeke, *From New Babylon to Eden,* 117.

[20] Baird, *Huguenot Emigration,* 2:400.

minister until the eighteenth century. Until then it relied on occasional visits by a minister, initially Daillé, to baptize, preach, instruct, and marry.[21] There is no evidence of the Walloon Van den Bosch ever going to New Paltz, and only limited evidence of contact with the community's members. Though recognized as a Walloon, he does not seem to have been strongly identified as one.[22]

The other Walloon church was in New York. It catered to the large community of Huguenots who lived on and around Manhattan Island, with Staten Island being the most significant nearby community. Daillé's remarks about Van den Bosch splitting off two parts of his church probably refer to the fact that he had begun to minister separately to the French Protestant community on Staten Island and possibly to some Huguenot settlers at Rye. (New Rochelle would not be settled until 1688, although Huguenots had begun buying land there in 1686.) How and with whose authority or approval Van den Bosch did this is hard to say. The French congregants seem to have played the decisive role, and Daillé was clearly not happy about it. Dominie Selijns confirms that Van den Bosch was serving the church on Staten Island by September 1686. Exactly how long he had been doing so is uncertain, but it was at least since the spring, when Daillé began to complain of it.[23]

Van den Bosch remained on Staten Island for about eight months. Exactly why he left is unknown. It seems that once again a mixture of personal troubles and conflicts with a local authority figure (Daillé) encouraged a move. About March 1688 "a French servant girl" from Staten Island arrived in Albany, who, as one Dutchman later told Van den Bosch, "paints you very black, on account of your former evil life at Staten Island."[24] There is no other evidence about Van den Bosch's life

---

[21] *Records of the Reformed Dutch Church of New Paltz, New York*, trans. Dingman Versteeg (New York: Holland Society of New York, 1896), 1-2; Ralph Lefevre, *History of New Paltz, New York and its Old families from 1678 to 1820* (Bowie, MD: Heritage Books, 1992; 1903), 37-43; Roth, "'where the walleons dwell.'" For Daillé see Butler *Huguenots*, 45-46, 78-79. Daillé made occasional visits but never lived there.

[22] For Van den Bosch's relations with the Walloons of New Paltz, see Evan Haefeli, "A Scandalous Minister in a Divided Community: Ulster County in Leisler's Rebellion, 1689-1691," *New York History* 88:4 (Fall 2007): 357-89.

[23] E. T. Corwin, *Manual of the Reformed Church in America*, 499 lists Van den Bosch as serving at Boston, 1685; Rye, 1686; Staten Island, 1686-1687; Kingston, 1687-1689, cited in Merritt, "French Church," who also adds "I have not been able to verify the statement as to Rye," 325. Selijns mentions Van den Bosch in *ERNY* 2:935, 645, 947-48.

[24] Wessel ten Broeck testimony, October 18, 1689, "Letters about Dominie Vandenbosch, 1689," Frederick Ashton de Peyster mss., Box 2 #8, New York Historical Society (hereafter cited as Letters about Dominie Vandenbosch). In 1922

on Staten Island, but judging from what he did afterwards in Kingston, one can surmise it involved a certain amount of drinking and sexual harassment.

Kingston and the Dutch Reformed Ministry

A new opportunity opened up in Kingston in the spring of 1687. The resident minister had died over the winter,[25] and Kingston had had a hard time attracting and holding on to a minister for most of the previous twenty years. It was a poor and isolated community, with the lowest ministerial salary in the colony. But it was better enough than Staten Island to encourage Van den Bosch to step out of the Anglican and Huguenot churches and into the Dutch Reformed Church. New York's leading Dutch Reformed ministers, Henricus Selijns and Rudolphus Varick, could not help but see an opportunity. Chronically understaffed, they were initially happy to have another minister for their churches. By June 1687 Van den Bosch had "subscribed to the formularies of" the Dutch Reformed Church and had become Kingston's fourth minister.[26]

Kingston's high society (such as it was) embraced Van den Bosch. One of the most prominent local colonists, Henry Beekman, boarded him at his house.[27] Another, Wessel ten Broeck, introduced him to the family of his brother, the Albany magistrate and fur trader Dirck Wessels Ten Broeck. In the course of visits and socializing between Albany and Kingston over the summer of 1687, Van den Bosch met Dirck's young daughter, Cornelia. On October 16, 1687, he married her in the Dutch Reformed Church at Albany.[28] Van den Bosch had finally found a degree of acceptance and the opportunity to settle down that had eluded him all of these years. Unfortunately, rather than comfort him, this brought out personal troubles that may well have been haunting him for years.

Dingman Versteeg compiled a paginated manuscript translation of the letters that currently lies with the original manuscripts (hereafter cited as Versteeg, trans.), p. 71 contains Wessel ten Broeck's testimony.

[25] The minister Johannis Weeksteen's last known signature is on the deacons' accounts of January 9, 1686/7, "Translation of Dutch Records," trans. Dingman Versteeg, 3 vols., Ulster County Clerk's Office 1:316. For more on Van den Bosch's time in Ulster and the broader context of his scandal, see Haefeli, "A Scandalous Minister."

[26] Ecclesiastical Meeting held at Kingston, October 14, 1689, Letters about Dominie Vandenbosch, Versteeg trans., 49; Selijns to Hurley, December 24, 1689, Letters about Dominie Vandenbosch, Versteeg trans., 78.

[27] He was living with the Beekmans in 1689, see testimony of Johannes Wynkoop, Benjamin Provoost, October 17, 1689, Letters about Dominie Vandenbosch, Versteeg trans., 60-61.

[28] "Albany Church Records," *Yearbook of the Holland Society of New York, 1904* (New York, 1904), 22.

Van den Bosch's letter to the bishop of London offers the first evidence of the mentality that would alienate him from Kingston's elite. His trope of unjust persecution by a powerful band of enemies, combined with implacable and brave resistance to their threats and machinations, did not reflect an aptitude for harmony and neighborliness. Perhaps it was a response to being a lone man without contacts, allies, or resources in the clannish colonies. Perhaps it was something deeper in his personality. Either way, it prevented him from settling down in any of the communities he served. He simply could not cooperate with people who disagreed with him. He reflexively interpreted any opposition or criticism as a conspiracy against him. For Van den Bosch it was always about power. Remarkably not self reflective and unable to recognize any faults of his own, his instinct was to stubbornly dig in his heels and resist rather than seek forgiveness and understanding.

For a Protestant minister, Van den Bosch also had a quirky sensibility. One Dutch dominie later complained that he had heard "a few expressions" of Van den Bosch's "which would better fit the mouth of a mocker with religion than of a Pastor." Another man reported that, when he went to have "his newly born infant entered in the baptismal record of the church," Van den Bosch had replied "that he came to him because he needed his ointment." Perhaps it was a joke, but it did not go over well.[29] Another local recounted how Van den Bosch told him about the ancient Romans' custom of beating their wives once a year "on the evening prior to the day they went to confession, because then, reproaching the men for everything they had done during the entire year, they [the men] would be so much better able to confess." Since Van den Bosch had quarreled with his wife the day before, he said he was "now fit to go to confession."[30] Another neighbor remembered Van den Bosch saying that "there were two kinds of Jesuits, viz one kind took no wives; and another kind took wives without getting married; and then Dom said: Oh my God, that is the kind of marriage I agree with."[31] These comments about magical ointments, confession (a Catholic sacrament), and Jesuits did nothing to endear Van den Bosch to his Calvinist neighbors.[32] The feeling was mutual. At one point, while

---

[29] Ecclesiastical Meeting held at Kingston, October 14, 1689, Letters about Dominie Vandenbosch, Versteeg trans., 51-52.
[30] Ecclesiastical Meeting held at Kingston, October 15, 1689, Letters about Dominie Vandenbosch, Versteeg trans., 53-54.
[31] Ecclesiastical Meeting held at Kingston, October 15, 1689, Letters about Dominie Vandenbosch, Versteeg trans., 68-69.
[32] Varick to Vandenbosch, August 16, 1689, Letters about Dominie Vandenbosch, Versteeg trans., 21.

drunk, he "slapped his behind and shoes, and filliped his thumb, and said, the Farmers are my slaves."[33]

The Scandal

Ulster County's population was a mix of Dutch, Walloons, Huguenots, and English. Linguistically, Van den Bosch was the perfect candidate to be their minister. Unfortunately, he was not the man for the job. Trouble began shortly before his wedding, when Van den Bosch got drunk and grabbed a local woman in an overly familiar way. Rather than doubt himself, he mistrusted his wife and began openly to suspect her fidelity. After church one Sunday in March 1688, Van den Bosch told her uncle Wessel, "I am much dissatisfied at the behavior of Arent van Dyk and my wife." Wessel answered, "do you think they are behaving together unchastely?" Replied Van den Bosch, "I do not trust them much." Wessel proudly retorted "I do not suspect your wife of unchasteness, because we have none such among our race [i.e. the Ten Broeck family]. But should she be such, I wished that a millstone were tied around her neck, and she died thus. ButI believe that you are no good yourself, as I have heard Jacob Lysnaar [i.e. Leisler] declare." Leisler had business contacts up and down the coast as well as special ties to the French Protestant community. He was in a particularly privileged position to hear any stories circulating about Van den Bosch, from the disgruntled Daillé to tales of the sort being spread by the French servant girl from Staten Island.[34]

By the fall of 1688 Van den Bosch was drinking regularly, chasing women (including his servant girl, Elizabeth Vernooy and her friend, Sara ten Broeck, Wessel's daughter) and fighting violently with his wife.[35] The turning point came in October when he started choking Cornelia one evening after he had administered the Lord's Supper. This finally turned Kingston's elite against him. The church elders and deacons suspended Van den Bosch from preaching, although he continued to baptize and perform marriages until April 1689. In December they began to take

---

[33] Wessel ten Broeck Testimony, October 18, 1689, Letters about dominie Vandenbosch, Versteeg trans., 71a.

[34] Wessel ten Broeck testimony, October 18, 1689, Letters about Dominie Vandenbosch, Versteeg trans., 70. Lysnaar is a common spelling of Leisler in colonial documents, David Voorhees, personal communication, September 2, 2004.

[35] Deposition of Grietje, wife of Willem Schut, April 9, 1689, Letters about Dominie Vandenbosch, Versteeg trans., 66-67; Marya ten Broeck testimony, October 14, 1689, Letters about Dominie Vandenbosch, Versteeg trans., 51; Lysebit Vernooy testimony, December 11, 1688, Letters about Dominie Vandenbosch, Versteeg trans., 65.

down testimony against him. It had apparently been decided to take the minister to court, because further testimony was collected in April 1689. One member angrily wrote to Selijns, demanding that something be done.[36] Stories of Van den Bosch's deeds spread. He complained of one of his parishioners who "blackened and vilified me in New York and on Long Island."[37] Something had to be done to restore order in the church.

How were the Dutch ministers to respond? Never before in the history of the Dutch Reformed Church in North America had the moral integrity of one of its ministers been challenged by his congregants. Until now the only disputes had been over salaries. In Europe there were institutions to deal with such cases—a court or a classis. America still had no ecclesiastical organization ready to deal with a badly behaved minister. Could the local courts handle the case?

Before anything could be done, New York was engulfed in a political revolution. In the fall of 1688 the Prince of Orange had invaded England with a Dutch army, compelling England's King James II to flee to France. After a few months England's Parliament named Prince William and his wife Mary (James II's daughter) as the new monarchs of England. This development called into question the government of the Dominion of New England appointed by James II. Since New York had been a personal colony of James II before being incorporated into the Dominion of New England, political authority there was particularly shaky. After news of the revolution reached New York in May 1689, a number of colonists demanded that the government created under James and the Dominion be replaced. The result was a local political revolution, since named after its figurehead, Jacob Leisler. Leisler's Rebellion disrupted and divided local government to the extent that it could not be relied upon to resolve the Van den Bosch case. Rather than going to court, the ministers would have to improvise.

Over the next several months, as Leisler's Rebellion unfolded, New York's Dutch ministers began to conceive of an unprecedented act of colonial church governance: bringing together representatives of the Dutch Reformed churches to resolve a dispute in one of them. In June the Reverend Petrus Tesschenmaecker, minister of Schenectady's Dutch Reformed Church, visited Kingston to inform the people that

---

[36] Laurentius Van den Bosch to Selijns June 21, 1689, Letters about Dominie Vandenbosch, Versteeg trans., 5-6; Hoes, ed. *Baptismal and Marriage Registers*, Part 1 *Baptisms*, 28-35 and Part 2 *Marriages*, 509.

[37] Laurentius Van den Bosch to Selijns May 26, 1689, Letters about Dominie Vandenbosch, Versteeg trans., 2.

Selijns had designated him to resolve the dispute. He proposed bringing in "two preachers and two elders of the neighboring churches." In July Van den Bosch and his principal accuser, Willem de Meyer, sent letters to Selijns, saying they would submit themselves to the judgment of the ministers and elders who would come and hear the case. But both qualified their submission to this committee. Van den Bosch submitted legalistically, "Provided the judgment and conclusion of said preachers and elders agree with God's word and with the Church discipline." De Meyer retained the right to appeal the decision to the Classis of Amsterdam, which had assumed authority over the Dutch churches in North America since the founding of New Netherland.[38]

Van den Bosch had ignited a debate over authority and power within the colonial Dutch Reformed Church. De Meyer took an anti-clerical stance; he did not trust the churchmen to discipline one of their own properly. He had heard a rumor of Selijns saying "that nobody should think that a Preacher, referring to Dominie Van den Bosch, could not as easily misbehave as an ordinary member." He understood this to mean "that a minister could not commit any faults (no matter how great they might be) on account whereof he could be absolutely deposed from office."[39] Rumor and insinuation were undermining ministerial authority.[40]

Dominie Selijns hoped for reconciliation. He feared the Van den Bosch affair might add to the schism developing in the colony's church over the new revolutionary government. Unfortunately, reconciliation was not the order of the day. Van den Bosch penned a long, defiant, letter to Selijns, denying that his enemies could prove anything against him and insisting that he was the victim of a slanderous campaign. His persecution complex leaps off the manuscript: "they dealt with me worse than the Jews dealt with Christ, excepting that they could not crucify me, which makes them feel sorry enough." He blamed his

---

[38] Laurentius Van den Bosch to Selijns, July 15, 1689 Letters about Dominie Vandenbosch, Versteeg trans., 3-4; Wilhelmus De Meyer to Selijns, July 16, 1689 Letters about Dominie Vandenbosch, Versteeg trans., 1.

[39] Ecclesiastical Meeting held at Kingston, October 14, 1689, Letters about Dominie Vandenbosch, Versteeg trans., 50; Laurentius Van den Bosch to Selijns, October 21, 1689 Letters about Dominie Vandenbosch, Versteeg trans., 38.

[40] Pieter Bogardus, who De Meyer charged with spreading the rumor, later denied it, Selijns to Varick, October 26, 1689, Letters about Dominie Vandenbosch, Versteeg trans., 37. The New York churches rebuked the "Upland" churches for giving credit to De Meyer's reliance on "hearsay," Selijns, Marius, Schuyler and Varick to the Churches of n. Albany and Schenectade, November 5, 1689, Letters about Dominie Vandenbosch, Versteeg trans., 43-44.

accusers for depriving his congregation of his preaching.[41] He assumed no guilt. True to form, Van den Bosch chose conflict over cooperation, undoing Selijns's hopes for reconciliation.

Ultimately, an "ecclesiastical assembly" was convened at Kingston in October 1689 to hear Van den Bosch's case. It was supposed to contain ministers and elders from all the Dutch churches. Distracted by the Revolution, the churches around Manhattan did not attend. The ministers and elders of Schenectady and Albany, who did attend, collected testimony about Van den Bosch for several days. Then one night they caught Van den Bosch stealing some of their documents. When he refused to admit the obvious, they refused to continue hearing his case. Claiming that he "could not with profit or edification" continue as minister of Kingston, Van den Bosch peremptorily resigned.[42]

Van den Bosch's resignation spared the colonial church from any constitutional dilemmas that might have been provoked by the need to depose him against his will. In a letter to Selijns—his last on the matter—Van den Bosch said that he "could not live in any further troubles, that they should look for another preacher, and that I should try to find happiness and quiet in some other place."[43] But he did not go away. On December 12, 1689, Ulster's Leislerian sheriff wrote to Selijns that Van den Bosch was still preaching and baptizing in the county and had even announced publicly "that he intends to administer the Holy Supper. . . . Many simple minded ones follow him." The sheriff requested a statement from Selijns "in writing" as to whether or not it was permissible for Van den Bosch to administer communion.[44] Selijns would write a number of statements to Hurley and Kingston over the next year, making clear the judgment of his church that Van den Bosch was unfit for the ministry.[45] But it made no difference. The colony-wide

---

[41] Laurentius Van den Bosch to Selijns, August 6, 1689, Letters about Dominie Vandenbosch, Versteeg trans., 7-17.

[42] Ecclesiastical Meeting held at Kingston, October 1689, Letters about Dominie Vandenbosch, Versteeg trans., 49-73; Dellius and Tesschenmaeker to Selijns, 1690, Letters about Dominie Vandenbosch, Versteeg trans., 32-34.

[43] See the correspondence in Letters about Dominie Vandenbosch, Versteeg trans., 36-44.

[44] De la Montagne to Selijns, December 12, 1689, Letters about Dominie Vandenbosch, Versteeg trans., 76.

[45] Selijns to "the Wise and Prudent gentlemen the Commissaries and Constables at Hurley," December 24, 1689, Letters about Dominie Vandenbosch, Versteeg trans., 77-78; Selijns & Jacob de Key to elders of Kingston, June 26, 1690, Letters about Dominie Vandenbosch, Versteeg trans., 81-82; Kingston's consistory to Selijns, August 30, 1690, Letters about Dominie Vandenbosch, Versteeg trans., 83-84; Selijns and consistory to Kingston, October 29, 1690, Letters about Dominie Vandenbosch, Versteeg trans., 85-86.

breakdown of authority in church and state under Leisler's rule allowed Van den Bosch to remain in Ulster until the spring of 1692.

The Classis of Amsterdam was bewildered. The affair was the first to invoke its authority over New York's Dutch ministers since the English conquest of 1664. Receiving a request for help from Selijns in June 1691, it asked deputies to research the matter. They found "no instance that the Classis of Amsterdam has had any hand in such business." Instead, local magistrates and consistories had always taken action. So the classis did not reply to Selijns. A year later, in April 1692, the classis finally wrote to say that it was sorry to hear about the troubles in Kingston's church, but that it did not understand them or know how to respond to them.[46]

After October 1690 there is little mention of Van den Bosch. He seems to have stayed on for another year and a half of so. At the latest he was gone by June 1692, though this was mentioned only briefly in the ecclesiastical correspondence from October 1692. Van den Bosch had "left Esopus and gone to Maryland."[47] He left behind his wife and a notoriously divided congregation. Once again he was on his own.

Maryland

Little is known about Van den Bosch's time in Maryland, the final and only fully Anglican phase of his career. One record has him administering a baptism in Cecil County on July 2, 1692. He was welcomed as a minister to the Church of England, which had just been made the established church of Maryland that June. Cecil County had been split into two parishes, North and South Sassafras. These were two of the original thirty Anglican parishes established in Maryland in 1692. Van den Bosch began ministering in North Sassafras, and in 1694 he was accepted as the minister of South Sassafras as well. He ministered to both parishes from 1694 until his death, which a local history (without citing direct evidence) puts at 1696.[48] Word of his death had certainly arrived in New York by that spring. Freed from the bonds of her unhappy marriage, his widow Cornelia married one of her former protectors, the blacksmith and consistory member Johannes Wynkoop, and had conceived a daughter by July 1696.[49]

[46] *ERNY* 2:1020-21.
[47] "Translation of Dutch Records," trans. Dingman Versteeg, 3 vols., Ulster County Clerk's Office, Kingston, New York 3:316-17; *ERNY* 2:1005-06, 1043.
[48] Merritt, "French Protestant Church," 327-29.
[49] There is no marriage record for Cornelia and Johannes preserved in either Kingston or Albany. But on March 28, 1697 they baptized a daughter, Christina, in Kingston.

North Sassafras parish today is based in the church of Saint Stephen in Earlville, which may well have been where Van den Bosch resided when he composed his last and most distinctive contribution to American history: a remarkably accurate map of the mouth of the Mississippi River and the Gulf Coast to its west. He drew it for Governor Francis Nicholson, a known patron of the Anglican Church who had been lieutenant governor of New York while Van den Bosch was there. Van den Bosch hoped to gain his patronage ("If this Labour of Mine hath the happiness to please yor Exy I will rejoice for it and I shall think my Pains not to have been Spent in vain"). In a letter dated "North Sassifrix, the 19th of October... 1694," "Lawrence van den Bosh" explained that he got the information about the region "on the left side of the Messacippi River from a French Indian."[50] Possibly a Shawnee, the man knew enough French to convey the information to Van den Bosch, whose linguistic skills came in handy once again.[51]

It seems quite fitting that the last evidence we have of Van den Bosch is of him dreaming of opportunity in the West and seeking the favor of a powerful male patron. Van den Bosch had come to America seeking opportunity. He found several opportunities, but he never found the political backing he clearly hoped for to protect him from those who criticized his behavior, whether personal or ecclesiastic. Unusually rootless for a colonial minister, Van den Bosch's life compels psychological analysis. His letters reveal what we would today call a narcissistic personality with some paranoid tendencies, both no doubt aggravated by the alcohol abuse all too common in the colonies. He also had difficulty with women. At the same time he was clearly charismatic, having a distinct appeal for at least certain individuals at important moments in his career. He was troubled, conflicted, and ambivalent about his place in early colonial society, and his experience is a reminder that even though there was a need for his talents—in

---

On their family, see Hoes, ed., *Baptismal and Marriage Registers,* Part 1 *Baptisms,* 31, 40, 49, 54, 61, 106. Johannes Wynkoop is noted as blacksmith, October 1692, Kingston Trustees Records, 1688-1816, 8 vols. (Ulster County Clerk's Office, Kingston, NY), 1:148.

[50] Lawrence van den Bosh, "Mississippi River and adjacent Gulf coast, 1694," Ayer Collection No 59, Newberry Library, Chicago, cited in W.P. Cumming et al., *The Exploration of North America, 1630-1776* (New York: G. P. Putnam's Sons, 1974), 151, with the map displayed as figure 226.

[51] Gregory A. Waselkov, "Indian Maps of the Colonial Southeast," in Peter H. Wook, Gregory A. Waselkov, and M. Thomas Hatley, eds., *Powhatan's Mantle: Indians in the Colonial Southeast* (Lincoln: University of Nebraska Press, 1989), 436-37, fig. 1, and 457-62, fig. 9, transcribes the text of the map's captions along with Van den Bosch's letter.

several churches—the the job of a pioneer minister was not for everyone. Apart from Maryland, where he apparently served without incident, his misadventures unsettled the first Huguenot churches, provoked New Englanders against the Anglican Church, and caused a minor constitutional crisis for the Dutch Reformed Church. He clearly had a knack for affronting Calvinist sensibilities. It is here, rather than in any theological or pastoral contribution, that his significance to religious life lies. The map, along with his wanderlust, suggests that his real potential lay elsewhere: as an explorer or adventurer, not in the settled Reformed ministry.

MEDIATORS

Dutch-Americans and Their Neighbors
in the Transitional Eighteenth Century

CHAPTER 10

Archibald Laidlie (1727–1779): The Scot who Revitalized New York City's Dutch Reformed Church

Joyce D. Goodfriend

The Reverend Archibald Laidlie clearly was not a typical Dutch Reformed clergyman in the American colonies. He was not Dutch and he did not affiliate with the Dutch Reformed church until well into his thirties when he was called to serve in New York City's Reformed church in 1764. Yet he had an enormous influence on the New York City congregation during the dozen or so years of his ministry there and, had he lived (he died in 1779), he surely would have played a major role in the church's development after the American Revolution.[1]

Explaining Laidlie's meteoric rise in New York City's Dutch church is something of a challenge, given that he was a Scot and a Presbyterian whose original church was the Church of Scotland. He was born in Kelso, Scotland, to William Laidlie and Jean Dickson in 1727.[2]

---

[1] I have examined Archibald Laidlie's impact on New York City's Dutch Reformed congregation in Joyce D. Goodfriend, "Archibald Laidlie and the Transformation of the Dutch Reformed Church in Eighteenth-Century New York City," *Journal of Presbyterian History* 81 (2003): 149-62. See also its biographical references.

[2] "A Memoir of the Rev. Archibald Laidlie, D.D. Late One of the Pastors of the Collegiate Reformed Prot. Dutch Church in New York," *The Magazine of the Reformed Dutch Church* 2 (May 1827): 33-37.

Archibald Laidlie
[Portrait owned by Collegiate Church, New York]

We can surmise that Archibald was a religious youth since he moved to Edinburgh to further his education and prepare for the ministry. In 1749, already in the Scottish capital, he began a spiritual diary that revealed his state of mind.[3] By this time he most likely had begun his studies at the University of Edinburgh. After receiving his M. A. degree, he served as a lecturer at Edinburgh.[4] In the Scottish capital, Laidlie likely came under the influence of a local minister named Robert Walker, who was associated with the Popular party in the Church of Scotland.[5] This situated him in the evangelical wing of Scottish Presbyterianism. Little else is known about Laidlie's early life other than that he had a brother, John Laidlie, with whom he corresponded after he moved to the Netherlands and later to New York. While in Vlissingen in 1761 he

---

[3] "A Memoir of the Rev. Archibald Laidlie."
[4] Hew Scott, *Fasti Ecclesiae Scoticanae: The Succession of Ministers in the Church of Scotland from the Reformation*. 7 vols. (Edinburgh: Oliver and Boyd, 1928), 7:545.
[5] *The Magazine of the Reformed Dutch Church* 2 (May 1827), 33. Ned C. Landsman, "Presbyterians and Provincial Society: The Evangelical Enlightenment in the West of Scotland, 1740-1775" in John Dwyer and Richard B. Sher, eds., *Sociability and Society in Eighteenth-Century Scotland* (Edinburgh: The Mercat Press, 1993), 196-97.

learned from his brother that their mother had died.[6] In a 1773 letter to his brother John, who lived in Kelso, he wrote about "my nephew William, your son" and sent greetings to "Sister [John's wife], & to Eliza [their daughter] and William.[7] He also mentioned receiving a letter from cousin John Dickson, uncle John's son.[8]

Ministry in Vlissingen

Undoubtedly the greatest gap in our knowledge of Laidlie's life and career concerns the period from the time of his graduation from the university to his appointment to a post at the Scottish Church in Vlissingen, the Netherlands in 1759. No records have come to light to indicate how he spent the years before he received the call from the Scottish Church in Vlissingen.[9] For whatever reason, he did not occupy a regular post in Scotland, and one can infer that he answered the call from the congregation in Vlissingen only as a last resort. More importantly, there is nothing in his life history to this point that even remotely suggests that he would become a star in New York City.

Laidlie made the most of his years as a minister to the small Scottish congregation in Vlissingen (1759-1763), deliberately setting out to curry the favor of clergymen and influential laymen. To play a role in local Dutch society, he had to school himself in the language and customs of the Netherlands. As he explained to his brother John in 1761, he needed to "Comply with the Customs of that people among whom providence has called me to live."[10] His satisfaction at his progress in adapting to his new life was evident in his boast to his brother the year before: "I have many kind friends ... especially some of the Magistrates, Ministers and other Dutch gentlemen of the best sort,

[6] Archibald Laidlie to John Laidlie, Flushing [the Netherlands], October 20, 1761. Archibald Laidlie Manuscripts, New York Historical Society. All Laidlie letters cited hereafter come from this collection unless otherwise indicated.

[7] Archibald Laidlie to John Laidlie, New York, November 5, 1773. In a letter written to John Laidlie from Amsterdam on December 1, 1763, Archibald Laidlie sends "kindest Comp[limen]ts to Sister, Niece and Nephew, to all my relations and friends." Archibald Laidlie to John Laidlie, Amsterdam, December 1, 1763.

[8] Archibald Laidlie to John Laidlie, New York, November 5, 1773. In a 1759 letter, he had referred to "Cousins Blackie and John Dickson." Archibald Laidlie to John Laidlie, Vlissingen, July 28, 1759.

[9] Prior to leaving for the Netherlands, he was admitted as a minister of the Church of Scotland on September 2, 1759. Scott, *Fasti Ecclesiae Scoticanae*, vol. vii, 545. On the Scottish church in Vlissingen, see William Steven, *The History of the Scottish Church, Rotterdam* (Edinburgh: Waugh and Innes, 1832) and Keith L. Sprunger, *Dutch Puritanism: A History of English and Scottish Churches in the Netherlands in the Sixteenth and Seventeenth Centuries* (Leiden: Brill, 1982).

[10] Archibald Laidlie to [John Laidlie], Flushing, the Netherlands, October 20, 1761.

whose acquaintance is both an honour and advantage to me, and as I begin now to speak Dutch, I can have both more pleasure and profit in their Company."[11] Laidlie's aspiration to move in elite circles may have been fulfilled in Vlissingen, but this was a small field on which to build a reputation. Much more significant is the fact that he had been noticed by the English ministers in Amsterdam who recommended him to the Classis of Amsterdam when a request came from New York City's Dutch Reformed Church for a minister who could preach in the English language.[12] The classis decided to propose Laidlie as the best candidate to meet the specifications of the New York congregation for "a good orator, used to elegant language, acquainted with men and books, ... orthodox in his principles, of an unblemished character, and affable in his behavior, whose piety is exemplary."[13] On October 3, 1763, he was "installed ... for the Holy Office in the church of New York" by the Classis.[14] This marked the critical turning point in the Scottish preacher's career. Not recognized in his homeland, he had transplanted himself to the Netherlands, where his assiduous efforts to please the locals while impressing the resident English clergy had paid off in his recognition by the Dutch Reformed church.

New York City

Still, Archibald Laidlie arrived in New York City in 1764 at the age of thirty-seven with much to prove. Although his sponsors in the Netherlands viewed him as a man of promise, his biography contained no evidence that would explain his phenomenal success in his new congregation. So we still must account for the astonishing success of a minister whose accomplishments to date were minimal compared to those of his peers.

Archibald Laidlie was well educated and assuredly well read in the works of Scottish and Dutch divines. He brought his library with him to his new post, shipping two boxes of books from Europe to New York.[15] But he made no claim to being a theologian, and none of his

---

[11] Archibald Laidlie to [John Laidlie], Flushing, The Netherlands, January 28, 1760.
[12] E. T. Corwin, ed., *Ecclesiastical Records of the State of New York*, 7 vols. (Albany: Lyon, 1901-1916), 6:3872-73. Hereafter cited as *ERNY*.
[13] "Call sent from Holland for a Minister to Preach in English ... January 10, 1763," *ERNY* 6:3855.
[14] *ERNY* 6:3907.
[15] Merchant Isaac Roosevelt of the New York City Dutch Reformed congregation was responsible for transporting two boxes of Laidlie's books from Europe to New York. Isaac Roosevelt Papers, Mss., Franklin Delano Roosevelt Library, Hyde Park, New York.

sermons were ever published. What made him stand out were his skills in the pulpit. Judging from contemporary commentary, Laidlie was an outstanding preacher. Whether his talents were fully appreciated by the transplanted Scots whose small congregation he served in Vlissingen is unclear, but once situated on a large stage and given more robust support, he blossomed as a charismatic preacher who drew hundreds of listeners, not all of whom were affiliated with the congregation. An Episcopalian named Elias Nexsen [Nixon] was reported to have been so "pleased and edified by the discriminating, powerful and savoury preaching of Dr. Laidlie" that "he and several others left the Episcopal for the Reformed Dutch communion."[16] It was not only adherents of the Church of England that were swept away by Laidlie's preaching. Samuel Auchmuty, the minister of Trinity Church, commented pointedly in October 1764 that Presbyterians were attracted to Laidlie. "Many of their greatest & most zealous Ladies have left them & have joined themselves to Master Ladley, & are contented for the present to hear him preach his Scotch true Calvinistic stuff, for two Hours upon a Stretch."[17]

From the outset, Laidlie got good reviews. On April 16, 1764, the *New York Gazette* reported favorably on his initial appearance in the city as the pastor designated to "officiate in the *English tongue*." The newspaper reported that "In the Afternoon Mr. Laidley with great Modesty, introduced himself to his Congregation at the New-Dutch Church to a prodigious crowded Auditory, making use of this Portion of Scripture, *Knowing therefore the Terror of the Lord, we persuade Men;* 2 Corinthians, Chap. V, Verse 11—which he handled with great Judgment, and Energy. His Application was extremely suitable; and concluded with a Charge highly becoming a Divine as not being afraid of the *Arm of Flesh* in endeavouring to reconcile Divisions."[18] Years later it was recorded that Margaret Beekman Livingston "was awakened under the first sermon the Rev. Sadly [Laidlie] preached in the Reformed Low Dutch church in New York, . . . nor she alone, but six or eight other respectable women."[19]

---

[16] *Christian Intelligencer*, June 18, 1831. Thanks to Firth Haring Fabend for this reference.

[17] Samuel Auchmuty to Dr. Samuel Johnson, New York, October 26, 1764, Hawks Collection, Mss. Archives of the Episcopal Church, Austin, Texas.

[18] *New York Gazette*, April 16, 1764. A portion of the sermon Laidlie delivered on April 15, 1764, is printed in "Religious Communications," *The Magazine of the Reformed Dutch Church* 2 (September 1827): 161-69.

[19] Elmer T. Clark, ed., *The Journal and Letters of Francis Asbury*, 3 vols. (London: Epworth, 1958), 3:242.

New York City's Dutch Reformed congregation had long been divided over the issue of the language of preaching. Since the 1740s congregants had debated the value of introducing English-language preaching to supplement Dutch-language preaching. Those who advocated calling a minister fluent in English, primarily members of the elite, were concerned about the gradual loss of younger members who could not speak Dutch and, in particular, "the offspring of the wealthiest members."[20] Unable to understand sermons preached in Dutch, these scions of the venerable Dutch families of the city and colony drifted to one of the many churches in New York City where English ministers held forth. To the dismay of its leaders, the congregation had become "a nursery for all the English denominations of Christians in this city, and those chiefly from our principal people, whereby most men in power belong to other congregations though lineally descended from Dutch parents."[21] The prospect ahead was sobering. As the congregation's size diminished, so would its wealth as well as its influence in public affairs.

Not all in the New York City church accepted this line of thinking. A substantial segment of the congregation—primarily artisans and laborers and their wives—rejected the argument that their congregation's imminent decline was attributable to the continuing use of Dutch in worship. Instead they traced the problem to the failure of church leaders to educate the children in the language of their ancestors. This group of congregants insisted that the only way to remedy the problem was to hold fast to tradition. In their eyes, preserving the true church order was dependent not only on adhering to the principles set forth at the Synod of Dort but maintaining Dutch as the sole language of preaching. In 1762 they stated unequivocally that they "would in no way consent that an English-preaching minister should come into our church. They desired to remain as they always had been."[22] Although the Amsterdam Classis turned down their petition that "no change or intermingling of languages be allowed in their house of worship," this did not diminish their zeal to retain time-honored ways. "We will protect our church in its doctrine and its language as far as lies in our power."[23]

Innovations in Preaching Style

What distinguished Laidlie from his fellow ministers—Johannes Ritzema and Lambertus De Ronde—other than his use of the English

[20] *ERNY* 6:3854.
[21] Ibid..
[22] Ibid, 3826.
[23] Ibid., 3880-81.

language was his evangelical style of preaching. To listeners familiar only with the formalistic sermons of orthodox preachers, this was eye-opening. John Henry Livingston, who became Laidlie's partner in the city's English-language ministry, praised his colleague's performance in the pulpit unsparingly. "He was a very acceptable preacher; bold and authoritative, commanding respect, fear, and love. The wicked trembled when he announced the terrors of the Lord, while the lambs of the flock were nourished and comforted, when he displayed the grace, care, and faithfulness of their divine and good Shepherd."[24] An early biographer described Laidlie as "one of the most spiritual, practical, and heart searching preachers of his day," a view seconded by a more recent writer who concluded that Laidlie "earned a reputation as an exceedingly earnest, direct, down-to earth, heart-searching, warm sermonizer."[25] No wonder that people flocked to hear him. In 1765 the elders and deacons related that Laidlie's work "is getting blessed in our congregation. It has caused a great stir among the dry bones of the valley, (Ezekiel 37)."[26] By 1767 the consistory was reporting that "the numbers of our Congregation who attend his preaching . . . are three times as many, as attend the Dutch service."[27] Laidlie continued to garner effusive praise from Dutch men and women of high status who had yearned for a distinguished speaker in their pulpit.

Laidlie took pride in his accomplishments. "I desire to mention with humility and Gratitude" he wrote his brother in Scotland in 1773, "that God remarkably blessed my Labours, and made his Word preached the happy and effectual means of Converting many." As he elaborated, he stressed his attentiveness to his work, a fact noticeable to all around him. Laidlie industriously fulfilled his ministerial duties in New York, devoting enormous amounts of time to teaching catechism classes, which were seen as critical preparation for communicants in the Dutch Reformed church. To highlight the differences between the Dutch Reformed church and the Church of Scotland, Laidlie informed

---

[24] John Henry Livingston quoted in Alexander Gunn, *Memoirs of the Rev. John Henry Livingston* (New York: Rutgers Press, 1829), 104-105.
[25] *The Magazine of the Reformed Dutch Church* 2 (May 1827): 34; Earl William Kennedy, "From Providence to Civil Religion: Some 'Dutch' Reformed Interpretations of America in the Revolutionary Era," *The Reformed Review* 29 (1976): 113. On Laidlie's preaching, see also Jack Douglas Klunder, "The Application of Holy Things: A Study of the Covenant Preaching in the Eighteenth-Century Dutch Colonial Church" (Th.D. dissertation, Westminster Theological Seminary, 1984), 133-37; 215-61.
[26] Elders and Deacons of the Church of New York to the Classis of Amsterdam, October 26, 1765, *ERNY* 6:4017.
[27] Consistory of the Dutch Reformed Church to Gov. Henry Moore, November 11, 1767, *ERNY* 6: 4104-06.

his brother that "it is a laudable practice in the dutch Church to admit none to the Lord's Table, but such as have been previously instructed in the knowledge of divine Truths agreeable to the plan laid down in the Heidelbergh Catechism, which is adopted by the Church of Holland." As a consequence, he continued, "I found myself under a necessity of having "no less than Seven different Companies of persons, Old & Young to instruct in the Knowledge of divine truths."[28]

Yet Laidlie did not stick precisely to the customary ways of imparting divine truths to New Yorkers. The year after his arrival he had already set in motion a plan to change the catechism used in teaching the doctrines of the Dutch Reformed church to one that more closely reflected his evangelical views. Lambertus De Ronde recounted that "Laidlie introduced a little catechism by Rev. Hellenbroek. This had been translated into English by a man named Low, a builder by trade. It was presented to the consistory with the intention that the young people should be catechized from it."[29] On July 29, 1765, "A translation into English of Domine A. Hellenbroek's Catechism by Petrus Lowe, had been presented" to the Consistory."[30] Evidently approved, the book was published by John Holt in 1765.[31] Abraham Hellenbroek (1658-1731) was a highly admired Dutch pietist minister whose 1709 catechism *Voorbeeld Der Godlyke Waarheden* [Specimen of Divine Truth] was circulated widely in both the Netherlands and America.[32] According to James Tanis, Hellenbroek "sought to change catechizing from a mental exercise to a spiritual exercise."[33]

Not only had Laidlie urged the adoption of a new catechism, but he had been instrumental in the appointment of a new catechist. This was an affront to his colleague, Lambertus de Ronde, who reported in September 1765 that "before the coming of Rev. Laidlie, I had over eighty catechumens (in English); but as soon as he came my 'System' was discarded.[34] The children were then put under the instruction of

---

[28] Archibald Laidlie to John Laidlie, New York, November 5, 1773.
[29] Lambertus De Ronde to the Rev. John Kalkoen, September 9, 1765, *ERNY* 6:4006.
[30] Ibid., 3999.
[31] A. Hellenbroeck, *Specimen of Divine Truths, Fitted for the Use of those, of various Capacities, who desire to prepare themselves for a due Confession of their Faith* (New York: John Holt, 1765).
[32] Hendrik Edelman, *Dutch-American Bibliography, 1693-1794* (Nieuwkoop: De Graaf, 1974), 110.
[33] James Tanis, "Reformed Pietism in Colonial America" in F. Ernest Stoeffler, ed., *Continental Pietism and Early American Christianity* (Grand Rapids, MI: Eerdmans, 1976), 52.
[34] Lambertus de Ronde, *A System: Containing, the Principles of the Christian Religion, Suitable to the Heidelberg Catechism; By Plain Questions and Answers. Useful for the Information of*

a newly appointed teacher, a tailor by trade."[35] In July 1766 de Ronde augmented his charge, stating that Laidlie "with our Consistory, appointed a Dutch tailor as a catechist in English, although this man had never before done any such work."[36] This man was Jakobus van Antwerp, whom the consistory had appointed "Catechist in the English language" on August 20, 1764. He was to "receive from the church £15, yearly, and from each catechumen two shillings per quarter."[37]

Laidlie was also an innovater in the practice of religion, setting up small devotional meetings for particular groups. Lambertus De Ronde disapproved of these "special meetings where women by themselves, and men, and youths by themselves expound the Scriptures by turns, repeat prayers from memory, discuss questions of conscience, etc."[38] Although conceding that "there is much clamor about sudden conversions of those who attend these meetings which have been organized," De Ronde remained skeptical of such "novelties."[39] De Ronde also censured Laidlie for deviating from Dutch Reformed practice, noting that he "was not willing to preach from Passion-texts or holiday sermons, as he ought to have done."[40] This criticism was echoed even by men counted among Laidlie's admirers, such as merchants Dirk Brinkerhoff and Abraham Lott, who admitted that the conduct of Dr. Laidlie with respect to the observance of holy days had given offence.[41] In a 1768 letter to John Henry Livingston, Lott asserted that there were "matters [such as observance of holy days], wherein [Laidlie] stands, in my opinion, wrong affected."[42] Posing a question designed to remind Livingston how far Laidlie had strayed from local practice, Lott asked "are you . . . such a stranger to the people of the Dutch Church of this

---

All Persons in the True Confession of Faith; and Necessary towards their Preparation for that Awful and Solemn Ordinance, the Lord's Supper. To Which is Prefixed, a Particular Address to Parents in General. Shewing the Relation they Stand under to their Children, to Instruct them in the Principles of the Christian Religion. And, to Which is Added, an Application of the Whole System. Shewing therein, the great Importance of Studying and Practicing Christian Religion; Being Both the Light of the World, and the Salt of the Earth. (New York: H. Gaine, 1763).

[35] Lambertus De Ronde to the Rev. John Kalkoen, September 9, 1765, *ERNY* 6:4006.
[36] Lambertus De Ronde to the Classis of Amsterdam, July 3, 1766, Ibid., 4063.
[37] Ibid., 3946.
[38] Lambertus De Ronde to the Rev. John Kalkoen, September 9, 1765, Ibid., 4006.
[39] Ibid.
[40] Ibid.
[41] Gunn, *Memoirs*, 199. In a footnote, Gunn explains that "Dr. Laidlie, it seems, had denied the obligation of these days, and though he usually preached upon them, would take other subjects than those selected for them by the Church of Holland."
[42] Letter from Abraham Lott to John Henry Livingston, November 1768, quoted in Gunn, *Memoirs*, 201.

city, as to imagine that the sticklers for those days are only to be found among those who speak Dutch?"[43]

Whatever reservations De Ronde and others had about Laidlie's way of doing things, the plain fact was that in a few years Archibald Laidlie had revitalized New York City's Dutch Reformed Church, bringing back into the fold many of the younger generation who had strayed because they could not understand the Dutch sermons, and recruiting not a few new members and listeners from other denominations. In 1767 Laidlie's backers asserted that "the work of the Lord, under the hands of Rev. Laidlie, is prospering so well that there is need of building a third church."[44] A church document recorded that "The North Church was opened for Divine Service on thirsday the 25 May 1769 by the Revd Mr Archibald Laidlie with a Suitable Discourse to a very Crouded audience, His Excellency Sir Henry More being present."[45] By this time the consistory had issued a call for another English-speaking minister, John Henry Livingston, to ease the load of Laidlie, "who preaches twice a week, and catechises four times."[46] In short, there is no disputing Laidlie's enormous popularity in New York City or the positive consequences of his English preaching in terms of increasing attendance at the church.

But was his outstanding performance as a preacher and a pastor the sole reason for his success? Did he possess other qualities that served him well in the tangle of congregational politics in New York City? An assessment of the ongoing internal division in the congregation after he took up his duties shows that Laidlie was extraordinarily adept at dealing with matters that could have derailed his career in an instant.

Maneuvering Through Conflicts

The triumph of the so-called English party in securing Archibald Laidlie's call to the New York pulpit did not erase the opposition to English preaching in the city's Dutch Reformed congregation. If anything, it intensified it. Using a variety of means—political and legal—they challenged the decision to call the Scottish minister and, after his

---

[43] Letter from Abraham Lott to John Henry Livingston, November 1768, 200.
[44] Thirteen members of the Church of New York to the Classis of Amsterdam, Feb. 18, 1767, *ERNY* 6:4082.
[45] "Journal of the proceedings of the Reformed Protestant Dutch Church" quoted in I. N. P. Stokes, *Iconography of Manhattan Island*, 6 vols. (New York: Dodd, 1915-1928), 4:795.
[46] Consistory to J. H. Livingston, New York, November 20, 1769, *ERNY*, 6:4172. For the call to Livingston, dated March 31, 1769, see *ERNY* 6:4145-46.

arrival, continued to protest his presence, not least by boycotting his sermons. "[T]he Dutch party have now entirely given over coming to church when I preach," Laidlie wrote, "and hear only Mr. De Ronde, whom they call their *wettige predikant* [lawful minister]."[47]

Laidlie was not unnerved by this tense situation, and the course of action he took reveals just how astute he was in the political sphere. Though he would have liked to fulfill the role of unifier of the congregation thrust upon him by the Amsterdam Classis, he quickly realized that he could not conciliate the aggrieved partisans of the Dutch language. "The great disappointment the Dutch party have met with, instead of reclaiming them, has added fury to their rage," he wrote to John Henry Livingston. "[T]hey think to revenge themselves upon me, though by their own confession, I am not the cause."[48] Faced with the animosity of a group of people whose social rank limited the influence they could exert on church affairs, Laidlie unsurprisingly kept his sights trained on the elite men who had backed his call. He knew from the outset that his patrons were "the richest and most respectable Merchants in [the] City" and he was determined to keep them in his corner as he carried on his ministry.[49] Obviously remembering the lessons he had learned in Vlissingen about the value of cultivating powerful people, Laidlie chose to ingratiate himself with the chief men of the congregation and their wives.

If Laidlie could not please everyone in the congregation, neither could he please all his ministerial colleagues. Preferring not to align himself with one side or the other in the bitter Coetus-Conferentie dispute that sundered the Reformed clergy in the mid-eighteenth century colonies, he elected to remain neutral, citing his unfamiliarity with the history of the conflict as the reason. This put him at odds with his fellow ministers in New York City, Ritzema and De Ronde, both of whom supported the Conferentie, which advocated maintaining the subordination of the American churches to the Classis of Amsterdam.

Laidlie's reluctance to ally with the Conferentie camp likely heightened his already strained relations with Lambertus De Ronde.[50] De Ronde initially had backed Laidlie's call, but turned into his greatest critic in New York. An ambitious man who perceived the

[47] Undated letter from Archibald Laidlie to John Henry Livingston, quoted in Gunn, *Memoirs*, 152.
[48] Ibid.
[49] Archibald Laidlie to John Laidlie, Amsterdam, December 1, 1763.
[50] On De Ronde's career in New York, see Joyce D. Goodfriend, "The Cultural Metamorphosis of Domine Lambertus De Ronde," *Hudson River Valley Review* 25 (Spring 2009): 63-73.

advantages of becoming bilingual in a city governed by the British, De Ronde had taught himself English, instructed catechism classes in English, attempted to preach in English, and indeed published two books in English. He was rewarded for his efforts by the ridicule of the congregational elite. The elders and deacons mocked the "passion which he has for preaching English, for which he is not in the least qualified."[51] De Ronde complained to the Amsterdam Classis, expressing his anguish at the consistory's design to have him preach only to the church's Dutch speakers. "Am I not to be allowed to preach the Gospel in this English tongue as well as in the Dutch? . . . am I only a Dutch speaking minister?" he railed "Well, [I] do, indeed preach in Dutch; yet, as a fact, I am able to speak, preach or write, in whatever language I choose." By default, De Ronde had become the leader of the Dutch party. In this role he leveled criticisms at Laidlie's evangelical preaching and his innovations in church practice, but to little effect. De Ronde knew which way the deck was stacked. Laidlie commanded the allegiance of the congregation's most prominent and powerful people. De Ronde concluded that his associate was immune to criticism. His "many adherents . . . dare not contradict him, and are ready to treat severely any one who opens his mouth against him."[52] Whether Laidlie encouraged his supporters to adopt such harsh tactics is unknown, but at least in De Ronde's eyes, Laidlie was untouchable. Dominie Ritzema, with a finger to the wind, cast his lot with Laidlie. He blamed the polarization in the church on "my colleague De Ronde [who] has united himself with . . . the Dutch party . . . and would like to see our beloved Laidlie expelled from the congregation."[53]

To assert that Laidlie's career prospered in New York is surely an understatement. His prestige was confirmed when he was awarded an honorary Doctor of Divinity degree by the College of New Jersey in 1770. Without question, Laidlie's talents as a preacher and his political skills were formidable, and he applied himself to his work with unparalleled diligence and enormous energy. Yet accounting for the rapid ascent of this transplanted Scottish minister in New York requires that we scrutinize the deliberate choices that he made as he adapted to his new environment. In doing so, we detect an unmistakable strain of opportunism in the man. One of the primary inducements for Laidlie accepting the call from New York was undoubtedly the ample salary.

---

[51] Elders and Deacons of the Church of New York to the Classis of Amsterdam, October 26, 1765, *ERNY* 6:4016.
[52] Lambertus De Ronde to the Rev. John Kalkoen, September 9, 1765, Ibid., 4006.
[53] Joannes Ritzema to the Classis of Amsterdam, September 10, 1765, Ibid., 4008.

Writing from Amsterdam in December 1763, he confided to his brother that "My stipend is about L200 Sterling, which in that Country is sufficient to enable me both to live genteelly and spare something; – the security for this sum is good and they give besides a free house and a quantity of wood to burn."[54]

Gaining Respectability

Once in New York City, Archibald Laidlie seems to have calculated the steps he should take to improve his standing in this distinctive milieu. We have already seen how he maneuvered to acquire friends in high places. Consistent with this pattern, he found a well-endowed heiress to marry in 1768.[55] Mary Hoffman, the daughter of Martinus Hoffman, a stalwart member of the congregation, brought a dowry of £1000. The minister apprised his brother that his father-in-law was "a Man of Considerable Property in this Country."[56] The couple lived in a style that advertised their social position. "We have three black servants and a White Girl to take care of the children," he informed his brother in 1773.[57] Archibald Laidlie's mahogany clothes press offers a tangible clue to the elegant furnishings with which the couple surrounded themselves. At some point after the Revolutionary War, Laidlie's widow presented this luxury item to Richard Varick, an eminent New Yorker who had been an officer during the American Revolution and subsequently became mayor of New York City. In his 1831 will, Varick bequeathed the cherished heirloom to Laidlie's grandson, the Reverend Richard Varick Dey.[58]

Laidlie married late, but he married well. And it was no accident that he chose to wed a Dutch woman. Once in New York, the Scottish minister made a conscious effort to socialize with well-to-do New Yorkers of Dutch ancestry and thereby to solidify his ties to the community that held the key to his fortunes. This meant disassociating

---

[54] Archibald Laidlie to John Laidlie, Amsterdam, December 1, 1763. The consistory's call to Laidlie, dated July 20, 1763, specified that "We promise to pay you ... L300 New York money, yearly, in quarterly sums." *ERNY* 6:3879.

[55] Archibald Laidlie and Mary Hoffman were married in New York City's Dutch Reformed Church on July 18, 1768. *Records of the Reformed Dutch Church in New Amsterdam and New York: Marriages from 11 December, 1639, to 26 August, 1801* (New York: New York Genealogical and Biographical Society, 1890), 229.

[56] Archibald Laidlie to John Laidlie, New York, November 5, 1773.

[57] Ibid., On October 5, 1770, Archibald Laidlie paid "Eight pounds" to Engeltie van de Water, a widow of the Out Ward of New York City for a Negro woman slave named Betty. See "Bill of sale for a Negro Woman Slave Called Betty," Laidlie papers.

[58] Will of Richard Varick, 1831, Mss., New York Historical Society.

himself from Scottish compatriots resident in the city. "There are many Scotch people here," he confided to his brother in 1765, but "as I belong to another congregation I have but little Acquaintance with my Country Men."[59] Although he could not bring himself to forego weekly meetings with New York's Presbyterian ministers, John Rodgers and John Mason, both of Scottish ancestry, and although he became a member of New York's Saint Andrew's Society in 1765, the year after his arrival, Laidlie deliberately sought to veil his Scottish identity.[60] No doubt his reticence to capitalize on his birthright was a consequence of the discomfort he felt when New Yorkers criticized his Scottishness. Samuel Auchmuty, the rector of Trinity Church, referred to him as "Ladley, the Scot[c]h Orator" and derided the "Scot[c]h true blue Presbyterian Eloquence at the Dut[c]h Ch[urch] Morning and Evening."[61] Sniping at Laidlie on account of his being a Scotsman was not confined to Anglicans. His colleagues Ritzema and De Ronde were indirectly mocking Laidlie when they defended three Reformed ministers who preached in German by stating that these men "ought not to be made any more contemptible on account of language than a Scotsman."[62] Rumors also circulated among the Dutch Reformed congregation's opponents of English-language preaching that Laidlie had "invited from Scotland a nephew of his to be schoolmaster, although there are plenty of schoolmasters in New York, and therefore, his object must simply be, as some think, to make a candidate of him there, and then to work him into the ministry."[63] Hoping to fend off such aspersions, the Scottish-trained minister did all he could to Anglicize himself. Spurning the company of local Scots was a price Laidlie was willing to pay if he could insert himself into the elite Dutch society of the city.

Laidlie's eagerness to identify as a certain kind of Dutch New Yorker is also illustrated in his renunciation of his Dutch language skills. When it had proved necessary for his social advancement in Vlissingen,

[59] Archibald Laidlie to John Laidlie, New York, May 8, 1765. At the time a Scottish Seceder Church existed in New York City. Joyce D. Goodfriend, "Scots and Schism: The New York City Presbyterian Church in the 1750s," in Ned C. Landsman, ed., *Nation and Province in the First British Empire: Scotland and the Americas: 1600-1800* (Lewisburg, PA: Bucknell University Press, 2001), 221-44.

[60] Samuel Miller, *Memoirs of the Rev. John Rodgers, D.D. late pastor of the Wall-street and Brick Churches in the City of New York* (New York: Whiting and Watson, 1813), 207; William M. MacBean, *Biographical Register of Saint Andrew's Society of the State of New York*. Vol. I 1756-1806 in Two Parts (New York: Saint Andrew's Society, 1922), 115.

[61] Samuel Auchmuty to Dr. Samuel Johnson, New York, October 26, 1764.

[62] John Ritzema and Lambertus De Ronde to the Classis of Amsterdam, October 29, 1765, *ERNY* 6:4020.

[63] Ibid., 4029-30.

Laidlie had made the effort to master the Dutch language. Now that he was ensconced in the circle of privileged English-speaking Dutch men and women in New York City, he chose to muffle his bilinguality. Early on there had been talk that Laidlie might preach at times in Dutch, but this expectation was soon dashed as the canny Scotsman sized up the landscape of church politics in New York.[64] Catering to the city's Dutch speakers was out of the question since it would mean alienating his elite backers who had specified in their call that they wanted "a good orator, used to elegant language" and a person whose "English dialect was pure and untainted, without any brogue of other languages."[65] Laidlie modeled himself as an Englishman to conform to the expectations of the city's Anglicized Dutch, whose plaudits he received along with a generous salary.

The American Revolution

Archibald Laidlie had carved out a place of eminence in the city's religious life. His prospects were bright and remained undimmed as the Revolutionary crisis unfolded. The Scottish-born minister left little doubt where his sympathies lay in the conflict with England. He used his pulpit to inspire congregants as they confronted British measures perceived as infringing on their liberties. At the time of the turmoil surrounding the Stamp Act, Captain John Montresor, a British Army officer stationed in New York, highlighted "a very sed[i]t[iou]s sermon preached by Mr. Ledly Minister N[ew] Dutch Church exciting people to Reb[e]ll[io]n."[66] On May 21, 1766, as part of a city celebration of the repeal of the Stamp Act, "the rector of the Reformed Dutch Church (Mr. Laidlie) gave a "congratulatory Discourse on the joyful occasion."[67] As the political quarrel with England intensified, Laidlie spoke out in support of the American position in a series of sermons on the Psalms that reflected his apprehension about the threat posed to American liberties by British rule.[68] On November 27, 1774, he addressed current

---

[64] The congregational committee that issued the call for an English preacher considered it a plus "in case he understood the Dutch language . . . as he might occasionally preach Dutch, and be in a capacity to converse with every individual of our congregation." Call sent to Holland for a Minister to Preach in English . . . January 10, 1763, Ibid., 3856.

[65] Call sent to Holland for a Minister to Preach in English . . . January 10, 1763, Ibid., 3855.

[66] Journals of Capt. John Montresor, 1757-1778" in *The Montresor Journals*, ed. G. D. Scull, *Collections of the New York Historical Society for the Year 1881* (New York: New York Historical Society, 1882), 350.

[67] Stokes, *Iconography of Manhattan Island*, 4: 765.

[68] Kennedy, "From Providence to Civil Religion," 113-14.

issues explicitly. "God's people, in time of publick distress when our Civil and religious priviledges are endangered, when the Iron rod of Tyranny and Oppression hang over our heads, should not behave as the Men of the World—No, we should be much in prayer—much in Confessing our Sins & the Sins of Magistrates, Ministers and all in power."[69]

Laidlie also acted behind the scenes to further the cause of the colonists in their battles against British authority. His private meetings with Presbyterian ministers John Rodgers and John Mason, originally designed for "cultivating friendship with each other, and for mutual instruction," changed in character "[t]oward the close of 1775," when the clergymen "agreed to suspend their usual exercises at these meetings, and to employ the time, when they came together, in special prayer for a blessing upon the country, in the struggle on which it was entering."[70] During the same years, according to Rodgers's biographer Samuel Miller, Laidlie belonged to a circle of New York City men, including Rodgers, Mason, and political luminaries William Livingston, William Smith, Jr., and John Morin Scott, who "made a number of useful publications on the impolicy and dangers of an American episcopate, and on subjects connected therewith."[71]

Laidlie's reputation among New Yorkers loyal to the Crown as a foe of British authority reinforces the picture of a minister committed to the stance of the revolutionaries. Writing in 1779, Charles Inglis, one of the city's Anglican ministers, remembered Laidlie as "a warm Presbyterian, & much prejudiced against the Church of England," adding that "he communicated his Warmth & Prejudices to his Adherents, who were the Majority, and have all proved violent Rebels."[72] Loyalist historian Thomas Jones expended an enormous amount of vitriol against Laidlie, describing him as "in his heart a presbyterian, in his principles of government a republican, an absolute enemy to monarchical government, and a most rancorous hater of episcopacy. He preached a doctrine, and endeavored to establish a system of politics in his congregation, extremely favorable to the wishes and designs of the republican faction in the province. . . . He soon introduced his own system of religion in the church, herded entirely with the Presbyterian

---

[69] Quoted in Kennedy, "From Providence to Civil Religion," 113.
[70] Miller, *Memoirs*, 207.
[71] Ibid., 192.
[72] Charles Inglis to the Society for the Propagation of the Gospel in Foreign Parts, New York, November 26, 1779, in John Wolfe Lydekker, *The Life and Letters of Charles Inglis: His Ministry in America and Consecration as First Colonial Bishop, from 1759 to 1787* (London: Society for promoting Christian Knowledge, 1936), 195.

parsons, the triumvirate [William Livingston, William Smith, Jr., and John Morin Scott], and other principal leaders of the puritanic conventicles."[73] Jones also corroborated Samuel Miller's assertion that Laidlie employed his pen in the cause of colonial rights. "This Laidly was a principal leader in the .... political papers which were published in New York in 1768, 1769, 1770, and 1771 under the signatures the 'American Whig,' 'Sir Isaac Foot,' and the 'watchman.'"[74]

As a supporter of independence, Laidlie could not remain in New York City after the British occupied it. His last known sermon to the New York City congregation was preached on July 7, 1776, just a few days after the Declaration of Independence.[75] He went into exile in Red Hook, New York, a place where the Hoffmans, his wife's family, held a good deal of property, and where he preached during the years between 1776 and 1779. Jack Douglas Klunder has identified twenty-three sermons that Laidlie gave in Red Hook, all but one of which had previously been delivered in New York City.[76] Laidlie's last sermon in Red Hook, according to Klunder's list, was given on April 10, 1779.[77] By then the Scottish-born minister was struggling with the long illness that finally took his life on November 14, 1779.[78] On September 10 of that year Margaret Beekman Livingston advised Albany's Dutch Reformed minister, Eilardus Westerlo, of Laidlie's impending death. "I am sorry to inform you, that my dear pastor, Dr. Archibald Laidlie is in a very bad state of health. I fear he will never preach again; he is now gone to Salisbury [Connecticut]."[79]

Mary Laidlie, the much younger widow of Archibald Laidlie, lived for another four and a half decades. When she died in 1825, her grandson, Richard Varick Dey, also a minister, delivered a discourse in New York's Middle Dutch Church to honor her. His remarks reveal that Archibald Laidlie was still revered among the city's Dutch Reformed as a teacher and as a man. "The memory of his piety and learning, in all things appertaining to the doctrines of salvation which he preached, is yet living in this congregation," Dey intoned. "Within these walls

---

[73] Thomas Jones, *History of New York During the Revolutionary War: and the leading events in the other colonies at that period.* Edited by Edward Floyd De Lancey. 2 vols. (New York: New York Historical Society, 1879), 1:21-22.
[74] Ibid., 1:23.
[75] Kennedy, "From Providence to Civil Religion," 114.
[76] Klunder, "The Application of Holy Things," 215-61.
[77] Ibid., 234.
[78] James Grant Wilson and John Fiske, eds., *Appletons' Cyclopaedia of American Biography* 6 vols. (New York: Appleton, 1888), 3:595.
[79] *Presbyterian Magazine* (1851): 525. Thanks to Rob Naborn for this reference.

he stood for many years, the herald of the cross. Here he exhorted the heedless, and encouraged the feeble-minded; here he wrestled with the Lord, in fervent prayer, for a blessing on the flock entrusted to his charge."[80] Laidlie was memorialized not only as a minister but as an exemplary human being. "In his private intercourse," Dey went on, "his manner of life is also remembered. He was humble without pretence; grave without severity; willing to acknowledge his own infirmities, and to cast the mantle of charity over the failings of others. 'He would rejoice with those who did rejoice, and weep with those who wept.'"[81] Dey reminded his audience that "It is now forty-six years since he went from among this people, to join the congregation of saints" but was quick to point out that "During the whole of that period, his surviving partner has attended the public worship of God in this house of Prayer, and communed at the table of her Lord."[82]

How Archibald Laidlie's career might have evolved in New York City if he had not succumbed to illness in the midst of the Revolutionary War must remain a matter of conjecture. Although all of the city's Dutch Reformed clergy—De Ronde, Ritzema, Laidlie, and the congregation's second English-language preacher, John Henry Livingston—supported the revolutionaries and went into exile at various spots in the Hudson valley, the conclusion of the war brought a definitive change in church policy as followers of John Henry Livingston came to dominate the congregation. From this point on it was clear that English was to be the language of worship in the city's Dutch Reformed Church. Against their will, the congregation's two Dutch-language preachers were compelled to retire, Dominie Ritzema expressing his dismay at the turn of events in a long letter he penned to the Amsterdam Classis in 1785 in which he reported "I and Rev. de Ronde were deposed by five elders and seven deacons."[83] With John Henry Livingston as its standard bearer,

---

[80] Richard Varick Dey, *A Discourse, Delivered in the Middle Dutch Church in Cedar-Street, N. Y. On Sabbath Evening June 12th 1825, On Occasion of the Death of Mrs. Mary Laidlie* (New York: Wilder & Campbell, 1825), 15.
[81] Dey, *Discourse*, 15-16.
[82] Ibid., 16.
[83] Rev. John Ritzema, Minister Emeritus of New York, to the Classis of Amsterdam, December 10, 1785, *ERNY* 6:4333. Soon thereafter, the consistory decided to respond to the needs of its Dutch-speaking members, issuing a call to Dr. Theodoric Romeyn of Schenectady to preach in the Dutch language. John Henry Livingston entreated Romeyn to accept the offer, explaining that "The number of Dutch families is not great; but lest you might fear that your usefulness should thereby be limited, the whole congregation is before you for parochial duties in English." Gunn, *Memoirs*, 289-290. After Romeyn declined this invitation, the consistory called Gerardus A. Kuypers to preach in the Dutch language. Kuypers, born in Curacao, finally accepted

the Dutch Reformed Church resumed its work in post-revolutionary New York City. There is little doubt that Archibald Laidlie would have been at Livingston's side as the church moved forward to make its mark in the new American nation.[84]

---

the call in 1789 and, preached in Dutch in New York City until 1803. Gunn, *Memoirs*, 294, note; John Knox, *The Death of the aged pious - - a blessing: a sermon occasioned by the death of the Rev. Gerardus A. Kuypers, D. D.: preached in the Middle Dutch Church, June 7, 1833* (New York: G.F. Hopkins, 1833), 13-14.

[84] In "Sanctuary Blessings," a sermon preached at the rededication of the Middle Dutch Church on July 4, 1790, John Henry Livingston asked rhetorically "But where is our LAIDLIE! Where is now that bold herald of the Gospel . . . His name still survives, and he, being dead, yet speaketh." He continued "Excuse this tribute of affection . . . which I owe to the memory of a man, who was once dear to me, as a fellow-labourer in this house, and whose ministry was highly acceptable, and greatly blessed to this people." *Select Discourses From the American Preacher, (A Work of which three Volumes are already published in America), by some of the Most Eminent Evangelical Ministers in the United States* (Edinburgh: Adam Neill and Company, 1796), 515.

CHAPTER 11

Gerrit Lydekker (1729-1794): A Tory Among Patriots

Firth Haring Fabend

Of the forty-one Reformed Dutch ministers in New York and New Jersey at the time of the American Revolution, only four were Tories. Three were foreign born (the Germans Johannes C. Rubel and John M. Kern); one was born in the Netherlands (Hermanus L. Boelen); and one was American-born (Gerrit Lydekker), pastor of the Reformed Dutch Church in English Neighborhood, in Bergen County, New Jersey.[1] Lydekker's career, as the only Tory minister in New York or New Jersey and was born and raised in America, indicates how theological principles had political consequences, for his life encompasses all the issues of the transition period that roiled the Reformed Church and the citizens of Bergen County in the decades from the 1730s through the Revolution.

Tensions among the Dutch in the American Revolution

Ten years before the outbreak of the American Revolution, just after the Stamp Act had caused so much indignation in the colonies,

[1] John W. Beardslee, III, "The Reformed Church and the American Revolution," in James W. van Hoeven, ed., *Piety and Patriotism: Bicentennial Studies of the Reformed Church in America, 1776-1976* (Grand Rapids, MI: Eerdmans, 1976), 21.

Gerrit Lydekker, c. 1775, [courtesy of the Seeley G. Mudd Manuscript Library, Princeton University]

the Classis of Amsterdam wrote a scolding twenty-three-page letter to the churches in New York and New Jersey, washing their hands of the churches' long-drawn-out bickering behavior. "We shall no more in the future treat with you," their High Mightinesses fumed. It was June 3, 1765.[2]

It was not taxes the churches bickered about, however, but rather the preferred mode of organization between two hostile factions within the Dutch Reformed Church in New York and New Jersey: the Coetus, a term for assembly, and the Conferentie, meaning conference, a conflict that the Amsterdam Classis had failed to reconcile. The original Coetus, unified but toothless, had been organized in 1738, at the suggestion of the Classis of Amsterdam, for the purposes of clergymen and their elders meeting annually and "agreeing together" on local issues as they arose. The Coetus, which did not actually meet until 1747, reorganized

---

[2] Alice P. Kenney studied eighteen Reformed congregations in the upper Hudson Valley and found a pattern of Tory/Conferentie Patriot/Coetus allegiance. As in the lower Hudson, religious beliefs and moral convictions in these communities often underlay the loyalty choices of individuals. "The Albany Dutch, Loyalists and Patriots," *New York History* 42 (October 1961).

in 1754 in the hopes of eventually becoming an independent classis that would have all the rights of the Classis of Amsterdam—that is, be equal to it as a sister classis within the Synod of North Holland. But the conservatives within the Coetus soon repudiated this move toward independence, and the more liberal ministers and their elders eventually withdrew from the body, wanting true autonomy, not mere permission to meet and agree together on local issues.

The issue of independence vs. subordination was paramount, but sub-issues that convulsed the two factions were the Coetus's desire to educate the clergy in an academy or seminary established on American soil, to license candidates for the ministry, and to ordain clergy in America. The Conferentie strenuously objected to these aspirations, even though as members of the original Coetus, they had already, beginning in 1741, voted to license and ordain five ministers. To further complicate matters, especially in eighteenth-century Bergen County, some Reformed ministers and congregants wanted "heart" religion, pietist preaching, spontaneous prayer from the pulpit, and less formality in general, while the more conservative ministers and congregants found ideas like the "new birth," spiritual regeneration, and deviation from Dutch traditions repugnant.[3]

All of these issues were exacerbated in the run-up to the Revolutionary War, as the desire for "independency" within the Dutch Reformed Church, and thus within all those communities in New York and New Jersey where the church was the primary cultural institution, mirrored the political desire of colonists to be free of Great Britain's rule. Patriots, particularly in the lower Hudson valley and the Hackensack valley, were motivated by a horror of losing their liberty to the tyranny of an "enslaving" King and Parliament, and Patriot churchgoers and clergy could easily see a like tyranny in the Classis of Amsterdam's determination to maintain control of the colonial church.

But also within the same communities and the same church, the "divine right of kings" was remembered, and for Tory churchgoers and clergy the horror was to dishonor the king. For them, a break from Great Britain was an affront to the rule of law and God, who had ordained, they believed, that the governance of the colonies belonged to the Crown and Parliament, with people duty-bound to defer and obey. Feelings eventually ran so high that the Coetus/Conferentie conflict evolved into a virtual civil war within the War of Revolution, again

---

[3] E. T. Corwin, ed., *Ecclesiastical Records of the State of New York*, 7 vols. (Albany: Lyon, 1901-1916), 6:3991-96. (hereafter cited as *ERNY*).

primarily in the lower Hudson and Hackensack valleys, with families and former friends and neighbors pitted against each other. Violence was endemic.

The final development that caused the Classis of Amsterdam in June 1765 to denounce the Dutch churches in New York and New Jersey was a five-year-long series of exchanges between Dominie Johannes Leydt of the Coetus and Dominie Johannes Ritzema of the Conferentie over Leydt's pamphlet, "True Liberty the Way to Peace." This pamphlet, which Leydt had published in August 1760, was addressed to the "Reverend Consistories of all the Dutch Reformed Churches in our Country." The peace to which he refers is the end of hostilities between Coetus and Conferentie. "I deem it to be my duty, and yours also," Leydt wrote, "to labor with such earnest zeal, that we (for the conservation of the liberty and the rights of the church of God) may attain unto a peaceful and a general union." Leydt's object was for full unanimity not only on the reunion question, but also on the overriding question of subordination vs. independence, and the lesser but still vexing ones of local training, licensing, and ordination.[4]

Family and Education

A look at the career of Dominie Gerrit Lydekker will illuminate the issues that underlaid the Coetus-Conferentie conflict and that complicated the course of the Revolution as it unfolded, particularly in Bergen County.

Born in 1729, Gerrit Lydekker was the fourth generation of his family in America. His great-grandfather, Ryck Lydekker, emigrated from Amsterdam in the service of the Dutch West India Company about 1650. His grandfather, Gerrit, was the father of Ryck II, baptized October 21, 1691, in the New York Reformed Dutch Church. Ryck II married Maritje Benson on April 19, 1718, in the same church. Their eleven children, of whom Gerrit was the sixth, and the first son, were all baptized at either Hackensack or Schraalenburgh, Gerrit at Schraalenburgh on May 7, 1729.

---

[4] Adrian C. Leiby has covered the Coetus/Conferentie topic in detail is his book *The United Churches of Hackensack and Schraalenburgh, New Jersey, 1686-1822* (River Edge, NJ: Bergen County Historical Society, 1976), and Dirk Mouw, "Moederkerk and Vaderland: Religion and Ethnic Identity in the Middle Colonies, 1690-1772" (Ph.D. dissertation, University of Iowa, 2009), goes into even greater detail. The violence is well described in another work by Adrian C. Leiby, *The Revolutionary War in the Hackensack Valley: The Jersey Dutch and the Neutral Ground, 1775-1783* (New Brunswick, NJ: Rutgers University Press, 1962).

The family seems to have been well off, for in his will Ryck Leydecker left his eldest son Gerrit a valuable farm of 400 acres between Overpeck Creek and the Hudson River in Hackensack, Bergen County.[5] Little is known of Gerrit's upbringing, except that he was of frail constitution and was a studious boy who studied Latin and Greek from his childhood, perhaps with his parents' intention that he eventually go into the ministry. Being the first-born son, with some sort of health issue and four elder sisters (one had died young), one can imagine that he was coddled and cosseted and made a pet of. His constitution, and his eventual occupation, would probably have precluded him from undertaking the hard work of farming himself, but it was the custom of the era and place that a farm of that size would have been worked by slaves and day laborers hired as needed, all supervised by an overseer. A drawing of Gerrit made in his forties shows him reading a book, with a pince-nez on his nose and a furrow on his brow. He wears a wig, in the contemporary style, which also indicates that he was a man whose pursuits were hardly those of an ordinary Bergen County farmer, but rather one with the resources and inclinations to spend his time in more contemplative pursuits.

The ministers of the Hackensack and Schraalenburgh Reformed churches that Gerrit attended as a boy were both well educated. Dominie Antonius Curtenius studied theology first at Groningen and then at Leyden. His colleague was John Henry Goetschius, who arrived in Hackensack in 1748 when Gerrit was nineteen years old. Goetschius has been described as a "learned, pious, and godly man, and a faithful and successful preacher of the Gospel . . . a man of profound erudition . . . and an accomplished theologian."[6] He was one of the founders of Queens College (Rutgers University today), trained a number of young men for the ministry, and in 1749 opened a school in Hackensack for the "Languages, as Latin, Greek, Hebrew, etc also the Arts and Sciences, Philosophy and Theology," which he advertised in the *New York Gazette* that year.[7] Gerrit was twenty years old at the time and undoubtedly was

---

[5] Johannes Leydt, "True Liberty the Way to Peace" (Philadelphia, 1760). The pamphlet and its successors were translated by the Rev. Maurice Hansen in 1887. His handwritten translation is in the Gardner Sage Library, New Brunswick Theological Seminary. A translation is also found in ERNY, 5:3762-3792.
[6] *Calendar of New Jersey Wills* (1761-1770), 4:249.
[7] E. T. Corwin, ed., *A Manual of the Reformed Church in America, 1628-1922*, 5th ed. (New York: Board of Publication of the Reformed Church, 1922), 347, 348; hereafter, *Manual*. Frederick W. Bogert, *Bergen County, New Jersey, History and Heritage*, 4 vols. (Hackensack, NJ: Bergen County Board of Freeholders, 1983), *The Colonial Days, 1630-1775*, 2:59.

a student in Goetschius's school. Two years later, at the age of twenty-two, he matriculated at the College of New Jersey (Princeton).

Churchman and Pietist

Gerrit Lydekker first appears in the printed record as the elder at the Coetus meeting in New York during the week of October 7-12, 1755, accompanying the minister of the churches of Hackensack and Schraalenburgh, John H. Goetschius. At the time Gerrit was a member of the Hackensack church, having joined after a public confession of faith on November 17, 1752, at age twenty-three.[8] He was elected to the office of elder without first having served as a deacon, the usual course, which indicates a high regard by church leaders for his religious "walk." The records indicate that he served two two-year terms until 1759 and then one more two-year term from 1762 to 1764. There was no rule in Reformed church order to prevent his serving another term at this point, and thus no cause for legal objection to it from his congregation, but he did not so serve. Why not?

Goetschius (himself one of the five ministers ordained on American soil by the Coetus in 1741) was a fervent pietist or New Lighter and was to become a notable Patriot in the War.[9] For Gerrit Lydekker, fresh out of Princeton, to have been his elder for six years, from 1755 to 1764, suggests that Lydekker was also a pietist, a follower of the Great Awakening, which had influenced the founding of Princeton in 1746, and where Lydekker would, of course, have imbibed Awakening ideas, style, and rhetoric.

Further support for his pietism is found in the essay, "A Discourse on the Greatness, and Praise of the Lord," composed and delivered by Gerrit Lydekker, A. B., and published in New York in 1766, a work that reveals no aversion to evangelical language or doctrine. Its message is "Be ye perfect" in order to inherit the kingdom. "Let all impenitent Sinners fly to Christ with the wings of an unfeigned Faith and with deep Repentence," Gerrit wrote. A long paean praising the perfection, omniscience, and omnipotence of God and urging its readers to study God's "two grand Volumes, or Books, namely the great Book of Nature and the greater supernatural Book of Grace, or the holy Bible,"

---

[8] ERNY, 5:3597. The "J" is a mistake for "G," for the church records indicate that Gerrit Lydekker, age twenty-six in 1755 and a recent graduate of the College of New Jersey (Princeton), was an elder that year. *Records of the Reformed Dutch Churches of Hackensack and Schraalenburgh*, Part II (New York, 1891), for the years 1755-1764.

[9] He was ordained on April 17, 1741, and reordained in 1748 to answer Conferentie objections to the validity of the 1741 rite. *Manual*, 347-48.

Lydekker's discourse is entirely within the conventional Awakening rhetoric of the day.[10]

If serving as elder with Goetschius and his published "Discourse" are not sufficient evidence of Gerrit Lydekker's progressive and pietist mindset in the 1750s, there is yet another clue to his loyalties. Just one year before he first became an elder, September 17-19, 1754, Dominie Johannes Ritzema and Dominie Samuel Verbrijck, respectively president and scribe of the then still-unified (but still ineffectual) Coetus, had recommended to Amsterdam that the American Dutch Reformed churches be allowed to establish their own long-desired classis on American soil. In doing so, they were simply conveying to their High Mightinesses what had been a unanimous decision by the Coetus.[11]

The Coetus made this momentous decision to ask for an American classis just as the controversy over the founding of King's College (Columbia) by a group of Episcopalian ministers was bursting onto the scene. The Reformed Dutch, ministers as well as congregants, grew mightily opposed to this plan, fearing that the proposed new college would be too closely affiliated with the Church of England and would be dominated by Anglican clerics and royal officials, who would likely try to establish an Anglican episcopacy in America. This was, of course, an unpalatable idea to the Dutch Reformed Church, which still remembered its own days as the "official" public church of New Netherland, its guarantee of autonomy by the Articles of Capitulation in 1664, and its incorporation by the Crown in 1696 with continuing guarantees of the Dutch right to liberty of conscience and the right to worship publicly according to their own customs and rules of church discipline.[12]

However, in an unforeseen outcome, a month after signing this letter recommending the establishment of an American classis, Ritzema,

---

[10] Gerrit Lydekker, "A discourse on the greatness, and praise of the Lord, composed and delivered, by Gerrit Lydekker, A.B.," in Isaac Sigfrid, John Henry Ringier, and Daniel Wyttenbach, *Theological theses: containing the chief heads of the Christian doctrine, deduced from axioms; composed and publickly defended in presence and under the direction of the very Reverend and most judicious John Henry Ringier, V.D.M. and professor of controversial divinity in the academy at Bern*. Published by Printed and sold by Samuel Brown at the foot of Potbaker's-Hill, between the New-Dutch Church and Fly-Market, 1766.

[11] *ERNY*, 5:3494.

[12] David C. Humphrey, *From King's College to Columbia, 1746-1800* (New York: Columbia University Press, 1976), especially Chapter 4; and Gerald F. De Jong, *The Dutch Reformed Church in the American Colonies* (Grand Rapids, MI: Eerdmans, 1978), Chapter IV.

who entertained hopes of being appointed a professor in the aborning Episcopalian college, changed his mind on the subject.[13]

The Coetus, enraged at Ritzema's change of face and lack of loyalty, demanded at its meeting the following year (October 7-14, 1755) that he turn over their minute book, the correspondence with Amsterdam, other papers belonging to the Coetus, and the treasurer's records. This order was agreed to *"without a dissenting vote."* In other words, in October 1755, Gerrit Lydekker, who was present as Goetschius's elder, voted with everyone else to agree that Ritzema must return the Coetus records to the Coetus. We should take this to be evidence that Lydekker was pro-Coetus and a supporter of Goetschius in October 1755.[14]

King's College Complication

In the interim, however, a new wrinkle had developed. Six months earlier, in April 1755, the Reverend Theodorus J. Frelinghuysen, Jr., called the Reformed Dutch ministers and consistories together "to take measures for seeking the establishment of a Classis and founding an Academy." This meeting was held in New York City in May 1755, and it authorized Frelinghuysen, in a direct rebuff to Ritzema's academic ambitions regarding King's College, to go to Holland to seek funds "for a University for the Dutch Church."[15] Ritzema, in his turn now thoroughly irked, pronounced the May 1755 meeting illegal and flatly refused to turn over the Coetus records. For the next nine years his correspondence, published in the *Ecclesiastical Records of the State of New York,* was involved primarily with four interrelated issues: the King's College matter, Leydt's pamphlets, the desire for English preaching in the New York Dutch churches, and the tendency of the Dutch churches to "independency."

Although he favored English preaching, Ritzema deeply feared the outcome of an independent Dutch Reformed Church with its own classis in America, especially one whose clergy were "given up to fanaticism" and "so-called 'preaching the spirit.'"[16] This is an indication that the Coetus-Conferentie split was not only of progressives against traditionalists, but that some or even perhaps many of the individuals involved were conflicted over all the issues, including English preaching.

---

[13] *ERNY*, 5:3499. Letter is dated October 17, 1754.
[14] *ERNY*, 5:3597-3610. Normally, the clerk kept the Minute Book, but since Samuel Verbryck, the clerk, had to travel back and forth from Tappan, it was perhaps thought prudent that the book stay in the city with the president.
[15] *ERNY*, 5:3541, 3546, 3551.
[16] *ERNY*, 6:3865.

Gerrit Lydekker was among the conflicted, and it was not the first, nor would it be the last time in his career that he was torn between opposing ideas.

Things came to a head at the session of the Coetus on June 20, 1764, when the Coetus, frustrated with Amsterdam's long-time recalcitrance on the classis question, withdrew from the meeting. At this point the Conferentie organized itself as "The Assembly Subordinate to the Reverend Classis," complete with elders. That same day Lydekker appeared before the newly organized group to request it to write on his behalf to the Classis of Amsterdam for permission to admit him to the qualifying examination to become a candidate for the ministry.[17]

Progressive or Conservative?

If Gerrit Lydekker was of a progressive and pietist bent, and an elder with the pietist Goetschius from 1755 until 1764, what caused him in June 1764 to become a public supporter of the Conferentie faction, now headed by the conservative Ritzema? As Adrian Leiby, a historian who has closely studied the issues, put it, "something happened."[18] What was it that happened to turn Gerrit Lydekker away from his one-time tutor and long-time minister Goetschius and to ally himself with Ritzema? The answer will become clear.

The day after his request for examination, the Conferentie duly wrote to the Classis of Amsterdam to recommend that they be allowed to examine Lydekker as a candidate for the ministry. They praised him "in the strongest terms" as having been taught from his youth in Latin and Greek, for having studied for four years at the College of New Jersey (Princeton), after which he spent another year and a half studying divinity, first under Goetschius (as we know from another source; they do not mention it) and then under Ritzema, and in Hebrew under Dominie Kals.[19]

They described Lydekker as "a student in theology" who had a "true desire to edify his neighbors." By this they meant "student" in the first *Oxford English Dictionary* definition of the word as "a person who is in engaged in or addicted to study," not that Gerrit, now age thirty-five, was still in school. But a delicate constitution ("weakness of body") had always kept him from undertaking the voyage to Holland for ordination, they wrote, and "Being convinced that the irregular ordination by

---

[17] *ERNY*, 6:3926.
[18] Leiby, *The Revolutionary War in the Hackensack Valley*, 35.
[19] *ERNY*, 6:3928.

the Coetus ministers was inconsistent with our [Reformed Church] constitution, he has never been able to unite with them. So he has spent six or seven years without any prospect" of a pulpit, they concluded.[20] (The six or seven years would date back to 1757, which would account for the eighteen months he spent studying with Ritzema and Kals after graduating from Princeton in 1755.)

Six months later, which was about as fast as transatlantic travel allowed at the time, the classis gave its permission for the "well-educated young gentleman" to be ordained in New Jersey (February 4, 1765), and the Conferentie, after many years opposing local ordination, did an abrupt about-face and, "knowing him to be properly qualified," ordained the man.[21]

These extraordinary developments took place in the midst of the five-year back-and-forth arguments running anywhere from 20 to 120 pages between Leydt and Ritzema. This had so exasperated the Classis of Amsterdam in 1765 that it finally washed its hands of the warring factions.

As we have seen, one of these arguments was the right of the Coetus to license and ordain clergy. But if the Conferentie was apparently *not* opposed to local ordination after all, having so expeditiously undertaken to ordain Lydekker, what was the real issue that had motivated its members to separate themselves from the Coetus in June 1764? And how did this relate to Gerrit's not staying on for a follow-up term, which could easily have been his, to his 1762 eldership in Goetschius's church? Either the office was not offered to him again, or he refused it. And what did it have to do with Gerrit Lydekker's conversion to the Conferentie? How conflicted was this man, and on how many different issues?

Perhaps Lydekker's change of heart had to do with sides taken in the King's College controversy, which still raged in 1764, and of which his mentor Ritzema was in the thick. Or perhaps it had to do with the language controversy that convulsed the Reformed Church upon the arrival in the early winter of 1764 of the Reverend Archibald Laidlie to preach in English in the New York Dutch Reformed congregations. Although Ritzema favored English preaching, many in the city and even more in Bergen County opposed it. Whether Lydekker sided with Ritzema and Laidlie in supporting the shift to the English language is not known, but it is more than probable. Gerrit Lydekker himself was

---

[20] Ibid.
[21] *ERNY*, 6:3973, 4011, 4013, 4028-29.

very Anglicized at this point in his life. In 1770 he married Elizabeth Coley, who was either the daughter or the sister of William Coley, a silversmith and jeweler in the employ of King George III, and he was soon best friends with English bishops and the English mayor of New York City.[22]

Subordination vs. Independency

But perhaps his change of heart had most to do with the long-simmering subordination vs. independency issue, which convulsed the Classis of Amsterdam particularly in 1763, as ample correspondence shows, and which was also finding resonance in the Revolutionary rhetoric beginning to be heard at this time. For example, in a letter to the Coetus on January 11, 1763, the classis wrote: "Brethren, consider what will be the result of your withdrawal from the Netherlands Church? Will it not be the beginning of the introduction of 'British' tyranny in the Church? . . . Would you not be the instrumentality of having your 'Dutch Church' liberties assailed, which you have enjoyed (from the English conquest) until now? . . . Try to prevent those bad results, which will confuse or completely destroy your congregations, by uniting together again in a Coetus subordinate to the Classis of Amsterdam."[23]

There is one shred of direct evidence to suggest that the best explanation for Gerrit Lydekker's switch in allegiance from Coetus to Conferentie in 1764 and from thence to Toryism was his conviction that, as the Classis of Amsterdam was the legal and lawful authority over the American churches, so the king of England was the legal and lawful authority over the American colonies. In neither case was independence an option for Gerrit. He was of a law-abiding nature, although in one matter that surfaced in 1776 his actions were legally ambiguous at best, as will be seen.

We have few direct words of Gerrit Lydekker to lead us to his most basic beliefs, much less to an explanation for his embrace of the conservative Conferentie ideology in 1764 and the Tory side in the War in 1776. But just as his highly pious "Discourse" of 1766 tells us that he was a New Light in his religious leanings, so an obscure footnote that

---

[22] John Wolfe Lydekker, "The Rev. Gerrit (Gerard) Lydekker, 1729-1794," *Historical Magazine* (1944): 305-306. John Wolfe Lydekker, archivist to the Society for the Propagation of the Gospel, was the great-great-great grandson of Gerrit Lydekker; hereafter, J. W. Lydekker, "The Rev. Gerrit . . . Lydekker." He was also the author of *The Life and Letters of Charles Inglis* (London: Church Historical Society, 1936).
[23] ERNY, 6:3853.

he inserted in his only other known publication gives a clue as to his political views.

This publication is his 1787 translation from the "low Dutch" of "A Treatise, in answer to the Proposed Question, What Arguments do Nature and Reason afford for the Existence of God; how far may we know this Being; and what moral Consequences can be deduced from it?" The author was Petrus Schouten.[24]

Schouten was a Roman Catholic priest with latitudinarian and Mennonite connections, which suggests that Lydekker was not so rigidly conventional in his personal associations as he seems to have been in other matters. It suggests perhaps that ideas were more important to him than maintaining inflexible notions of personal loyalties—a trait that may explain why he was loyal to both Goetschius and Ritzema almost at the same time. An intellectual, he saw in certain men ideals and ideas he could relate to, and he was thus capable of being pulled in different directions simultaneously.

In Schouten's chapter starting on page 133, "Concerning the Love to the Public," he asserts that "If you reverence, honor and obey the Magistrates, and circumspectly refrain from all that may disturb the peace; [and] earnestly pursue your calling [etc.], . . . will you not then also do as much for the General Welfare, or Good of the Public?"

Immediately after the phrase "If you reverence, honor and obey the Magistrates," Gerrit inserted his gratuitous footnote: "In proof and confirmation of the doctrine here advanced by our great and learned Author [Schouten], Vis. that we ought to be good and loyal subjects, I shall adduce the subsequent arguments [for this doctrine] from the sacred Scriptures." Here he cites Romans 13:1-7, Ecclesiastes 10:20, Exodus 22:28, Proverbs 19:12, and Matthew 22:15-21. (The relevant phrases are, respectively: From Romans, "Let every person be subject to the governing authorities [as] . . . instituted by God . . . for the authorities are ministers of God." From Ecclesiastes, "Even in your thought, do not curse the king." From Exodus, "You shall not revile God, nor curse a ruler of your people." From Proverbs, "A king's wrath is like the growling of a lion." And from Matthew, "Render unto Caesar the things that are Caesar's, and to God the things that are God's.")

---

[24] Peter Schouten, *A Treatise, published by the Society of Edam, for the Good of the Public: in Answer to the proposed question, What Arguments do Nature and Reason afford for the Existence of God; how far may we know this Being; and what moral Consequences can be deduced from it?* Translated from the Low-Dutch, by the Reverend Gerrit Lydekker, A. B. (London: Printed for the Translator ... 1787), 135.

Finally, he cites the "sacred Injunction of St. Peter, in his First Epistle, chap. ii.13-17," which he quotes verbatim from the King James Version of the Bible:

> 13. Submit yourselves to every ordinance of man, for the Lord's sake: whether it be to the King, as Supreme;
> 14. Or unto Governors, as unto them that are sent by him for the punishment of evil doers, and for the praise of them that do Well.
> 15. For so is the Will of God, that with well-doing ye put to silence the ignorance of foolish men:
> 16. As free, and not using your liberty for a cloak of maliciousness, but as the servants of God.
> 17. Honour all men. Love the brotherhood. Fear God. Honour the King."

He ends:

> That we may one and all be induced to love, fear and obey, the amiable the tremendous God, and honour the King, and receive eternal, perfect felicity, which is the sure, great, and most gracious reward of keeping the Divine Commandments, is the sincere wish, and most earnest prayer of THE TRANSLATOR.

We have to conclude that Gerrit Lydekker, no doubt influenced by the acrimonious arguments in the Leydt/Ritzema pamphlet war and the outrage of the Classis of Amsterdam at being "abused," "scorned," and "slandered" by the Coetus ministers, who had approved Leydt's publications, had espoused the intellectual argument that God's earthly authorities were not to be defied. In other words, it was not presumption or arrogance that led Lydekker to insert his views on civil obedience into Schouten's treatise, but rather the "true desire" of this "well-educated gentleman preacher" and "student of theology" to edify his readers, a desire so strong that it overwhelmed and superseded the customary self-effacing role of translator. Even four years after the end of the Revolution, apparently, the tensions of that conflict were still vivid in his mind, and he remained convinced that the king of England had been the rightful ruler of the American colonies, just as the Classis of Amsterdam had been the rightful authority over the American Dutch Reformed churches. Though the Coetus/Conferentie conflict had been theoretically healed in 1771 in the Plan of Union, the plan was only a Band-Aid on the conflict in Bergen County and adjacent Orange County. It immediately re-emerged in the Revolution, and it persisted for decades. As we know, it even re-erupted in 1822 in the schismatic so-called True Reformed Dutch Church in Bergen County, which was very detrimental to the Reformed Dutch Church's progress as a denomination.

The Consequences of Merging Religious and Civil Loyalties

Some accounts of Gerrit Lydekker's career prior to the Revolution say that he was "called" to the North Branch Reformed Church in 1767. But this church "removed to Readington" in 1738, and the published history of the Readington Reformed Church makes no mention of Lydekker among its ministers. The Reverend Dr. Jacob Rutsen Hardenbergh, a fervent pietist and later patriot, was in the Readington pulpit during these years—years that were colored by a deep split in the congregation between "Coetus men" and those favoring subordination, known as the "malcontents." The conclusion is inescapable that, at most, Gerrit Lydekker ministered to the malcontents within the congregation, not to the main body, and, according to Corwin's *Manual*, only in the year 1767.[25]

In 1770 Lydekker was called to the newly formed church at English Neighborhood. Here he remained until 1776, that fateful year, the year that finds him praying for the king and the royal family from the pulpit in disobedience of the express dictate of the Congress that to do so was an act of treason. In his congregation that year was Charles Inglis, minister at Anglican Trinity Church, who had fled the city. That was also the year that Gerrit Lydekker took into his very household David Matthew, Esq., former Tory mayor of New York City. The presence of these two Tories in their midst was anathema to local Patriots, but Lydekker's loyalties to the king as God's deputy on earth were so strong, his principles so founded in his interpretation of Holy Writ, that he defied the new American authorities and risked his property, if not his life, in their defense.

When the war broke out that year, Gerrit fled Bergen County for British-held New York City, where the Reverend Inglis granted him the use of St. George's Chapel at Trinity Church and where he ministered to the Dutch Loyalists in the city for the duration of the war. Meanwhile, Bergen County Patriots looted his home, and the authorities seized his farm of 400 acres, plus another parcel of ten acres. He testified later that his losses amounted to £2,523/6.8. After the war, when he resettled in

---

[25] Henry P. Thompson, *History of the Reformed Church, at Readington, N.J., 1719-1881* (New York: Reformed Church in America, 1882); and Corwin, *Manual*, 405.

England, the British government compensated him for approximately half of this amount and gave him a small annuity.[26]

From this period in his life we have first-hand descriptions of his character. The first bishop of the Anglican Church in America, Samuel Seabury, said of him: "He was obliged . . . on account of his Loyalty, to take Refuge in this City [New York] . . . [and] he is a Gentleman of Character, Worth and Reputation."[27]

And Charles Inglis of Trinity Church, the first English colonial bishop, wrote of him: "he always appeared to me . . . a firm Loyalist, who detested & opposed the American Rebellion; That he bore a very fair, respectable Character [and] officiated to a Dutch Congregation, the Members of which were warm Loyalists; That from good Information, I have been assured that he owned & was in Possession of a valuable Farm in New Jersey, which was confiscated & sold by the Rebels."[28]

In his own words, Gerrit Lydekker, before sailing to England in December 1783, appealed to Sir Guy Carleton, commander in chief of the British forces, for financial support. Speaking of himself in the third person, he wrote:

> . . . at the moment he is about to quit his Native Land perhaps for ever, & to go into a Strange Country: he sees with double Force his deplorable Condition, stripped of all his Property, & even destitute of Money to discharge his just Debts, which as an honest Man, & a Christian it is his Inclination & Duty to do. He has not even the Means of purchasing those little Articles which are absolutely necessary for the Comfort & Convenience of his Wife & 3 Children, during so long a Voyage. Thirty or Forty Pounds Sterling, in this hour of Distress, would revive the Hearts of a drooping Family, & cause your Memorialist once more to lift up his despondent Head, & look the World in the Face.

Carleton allotted him 100 pounds.[29]

Some months later, now in England, Gerrit Lydekker addressed a request for support to the commissioners appointed by Parliament to inquire into the losses and services of the American loyalists. From the beginning of the war, he noted, he had become "very obnoxious" to the Americans because of his known attachment to the king, so that

---

[26] *ERNY*, 6:4304-05. Also J. W. Lydekker, "The Rev. Gerrit . . . Lydekker," 306-14.
[27] J. W. Lydekker, "The Rev. Gerrit . . . Lydekker," 309.
[28] Ibid., 312.
[29] Ibid., 310-11.

he was "obliged to quit his very comfortable Habitation, his Family & Congregation, & remove to the City of New York ... for Security to his Person." All his property was confiscated, and "the distressed Situation that his Family now labours under from pressing Want" requires him to ask the commissioners to make such support as "in their Wisdom & Justice shall appear consistent with his calling & Family." He was granted about half the amount of his claim, together with a small annuity. Gerrit Lydekker lived for ten years after arriving in England. He died on June 28, 1794, at his son's house in Pentonville, in northwest London, at the age of sixty-five.[30]

In sum, Gerrit Lydekker, Bergen County Tory and Reformed Dutch minister, made a decision to remain loyal to King George III—in his own words to "honour the King" as his civil authority, in the same way that he honored the Classis of Amsterdam as his ecclesiastical authority. He was not unique in this; it was the thinking of many principled loyalists who lost all their worldly goods in the Revolution by choosing King over Congress. This was the intellectual link that connected Conferentie supporters with the Tory cause and the moral link that connected both Tories and Patriots to their loyalty choices.

For his political views, though they were based on his interpretations of Holy Scripture, Gerrit Lydekker was denounced as a traitor, suffered the loss of his real property in Bergen County, and when the British lost the war had to flee his native land, where his ancestors had settled 130 years before. He was a man of principle and committed to his deepest beliefs about authority and order. But he was also a complicated man, often pulled in opposing directions by conflicting forces. Whether for safekeeping, as his great-great-great grandson has suggested, or in anger at his treatment by Patriots and the loss of his worldly goods, as others have maintained, he took with him when he fled to New York City the records of his congregation at English Neighborhood. These have never resurfaced, much to the distress of local historians and of persons trying to establish their genealogies through baptismal and marriage records.[31]

---

[30] Ibid., 310-12.
[31] W. Woodford Clayton and William Nelson, eds., *History of Bergen and Passaic Counties* (Philadelphia: Everts and Peck, 1882). The authors quote from the records of the churches of Schraalenburgh and Hackensack, subsequently published by The Holland Society of New York, that Dominie Lydekker, in moving to New York in 1776, "took with him all the papers and writings belonging to the congregation," 249.

CHAPTER 12

Eilardus Westerlo (1738-1790): From a Colonial to an American Pastor

Robert Naborn

Introduction

The path of Dominie Eilardus Westerlo's life, guided from birth by the Reformed Dutch faith, led to the congregation of Albany, New York, thousands of miles from his place of birth. He was considered a powerful man in Albany, and his *Memoirs*[1] provide much information and personal reflection on his life.

The information about his life is based in large part on his unpublished *Memoirs*. Until recently, only one person appears to have had access to this document: Hermanus Bleecker (1779-1849). This Albany native and representative, chargé d'affaires to the Netherlands from 1839 to 1842,[2] eulogized Eilardus Westerlo in 1843.[3] Bleecker's

---

[1] They have been found in three parts. The first two are in the *Historic Cherry Hill* archives in Albany; the third in the *Albany Institute of History and Art* archives. I will refer to them to in this paper as *Memoirs*.

[2] Bleecker invited John Romeyn Brodhead to come to the Netherlands as his personal secretary in 1841, and he then assisted him in securing seventeenth-century documents in Great Britain, France, and the Netherlands.

[3] William B. Sprague, ed., *Annals of the American Pulpit, or Commemorative Notices of*

Pulpit in the Albany Dutch Reformed Church, c. 1657. The inset shows how the hourglass was close to the top of the staircase.
[from: Alice P. Kenney, *Stubborn for Liberty, the Dutch in New York*. (New York: Syracuse University Press, 1975), 120. inset from George Rogers Howell and Jonathan Tenney, eds., *Bicentennial History of Albany. History of the County of Albany, New York, from 1609 to 1886* (New York: W. W. Munsell & Co, 1886) 770.]

information was based on Westerlo's diaries, written between 1770 and 1790.[4]

It was not until 1984, almost two hundred years after Westerlo's death, that the Reverend Howard Hageman reintroduced Eilardus Westerlo to the world.[5] The title of Hageman's lecture, "Albany's Dutch Pope,"[6] although somewhat tongue-in-cheek, was intended to express Westerlo's importance in eighteenth-century Albany. It should be seen as Hageman intended it, a "simple effort to revive the memory of someone who meant a great deal in the development of this city in one of the critical periods of its history."[7]

Distinguished American Clergymen of Various Denominations, From the Early Settlement of the Country to the Close of the Year Eighteen Hundred and Fifty-Five. With Historical Introductions (New York: Robert Carter & Brothers, 1869), 9:29-33.

[4] This would suggest the three parts of the *Memoirs* were still together in 1848.
[5] It seems Hageman had no access to the memoir sections of 1782-1790. He referred to them as "an unpublished autobiography which can no longer be found."
[6] It appeared under this title in *De Halve Maen* a year later [Howard G. Hageman, "Albany's Dutch Pope," *De Halve Maen* 58:4 (1985): 8-10, 20-21.
[7] Hageman, *Pope*, 21.

Westerlo's life can easily be divided into four parts. His formative years in the Netherlands, from October 1738 until his voyage to America in the summer of 1760, form the first part. The second part begins with his arrival in the New World in September of 1760 and ends with 1768, the year of his regeneration experience. In the third part we see the first effects of his rebirth until 1775, the year of his marriage, on the eve of the American Revolution. The fourth part covers his time during the war and the post-war years until his death in 1790.

Formative years (1738 – 1760)

When Eilardus Westerlo was born on October 30, 1738, his father, Isaac, born in Oldenzaal in Overijssel, was the minister of the Dutch Reformed Church in Kantens (Groningen), having begun his career in Oosterhesselen (Drenthe). Eilardus's mother, Hillegonda, was born in Dalen, five miles south of Oosterhesselen. Isaac was a junior colleague of the minister in Dalen, Eilardus Reiners, Hillegonda's father. It is likely that Hillegonda and Isaac met through him.

Eilardus Reiners was one of five sons of the Reverend Lubbertus Reiners (1629-1720), all of whom were ministers, and he was the one to succeed their father in Dalen. He had come from Neuenhaus (Nieuwenhuis) and Veldhausen (Veldhuizen), in what is now Germany, barely ten miles North of Denekamp (in Overijssel).[8]

Westerlo gave an account of his own birth and the first days of his life:

> At the solemn baptism I was given the name Eilardus,[9] after my mother's father, in his lifetime minister in Dalen, Eilardus Reiners, a man whose descent and memory are blessed, and whose name my parents must have determined, among other things, to single me, their eldest son, out early on and starting in my youth, for the same Holy service – *Elevate, oh my soul, thy fathers' God!*[10]

In 1739 his father was called to Denekamp, whose Dutch Reformed population formed a minority among the Catholics, as was the case in his native Oldenzaal. When he was almost ten years

---

[8] Not to be mistaken for Veldhuizen in Drenthe.
[9] Interestingly enough, the first name "Eijlerd" was also in use on his father's side of the family: one of the men Eilardus Westerlo dedicates his disputatio to is Joh[an] Ei[j]l[ard] Borgherinck [Borgeringh], identified as a relative. Westerlo's paternal grandmother was Lucia Borgeringh, and I found one document mentioning an "Eil. Borgeringh" in Oldenzaal, possibly the father of both Lucia and Johan Eijlard.
[10] *Memoirs*, January 17, 1770.

old, Eilardus was sent to a grammar school in Oldenzaal,[11] some ten kilometers southwest of Denekamp. Eilardus boarded with two of his mother's cousins, Aleijda and Gesina Reiners, daughters of the late Reverend Arnoldus Reiners. Since a census was conducted in Denekamp in 1748 and shortly thereafter in Oldenzaal, we have a complete picture of Eilardus's family situation in both locations. In Denekamp "Eilard" was the eldest of six children under the age of ten, and the family had two maids;[12] in Oldenzaal, "Eijlerd" was no longer considered younger than ten, but one of two "free persons, boarders or otherwise, living in the household," the other being Jan Bavink.[13]

Life in the Reiners sisters' household seems to have given rise to another deeply religious experience for Eilardus. His own words suggest a life in which the Dutch Reformed teachings kept him from too many youthful indiscretions:

> It was a family in which, in the evenings, I was especially expected to publicly read aloud some passages from the Holy Bible in sequence, and sometimes one or another edifying sermon. There I also often heard mention of the dear truths of Christianity, which was a blessed means to keep me away from the many temptations of youth, although I will always have reasons enough to pray every time *Lord, remember not the sins of my youth*.[14]

In 1750, when he had been away from home for two years, Eilardus's mother died in childbirth, causing him to worry about his academic future because of the family's financial insecurity. In 1754, when he was almost sixteen, Eilardus matriculated at the University of Groningen, the alma mater of his father, both grandfathers, and several great-uncles.[15] Eilardus's fear that his father did not have the means to

---

[11] Van Lieburg confirms this was a logical step for prospective theology students. Fred A. van Lieburg, *Profeten en hun Vaderland. De Geografische Herkomst van de Gereformeerde Predikanten in Nederland van 1572 tot 1816* (Zoetermeer: Boekencentrum, 1996), 74.

[12] Genealogische Werkgroep Twente, *Volkstelling Stad en Gerigt Ootmarsum (1748)* (Oldenzaal: Stichting Jaarboek voor Twente, 1998), 2:18.

[13] Genealogische Werkgroep Twente, 1995, *Volkstelling van Oldenzaal Stad (1748)* (Oldenzaal: Stichting Jaarboek voor Twente, 1995), 29. Westerlo does not mention this Bavink, but the Baving family genealogy [www.arendarends.nl/Peize/Peize%20 families/Baving.htm] shows a Jan Baving (1740-1810), son of Lucas Baving and Casparina Reinders (who died in 1740), which may mean Eilardus was boarding with a cousin at the Reiners sisters.

[14] Psalm 25:7. Westerlo's words are taken from his *Memoirs*, January 17, 1770.

[15] "Isacus Westerlo, Tubantinus [=from the Twenthe district of Overijssel], Literarum" was registered on September 25, 1725, "Jean Westerlo, Suollanus [=of Zwolle], Jur." on November 6, 1697, and "Eijlardus Reiners, Drenthius, Theol." On September

send him to the university seems unfounded; there is no record of his father receiving financial aid for his son's education, although it was not uncommon for ministers to receive this. The fact that Isaac was not a minister of the Classis of Groningen may have prevented him from receiving funds for his son's education in that city, or perhaps, contrary to Eilardus's assumptions, there was no need for such assistance. As far as can be ascertained, none of his siblings attended a university, and none of them pursued a career in the ministry.[16]

Not much is known about Eilardus's life at the university. It is likely that he took courses in Dogmatic Theology, Theologica Practica, Emblematica, Typica, Profetica, Elenctica, Exegetica, the Formulae [of Concord], the Canons of Dort, and the Liturgy. In 1759 he defended his *disputatio*, one of the requirements of his study of theology.[17] It was a public academic exercise[18] to test the student's progress in a session presided over by a professor. The student defended printed theses, which were often based on material that had been covered during the professor's lectures.[19] Often, but not always, the professor would bundle the *disputationes* of his students and publish them under his own name.[20] Daniel Gerdes did so several times once a subject had been covered by his students. Westerlo's *disputatio*, chapter XV (of sixteen) on the First

---

15, 1694 [Historisch Genootschap te Groningen, *Album Studiosorum Academiae Groninganae* (Groningen: J. B. Wolters, 1915), 139, 144, and 173].

[16] Much later his half-sister, Hillegonda Willemina Westerlo (1754-1841), married Jacobus van Loenen, minister in Dalen.

[17] "Eilardus Westerlo, Transisalanus [=from Overijssel], verdedigde, 7 april 1759, te Groningen, eene Disputatio exegetica XVI, [in cap. XV. ad Corinthos], en droeg die op aan de hoogl. Gerdes en Ruckersfelder, te Gron. en te Dev., en aan Joh. Eilardus Borgherinck, civit. Daventr. trib., praeposit. Oldensal. praet. [=civil administrator of Deventer, praetor of the countryside court in Oldenzaal) etc." Nederlands Genootschap voor Genealogie en Heraldiek, Heemkunde en Geschiedenis, *De Navorscher* (Amsterdam: J. C. Loman, Jr., 1880), 486.

[18] It was a so-called *disputatio exercitii gratia*, a rhetorical exercise for the student, as opposed to the *disputatio pro gradu*, which served as the last requirement of one's studies, for obtaining a doctorate, for example. Disputations of the first category were presented far more often than those of the latter. Westerlo's was one of only 28 *disputationes exercitii gratia* in theology at the University of Groningen between 1751 and 1760. See Jacob van Sluis, "Disputeren in Franeker en Groningen," in H.A. Krop, et al., eds., *Zeer Kundige Professoren. Beoefening van de Filosofie in Groningen van 1614 tot 1996* (Hilversum: Verloren, 1997), 47-56.

[19] See Ferenc Postma, ed., *Disputationes Exercitii Gratia. Een Inventarisatie van Disputaties Verdedigd onder Sibrandus Lubbertus, Prof. Theol. te Franker 1585-1625* (Amsterdam: VU Uitgeverij, 1985), xv.

[20] Professors also frequently used disputations for political ends. See, for example, Edwin Rabbie, ed., *Hugo Grotius: Ordinum Hollandiae ac Westfrisiae Pietas (1613)* (Leiden: Brill, 1995), 3, 4, 7.

Letter of the Apostle Paul to the Corinthians, was thus published in Groningen in 1759.

In March 1760 Westerlo took his preparatory and peremptory exams, the exams required by the Reformed Church. His professors, Daniel Gerdes and Michaël Bertling, had selected him for the congregation in Albany, in North America. Westerlo showed up with his testimonials, necessary to be admitted to the preparatory exam. It was not the classis, but the theological faculty who presided over this exam. The *Acta Synodi Groninganae* simply state: "Praeparatorie Geëxamineerde de Theolo. Faculteit d. Eilardus Westerlo den 17 Meert 1760."

The successful examination admitted him into the pulpit, and he was thus entitled to seek a post. He took the peremptory exam almost two weeks later, after which he was ordained for his position, some three thousand miles away.

The request to Gerdes and Bertling had been submitted through an agent, Daniel Crommelin, who was in contact with merchants in Albany and New York City at the time.[21] The use of agents was not uncommon, and the reason to bypass the Classis of Amsterdam, at least initially, was not necessarily to spite the classis. Historian Dirk Mouw has found that agents were viewed by congregations as "best suited to act in the interests" of the congregations, suggesting the classis was not in a position to act in the best interests of the churches overseas.[22] Indeed, one may doubt that the members of the Classis of Amsterdam had the information, knowledge, insight, and commitment necessary to assess a person's ability to function as a minister in colonial American society, although the same might be said about professors at universities in the Netherlands. Congregations also often had a difficult time verbalizing what kind of person they needed.

At the time the consistory in Albany sent the call to Groningen in 1759, the congregation may have had several reasons not to get the

---

[21] Daniel Crommelin (1707-1789) was born in New York, where his father Charles, a British immigrant with French roots, set up the Holland Trading Company in 1720. Daniel moved to the Netherlands when he was seventeen, to set up an international trading company in Amsterdam.

[22] Dirk Mouw, "Recruiting Ministers: Amsterdam, New York, and the Dutch of British North America, 1700-1772," in G. Harinck and H. Krabbendam, eds., *Amsterdam-New York: Transatlantic Relations and Urban Identities Since 1653* (Amsterdam: VU Uitgeverij, 2005), 90-91. He estimates that calls through agents account for one quarter (23) of the calls sent to the Netherlands between 1700 and 1772. Interestingly enough, Mouw mentions Gerdes and Bertling as being involved in a call from Schoharie in 1762, but not the one from Albany in 1760. The records show there was such a call from Schoharie, with involvement of Westerlo, but it never materialized. Mouw, *Recruiting*, 96 n19.

Classis of Amsterdam involved: Dominie Theodore Frelinghuysen had left Albany to meet with the classis, ostensibly to request permission from the Classis of Amsterdam to establish a classis and an academy in America. It would have appeared odd, to say the least, if Albany were to petition the Classis of Amsterdam for a new minister at the same time its current minister was in Amsterdam. The Classis of Amsterdam never received such a request from Albany, nor did Albany ever send an official letter explaining the dismissal of its minister Frelinghuysen.

The second largest Dutch Reformed congregation in North America must have been an attractive possibility for ministers already in America, but the fact that the Albany consistory had dismissed Frelinghuysen under a cloud of controversy may have made this position less than desirable. One third of the congregations in New York and New Jersey were without a minister at the time that the blank call was sent to Groningen,[23] also an indication that it was not easy to find a minister in North America. Since the consistory sent the letter of call so soon after Frelinghuysen had left for Holland, it does not seem plausible that it spent a long time weighing the possibility of calling one of the ministers of smaller congregations in New York or New Jersey. They were likely looking for a candidate without involvement in these conflicts—one with a clean slate.

Whatever the advantages the consistory of the Albany church saw in bypassing the Classis of Amsterdam and in using an agent, it was by all standards the most expensive method of acquiring a new minister. The invoice presented by Daniel Crommelin toward the end of 1760[24] shows that the total costs of bringing Westerlo to New Netherland amounted to ƒ892.90, approximately €9,000 in today's money. More than a third of it was a ƒ300 "assignation" to Professor Gerdes.[25]

Gerdes received a substantial sum of money, but it is not likely that the sum was large because of stipulations made by the consistory

---

[23] Of the 81 congregations, 27 had no minister. In his analysis of eighteenth-century Reformed ministers in the Netherlands, Van Rooden concludes that there was a permanent surplus of proponents until 1775. Peter van Rooden, "Van Geestelijke Stand naar Beroepsgroep. De Professionalisering van de Nederlandse Predikant, 1625-1874," *Tijdschrift voor Sociale Geschiedenis* 17 (1991): 365-67, n10.

[24] Document 43-11 in the archives of the First Church in Albany. The invoice is difficult to follow: Dutch guilders and British pounds sterling are added up to yield the mentioned total of ƒ892.90 [=892 guilders and 18 stuivers].

[25] The Church had to borrow £165 New York currency from its Poor Fund to pay its debts incurred in calling and bringing over Eilardus Westerlo. Edward T. Corwin, ed., *Ecclesiastical Records of the State of New York*, 7 vols. (Albany: Lyon, 1901-1916), 5:3800 (hereafter cited as *ERNY*). Also Document 43-1 in the archives of the First Church in Albany.

about the candidate's convictions. Although Frelinghuysen had been explicitly commissioned by the Classis of Amsterdam to convince the Albany consistory to join the Coetus in 1745,[26] these stipulations probably did not concern the possible candidate's position in the Coetus-Conferentie conflict:[27] the Albany congregation was split over the issue, and a candidate in Groningen could not have been aware of the conflict. Gerdes must have been asked to analyze the candidate's character, making sure that his personality would fit in a congregation whose split was worsened as a result of its current minister having made his convictions (read: those of the Classis of Amsterdam) clear.

In other words (even though the consistory in Albany was not thinking in these terms), the young pietist minister Eilardus Westerlo, with a family background in the Dutch Reformed Church and having shown the zeal and character needed to lead a congregation that was in turmoil, was seen as the perfect candidate to be the minister of the second-largest congregation in North America, and Albany was willing to pay for professor Gerdes' service. What made this call to Groningen special is that, in addition to bypassing the Classis of Amsterdam and using an agent, Albany had not told its minister at the time, Theodore Frelinghuysen, that he need not return. In any case, he appeared to be fighting his dismissal in the Netherlands, spending two weeks in Groningen,[28] after which nobody seems to have heard from him again.

In a letter from New York City to his wife, on the eve of his sudden departure, dated October 5, 1759, Frelinghuysen spoke of "an important affair which the Lord hath put in [my] heart" for which he had to go to Europe. The letter and its post scriptum show that the possibility that he might not return was on his mind.[29]

The ship that carried Westerlo across the North Atlantic Ocean must have left towards the end of June 1760. Its first stop was Texel, to prepare for the voyage, just as Henry Hudson's *Halve Maen* had done some one hundred fifty years earlier.[30] His call, crossing, arrival, and

---

[26] ERNY, 5:3423.
[27] In short, the conflict, which was not fully resolved until after the Revolution, centered around those wanting to establish some type of classis in North America, with the authority to examine and license candidates for the ministry, and to ordain ministers on the one hand, and those wanting to remain subordinate to the Classis of Amsterdam.
[28] Letter by Gerdes to Crommelin, May 10, 1760. RCA Archives, Sage Library in New Brunswick, NJ.
[29] ERNY, 5:3738-39.
[30] Carel De Vos van Steenwijk, who met Westerlo in Albany in 1784, gave a more elaborate account of his 15-week crossing in 1783. Carel de Vos van Steenwijk, *Een Grand Tour naar de Nieuwe Republiek: Journaal van een Reis door Amerika, 1783-1784*, ed.

beginning in Albany carried importance for Westerlo; he mentioned their dates more than once in his *Memoirs*. Only once did he give an account, albeit a brief one, of his voyage across the North Atlantic Ocean:

> Twenty-three years ago I first arrived in this city through Divine mercy, having been upwards of fourteen weeks on the vessel in my passage from Europe, and experienced the Lord's preserving and protecting goodness. Already when we had just left Holland we saw a French privateer (for it was then wartime)[31] near upon us but happily pursued by an English man-of-war, and not allowed to take us, and when laying ready at Stromnitz in the Orkneys, we got information of another on that coast and were prevented from being captured, and afterwards we escaped once more by safe sailing. Thus, the Lord's eye was upon poor me that I should not be carried into an enemy's land, and he brought me safely here, where I was received in friendship by the inhabitants, and preached the next Lord's Day from Romans 1:15.[32]

New York City minister Johannes Ritzema, whose son Rudolphus may still have been at Groningen University when Westerlo left in the spring, was the first to welcome Westerlo to the New World in early October 1760.

We do know that the Classis of Amsterdam was not happy with the way Westerlo was sent to America. On October 3, 1763, the Classis of Amsterdam wrote to the "Ministers who call themselves the Conferentie," and, while admonishing them to adhere to the Classis of Amsterdam as a "Higher Assembly," they added:

> You will also inculcate this on those new brethren who you have recently sought and obtained from the Faculty of Groningen.[33]

Wayne te Brake (Hilversum: Verloren, 1999), 35-38. Westerlo only mentions meeting ambassador Van Berckel and the fact that the latter stayed at the Westerlo's and then traveled with Westerlo and Governor Clinton to Kingston [*Memoirs*, August 8, 1784], whereas De Vos van Steenwijk notes that he and Westerlo both spent their youth in and around Oldenzaal, and that he was able to update Westerlo on the school there. See De Vos van Steenwijk, *Tour*, 167-170.

[31] The Seven Years' War (1756-1763) between the French and the English is the European counterpart of the French and Indian War (1754-1763) in North America.

[32] *Memoirs*, October 13, 1783.

[33] ERNY, 6:3896. Corwin adds the names of Cook [Cock?], Meijer, and Kern in parentheses, but it can only be that the Classis was referring to Westerlo and Cornelis Blauw [matriculated at the University of Groningen in 1749; arrived in America in 1762, to preach at Pompton Plains, etc.] in addition to Meijer: Gerard Daniel Kok (Cock) didn't arrive until 1764, did not graduate from Groningen, and

[The only two ministers to have come over recently were Eilardus Westerlo and Hermanus Meijer] These gentlemen, although passing through our city (Amsterdam), did not address themselves to us. We also think it highly befitting that you should seek for ministers whom you may require (in America), through the Classis of Amsterdam, or their committee *Ad Res Exteras*, or at least through members of that Classis to whose care the New York churches are committed. Or if any are sent to you from other quarters, they should refer themselves to us in order to receive our exhortations how to carry themselves properly and in due subordination to our Classis.[34]

Finding His Place in the New World (1760 – 1768)

Although the first comprehensive census in America was not conducted until 1790, unofficial figures show that in 1760 Albany had more than doubled in size since the British had taken over the colony of New Netherland in 1664 and changed Beverwijck's name to Albany.[35] Albany was definitely more than "a Dutch outpost in an English colonial society."[36] It was still an important town for trading with the Indians,[37] and it seemed to have maintained much of its Dutch character and flavor.

By one historian's assessment, Westerlo's transition from a twenty-one-year-old recent graduate in the Old World to the minister of a large congregation in the New World appears to have gone well:

---

the classis had examined him [Corwin, *Ecclesiastical*, 3832-33] and approved of his call from Rhinebeck and Camp, NY, in September of 1762 [Corwin, *Ecclesiastical*, 3820], and Johann Michael Kern did arrive in New York in October 1763, but he graduated from Heidelberg, in Germany. Both Cock and Kern preached in German, in German Reformed Churches.

[34] ERNY, 6:3896-97.
[35] The British "found a village with more than a thousand people." Janny Venema, *Beverwijck: A Dutch Village on the American Frontier, 1652-1664* (Hilversum/Albany, NY: Verloren/State University of New York Press, 2003), 24. Not all figures are reliable: Andrew Burnaby, vicar of Greenwich, found the 1759 figure to be 100,000. Andrew Burnaby, *Travels Through the Middle Settlements in North-America in the Years 1759 and 1760* (Dublin: R. Marchbank, 1775), 138, a figure copied by subsequent travelers through the area. This figure was certainly far off: most estimates of the number of inhabitants in New York City around 1760 do not surpass 18,000.
[36] Hageman, *Pope*, 20.
[37] In 1787, when Westerlo advertised the sale of the Church's pasture lots on behalf of the Consistory, he mentioned that the city of Albany was one "affording the most facile and commodious intercourse with Niagara, Detroit, & Michillimackinac, the three great Indian marts ..." Document 64-5 in the Archives of the First Church in Albany. It was not until 1797 that Albany became the capital of the state of New York. In 1786 it was the sixth city in size in the United States.

Eilardus Westerlo [was] a brilliant and tactful young divine from the University of Groningen, who healed the schism in the church so effectively that the Common Council awarded him the freedom of the city a year after his arrival.[38]

Since the Common Council, and the seats of government of Albany in general, were often still occupied by people of Dutch descent who were also influential in the Dutch Reformed Protestant Church, and vice versa,[39] it was very important to be accepted by these bodies. Young Westerlo achieved just that in a congregation that was (and would remain for several more years) split over the Coetus-Conferentie issue.

In 1763 Dominie Hermanus Meijer, a fellow Groningen graduate, arrived in New York to become the minister of the Dutch Reformed Church in Kingston. Meijer, originally from Bremen, matriculated in September 1757, and it is likely that his situation in 1763 was similar to Westerlo's in 1760: receiving a call just when he was about to finish his studies. He indicated that professors in Groningen (and *not* the Classis of Amsterdam) had sent him.[40] It is also very likely that the call to Meijer was issued through Crommelin in 1763.[41]

On December 22, 1774, Westerlo mentioned Meijer as the last one of a list of friends in New York and New Jersey who had helped him, adding that he "should have mentioned [him] first." When Meijer's consistory in Kingston refused to give him the testimonials needed for him to become minister elsewhere, Westerlo's help revealed his understanding of the role of the church, both in New York and in the Netherlands, and his adherence to the Canons of the Synod of Dordrecht of 1618/1619.[42]

The call to Hermanus Meijer that caused Westerlo to act was issued in the spring of 1768. That spring proved pivotal in Westerlo's religious life. In his *Memoirs* he noted that, in early 1768, "new and strange doctrines in this congregation were introduced, even by those

---

[38] Alice P. Kenney, *The Gansevoorts of Albany: Dutch Patricians in the Upper Hudson Valley* (Syracuse, NY: Syracuse University Press, 1969), 45.

[39] The members of the Common Council that October 1761 were Peter Lansing, Frans Pruyn, Cornelis Ten Broeck, Volkert Douw, Abraham Ten Broeck, Henry I. Bogart, Jacob van Schaick, Marte Mynderse, and John Hansen. Joel Munsell, ed., *Collections*, 128, all also members of the Dutch Reformed Church.

[40] ERNY, 6:4021.

[41] *Memoirs*, December 27, 1783.

[42] See Robert A. Naborn, "Eilardus Westerlo on Hermanus Meijer's Call to Caughnawaga," in Margriet Bruijn Lacy et al., eds., *From De Halve Maen to KLM: 400 Years of Dutch-American Exchange*, (Münster: Nodus Publikationen, 2008), 149-58, for a full discussion of Westerlo's involvement in this call.

whom it does not behoove." It made him decide to dedicate several sermons "to the first principles of the doctrine of Christ," but he also became convinced that he was filled with "sinful vices in [his] heart," which made him "reform [himself]" by trying to purify [himself] completely," knowing that he "had to be reborn for that."[43]

On April 20, 1768, Westerlo's "incessant prayers, by day and by night" were heard. While reading in Thomas Boston's *Human Nature and its Fourfold State* he felt renewed, and, just as Boston had written, "the world will probably be in flames," Westerlo got up to see a large fire in the woods. As soon as he realized what it was (he did not elaborate), he lay himself down to pray. After having gone downstairs for a drink, he was driven to read Psalm 25, which calmed him down.[44]

Towards Independence for America—and for the Church in America (1768-1775)

The Coetus-Conferentie schism and the desire for reconciliation kept Westerlo working cautiously at maintaining good relations with his congregation. When John Henry Livingston brought the so-called Plan of Union from the Classis of Amsterdam in 1770, he invited all the congregations in New York and New Jersey to a "General Convention of the Reformed Churches" in New York City in October 1771. After this meeting it became clear that several congregations were not ready (yet) to join this union, most notably Albany. Westerlo did sign the Articles of Union in 1772, but only on behalf of the Schagticoke church, which he supplied in those years.

In the years following the 1771 meeting, the Albany congregation, including meetings of its great consistory,[45] remained divided. On September 17, 1773, a large number of members of the Albany congregation submitted a letter of remonstrance, in English and in Dutch, with many signatures attached.[46] They protested both against the plans they believed were afoot in the consistory for their congregation to join the union, and the fact that the synod would

---

[43] *Memoirs*, January 17, 1770.
[44] Ibid..
[45] A meeting with all past and present consistory members, convened for important matters.
[46] Document 52-2 in the archives of the First Church in Albany. How many members signed will probably never be established with certainty: some names appear several times, and more than once a series of names is written down in the same handwriting. Also, the total number indicated on the documents themselves (173 on the English document) is exceeded by the actual tally: 246 on the English, and 57 on the Dutch document.

meet in the Albany church on September 21. This letter followed the September 9 consistory meeting and a September 15 letter to the Albany Corporation, i.e., the mayor and aldermen of Albany, anticipating unrest during the September 21 assembly meeting.

On January 5, 1774, Westerlo wrote a letter to his congregation in Albany as a personal attempt to convince the congregation that joining the union would be in its best interest, or even the most logical step to take by the congregation.[47] He showed himself to be such a strong advocate of the Plan of Union that the position he was considered to have taken in October 1771, that of one of the "neutral brethren," must have reflected that of his congregation and not his own attitude toward the Plan of Union. Since the other "neutral" member on the committee to draw up "a formula of union" was John Henry Livingston,[48] it is clear that the neutrality referred to here was the position in the Coetus-Conferentie schism and not the one toward the Plan of Union. It was not until 1785 that the Albany congregation joined the union.

Toward the end of December 1774 Westerlo explained in his *Memoirs* why he had had "sufficient reason to live happily in this congregation." Among other factors, he cited the unsolicited call he received to the Albany congregation, divine guidance in the ways of the Lord, the awakening of his soul through the mercy of the Lord, and the love and respect he received from dear friends who held firm to the gospel, and "the sweet harmony" he enjoyed "with his honorable Consistory."[49]

In the summer of 1775 there occurred a big change in Westerlo's life. He married the widow of patroon[50] Stephen van Rensselaer II, Catherine Livingston, a daughter of Philip "the Signer" Livingston, on July 19, 1775. This changed Eilardus from a seemingly lonely bachelor pastor to someone near the center of power in Albany. The marriage took place at the Van Rensselaer manor. Dominie Elias van

---

[47] In Albany Institute of History and Art archives, Westerlo Papers.
[48] *ERNY*, 6:4212.
[49] *Memoirs*, December 22, 1774.
[50] A patroon was a landholder in New Netherland who, by the West India Company charter of 1629, and under Dutch colonial rule, was granted proprietary and manorial rights to a large tract of land in exchange for bringing 50 new settlers to the colony. Stephen van Rensselaer inherited his patroonship from Kiliaan van Rensselaer (about 1585-1643), who established Rensselaerwyck, the largest and most successful patroonship in New Netherland. It covered almost all of present-day Albany and Rensselaer counties, and parts of present-day Columbia and Greene counties in New York State. Westerlo's oldest stepson, Stephen van Rensselaer III (1764-1839), is also known as "the last patroon."

Bunschooten, later a great benefactor of New Brunswick Theological Seminary, officiated.[51]

Westerlo had thus become a member of two of the most influential families in the Hudson valley—or three, if one counts the Ten Broeck family as well.[52] Given the Dutch church's impact on city matters, The Reverend Dr. Howard Hageman may not have been too far off in calling Westerlo "Albany's Dutch Pope." In any event, Westerlo's new standing was evidently adequate to inspire him to draw up a will less than six weeks after the wedding.

In November of that same year, 1775, Eilardus Westerlo and his colleague John Henry Livingston became brothers-in-law when the latter married Catharine's younger sister Sarah in Kingston, New York. This may have even further increased Westerlo's influence or standing within the Dutch Reformed Church, although he was still in the difficult situation of representing a congregation that had not joined the union.

Independence, and Rebuilding the Dutch Church (1775-1790)

How much could Westerlo write between 1775 and 1781? There was a scarcity of paper, and maintaining a diary may have been risky. It is clear that Westerlo decided at some point during the period to start writing more regularly. At least 112 pages (in Dutch) are missing.

The political situation in Albany during the first years of the Revolutionary War was unsettled. There was an official government, the Common Council, also known as the Corporation, but real power was already in the hands of the pro-Revolutionary men organized as the so-called Committee of Correspondence and Safety. This group arrested the mayor and city clerk when they celebrated the king's birthday on June 3, 1775. The Committee of Correspondence was financed by many of the citizens of Albany.[53]

The British targeted the Dutch Reformed clergy, and sources indicate that Westerlo fled Albany, at least at times. He may have taken his family to Salisbury in Connecticut, on the border with New York and Massachusetts, where the Van Rensselaers owned a farm.

---

[51] Van Bunschooten had studied under Hermanus Meijer, and he was one of the first to be ordained by the General Synod of the independent Dutch Reformed Church in America, in 1773. In 1775, he was minister of the church at Schagticoke.

[52] Abraham Ten Broeck was a great-uncle and the official guardian of Stephen van Rensselaer III.

[53] Westerlo donated a small sum too, which was probably not a risk-free move on his part [See James Sullivan, ed., *Minutes of the Albany Committee of Correspondence, 1775-1778* (Albany, NY: The University of the State of New York, 1923).

Westerlo was still often in Albany as well: baptisms, marriages, and other services were still performed, although not regularly. In the literature, Westerlo is invariably referred to as a patriot minister preaching against the British, but no direct sources are given. Historian Alice Kenney quotes from a letter Leonard Gansevoort wrote to his brother Peter after Philip Schuyler's army had stopped by on its way to invade Canada, on August 28, 1775:

> General Schuyler has yesterday been in the Dutch Church and desired the prayers of the Congregation for himself and the army under his command which he received, and I sincerely lament that you were not present that you might have heard it. Mr. Westerlo's prayer was so very pathetic and so well adapted that he drew tears from the eyes of almost all there present. May God grant that a happy reconciliation take place upon constitutional principles and prevent the further effusion of blood.[54]

In early 1776 Westerlo decided to draw up a genealogy of his family. It shows that he was fairly well informed of his relatives' situation in the Netherlands. The year "1776" is written across the top, but his (expected) child, Rensselaer, born on May 6, 1776, is not included, which is an indication that Westerlo probably wrote it in early 1776 and that he never revisited this document.[55]

Westerlo is linked to a number of important events in the second half of the war. On December 14, 1780, he officiated at the wedding of Alexander Hamilton, then assistant to George Washington (and in 1791 the first Secretary of the Treasury), and Elizabeth (Betsy) Schuyler, a daughter of General Philip Schuyler, held at the Schuyler mansion in Albany. In June 1782 Westerlo had the honor of addressing George Washington and other dignitaries in a sermon (in English) delivered in the Dutch Reformed Church.

With the end of the War of Independence the churches started the reconstruction of their congregations and their church buildings. This is also the time Westerlo began his *Memoirs* in a diary-style form, also switching to English, and when he started preaching in English in addition to Dutch.

The Issue of Dutch Versus English

How did Albany, the Dutch Reformed congregation and consistory of the city, and Westerlo himself, deal with the English/Dutch language

---

[54] Kenney, *Gansevoorts*, 90. She adds: "Dominie Westerlo conducted daily services of prayer for preservation from the hand of the invader" Kenney, *Gansevoorts*, 105.
[55] The document is in the archives of *Historic Cherry Hill* in Albany, NY.

issue? Many scholars have noticed the gradual demise of the Dutch language among the descendants of Dutch colonists in New York and New Jersey, not only in its daily use, but also, more slowly, in the Dutch Reformed churches.

It is rather remarkable how long the Dutch language persisted in some parts of North America. Albany is an example of an area where Dutch survived long into the British reign. In Albany the Dutch language even outlived the British reign, only to succumb to English after the Revolution. When Westerlo received his call in 1760, there was no debate in Albany whether the new minister should also be able to preach in English. Less than three years later the largest consistory in North America (New York City) sent a call to the Reverend Archibald Laidlie, educated at the University of Edinburgh and minister at the Scottish Church in Vlissingen (Flushing) since 1759, specifically asking him to preach in English.

On March 12, 1782, after more than twenty years in Albany, Westerlo decided to try his hand at preaching in English. Two months later he abandoned Dutch in his *Memoirs* as well: "Blessed be the Lord, ... who ... enabled me to perform his public worship in this language, in which I now also begin to remember in this diary his loving kindness towards me, conscious, that perhaps my own children will be best able to understand my notes and render thanks to our God for the innumerable mercies they have received in their youth and infancy."[56]

Westerlo went on to report that his congregation "appeared to be satisfied and even glad with this his undertaking" (i.e., preaching in English), and, looking back on the year past, he saw even more than one benefit: he thanked God "for His enabling and encouraging me to preach even in the English language, which has excited at least the Presbyterian congregation to attend and procure a minister for themselves, whom I hope the Lord will bless."[57]

When the need for English preaching on a weekly basis was felt in the congregation, the consistory on February 2, 1786, decided to "try a subscription for calling an assistant minister to preach in the English language." It took more than a year to find such a person. The Reverend John Bassett, who had been a student under John Henry Livingston, was appointed to be both minister and president of the fledgling Albany Academy.[58]

No Dutch-speaking replacement was ever hired following Westerlo's death, and the consistory meeting minutes have been kept

[56] *Memoirs*, May 22, 1782.
[57] *Memoirs*, December 31, 1782.
[58] *Memoirs*, November 27, 1787.

in English since early 1791. The power of the Dutch in Albany had been waning following the American Revolution.

After Albany joined the union in May 1785, Westerlo was elected president of the General Synod in October of that year. From New York, where he "was received by [his] friends with many tokens of pity and love," Westerlo accompanied John Henry Livingston to Princeton, "where [he] was publicly honored and unexpectedly obtained the honorary degree of our profession."[59] The trustee minutes simply state the resolution of September 28, 1785, "that the Revd Erlardus Westeloe [sic!] of Albany, the Revd Jonathan Edwards, of New Haven, the Revd Henry Purcell of Charleston in South-Carolina, be admitted to the degree of Doctor of Divinity."[60]

Since his first contact with the Reverend Dr. Ezra Stiles of Yale College, when Westerlo sent a letter in Latin successfully requesting acceptance of his stepson Philip van Rensselaer into the college in May 1782,[61] Stiles and Westerlo regularly wrote to each other in Latin. Although they never met, they considered each other friends. Stiles is often quoted as saying that Westerlo "wrote Latin in greater purity than any man he had ever known."[62]

1785 was also the year Westerlo and his family had to move out of the Van Rensselaer manor, because Stephen van Rensselaer III (Harvard, 1782) had come of age. The church had a parsonage built for Westerlo and his family: his wife; their three children, Rensselaer, Catherine, and Johanna; and the two remaining stepchildren, Philip and Elizabeth van Rensselaer. The house was located on Market Street, which was one of the streets intersecting with the 1715 Stone Church in the city's center.

In the second half of the 1780s Westerlo's health was in decline; and the loss of his youngest daughter, Johanna, who was almost five, to a mysterious intestinal disease in 1788, also had an impact on his health. He visited Saratoga Springs, which restored his strength somewhat, but not enough to stop the decline.

Westerlo's final efforts were again for a religious cause. In early 1790 his translation of Robert Alberthoma's book of catechisms was published,[63] and he was getting ready to translate *Gods Onfeilbare*

---

[59] *Memoirs*, October 13, 1785. From New York, he also wrote to his wife with this news, in a letter dated October 4, 1785.
[60] *General Catalogue of Princeton University, 1746-1906* (Princeton University, 1908), 251.
[61] Franklin B. Dexter, ed., *The Literary Diary of Ezra Stiles*. Volume III: January 1, 1782-May 6, 1795 (New York: Scribner's, 1901), 20.
[62] E. T. Corwin, *A Manual of the Reformed Church in America, 1628-1902* (New York: Board of Publication of the Reformed Church in America, 1902), 907.
[63] It appeared as Robert Alberthoma, *Principles of the Christian Religion, as Taught in the Reformed Protestant Dutch Churches* (Albany, NY: Charles R. & George Webster, 1789).

Waarheden Voorgestelt in eene Verklaringe over den Heidelbergschen Katechismus [*God's Infallible Truths Shown in an Exposition about the Heidelberg Catechism*] (Amsterdam, 1736), by his great-uncle Hermannus Reiners, but this plan never came to fruition.

Eilardus Westerlo passed away on December 26, 1790, having lain in a sickbed for several weeks. In his last diary entry, dated December 4, he described his rough night, with a sudden cold chill, when he was "awakened by the thought that I was struck with an apoplexy." Westerlo's last words on paper were "May I live a life of faith and Holiness, and be found in peace. Amen."

Conclusion

The Reverend Dr. Eilardus Westerlo (1738-1790) held but one full-time position during his lifetime. He was minister of the Reformed Protestant Dutch Church in Albany for thirty years, during which time his adoptive country became independent from Great Britain, and during which time his church became independent from its mother country and from the Classis of Amsterdam.

Westerlo played an important role in successfully guiding the Dutch Reformed congregation of Albany, the second largest in North America, through many changes and difficulties. It is amazing to think how two professors, thousands of miles away and unfamiliar with the situation in Albany, and faced with a limited number of students from which to make the choice, appear to have chosen the right person for the job.

This twenty-one-year-old recent graduate from the University of Groningen immediately understood the issues at hand in Albany: a congregation with some strong-willed, powerful, and politically connected members, divided first in the Coetus-Conferentie dispute and later over the Plan of Union. The American Revolution was another problem that required careful handling, as did the gradual switch from Dutch to English.

It would seem that Westerlo was not a power-hungry figure, as is suggested by Hageman's application of the term "pope," but rather a careful and successful shepherd of his flock. The Albany congregation, one of the most prominent of the Dutch Reformed congregations, did not fall apart over the divisive colonial issues between 1760 and 1790, and it was Westerlo who accomplished this.

SUCCESSORS

The Colonial Legacy for the New Denomination and the
New Immigration in the Nineteenth Century

CHAPTER 13

John Henry Livingston (1746-1825): Interpreter of the Dutch Reformed Tradition in the Early American Republic

John W. Coakley

The Reverend John Henry Livingston was born and raised in Poughkeepsie, New York. He graduated from Yale in 1762 and afterward read law for a time. Then, following a conversion experience in 1764-5, he felt a call to the ministry. He traveled to the Netherlands in 1766, received his theological education at the University of Utrecht over the next four years, and then was ordained by the Classis of Amsterdam. In 1770 he sailed back to America, where he served as a Dutch Reformed minister until his death fifty-five years later.

Livingston played a prominent role in the transition that the Dutch Reformed congregations in America underwent during his lifetime, from being a part of the national Dutch church that was anomalously placed in British colonial society, to becoming a self-governing church with its own place in the new American republic—a church that however, still called itself "Dutch" and valued its faithfulness to Dutch traditions of belief and practice. Specifically, he helped create two crucial conditions that made that transition possible: first, a constitutional basis for the new church, and, second, an institution whereby the new church could educate and certify its own clergy. In

Portrait of John Henry Livingston D.D.
by Gilbert Stuart, 1795, oil on canvas
[Collection of the New-York Historical Society]

both respects the fact of Livingston's Dutch education was essential to his position and influence, even as he became the very embodiment of the church as a new American entity.

Youth

Livingston's choice to prepare for the ministry in the Dutch church as distinct from some other church appears to have been a self-conscious decision, not the natural expression of a sense of identity with the Dutch tradition.

Livingston belonged to an "aristocracy," as Cynthia Kierner has characterized the Livingston family—that is, a family who, by the time of his birth, was clearly "distinguished culturally from their humbler neighbors," in wealth and manners.[1] The founder of the dynasty had been Robert Livingston (1654-1725), a Scotsman brought up in the Netherlands who arrived in the New York colony in 1675. By 1686 he

---

[1] Cynthia Kierner, *Traders and Gentlefolk: The Livingstons of New York, 1675-1790* (Ithaca: Cornell University Press, 1992), 129.

had assembled the 160,000-acre tract called Livingston Manor, which established the family's wealth. By the time of John Henry's birth in 1746 the Livingstons were also poised to become a political force in the New York colony as the leaders of one of the two great rival New York political factions in the decades before the Revolutionary War. The other faction, associated with the Delancey family, was as closely identified with Anglican privilege as the Livingstons were identified with Protestant dissent.[2] John Henry's branch of the family was the least prosperous; his grandfather was Robert's youngest son Gilbert, whom Robert had rescued from bankruptcy, severely reducing his inheritance in consequence. But Gilbert's son Henry, John Henry's father, did become a man of substance as clerk of Dutchess County and member of the colonial assembly. This was owed to the patronage of Henry's uncle, Henry Beekman, rather than to the Livingston patrimony.[3] Nonetheless, John Henry maintained correspondence with Livingstons of other branches of the family throughout his life and also married into one of those branches in 1775. His wife was his second cousin Sarah, the sixth child of his father's first cousin Philip Livingston, a wealthy New York merchant, signer of the Declaration of Independence and sometime elder of the Dutch congregation of New York. When Philip died in 1778, he left extensive properties to Sarah and her husband, and John Henry managed these as an adept man of affairs in the family tradition.[4]

Livingston's immediate family belonged to the Dutch congregation of Poughkeepsie, but the Dutch church figures apparently only slightly, and, by implication, negatively, in his own account of his religious formation. That account forms part of a memoir of his early years written in 1818, the year he turned seventy-two; the manuscript itself is lost, but Alexander Gunn incorporated large excerpts of it into his 1829 biography.[5] We learn from the memoir that the decisive event

[2] Ibid., 175-76.
[3] Ibid., 60-61.
[4] Philip Livingston Estate Documents, Box 5, New York Historical Society.
[5] Gunn described the manuscript, then in the possession of Livingston's son Henry Alexander Livingston, as "of about fifty or sixty pages letter paper" (Alexander Gunn, *Memoirs of John H. Livingston prepared in compliance with a request of the General Synod of the Reformed Dutch Church in North America* [New York: Rutgers Press, 1829], 8). Assuming the same word-density as Livingston's letters, which is approximately 250 words per page, the memoir would have been between 12,500 and 15,000 words in length. Gunn's quoted excerpts, all in chapters 2, 4, and 5 of the *Memoirs*, total about 6800 words. Also the high degree of personal detail throughout those chapters, in contrast to the rest of the book, suggests Gunn's reliance there on the manuscript even when he is not quoting it.

in his spiritual life was an awakening or conversion that occurred in 1764, two years after his graduation from Yale, when a serious illness had made him lay aside his legal studies. In his earlier youth, Livingston says, "the amount of benefits resulting from early parental instruction, and from all the ordinances and sermons I had heard during my whole life, was nothing more than some confused ideas of truths, which I did not understand, or believe." Gunn informs us that he could not "intelligently unite" in worship at the family's church anyway because he did not know Dutch. (He became fluent only later, in his Utrecht years.)[6] But now as an eighteen-year-old, Livingston says, he read Bunyan and Doddridge, who impelled him to a careful study of the scriptures. This in turn impressed upon him the divinity of Christ and the truth of the doctrine of justification, which led him to an experience of grace and the conviction that he was a child of the covenant. Then he heard a sermon by the British revivalist George Whitefield, who spoke a word of assurance directly, as Livingston thought, to himself.[7] In all of this, the stated influences upon him, we notice, were not from the Dutch church in particular but from the broader evangelical culture. Following closely upon this awakening, Livingston decided, after protracted deliberations, to enter the ministry; and again the Dutch church does not figure in his account of this decision.[8]

It is only *after* Livingston reports his decision to become a minister that the Dutch Church enters the narrative of the memoir. Now that he was resolved on the ministry, he says, there were three churches in which he might have sought ordination: the Episcopalian, the Presbyterian, and the Dutch Reformed, all of them genuine possibilities (although he cannot help making a negative comment on the Episcopalians' "popish bigotry" and "frivolous affectation of superiority"). He is at pains to picture the Dutch church therefore as a matter of conscious choice for him, which he chose for precise reasons: because it was his family's church, because its doctrines and practices were "evangelical," and also because he felt he could be an "instrument" of God to help mend the "unhappy schism and controversy" caused by the Coetus-Conferentie dispute, which at that moment "threatened the annihilation of that whole denomination."[9] His health improved after this. Then in the summer of 1765, with his conversion and call behind him as well as his decision for the Dutch church—and also after he had begun to read

---

[6] Gunn, *Memoirs*, 47, 45, 161.
[7] Ibid., 62-63.
[8] Ibid., 69-73.
[9] Ibid., 113-14.

"historical, poetical and other works, calculated to improve him in general and polite literature," in preparation for a ministerial career—he had what Gunn calls "his first interview" with Archibald Laidlie, the recently called English-language minister of the Dutch church of New York City. Thereafter Livingston began to see the minister "daily." Laidlie was soon convinced of his seriousness of purpose and advised him to undertake his theological studies at a university in the Netherlands.[10]

Livingston's consistent picture of his crucial religious formation as something that happened apart from the Dutch church, and of his coming to that church therefore fully formed and bringing his gifts *to* it, dates, it is true, from fifty years after the fact. It shows us the aged Livingston's desire to think of himself as the church's patron rather than its product. Nonetheless, a letter has survived that he wrote at the time, just before his departure for the Netherlands, which, if it does not precisely confirm the details of the later account, at least displays a sense of self consistent with it. The letter is to his younger brother Henry. With his own recent conversion fresh in his mind, he tells Henry how "noble" it is for a young man like himself or Henry to have "glowing ambition and secret desire and hope of shining in the world. And join to this religious principles: a strong desire of serving his God, and throwing his mite of abilities and faculties in the service of his Master and for the good of his fellow creatures."[11] There is a sense here that *noblesse oblige*. Cynthia Kierner, in her study of the Livingston family, has taken a phrase from this letter—that youth is a time "to prepare for future usefulness"—as an exemplary expression of the family's patrician sense of obligation to society.[12] Livingston here understands his conversion as something that undergirds his frank "ambition," his desire to "shine," which he is fulfilling by choosing the path he is about to set out on, namely to make his contribution to the Dutch church.

Livingston in Utrecht

Having taken Laidlie's advice to study in the Netherlands, Livingston traveled there, arriving on June 20, 1766. He chose to enroll at the University of Utrecht, in part because of the reputation of the theology professor Gisbert Bonnet, and he began his studies that fall.[13] He was to stay until June 1770. These years formed him as a theologian

[10] Ibid., 120-22.
[11] John H. Livingston to Henry Livingston, February 4, 1766. Livingston Family Papers, New York Public Library.
[12] Kierner, *Traders and Gentlefolk*, 145.
[13] Gunn, *Memoirs*, 124-25, 161.

and also marked the modest beginning of his active involvement in the affairs of the Dutch churches of America.

Livingston's experience at Utrecht stimulated both the pietistic and the rationalistic strains in his thinking that would always afterward characterize him. In the memoir he lists his pious Dutch friends by name, describes his edifying visits to the influential pietist minister Gerardus van Schuylenborgh and his wife in the village of Tienhoven, tells of his successes in helping three persons along toward their own experiences of conversion, and recalls what seems to have been an international conference of devout persons who gave testimony of their conversions.[14] As for his rationalism, here he was strongly influenced by his mentor Bonnet, who, though he defended the Reformed faith against what he saw as the encroaching skepticism of the age, allowed a much larger place in his system for a natural theology than is found in earlier Reformed divines such Calvin or the seventeenth-century Voetian theologian Johannes à Marck, whose textbook Bonnet used; moreover he defended the supernatural authority of the Bible on rational grounds.[15] For Livingston, this "supernatural rationalism"—the affirmation of the accessibility of religious truth to the reasoning mind, albeit inadequate of itself for salvation—was to constitute the ground base of his own theology, as it frequently appears in his sermons as well as in his 1784 inaugural discourse as a professor of theology in America and later in his lectures at New Brunswick.[16]

Livingston also cultivated at Utrecht an interest in issues of religious liberty. Bonnet, who was then participating in a public debate on the subject, again influenced him. Joris van Eijnhatten has recently placed this debate in the context of the eighteenth century transition in the Netherlands *from* a "Christian commonwealth"—that is, a society that assumed the idea of an established church, albeit "mitigated" in the Dutch case by concessions to domestic peace—*to* what he calls a society of "civic diversity," a genuinely religiously plural society in which religious affiliation was based on the free choices of well-informed citizens. Bonnet stood precariously between these options; he argued for an established church, but he also argued for freedom of conscience,

---

[14] Quoted in Gunn, *Memoirs*, 163, 126-30, 169-73.
[15] Van den End, *Gisbertus Bonnet*, 92-100.
[16] John H. Livingston, *Oratio inauguralis de veritate religionis christianae* (New York: Samuel and Johannes Loudon, 1785); Ava Neal, *Analysis of a System of Theology Composed Chiefly from Lectures Delivered by the Late John H. Livingston* (New York: J.F. Sibell, 1832); see John W. Coakley, "John Henry Livingston as Professor of Theology," in James Hart Brumm, ed., *Tools for Understanding: Essays in Honor of Donald J. Bruggink* (Grand Rapids MI: Eerdmans, 2008), 189-200.

and moreover argued that those who did not agree with the doctrine of the established church not only may but *should* leave it, thus asserting in effect precisely the individualized notion of religious authority that would support the "civic diversity" he otherwise opposed.[17] Livingston's doctoral dissertation, which he defended just before he returned to America in 1770, also asserts the liberty of conscience. He used the vocabulary of Reformed covenant theology to argue that the theocracy of the Old Testament, with its limitation of the liberty of citizens, is a unique and inimitable exception to the principle of liberty of conscience. He explained this principle in terms that echo the defense of that principle by John Locke, and which Livingston considered consonant with the covenant of grace.[18] Livingston also still thought, like Bonnet, in terms of the government's legitimate interest in supporting religion, if not a particular church, as indeed did most of his Presbyterian compatriots in the era of the American Revolution. The Livingston party in the New York colonial legislature had also assumed this stance even in its opposition to the Anglican establishment—as when later, in 1777, John exhorted his cousin Robert R. Livingston to include some provision in the New York State constitution for the "encouragement of religion and virtue."[19]

Livingston in his Netherlands years also retained his earlier interest in the mending of the schism between the Coetus and Conferentie factions in North America. To what extent he did so, however, is open to question. Historians on the American side began within a few decades (as will be noted below) to exaggerate his role: he would be said, for instance, to have personally persuaded the members of the Classis of Amsterdam to propose an end to the schism and to establish a plan for theological education in America for the Dutch churches.[20] But quite apart from the unlikelihood that a young theological student could exercise such influence, whatever his gifts and social connections, the surviving evidence suggests that his role was much more modest. Indeed, as Dirk Mouw has recently argued, signs of the softening of the classis's

---

[17] Joris van Eijnatten, *Liberty and Concord in the United Provinces: Religious Toleration and the Public in the Eighteenth-Century Netherlands* (Leiden & Boston: Brill, 2003), 70-91.

[18] John H. Livingston, *Specimen theologicum inaugurale exhibens observationes de foederis sinaitici natura ex ejus fine demonstrata* (Utrecht: J. Broedelet, 1770); see John W. Coakley, "John H. Livingston and the Liberty of the Conscience," *Reformed Review* 46 (1992): 119-35.

[19] John H. Livingston to Robert R. Livingston, February 28, 1777. Robert R. Livingston Papers, reel 1, New-York Historical Society.

[20] E.g., David D. Demarest, *History and Characteristics of the Reformed Protestant Dutch Church* (New York: Board of Publication, 1856), 91-92.

strong resistance to the Coetus's claims to classical authority and to its efforts to establish an American academy appeared as early as 1764—at a time, that is, before Livingston's journey to the Netherlands—and it was certainly well under way by 1766, when he arrived.[21] A considerable body of official sources demonstrate the classis's manifest change of heart beginning in the spring of 1768. This includes the classis's first attempt at proposing a plan of union and the various communications among the classis, the Synod of North Holland, and the American parties about the matter. In the document collection assembled by E.T. Corwin,[22] Livingston's name nowhere appears.

To suggest that he had little influence on the decisions of the Classis of Amsterdam is not to deny Livingston's interest in the matter of the Coetus-Conferentie controversy or the possibility of some minor influence on events. There is no reason to doubt that, as he implied in the 1818 memoir, he had hoped even at the time of his decision in 1765 to cast his lot with the Reformed Church, that he might somehow help "compromise and heal" its "dissensions."[23] Gunn, apparently depending here on the 1818 memoir, says that John Witherspoon wrote Livingston asking for help to find accommodation when he came to Utrecht in 1768 shortly before taking up the presidency of the College of New Jersey at Princeton, and that Livingston introduced him to Bonnet. Then he quotes Livingston, apparently from the memoir, describing an interview with Witherspoon, who expressed a wish for "the two churches of Holland and Scotland" to "co-operate in promoting the best interests of the Gospel in America." Gunn also quotes a subsequent letter from Witherspoon that thanks Livingston for "the pains you have taken in the affair of the union."[24] The plan of union for the American churches that then was entered into the classis minutes for June 6 contained the proposal that the Americans install one or two Dutch professors at Princeton instead of attempting to establish their own academy. Gunn reasonably hypothesized that this idea (ultimately rejected by all the American parties) had been Livingston's, and that Witherspoon had conveyed it to members of the classis.[25] If that is so, then Livingston was no mere observer of the classis's deliberations, though he can hardly have been a major player.

[21] Dirk Edward Mouw, "*Moederkerk* and *Vaderland:* Religion and Ethnic Identity in the Middle Colonies, 1690-1772" (Ph.D. diss., University of Iowa, 2009), 453-67.
[22] I refer here to the documents in *ERNY*.
[23] Quoted in Gunn, *Memoirs*, 114.
[24] Ibid., 185-86.
[25] Ibid., 192.

Livingston's stay in the Netherlands came to an end in 1770. The Classis of Amsterdam had examined and licensed him to preach in the summer of 1769 and then examined him again and ordained him on April 1, 1770, after he had accepted a call from the New York City consistory.[26] He defended the dissertation on May 16, 1770, and left the Netherlands early in June. After a month's sojourn in England he sailed again for America, reaching New York on September 3.[27]

The Constitution of an American Church

Once in America again, Livingston served the New York congregation over a span of forty years (1770-1810), with a seven-year hiatus during the Revolutionary War (1775-83), when he ministered to various congregations upstate. Then he spent the last fifteen years of his life (1810-1825) in New Brunswick, New Jersey, helping to establish the infant theological seminary there. He never made a return journey to the Netherlands (indeed no evidence suggests that he would have expected to do so), although he retained many correspondents there.[28] Still, his Dutch education—of which he remained proud[29]—was to have an important legacy in his career, especially with regard to the very two questions in the church's life that had been most at issue in the Coetus-Conferentie dispute and now required definitive answers: first, the question of its constitution, i.e., how to understand and embody the church's authority; and, second, the question of the "professorate," i.e., how to prepare its clergy.

As for addressing the question of the constitution, that is, the configuration of the church's authority, the Americans' first step was to reconcile, now with the classis's blessing, the Coetus and the Conferentie factions. Here Livingston had a conspicuous role. The decisive event was the convention of ministers and elders called by the consistory of the New York church in October of 1771, which drafted and proposed to the churches the "Articles of Union" that were then ratified by most of the churches in another convention the following year. This document declared that the American churches would follow the church order of Dort; established a "particular" and "general" assembly or body, thus avoiding the terms "classis" and "synod" in deference to the wishes of the Classis of Amsterdam; and made provision for the

---

[26] E. T. Corwin and Hugh Hastings, eds., *Ecclesiastical Records of the State of New York*, 7 vols. (Albany: Lyon, 1901-1916) 6:4182-83. Hereafter cited as *ERNY*.
[27] Gunn, *Memoirs*, 212-14.
[28] Ibid., 275-76.
[29] Ibid., 517-18 (testimony of Prof. Samuel Miller of Princeton).

professorate.[30] Livingston, as president *pro tempore* of the consistory, signed the invitation to delegates and chaired the convention itself.[31] He clearly had a place of honor. But again subsequent tradition has tended to exaggerate his role; no documentary evidence supports the frequently repeated later claim that it was he who brought the substance of the Articles with him from the Netherlands and disclosed it at the convention. It is true that he was on the drafting committee of the convention and no doubt had much to do with fashioning the document.[32] But probably the reason for the choice of Livingston as host and convener was precisely his innocence of the Coetus-Conferentie dispute, in contrast to the other three ministers of the New York church; for Johannes Ritzema and Lambertus De Ronde had participated in the Conferentie, and Archibald Laidlie's official neutrality had sparked controversy.[33]

The ratification of the Articles of Union was not, however, the end of the constitutional process for the American Dutch churches.[34] Another step was necessary, namely to adapt themselves to the new American political situation created by the Revolution. Here Livingston took the lead.

Livingston's concern with the question of the church's place in the new American order reflected the interest in issues of religious liberty evident earlier in his doctoral dissertation. In a letter of March 1788 to his colleague Dirk Romeyn of Schenectady, he expressed his conviction that the state must guarantee the liberties of religious organizations and that those organizations must in turn make public witness of their own structures of accountability. American churches, he said, were necessarily making the transformation from "appendages of national Churches in Europe" to "national Churches themselves in this new Empire." In the case of the Dutch denomination, this required that "we should revise some articles in our fundamental agreement respecting our church government of 1771 [the Articles of Union], and see whether some of those articles do not militate against our independent state."[35]

---

[30] *Acts and Proceedings of the General Synod of the Reformed Protestant Dutch Church in North America, vol. 1* (New York: Board of Publication of the Reformed Protestant Dutch Church, 1859), 9-20; *ERNY*, 6:4212-18.

[31] Ibid., 7; *ERNY*, 6:4209.

[32] Ibid., 8. See Gunn, *Memoirs*, 225n.: "the Doctor himself was, without doubt, the author of this plan, or of the greater part of it"

[33] On Laidlie's place in the controversy, see Mouw, "*Moederkerk* and *Vaterland*," 449, 454, 569-70, and Joyce Goodfriend's essay in this volume.

[34] On the history of the constitution, see also Daniel J. Meeter, *Meeting Each Other* (Grand Rapids, MI: Eerdmans, 1993), 31-55, 145-58.

[35] Gunn, *Memoirs*, 298-99.

He cites no examples, but presumably had in mind at least Articles 23 and 24, which established, in cases of disputed doctrine or the discipline of ministers, the right of appeal to the Classis of Amsterdam and the Synod of North Holland, whose decisions would be binding.[36] The issue, then, was the American Dutch churches' independence and self-accountability—the necessity of making clear that this was a "national church" of the United States, not subject to foreign authority.

Then over the years from 1788 to 1793, with leadership from Livingston, the American Dutch church produced the sort of constitutional document he had begun to envision. The project unfolded gradually. In October of 1788 the General Synod appointed a committee, which included Livingston, to publish the Church Order of Dort and the doctrinal standards in English. The stated rationale—that "the circumstances of our churches, especially in relation to the general protection of the civil authorities in freedom of worship, necessarily demand" such a publication—echoes the letter to Romeyn.[37] Then in October 1790, the translations being finished, the General Synod began to consider a substantive revision to the church order. A committee made up of the ministers in the New York church—thus including Livingston—was charged to interpolate "observations" into the translated text to explain it. Then, probably following Livingston's suggestion,[38] the plan was changed to leave the church order intact and constitute the "observations" as a separate document of "explanatory articles" adapting the church order to American circumstances. Livingston then presented to the General Synod of October 1792 the finished set of "explanatory articles" on the church order, which, the minutes imply, was the product of his own pen. ("Professor Livingston reported, that he had completed the work intrusted to him.")[39]

In the previous May the General Synod minutes had identified the project in terms consistent with Livingston's original idea, declaring that the prospective publication, in addition to serving the needs of the church itself, would "satisfy the desires of the civil government," since it would make public the "basis" as well as the actual practice of the church's order and "thus, the different charters [of local churches] may be ratified."[40] Livingston, along with his New York colleagues William Linn and (elder) Peter Wilson, were charged to see the work through

---

[36] *Acts and Proceedings*, 12.
[37] Ibid., 184-85.
[38] The idea appears in a letter to Romeyn, May 1, 1792. Gunn, *Memoirs*, 317.
[39] *Acts and Proceedings*, 235.
[40] Ibid., 218.

the press. Livingston then "exhibited" the published volume, entitled *The Constitution of the Reformed Dutch Church in the United States of America*, containing the translated church order and the new "Explanatory Articles," as well as translations of the Dutch church's doctrinal standards and liturgy, at the General Synod of October 1793.[41]

The "Preface" to the volume sums up its significance in terms of the task Livingston had begun with, that is, to define the authority of the American Dutch church in the context of the new American nation. It stands as Livingston's most mature expression on the subject. It also significantly broadens the context of the task—to include an expression of millennial hope. Thus after asserting that the church is "a bond of union wholly voluntary, and unattended with civil emoluments or penalties" and "cannot be considered as an infringement upon the equal liberties of others"—and (so we gather) is worthy of the society's, and thus the state's, trust—he points out the major change the church is now making in the Church Order of Dort: anything relating to "the immediate authority and interposition of the Magistrate in the government of the Church [as in Europe]... is now entirely omitted." Then he envisions the consequences of this change in theological and, more precisely, eschatological, terms. The situation in America to which the Dutch church has now adapted itself, he says, will finally make possible a "fair trial" to demonstrate "whether the Church of Christ will not be more effectually patronised" in a situation where consciences are truly free—a situation which may well lead to the "triumph of the Gospel and the reign of peace and love."[42] Here then, in effect, is where the millennium comes in—as the likely consequence of a repositioning of the church in society.

Livingston's efforts to rethink the church's constitution came to an end with its publication in 1793. But there is an important sequel in his career that, though beyond our present concern, requires at least a mention: his advocacy for missions. The theme of the connection between the advent of religious freedom and the millennial hope of the evangelization of the world appears repeatedly in his sermons from the mid-1790s onward—that is, from about the time of the "Preface"—and then eventually in the published version of his influential sermon to the New York Missionary Society, "The Triumph of the Gospel," in 1804.[43]

[41] Ibid., 245.
[42] *The Constitution of the Reformed Dutch Church in the United States of America* (New York: William Durell, 1793), vi.
[43] E.g., sermons of January 1, 1795, February 19, 1795, and March 5, 1797, John H. Livingston Papers, doc. 7, doc. 89 (sec.22), and doc. 33, Collegiate Church

Professor Livingston

In the matter of clergy education, or the "professorate," Livingston's role was not that of a theoretician, as in the case of the constitution. Rather, as the first and—for for much of his career—the only occupant of the office of "Professor of Theology," he was the chief embodiment of the church's clergy education. In this sense, although neither his tenure in the office nor his competence was challenged—overtly, anyway—still he stood in the middle of a considerable debate about how and where the professorate was to be given a permanent form, a debate that continued almost to the end of his life.

Several issues were involved in that debate, issues that were often entangled with each other. One was whether the work of the professorate would not be better spread among learned ministers rather than focused in one person, and thus whether a settled academy was really desirable. A related issue was whether locating the professorate in a particular place would disadvantage the regions of the church distant from it. There was also the issue of whether the metropolis of New York was or was not a desirable location for theological students. And then—intimately connected to all of these, and complicated by the tight economy of the decades after the Revolutionary War—there was the problem of motivating donors to provide funds. More work needs to be done before we can describe very precisely the passions, convictions, interests, and jealousies that underlay these issues. But it is clear that resolving them was, in the end, essentially a political problem, a matter of negotiations around perceived common interests, and the creation of a majority in the General Synod with the will to act. In this sense the issue of the professorate was arguably the major ground on which the church found its particular political shape in its formative years.

Livingston became the church's Professor of Theology in 1784. The appointment was a direct consequence of his education at Utrecht. The Articles of Union in October 1771 called for one or two professors to be appointed "from the Netherlands." But when the Classis of Amsterdam approved the Articles the following April it suggested that the Americans "might find in their own body a suitable person, who although not born in the Netherlands, has studied and received his

---

Corporation Archives, New York; John Henry Livingston, *The Triumph of the Gospel. A Sermon delivered before the New-York Missionary Society at their Annual Meeting, April 3, 1804* (New York: T. & J. Swords, 1804), 21-22; see John W. Beardslee III, "John Henry Livingston and the Rise of American Mission Theology," *Reformed Review* 29 (1976):107.

ordination there."[44] Then on June 8, 1774, on receiving the General Body's request for nominations, the classis consulted the Utrecht faculty, specifically mentioning Livingston as the name that "occurs first to our minds" for the American position. Professor Bonnet, on the faculty's behalf, replied immediately with an endorsement of Livingston, citing his "peculiar acquaintance with the languages, names and circumstances of the country."[45] The General Body at its April 1775 meeting received the classis's recommendation of Livingston with a copy of Bonnet's letter and intended to take action at its October meeting. By October, however, the Revolutionary War had begun, and the matter was put off "by reason of the pitiful condition of our land."[46]

Not until October 1784 did the General Body (which would begin calling itself the General Synod in the following year) take action, forming a "commission to draft the resolutions of this Rev. Body in relation to the professorate." However that commission did not nominate Livingston directly but proposed only that a professor be appointed "in the City of New York" and that, because of the broader church's lack of funds, the New York consistory be asked to make some "arrangement" to support him themselves. Clearly the candidate would be Livingston, who was the only minister in the New York church, and the oddly indirect method of nominating him, whatever else it might mean, suggests that the General Body had no funds to support him. The body then did unanimously elect him, and the following May he gave his inaugural lecture in the old Dutch Church on Garden Street in New York.[47] But the New York consistory meanwhile declined to provide any assistance.[48] So Livingston took up the position without pay and without any adjustment to his pastoral responsibilities. This was an inauspicious beginning for the professorate.

Over the next few years, as resources remained scarce, efforts to raise funds for the professorate competed with appeals from the trustees of Queens College, to the benefit of neither institution. The synod vacillated as to how to accommodate Queens. In May 1791 it undertook to raise a "subscription... through all our congregations" for the professorate, leaving the trustees to solicit for the college on their own.[49] Then in October it changed course and agreed to solicit

[44] *ERNY*, 6:4237.
[45] *ERNY*, 6:4277-79.
[46] *Acts and Proceedings*, 61.
[47] Ibid., 123-25, 135.
[48] New York Consistory Minutes, Liber G, 41 (October 8, 1784), Collegiate Church Corporation Archives, New York.
[49] *Acts and Proceedings*, 215-16.

funds for the college, on condition of a pledge from the trustees to call a professor of theology of the synod's choosing who would also serve as president of the college.[50] But by October 1793 the trustees had begun to consider joining forces instead with the Presbyterian college at Princeton; and the synod, highly displeased, returned to the earlier plan of a subscription for the professorate alone.[51] Through all of this, fundraising was unsuccessful.

Meanwhile, another question had arisen to complicate the establishment of the professorate, namely whether it was after all desirable to locate the professorate in New York City. The synod of October 1786 "unanimously concluded," because of the expense incurred by students to maintain themselves in the city, to appoint "one of our brethren in the country"—specifically Hermanus Meyer of Pompton and Totowa, New Jersey—as "Lector" to prepare students there and then send them on to Livingston for the "completion" of their studies.[52] Meyer died in 1791, and the synod of the following October replaced him with two others, Solomon Froeligh of Hackensack and Dirk Romeyn of Schenectady.[53]

In the mid-1790s Livingston and others made a concerted effort to reinforce the role of the elected professor and to push the synod to establish it on a more solid footing, in a way that responded also to concerns about locating the professorate in New York City. Already in 1791 he had asked his consistory to consider reducing his pastoral duties to allow him to "attend the due discharge of his office as Professor," but without result.[54] Then in June 1794 the synod adopted, likely with Livingston's influence, a far-reaching proposal that called for Queens College to move closer to New York City, specifically to Bergen or "still further to the north," so as to incorporate the professorate in a manner convenient to theological students; and in the (probable) event that this would be impracticable, for a "Divinity Hall" unconnected with a college to be established for the professorate in a village such as Flatbush where living costs would be low, but near enough to New

---

[50] Ibid., 224-25. Livingston himself had long been open to locating the professorate at Queens, but conceived the college as ideally a "divinity hall," i.e., emphasizing theology rather than liberal arts (Gunn, *Memoirs,* 303-06) and eventually as president of Queens he initiated an experiment, ultimately unsuccessful, to change the college accordingly (ibid., 421-30).
[51] *Acts and Proceedings,* 249-50, 252.
[52] Ibid., 147-48.
[53] Ibid., 241.
[54] New York Consistory Minutes, Liber G, 203-05 (February 2, February 8, and February 11, 1791).

York City to "reap all [its] advantages." The synod also called on the New York consistory to reduce Livingston's duties so as to allow him to relocate to that place, and it promised to raise money to contribute to his support.[55] The consistory was still reluctant, but after extensive conversations with Livingston from September of 1794 until July of 1795 it agreed to the plan: he would preach once per Sunday, which was half his usual service, and could have his full job back if the new arrangement did not work out.[56]

The plans did not work out. Livingston reported to the synod in May of 1796 that he had now "removed to Long Island" and was proceeding with the plan.[57] But within a few months he wrote them another letter, this one long and dismal, rehearsing the history of the professorate and the sacrifices he personally had made for it over the years, including the recent move, but lamenting that the synod had not come up with the promised financial support. "The Professorate remains thus entirely forsaken, and no measures are pursued, or even proposed, to countenance and assist the institution." If the necessary "measures" for support of the professorate "are suffered to slumber much longer, the whole institution will sink into oblivion, and all the benefits to be expected from it be inevitably lost." He asked for a "candid reply."[58]

The synod responded at first by renewing its resolve to raise a subscription for the professorate, but the next year it made a substantial response, this time corroborating Livingston's sense of its failure: the synod wished him to "continue to discharge the duties of the office" but believed it "not expedient, under present circumstances, to take any further measures for the support of the professorate." Then the synod went farther. It elected Froeligh and Romeyn as *Professors* of Theology (not merely lectors, i.e., assistants to the professor) alongside Livingston—thus not just acknowledging the status quo of diffused and uncompensated instruction, but reinforcing it.[59] In January 1798 Livingston arranged with the consistory to return to Manhattan and resume all his pastoral duties.[60]

After this the status quo remained unaltered until May 1804, when the General Synod began another attempt to change it. This attempt

[55] *Acts and Proceedings*, 260-63.
[56] New York Consistory Minutes, Liber H, 8-15 (April 23, 1795), 26-29 (July 16, 1795).
[57] *Acts and Proceedings*, 458.
[58] Ibid., 464-66; cf. Gunn, *Memoirs*, 350-56.
[59] *Acts and Proceedings*, 467, 269-70.
[60] New York Consistory Minutes, Liber H, 115-17 (January 17, 1798). He had returned to Manhattan by March 1; ibid., 119.

would meet with greater success, owing to a consolidation of influence by the southern regions of the church, likely led by the New York City consistory with the involvement of Livingston. Two regional particular synods had been established in 1800: that of Albany, in the north, and that of New York (which included the churches of New Jersey) in the south. The General Synod minutes of May 1804 report that the New York Synod had "enjoined it upon their delegates to the General Synod to request that the Professorate be restored to the plan on which it was first established, and on which it continued till the year 1797," that is, before the election of the second and third professors. The General Synod then, apparently on the strength of those delegates' votes, proceeded to a new election of a single professor, on the understanding that the other two professors would remain in office "during their natural lives" but would not be replaced. Livingston was once again elected, though not unanimously, from a slate of five nominees.[61] Two years later all of this was challenged, when a motion was made not only to return to the status quo of three professors but actually to augment it by appointing a fourth under "auspices" of the Albany Synod. But this recommendation was defeated; once again the southern interests had the votes.[62] Then the trustees of Queens had worked out a plan with the Particular Synod of New York for a "covenant" between the trustees and the General Synod, which was duly enacted at the May 1807 General Synod meeting. This covenant called for funds raised for the professorate to be held by the trustees, who would in turn be "bound," when these were sufficient, to issue a call to the person "nominated and chosen by the General Synod"—in effect, Livingston—to teach at Queens, and that a separate board of "Superintendents of the Theological Institution in Queens College" would be established to oversee the education of theological students. The covenant also committed the synod to raise funds for a theological library and a new building to be shared by the college and the "theological institution" at New Brunswick.[63]

The covenant became an effective basis for establishing the professorate in New Brunswick. On the strength of it Livingston moved there in 1810, to serve as professor of theology and president of the college until his death. Other plans for the professorate continued to be rumored for several years, but a fundraising campaign spearheaded by

---

[61] *Acts and Proceedings*, 333-34 (committee report), 339 (election of Livingston).
[62] Ibid., 344-45, 347.
[63] Ibid., 365-66.

Livingston himself in 1820 secured an endowment adequate to allow it to remain in New Brunswick.[64]

Thus the professorate was finally more or less securely established in New Brunswick after more than fifty years of debate following the adoption of the Articles of Union. Through this debate the alliances among interests eventually emerged that were necessary for the church to commit itself to a particular educational institution in a particular place. As for Livingston, if we do not precisely hear his voice at every point in this debate, we can almost always discern his presence.

Livingston and Historical Memory

The story of the professorate, or, more precisely, the part of the story that moved toward resolution, also appears to have affected Livingston's own story, i.e., the way he would be remembered. It seems to have been more or less at the moment when the synod's covenant with Queens College was being formulated that a narrative began to take shape that retrospectively gave him a major role in the resolution of the Coetus-Conferentie controversy and made him, in effect, the central figure in the founding of the American church.

We find a hint of this new narrative in an "Address" that appears in the minutes of the 1807 synod for distribution to the congregations as an appeal for funds to support the new covenant between the synod and the trustees of Queens College.[65] The document presents "a detail of facts" regarding the history of the church with a focus on the professorate. Though oddly it does not name Livingston in its account of the end of the Coetus-Conferentie controversy, it refers to "a person who, during his residence in Holland, in 1766, and following years, had obtained the acquaintance and confidence of many of the principal ministers of the Church of Holland" and "gained their approbation to a plan for forming an ecclesiastical constitution in America."[66] No doubt readers would have identified the current professor in this description.

The new narrative also appeared in a fuller form that same year of 1807. This was in an installment of a set of influential "Sketches" of the history of the American Dutch churches in the *Christian's Magazine*, a journal edited by John Mitchell Mason, a prominent minister of the

---

[64] Howard G. Hageman, *Two Centuries Plus: The Story of New Brunswick Seminary* (Grand Rapids: Eerdmans, 1984), 42-43; Gunn, *Memoirs*, 405-11.
[65] *Acts and Proceedings*, 368-78. This "Appeal" was signed by the ministers John Abeel, Jeremiah Romeyn, and Gerardus Kuypers; Abeel and Kuypers were Livingston's colleagues in the New York church.
[66] *Acts and Proceedings*, 372. See Mouw, "*Moederkerk and Vaderland*," 498-99.

Associate Reformed Church. Dirk Mouw has recently called attention to the importance of these articles as signaling a new perspective on the history of the Dutch churches. In the context of interpreting the Coetus-Conferentie schism as a contest between American freedom and Old World tyranny (an interpretation which, as Mouw argues, would not have been shared by the principals in the controversy three decades earlier, and which was itself not shared by the authors of the "Address"[67]), the anonymous author presents Livingston outright as the healer of the schism and by implication the father of a new American church. He is pictured as the one who persuaded the members of the Classis of Amsterdam to act for the "accommodation of ecclesiastical differences in *America*" and who prevailed upon the Synod of North Holland to constitute the classis as a "permanent committee" for the purpose, and who then was responsible for the Articles of Union and the convention that endorsed them.[68]

The "Sketches" in the *Christian's Magazine* were to be remarkably influential; their narrative of the colonial period and its aftermath fundamentally shaped the way the story of the Dutch Reformed churches in America has been told ever since.[69] And Livingston was at the center of that narrative. Though his place in the narrative is (as I have suggested above) not well supported by the surviving evidence of the years around 1770, it was still probably not without some basis in fact. Livingston surely had personal contacts among the clergy when he was in the Netherlands; moreover he was a close associate not just of the writers of the "Address" but also of the editor of the *Christian's Magazine*. It is likely that both accounts had at least his tacit approval, even though he was not to make the same claims for himself in the 1818 memoir (or Gunn would surely have reported them). There was *something* there to be remembered, and what was occurring around 1807 was an attempt to make that memory central, to organize the story now, in part at least, around Livingston.

Why did this new narrative emerge about the church's formative moment? A full answer is not possible here, but surely one motivating element was the renewed attempt around 1807 to establish the professorate once and for all by placing the professorate at Queens College. Livingston stood not only as the incumbent professor but also as the link with the early formative events of the church, the memory

---

[67] Mouw, "*Moederkerk* and *Vaderland*," 495-98.
[68] Anon., "Brief Historical Sketches of the Reformed Dutch Church in the United States [third installment]," *The Christian's Magazine* 3 (1807): 266-73.
[69] Mouw, "*Moederkerk* and *Vaderland*," 499-502.

of which was fast receding. Accordingly, he served as a powerful symbol of that continuity, and a useful one, at least for those who were telling the story.[70]

If the story about Livingston that was already being told by the end of his life exaggerated his contribution toward the ending of the Coetus-Conferentie dispute, still by anyone's reckoning he had a pivotal place in the process of formation of the Reformed Protestant Dutch Church in North America over its first few decades. That was a process that required the church both to establish its institutions and to rethink its relationship to Dutch tradition, even as that tradition remained essential to its identity. Livingston's Dutch education not only placed him at the center of the politically complex establishment of theological education but also shaped his intellectual development and accordingly his influence on the church in its new American form. On the other hand, Livingston's family heritage was not predominantly Dutch, and for all his perseverance in the Reformed ministry he retained a conviction, as the 1818 memoir shows, that his commitment to the church was a matter of his own conscious choice, not a function of an already-established identity. In this sense Livingston stands for the Dutch churches' emergence as an American "denomination"—a church of its own, convinced of the truth and purity of its inherited doctrine and discipline, but acknowledging itself to be but one religious expression among many in a free society, openly available to the discriminating choice of citizens.

---

[70] On Livingston's "patriarchal" persona at New Brunswick, see Coakley, "John Henry Livingston as Professor of Theology," 194-95.

CHAPTER 14

Cornelius van der Meulen (1800-1876): Builder of a New Dutch American Colony

Hans Krabbendam

While most contributions in this volume deal with Dutch clergy in North America before the American Revolution, it makes sense to conclude with an essay that extends that horizon and expands the definition of "colony." Carrying the story into the nineteenth century and to a Dutch settlement in the Midwest, the *Kolonie*, as it was then known, provides a perspective that highlights some of the unique features and trends of the earlier history of Dutch clergy in North America. Such a perspective also sheds light on the consequences and outcomes of those earlier events and patterns and reconnects two stories that are often told without reference to each other.[1]

Specifically, the life of the Reverend Cornelius van der Meulen is relevant for five reasons. The first is that he represented a new type of colonial clergy. He was not only a pastor, but also an immigrant leader.

---

[1] I would like to thank my co-editors Leon Van den Broeke and Dirk Mouw for their critical reading of this essay and their many useful suggestions. I used parts of my earlier publication on Van der Meulen, "Forgotten Founding Father: Cornelius VanderMeulen as Immigrant Leader," *Documentatieblad voor de Geschiedenis van de Nederlandse zending en overzeese kerken* 5.2 (Fall 1998): 1-23.

Cornelius van der Meulen
[Archives, Calvin College,
Grand Rapids, Michigan]

This adds a new component to the category that has been investigated in the foregoing essays. He was one of the most visible immigrant leaders of the 1840s, and he sought to channel the Dutch immigrants into a new society. But he envisioned a role for them in that new setting that was firmly rooted in the past, seeking continuity with both the Pilgrims and the colonial Dutch.

In this respect, however, Van der Meulen is a better subject than his more illustrious colleagues, the Reverends Albertus Van Raalte and Hendrik P. Scholte. They stand out as academically trained, but they were the exceptions rather than the rule. Indispensable as the strategists of the new mass immigration and the main contacts with American society at large, they were not archetypes of the hundred or so Dutch ministers who came to serve congregations in America. Cornelius van der Meulen did play a part in these highly visible activities and was close to the leadership, but he was also a typical minister. As with most of his lesser known colleagues, his attention was more often focused inward rather than outward, tying the Dutch in the Midwest together. If Van Raalte acted as the Secretary of State of the *kolonie*, Van der Meulen was its Secretary of the Interior, attending to the vitality and cohesion of the settlement. His education likewise resembled that of the majority of Dutch ministers who served immigrant churches in America, such as the

Reverends Marten Ypma and Seine Bolks—though the commonalities and patterns in the training and career paths of such men needs further study.

A second reason for selecting Van der Meulen is that he personally connected the recent immigrant Dutch to the descendants of the colonial Dutch. He sought the support of the established Dutch-American communities on the Atlantic seaboard and embraced their institutions and traditions. He sent his two sons to the East Coast to be educated and trained as ministers. This precedent was followed by scores of candidates who carried this American legacy into the midwestern churches. The Dutch-American subculture in the Midwest could only have been founded as a result of a joint effort. He was the perfect team worker, who established and nurtured the connections necessary for the stability and survival of the *kolonie*.

A third argument for examining Cornelius's life was his success in laying the foundations for the vitality of Dutch settlements in two urban centers, Chicago, Illinois, and Grand Rapids, Michigan. While the career patterns of Dutch Reformed ministers in the early years revolved around rural places, the cities quickly emerged as the centers of growth after the Civil War. These proved to be indispensable links in the formation of a strong Dutch subculture, and Van der Meulen recognized their potential at an early stage.

A fourth reason for studying this man is that he was highly regarded as a spiritual authority, amply demonstrated by the fact that he was called the "Apostle of Zeeland" and later an "Aaron" to Van Raalte, the "American Moses" or the "Apostle of the Colonists." This reputation helped set a new standard in the New World. An understanding of his piety is the key to his life, as the source of his motivation, and the basis of the high regard in which he was held by his flock. Moreover, his brand of pietism provided a smooth link to American evangelical theology.

Finally, these qualities shaped his role as a constructive and unifying force rather than as a divisive one, which explains his unreserved loyalty to the Reformed Church in America. This last assessment could (justifiably) be met with a measure of surprise, since he was, after all, a Seceder who had helped split the powerful *Nederlands Hervormde Kerk* and had even separated himself from his native land. How can that be explained? How are these breaks harmonized with his reputation as a builder?[2]

---

[2] A brief note on the sources. Van der Meulen left few primary documents. In addition to church records at various levels, a unique collection of testimonies of relatives and close friends, called the "Remembrances," was published immediately after his

To answer such questions, I will examine his spiritual formation, his view of the church, and his idea for a new community, and I will end by considering his own evaluation of his achievements upon his return to the Netherlands. This journey near the end of his life also offers the opportunity to assess Van der Meulen's life from a different vantage point, since it enables us to gauge his significance to the community he left behind in the Netherlands.

Personality

Cornelius van der Meulen was a doer, not a writer. The key to understanding the choices he made is his life story. Our attention is immediately drawn to death, which hovered as a constant threat and frequent reality in his family life. Though he was far from unusual in having grieved the deaths of many loved ones, these experiences intensified his affection for his surviving family members and deepened his empathy for the people of his congregations. This, in turn, earned him much sympathy and admiration from his circle of church members.

When Cornelius was born on December 15, 1800, in the town of Middelharnis, on the island of Flakkee, close to Rotterdam, death had already taken its toll in his family. Cornelius's parents had nine children, but only he and his older brother Eliza, born in 1793, survived. Their mother died when Cornelius was five years old, and their father, who never remarried, died when Cornelius was twenty-six. One year later Cornelius married Elizabeth Geertrui van de Roovaard, a woman from the same region. The tragedy of early death repeated itself in the next generation. Though Cornelius was strong as an ox, he had to bury nine of his twelve children, five in the old world and four in the new. These events were not unusual and could have made him bitter, but they made Cornelius a mellow man.[3]

Cornelius's father had a variety of jobs, beginning as a laborer and later working as a contractor for Middelharnis, a town with a

---

death in 1876. Even though it was meant as an eulogy, this collection of careful and detailed observations helps us to document the key moments in his life as well as his standing in the community. No dissenting voice was heard except among the True Brethren in the later Christian Reformed Church. *Ter nagedachtenis van Rev. Cornelius van der Meulen* (Grand Rapids, MI: De Standaard Drukkerij, 1876). Although his official name was Cornelis, I use the anglicized form Cornelius as a matter of consistency.

[3] Julian H. VanderMeulen, "Genealogy VanderMeulen family," chart 1, Herrick Public Library, Holland, MI. This genealogy is not fully reliable and has some dates wrong, such as the birth date of Annetje Elizabeth (correct is February 20, 1828) and the death of Anna (correct is March 8, 1849). The wedding date of his parents Jacob and Anna is May 8, 1785.

population of three thousand. Almost all of its citizens belonged to the *Hervormde Kerk*, with small minorities of Jews (fifty) and Roman Catholics (one hundred). Most inhabitants made their living as farmers (growing wheat or potatoes) or as fishermen.[4]

Although he later described his father as a wise and pious man, Cornelius himself was originally not as interested in religion as he was in many other things. As a young man he never severed his ties with the church, though he preferred a comfortable life outside of it. This situation did not last long. His firstborn daughter died within six months of birth in 1828. An even greater tragedy happened in Rotterdam, where he had moved to work as a commissioner. His two infant sons succumbed to the city's first cholera epidemic. This blow made Cornelius return to his native town and re-evaluate his life. Although he had appreciated the gifted preachers in the *Hervormde kerk*, he found no comfort there. He turned to an informal group of pious people, which he joined and soon led. He presented his children to a traveling independent minister by the name of Budding for baptism. Thus he became part of the secession movement in its early phase, not as someone who declared the *Hervormde Kerk* bankrupt, but as a seeker who felt closer to God in a voluntaristic assembly of believers seeking an experiential knowledge of God than he did in the formal structure of the national church. It was his need for spiritual comfort that drew him back, and a comforter he would become.

Life did not become easier. As a practical man with experience in various occupations, Cornelius was soon elected an elder by the members of the seceded congregation in Middelharnis. He also preached in neighboring towns and was considered the leader of the local Secession. This came at a price. His neighbors rejected him as a troublemaker, and even people in his own seceded denomination were suspicious of his motives, fearing he was in it as a career path and not out of calling. Yet, his sense of calling was strong, and he decided to get more education before officially entering the ministry.[5]

Cornelius presented himself to the most learned of Seceders, Dominie Hendrik P. Scholte (1805-1868), the wealthy, Leyden-educated, cosmopolitan publicist, and visionary minister. His instructor, however, did not much care about his intellectual training and instead put him straight to preaching. When Van der Meulen studied, he did not so much

---

[4] A.J. van der Aa, *Aardrijkskundig woordenboek der Nederlanden*, 13 vols. (Gorinchem 1846), 7:920-27.
[5] Fred A. van Lieburg, "Kleine professoren, halve dominees, fijne dokters. Oefenaars op de pastorale markt in de vroegmoderne tijd," *Documentatieblad Nadere Reformatie* 22 (1998): 1-26.

devote his time to biblical exposition or the classical languages, but to church polity and church history. Later he realized that his doctrinal education had hardly surpassed that of a Sunday school student who had mastered his catechism.[6]

This odd specialization can be explained by the nature of the Secession, which blamed the *Hervormde Kerk* for not guarding the church against impure doctrines and practices. As other new religious groups, the Seceders struggled with the proper church order, the 1619 Dort Church Order or its more contemporary adaptation, which ironically turned them not only against the main church but also against each other. Van der Meulen tried to minimize the damage these sharp discussions could bring.

In these early years of the Secession, the leaders were grouped around three strands of thought that united them with some Seceders and divided them from others, depending on their views on spirituality, church organization, and the relationship between church and state.[7]

Ideals for the Church

The first group had an experiential strand with roots in the Further Reformation of the seventeenth century and Reformed pietism of the eighteenth century. Dominies Hendrik De Cock and Simon Van Velzen shared many of the experientialists' theological ideas, but they also insisted on Calvinist orthodoxy, strict adherence to the church order of Dordt, and a theocratic state. They trained about three quarters of all new Seceder ministers in the period between 1836 and 1846, who were rooted in conventicles and religious exercises.

A second group had a broader horizon. They were orthodox and confessional but did not place experiential religion at the core of their belief system. The leaders in this group were Dominies Anthony Brummelkamp and Albertus C. Van Raalte. They advocated flexibility regarding the Church Order of Dordt and favored some distance to the state.

The third group was mainly inspired by the Dutch Awakening, the *Reveil*. Its main spokesman was Hendrik P. Scholte, whose purpose was not to restore the traditional church order but to establish Bible-believing congregations of confessing Christians, with an emphasis

---

[6] *Nagedachtenis*, 142.
[7] Melis te Velde, "The Dutch Background of the American Secession from the RCA in 1857," in George Harinck and Hans Krabbendam, eds., *Breaches and Bridges: Reformed Subcultures in the Netherlands, Germany, and the United States* (Amsterdam: VU University Press, 2000), 85-100.

on personal faith, the spread of the kingdom of God, and the second coming. They were the most congregational in organization, resisting strong synodical authority and advocating separation between church and state.

The new church spent much time and energy defining the boundaries of the group of (true) believers, and they consequently disagreed about the core of the sermon: should it preach judgment or grace? Sermons that prodded listeners to grasp the buoy of faith were regarded as Arminian, because they ascribed the power of faith to people instead of to God alone. The middle ranks of Van Raalte and Brummelkamp joined Scholte in his refusal to limit the gospel to a passive resignation and supported his efforts to find or create common ground with other believers. The first group saw this attitude as a standing invitation to impurity in the church. Van der Meulen sided with Van Raalte and Scholte and regretted the strict policing of the boundaries, which led to bitter internal divisions.

For practical and theological reasons, the members of the second and third groups were most likely to emigrate. Their horizons were broad, they were more flexible about entering new arrangements, and they allowed for more individual freedom. Emigrants from the first group were suspicious of innovations. Proposals to introduce hymn singing, to open the Lord's table to outsiders, to abandon Christian holidays, or to make preaching from the Heidelberg Catechism optional, were red flags. Van der Meulen did not belong to this group of traditionalists. He decided not to wear the old costume or sing the sixteenth-century translations of the Psalms, fearing superstitious attachment. His theology was orthodox and conventional, but his practice was flexible when he saw traditions impeding the conversion of seekers.[8]

Building a Community

After apprenticing in Rotterdam and his native Middelharnis, Van der Meulen's main mission field was in the province of Zeeland, where he began his ministry in the summer of 1841. As a kind of itinerant preacher he served the twelve seceded congregations in the province. After several of these had acquired their own ministers, he concentrated on the congregation in Goes but continued to travel around. His formative

---

[8] He published a letter describing a conversion experience of one of his Dutch parishioners, "Overlezenswaardige brief dien wij onze vrienden en geburen volstrekt moeten laten lezen," *De Hollander*, December 29, 1852.

period as a preacher took place in depressed times: economically, politically, and spiritually. The first two were beyond his influence, but in the religious realm he found great satisfaction. His practical sermons found a welcome reception, and the apex of his ministry was a mass conversion following a sermon in Axel.[9] When disaster struck in 1845—the potato blight hit Europe hard and droughts destroyed the other crops—he called for a public day of thanksgiving, fasting, and prayer to heed God's judgment, while blaming the government for being passive and lax. Though his horizons were broad—he explicitly listed the signs of revival elsewhere in Europe and as far away as China—he warned believers that they should not emigrate for the wrong, worldly, reasons, such as to escape God's judgment or to avoid helping others in greater need.[10] Van der Meulen's friends and colleagues convinced him that the best argument for emigration was the apparent inevitability of God's judgment. They saw emigration as a way out of the current spiritual and social depression, and they persuaded him to join the group that planned to leave for America. It was a providential escape.[11]

The story of the Zeeland departure in 1847, when 457 people left on three ships, has frequently been told. Important to note here, however, is that Van der Meulen functioned as the conscience of the group. He was perfect for the job, thanks to his many regional connections, his flexibility, his great social skills, and his humor. These qualities positioned him as a magnificent mediator in the many disputes that the emigration enterprise caused. He followed the Zeelanders who had decided to join Van Raalte in Michigan, where they arrived in the summer of 1847.

His irenic intent was evident in his suggestion to call the settlement "Brothertown" because all provincial groups had to live cordially together. This proved that though he had strong ties to the province of Zeeland, he was not a provincial chauvinist. The name Zeeland ultimately won out, simply because it proved a better advertisement, as subsequent years would confirm. The early history of Zeeland has been told elsewhere, so it is unnecessary to repeat it here. Suffice it to say that it took five years of hardship to establish a viable colony. Van der Meulen shared his meager means with his neighbors in order to prevent the first settlers from abandoning the colony. This personal

---

[9] *Nagedachtenis,* 39-43.
[10] C. van der Meulen, *Verneder u dan onder de krachtige hand Gods. Opwekking tot het houden van eenen algemeenen dank- vast en bededag op Woensdag, den 25sten Februarij 1846* (Amsterdam: Hoogkamer & Comp., 1846), 4 and 8.
[11] *Nagedachtenis,* 75.

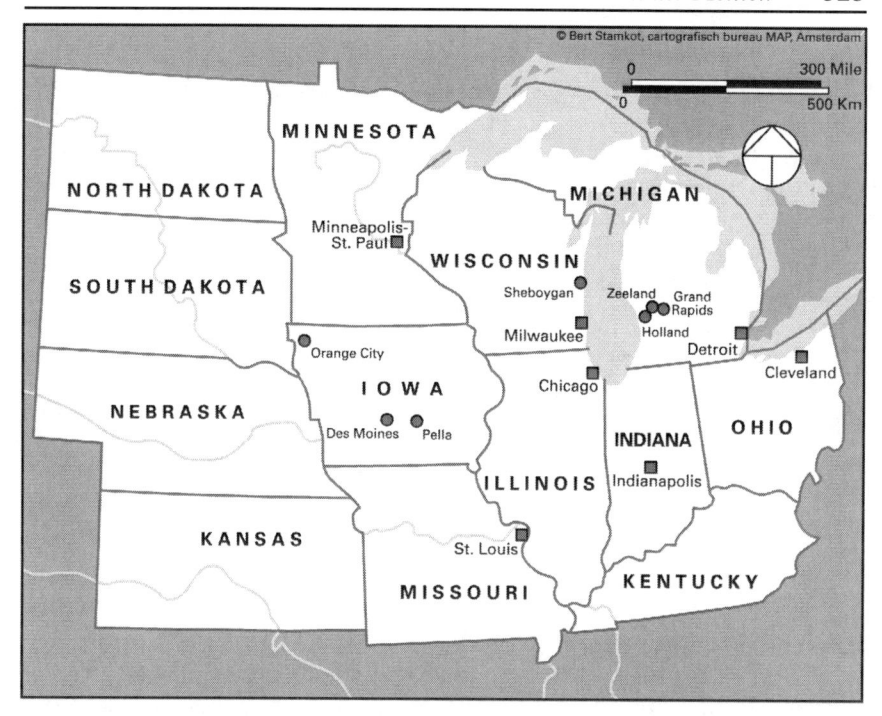

Map 4: Nineteenth-century Dutch settlements in the American Midwest

commitment stole the hearts of his community, and he was elevated to saintly status as founding minister. After he had secured stability at home, his attention moved to the community at large. Thanks to his strong constitution, he could assist the other churches as well.[12]

Wider World

By 1852 the Michigan *kolonie* had proved its viability, and Van der Meulen could spread his wings. In the spring of that year he asked the Board of Domestic Missions on behalf of Classis Holland for funds to travel to Pella to establish a Reformed church there after the Reverend Henry P. Scholte had alienated himself from his congregation. He was awarded $25, but more urgent duties in Michigan prevented him from going. Instead he used the money to defray the costs he had incurred to

---

[12] Ibid., 80 and 105. He was a physically strong man and not afraid to travel. According to his son he only missed two Sundays services in his active life, due to an accident with his horse and buggy. How personality mattered is shown by his successor in the First Reformed Church in Zeeland, Herman Stobbelaar, who gave judgmental sermons and lacked self-criticism and sensitivity to the spiritual traditions of his parishioners. VandeLuyster recorded his version of the clash with Stobbelaar in

put the troubled churches in Rochester and Buffalo back on their feet.[13] Examples of similar problem-solving operations in the immigrant churches are numerous.

During his first decade in the United States Van der Meulen had strengthened the links between his constituency and a national support group, which led to full integration into the Reformed Church in America. With the founding farmer of Zeeland, Jannes van de Luyster, he attended the General Synod of the Reformed Church in June of 1855 to promote the Holland Academy and ensure that its graduates could enter the seminary at New Brunswick, New Jersey. His success inspired him to report favorably about the denomination.[14] He found the church to be reliable in doctrine, though its practices were not perfect (e.g., laxity regarding weekly sermons on the Heidelberg Catechism as well as church discipline). He concluded to his satisfaction that the students at the seminary were faithfully taught the traditional Reformed doctrines.[15] The next year he wrote a Dutch pamphlet with his colleagues Albertus Van Raalte and Pieter Oggel about the *Hollandsche Gereformeerde Kerk in Noord-Amerika* to introduce new immigrants to the history, doctrines, and government of this church. He used biblical metaphors to confirm its strengths: the church was as the glorious city Zion, and its mission boards and educational institutions were its palaces and towers.[16]

---

a memo, Joint Archives of Holland, VandeLuyster Collection, box 1, folder "1861." After Stobbelaar had accepted a call to Town Holland, Wisconsin, a sizeable minority of 14 proposed to call Van der Meulen back (minutes January 25, 1865).

[13] Reformed Church Archives, Correspondence of the Board of Domestic Missions box 14, folder "Reports of Aided Churches." Van der Meulen traveled to Pella in September 1857. The money was also used to cover his medical expenses after an accident

[14] *The Acts and Proceedings of the General Synod of the Reformed Protestant Dutch Church in North America, convened at the City of New-Brunswick, June 1855* (New York: Board of Publication, 1855), 581-82.

[15] *Classis Holland Minutes* 179 and 180; Johannis Marckii, *Chrisianae Theologiae Medulla* (Trajecti ad Rhenum 1742). See *Catalogue of the Theological Seminary and Rutgers College Libraries, New Brunswick, NJ* (New Brunswick, NJ: Press of J. Terhune and Son, 1854) shows no titles in Dutch. Howard Hageman, *Two Centuries Plus: The Story of New Brunswick Theological Seminary* (Grand Rapids, MI: Eerdmans, 1984), 64-73. The Zeeland church contributed $ 18.70 to the furnishing of Hertzog Hall.

[16] C. Van der Meulen, A.C. Van Raalte, and P.J. Oggel, *Beknopte verhandeling over de geschiedenis, leer en regering der Hollandsche gereformeerd Protestantsche kerk in Noord-Amerika* (New York 1857). *Nagedachtenis*, 89. The Board of Publication of the RCA commissioned one thousand copies. Van der Meulen's enthusiasm for the RCA was not shared by everyone. He was reported to have said in 1855 that the fathers of the Secession of 1834 had been haughty when they announced that they were the only true church, and that members of other churches had joined in a communion service. Moreover, he persisted in the distribution of tracts, which suggested general

Education was a key concern for the colony, and Van der Meulen was one of its strongest supporters. This was not only so because the Dutch ban on parochial schools was one of the chief complaints of the Seceders, but also because most immigrants had left the Netherlands to improve the lives of their children.[17] Van der Meulen strongly supported Van Raalte's plan for a school and set out to find funds and support. He appealed to the churches with strong biblical pleas: Where should the "Elkanahs and Hannahs" who promised their Samuels to God's service go? What answer should they give to the question that Bathsheba posed for king David when he was old and his succession had not been arranged? The response to his appeal was positive. The Dutch immigrants recognized that there were openings in the U.S. for civil servants and that the Dutch could occupy these positions. Without proper education the mission "to spread the light of the gospel in the dark places of the earth" could not be accomplished. Therefore a school should serve the entire region and not only the town of Holland, and it ought not only provide for ministers, but for all kinds of civic functions.[18]

Since Van der Meulen belonged to the older generation, having emigrated in his forty-seventh year, his focus was clearly on the next generation. In 1852 his two sons were eighteen and fourteen years old and ready for more schooling. In September 1854 he accompanied his oldest son Jacob, with two other Dutch students, to New Brunswick, where they became part of the small student body of fifty in the preparatory school of Rutgers College and fifty at the seminary, taught by three professors.[19] The senior pastor had promised God his son for

---

atonement, though the classis had found them incompatible with the Calvinist tradition. Van der Meulen defended his act with the argument that the tract was useful to reach the unconverted, though not to teach the believers. According to a memoir of Jan Gelok documenting his departure from the Reformed Church, dated Winter 1864 and filed in the Minutes First CRC Grand Rapids, book 1, Heritage Hall, Calvin College. (Hereafter cited as HH). See also the Minutes of the Hollandsch Gereformeerde gemeente van Holland vol. 2, 31 August 1858: brother Wilterdink resigns his membership from the congregation because children of non-members are baptized and Van der Meulen preaches that these children are part of the covenant. *Classis Holland Minutes* (Grand Rapids: Eerdmans, 1950), 203.

[17] *Classis Holland Minutes*, September 1, 1852, 100-07.
[18] Hope College, Joint Archives of Holland, Minutes Classis Wisconsin RCA, April 9-10 and September 10, 1862.
[19] Letter A.C. Van Raalte to Garretson, September 19, 1854. The first group of Dutch students were Jacob Vander Meulen, Rutgers, 1858, and New Brunswick Theological Seminary (NBTS), 1861; Christiaan Vander Veen, same year; John Vander Meulen, Rutgers, 1859 and NBTS, 1862; John H. Karsten and Egbert Winter, Rutgers, 1860 and NBTS, 1863, John Howard Raven comp., *Biographical Record of Theological*

the ministry after his other four children had died.[20] Both sons served first the new immigrant communities in Wisconsin and later filled the most prestigious pulpits in Michigan—in Holland and Grand Rapids. They were shaped by the East and respected by the West. Their father remained interested in education, as is proven by the special attention (and appreciation) he had for the academic program and standards of the seminary in Kampen, the Netherlands, when he visited his old country in 1869.[21]

Similarities to American Religious Culture

Van der Meulen always preached in the Dutch language. This was not a conscious rejection of English but was a result of his inability to use the language effectively. Rare testimony comparing the oratorical skills of Van Raalte and Van der Meulen in 1852 shows a preference for the latter: "Rev. VanderMeulen seems by far to be the best liked of the two... as well on as off the pulpit. The cause is that he quickly acquired the American manners and customs, which makes him speak freely, while the other is rather confused and thinks he knows everything and that every one must follow him."[22] One should not attach too much weight to this personal judgment, since it might very well mean that the author disliked Van Raalte and preferred the impromptu style that Van der Meulen had acquired already in the Netherlands. It does, however, reveal why Van der Meulen made an easy transition to American-style behavior. He promoted the teaching of English early on and became an American citizen as soon as he could. He was not afraid of American influences, and he incorporated familiar ones while resisting those that were far beyond his experience.[23]

His gift for selecting relevant Bible passages and applying them to specific situations enabled Van der Meulen to touch hearts and souls. He used a variety of opportunities to make spiritual appeals. Audiences made donations readily after one of his moving addresses. The favorite stories told by his sons about their father included those

---

Seminary New Brunswick 1784-1911 (New Brunswick, NJ, Printed for the Seminary by the Rev. Archibald Laidlie Memorial Fund, 1912), 146, 151, 154-55. These are the first five graduates from Rutgers and NBTS and who had graduated from Holland Academy. After theological education began at Hope College in 1866, few students of the colony went East for their seminary education.

[20] *Nagedachtenis*, 25.
[21] Ibid., 144.
[22] Argus from Grand Rapids in the *Sheboygan Nieuwsbode*, February 17, 1852.
[23] Joint Archives of Holland, Van der Meulen Papers, file 6, Naturalization Record October 5, 1852.

of the conversions of young people.[24] The premature deaths of his two daughters in 1857 were followed by a revival in his church. This interest in revivals remained until the end of his life, and just before he died he went to listen to the revivalist Earle.[25] So, in his behavior he resembled the American revival preachers even though he was not theologically influenced by them.

Part of his appeal came from the fact that he took his own medicine: he applied these texts to himself as well. For example, he took the text of his 1859 New Year's Eve sermon on Exodus 4:20b (about Moses who took his staff at hand to return to Egypt) as a sign; it prompted him to accept a call to Chicago. He had become deeply rooted in West Michigan, where he owned hundreds of acres of land and his own homestead (which he did not sell until 1875). He was surrounded by friends and relatives and served a large congregation with three hundred full members, which had become fully self-supporting in 1856. Chicago, on the other hand, had only a small congregation of fifty members amidst a large number of unaffiliated Dutch immigrants. Van der Meulen realized the potential for growth and reasoned that if the fish were unwilling to come to the net, he would take the net to them. He set up a series of Thursday evening services that drew more people to the church, inspired the members to raise funds to build a new edifice, and collected a $400 grant from the Board of Domestic Missions of the Reformed Church in America. Although his pastorate lasted only two years, it was sufficient to put the church back on its feet. This kind of activity was typical for the revered minister; before facilitating the Chicago edifice, he had dedicated seventeen others. This result was what he had in mind, and he could move on to the next hotspot.[26]

An urgent call from Grand Rapids brought him from the Windy City to the Furniture City in 1861. Van der Meulen had known Second Reformed Church from its beginning. A fellow student under Scholte, the Reverend H.G. Klijn, its first minister, had continued to serve the

---

[24] *Nagedachtenis*, 82-84.
[25] Ibid., 22.
[26] Zeeland Historical Society, Zeeland, Michigan, "Eerste kerkeraadsboek Gereformeerde Kerk Zeeland, Michigan," Minutes February 25,1859. *De Hollander*, July 11, 1860. Letter Mrs. Budde to Wormser, late 1860 or early 1861 Johan Stellingwerff, Robert P. Swierenga, ed., and Walter Lagerwey, trans., *Iowa Letters: Dutch Immigrants on the American Frontier* (Grand Rapids: Eerdmans, 2004), 482. Letters C. Van der Meulen to John Garretson, February 17 and May 9, 1859, Board of Domestic Missions. The correspondence of the Board of Domestic Missions, Reformed Church in America, Reformed Church Archives, box 15, fldrs. Jan-Mar, Apr-Dec. 1859.

church as its main counsel, preaching there once every month for its first five years. In 1857 the church had split over the issues that led to the founding of the Christian Reformed Church, and the congregation felt very much discouraged when the membership dwindled to eighty souls. Van der Meulen teamed up with his friend, the entrepreneur Frans van Driele, who was the leading elder. He evaluated the spirit of the younger generation, and they persuaded him that there was a future for that congregation, and it proved to be true during the decade of his ministry. In Grand Rapids Van der Meulen organized his first revival, which took place in January of 1870. It was adapted to suit congregational preferences and was limited to one week of prayer meetings and daily sermons. Despite the twenty recorded confessions of faith, he hesitated to continue, fearing it resembled a Methodist revival.[27] Nevertheless, it proved he had fully adapted to the style of American preachers.

Return to the Netherlands and Evaluation of His Role

Just before the event signaling the culmination of his adaptation to his adopted homeland, Van der Meulen had the opportunity to evaluate the immigration enterprise by returning to the land of his birth. Again a personal loss prepared him for this move, which he made as he approached his seventieth birthday. His wife died during a church service in February 1869. To help him recuperate from this loss, his consistory granted the old pastor a vacation of several weeks. The Classis of Holland had decided to reconnect with the seceded churches in the Netherlands, which would meet in June of 1869 in Middelburg, the capital of the province of Zeeland. The fact that it commissioned its own representative to the Dutch synod was a sign of the relative independence of the Holland Classis. Thanks to an official request from the Dutch Seceders to the Reformed Church in America, the Synod of Philadelphia cabled him that he could act as the official representative of the American church.[28]

The timing of this trip was important because both sides of the Atlantic had to assess the future of the relationship between the old country and the immigrants: would the next generation maintain these contacts?[29] The 1869 Middelburg Synod of the Seceders was crucial

---

[27] According to Frans Van Driele in *Nagedachtenis*, 126.
[28] It had done something similar in 1866 when classis Holland had sent a letter which Van Raalte presented to the members the synod of the Seceders in Amsterdam.
[29] It also might have been prompted by the name change of 1867, when the word 'Dutch' was dropped and the denomination continued as the Reformed Church in America; W. van 't Spijker, "The Christian Reformed Church and the Christelijke

because it united the various seceded factions into one Christian Reformed Church. For Van der Meulen personally it was a a time of celebration and reunion. From Rotterdam he traveled by steamboat with his former colleagues and friends Anthony Brummelkamp, Helenius De Cock, and Nicholas Dosker to the capital of Zeeland.

His own festive mood was matched by the warm and open atmosphere at the synod, which lacked all traces of sectarianism. He was so touched by the cordial spirit of the meeting that it struck him that the Millennium must have arrived. The flood of attention and invitations reassured him that he was fully recognized and accepted as their old pastor. Rumors of his alleged liberalism proved false. Thirty years earlier he had been alone in the Province of Zeeland, poorly trained, despised and fined by the authorities; and now he returned to an area served by sixteen seceded ministers, and the civil leaders all came to listen and talk to him. Twenty-two years after his emigration Van der Meulen announced that the new colony had matured. This contrast between the time of his departure and his present reception was a justification of his choices.

He deferred questions about the purity of the Reformed Church and turned the tables. He told the seceded believers in the Netherlands that his presence as the official representative of the Reformed Church represented a badge of honor for the Dutch church because it demonstrated that this new denomination was not sectarian but was true to its Calvinist character.[30] He confirmed that the Reformed Church in America and the Christian Seceded Church in the Netherlands were completely similar in doctrine and church government.[31] He told his old church that this foreign recognition meant they were considered the true guardians of Calvinism in the Netherlands. Privately, he expected that the growth of the Seceders would help the Netherlands to return to its Calvinist moorings.

To the very end Van der Meulen proved himself to be a true immigrant leader. He joined a group of new immigrants on their sober trip overland via Canada to Michigan instead of taking a comfortable

---

Gereformeerde Kerken in Nederland," in Peter De Klerk and Richard De Ridder, eds., *Perspectives on the Christian Reformed Church: Studies in Its History, Theology, and Ecumenicity* (Grand Rapids, MI: Baker, 1983), 367; Gerald F. De Jong, "The Controversy over Dropping the Word Dutch from the Name of the Reformed Church," *Reformed Review* 34 (Spring 1981): 158-70.

[30] *Nagedachtenis*, 140-42.

[31] *De Bazuin*, 27 August 1869. *Handelingen en verslagen van de Algemene Synoden van de Christelijk Afgescheidene Gereformeerde Kerk (1836-1869)* (Houten/Utrecht: Den Hertog, 1984), 986, 1021.

train ride. In September 1869 his cousin Willem, the only living son of Cornelius's brother Eliza, emigrated with his family to Grand Rapids, where he worked as a porter and in the furniture industry.[32]

Rejuvenated by this joyful reunion, Van der Meulen returned to Grand Rapids and soon married a widow, Frouke VanderPloeg, in February 1870. He continued to work until 1873, when he retired. In addition to hardships, he experienced many satisfying events in his life. He lived to see his two sons become respected ministers, as did a number of men from his flock in the old country: Adriaan Zwemer, James Moerdijke, Arie Cz. Kuiper, W.P. de Jong, Hendrik Uiterwijk, and James de Pree.[33] He loved his office and continued to preach until the very end. He died peacefully in Grand Rapids on August 30, 1876, and was mourned by the entire colony.

His funeral was a public event. His body was carried by train from Grand Rapids to Zeeland. In his home town all stores and factories closed, and many mourners came to pay tribute. That his death ended an era is illustrated by the fact that the classis decided to place a marker at his grave. Within a month after his death the two regional bodies to which the churches of Zeeland and Grand Rapids belonged began taking their minutes in English instead of Dutch. James de Press wrote in the *Christian Intelligencer*, the magazine of the Reformed Church in America, "With myself, many of those who then constituted the youth of Zeeland look upon the departed brother as their spiritual father."[34]

Conclusion

Historian James Bratt, in an article in the year 2000, characterized the role of one of the leading Christian Reformed ministers: "The challenge of a religious *leader* is to deploy spiritual resources effectively in concrete situations."[35] This is exactly what Cornelius van der Meulen

---

[32] Julian van der Meulen, "Genealogy," VI 1 and VI 2. His children quickly assimilated and married outside the Dutch clan. *Nagedachtenis*, 147-48.

[33] Henry S. Lucas, ed., *Dutch Immigrant Memoirs and Related Writings* (rev. ed.; Grand Rapids, MI: Eerdmans, 1997), 2:413-14, 420-22, 447. *Nagedachtenis*, 93-94.

[34] *Classis Holland Minutes*, September 13, 1876; Joint Archives of Holland, Minutes Classis Grand River, September 20, 1876. James de Pree, "The Late Rev. C. Van der Meulen," *Christian Intelligencer* September 28, 1876, 3-4. *Historical Souvenir of the Celebration of the Sixtieth Anniversary of the Colonization of the Hollanders in Western Michigan. Held in Zeeland, Michigan, August 21, 1907* (Executive Committee, 1908), 36.

[35] James D. Bratt, "Lammert J. Hulst: The Pastor as Leader in an Immigrant Community," in Hans Krabbendam and Larry Wagenaar, eds., *The Dutch-American Experience: Essays in Honor of Robert P. Swierenga* (Amsterdam: VU University Press, 2000), 209-21, quotation on page 215.

did. His prestige rested on a foundation of humble origins, hard labor, community service, patriarchal appearance, and successful efforts in maintaining personal links with his pre- and post-emigration circles. Van der Meulen was the prototype of a new minister needed for serving a new colony founded at a time of mass migration. His strong constitution, stable personality, emphatic manner, great mobility, and practicality prepared him for a pioneering role in the Midwest and earned authority built on reliability. During his leadership in Michigan he prepared the Protestant Dutch immigrants for the next phase, when the balance shifted from rural towns to emerging cities. Without his gifts the immigrant churches would have found it much more difficult to spread from the rural areas into the cities.[36]

His own conversion experience after dramatic family events made him turn to the Seceders as a source of spiritual nourishment instead of the established *Nederlandse Hervormde Kerk*, but he never totally rejected the old church. This experience helped him to seek cooperation with others wherever possible. The Secession coincided with his own spiritual awakening and drew him into a pioneering role that would harmonize with key elements of American evangelicalism. His limited training was enough to prepare him for the pulpit. While he was a passionate preacher who delivered practical sermons, his real strength lay in his close identification with his parishioners. After he had shared his concerns about immigration taking place for the wrong reasons, he came to view the move as an opportunity for growth.

Van der Meulen's legacy is to be found chiefly in the United States, but not exclusively so. The irenic minister helped the early immigrants to regain their self-respect and self-confidence by creating stable communities. Only seceded ministers such as Van der Meulen could organize a viable Dutch church in the Midwest. They were used to harsh conditions, possessed a broad authority in religious and practical matters, and developed new networks. His contacts with both the East Coast and the old country kept the old sources of support open and offered havens for new immigrants. He was particularly effective in tying urban and rural settlements together, a connection that would prove crucial for the survival of the churches and the colonies. He promoted education as an instrument for further expansion, and he approached the issue of language as a practical matter. His return to the old country

---

[36] Charles Scott, "Its Missionary Work at Home," in *Centennial Discourses: A Series of Sermons Delivered in the Year 1876, by the order of the General Synod of the Reformed (Dutch) Church in America* (New York: Board of Publication of the Reformed Church in America, 1877), 501-30, esp. 516.

helped him to confirm the wisdom of his decision to emigrate. In turn, however, his success and that of his cohorts in the United States helped to strengthen the position of the Christian Reformed denomination in the Netherlands. He saw his endeavors in the United States as a promise that orthodoxy could be restored even in the Netherlands as it had happened in America.

When in late 1876 the last examples of this type of colonial minister, Van der Meulen and Van Raalte, died within a period of three months, it signaled the end of an era. At that point the basic infrastructure of the Dutch immigrant churches in the Midwest had been completed. The educational institutions were in place to train the new generation of leaders who would be responsible for the integration of later waves of immigrants.

INDEX

Abeel, John, 312
Abrahams, Maritje, 183
Adriaensen, Marijn, 92
Advice, Broad, 97
Aelbertsz, Gijsbert, 81, 86
African Americans, 28, 90, 127, 128. See also Slavery
Albany, description of, 284; First Reformed Church in (*illus*), 104; participation in the Plan of Union, 286-87; pulpit in the Dutch Reformed Church of (*illus*), 276
Alberthoma, Robert, 291
Alutarius, Henricus, 87
à Marck, Johannes, 300
American Revolution and the Reformed church, 259-62; in Albany, 288-89
Ames, William, 151
Amsterdam, supervision of churches by, 6-8
Andros, Edmund (Governor), 115, 138, 157, 224

Anglicans in Maryland, 233-34
Apostle of New Jersey. *See* Bertholf, Guiliam
Apricius. *See* Price, John
Arnold, William Harris, 66
Articles of Union, 286, 303-04, 307
Auchmuty, Samuel, 243, 252

Badius, Otto, 90
Baerents, Engeltje, marriage to Bastiaen Krol, 46
Baerents, Wige (Ytje), marriage to Bastiaen Krol, 48
Bancker, Margaret, 182
Bassett, John, 290
Bastiaensz, Jan, 49, 50
Batavianization, 5
Bavink, Jan, 278
Beekman, Gerardus, 189-90
Beekman, Henry, 227, 297
Benson, Maritje, 262
Bertholf, Crijn, 200-01

Bertholf, Guiliam, 6, 8, 18, 140, 167, 192–93, 197–216; and Frelinghuysen, 214–15; and Leisler Rebellion, 204–05; arrival in New York, 202–03, 208–10; at Bergen, 209–10; at Hackensack, 204–06; baptism of, 200; clash with Selijns, 199–200, 202–03, 205, 210–13; early life and education, 198–201; handwriting of (*illus*), 198; later years of, 213–16; ordination in Zeeland 206–208
Bertling, Michaël, 280
Blauvelt, Willem Albertsz, 45
Bleecker, Hermanus, 275
Blom, Hermanus, 125
Boelen, Hermanus L., 259
Bogaert, Andries, 178
Bogaert, Cornelis, 86
Bogaert, Willem, 81
Bogardus, Everardus, 11, 22, 44, 61, 63, 78, 79–100; (*illus*), 80; and conflict with Kieft, 91–96; and call to ministry, 84–85; and drinking, 97–98; and relationships with Lucas Zas, 84–85; and religious environment of Woerden, 85–86; as a comforter of the sick, 88–89; colonial experience of, 90–96; death of, 100; dream of, 88; early spiritual experience of, 81–83, 85–88; education of, 88; entry into public life, 87; ordination of, 89; pietism of, 98–100; reassessment of, 97–100; traditional assessment of, 96–97
Bolks, Seine, 317
Bonnet, Gisbert, 299–300, 302, 308
Boston, Thomas, 286
Brandt, Marten Jansz, 88
Bratt, James, 330
Breeden-Raedt, 91
Brinkerhoff, Dirk, 247
Brodhead, John Romeyn, 61–62
Brouwer, Jan Jansz, 70
Brummelkamp, Anthony, 320–21, 329
Buddingh, Derk, 62
Burgers, Abraham, 178
Burgers, Grietje Jans, 179
Burgers, Sara, 183
Burgess, John, 151

Burgher Household, The, 84

Call, process of a, 2–4, 7, 12–13, 17–18; use of an agent for, 280–81, 285
Carleton, Guy, 273
Carstenszen, Laurens, 183
Cats, Jacob, 123
Ceporinus, Petrus, 106
Christian Reformed Church, 328–29
Christouel, Anneken, 40
Classis, desire for in America 266–67
Cocceius, Johannes, 21, 123, 187
Coetus-Conferentie conflict, 8, 14, 31–32, 116, 249, 260–62, 265, 282, 298, 301–02, 312
Coley, Elizabeth, marriage to Gerrit Lydekker, 269
Comforter of the Sick, 38, 44; duties of, 42–43, 89, 106
Concord, The, 41
Conscience, freedom of, 42
Consistory, selection of, 5
Conventicles, 22
Covenant in Dutch Theology, 21
Cralingius, Jacobus, 87
Crespel, Anthonij, 202
Croesen, Gerrit Dirckz, 127
Crommelin, Daniel, 280–81, 285
Curtenius, Antonius, 263

Daillé, Pierre, 221, 224–25
Danckaerts, Jasper, 110, 161, 165–67
Davits, Abraham, 181
Davits, Dieuwertje, 181
de Beauvois, Carel, 128–29
De Cock, Helenius, 329
De Cock, Hendrik, 320
De Eendracht, 41
de Forest, Jesse, 40
de Jong, W.P., 330
de Labadie, Jean, 111, 199
Dellius, Godefridus, 117, 136, 139, 175, 191–92, 205, 210
de Marees, Janneke, 121
de Meyer, Willem, 231
de Niet, Johan, 106
de Pree, James, 330
de Riemer, Margaretha, 143; marriage to Henricus Selijns, 137

De Ronde, Lambertus, 244, 246–47, 249, 252, 256, 304; and conflict with Laidlie, 248
De Schelvis, 45
de Sille, Nicasius, 126
de Vries, David Pietersz, 64, 91
de Witt, Johan, 133
De Witt, Thomas, 62–64
Dey, Richard Varick, 251, 255–56
Dickson, Jean, 239
Dickson, John, 241
Dinclagen, Lubbert, 91
Disciplinary process in America, 230–32
Dordrecht, synod of, 11, 16, 20, 69, 83, 116; church order of, 305
Dosker, Nicholas, 329
Double predestination, 83
Drisius, Samuel, 114, 126, 129, 134
du Bois, Benjamin, 15
du Bois, Gualtherus, 142–43, 214
du Bois, Jonathan, 15
Dutch language, in North America, 23–25; in worship, 289–92; survival in Albany, 290; opposition to worship in English, 244, 248–52
Dutch Reformed Church, establishment of, 37–39, 60–62, 68
Dutch Reformed Church in the fort (*illus*), 2

Earl Willem VI, 180
Edwards, Jonathan, 291
Eekhof, Albert, (*illus*) 60, 39, 48–49, 60, 67–69, 76
Eendracht, 77
Egberts, Annetje, 40, 49
English conquest in 1664, 7
English language, in Albany congregation, 290; in worship, 289–92; preaching in New York, 244, 248–52, 256–57. *See also* Laidlie, Archibald
Enkhuijzen, Roldanus of, 180
Essenius, Andreas, 122

Flying Fish, 190
Fordham Manor transfer to Reformed Church, 137
Freeman, Bernardus, 167, 214

Frelinghuysen, Ferdinandus, 15
Frelinghuysen, Henricus, 15
Frelinghuysen, Jacobus, 15
Frelinghuysen, Johannes, 15
Frelinghuysen, Theodorus Jacobus, 1, 15, 22, 214
Frelinghuysen, Theodorus J. Jr., 266, 281–82
Froeligh, Solomon, 309–10
Fryenmoet, Johannes Casparus, 14

Gansevoort, Leonard, 289
Ganesvoort, Peter, 289
Geldorpius, Gosuinus, 51
Gerdes, Daniel, 279–82
Glorious Rebellion, 163, 230–31
Goethals, Gregorius, 70
Goetschius, Johannes Henricus, 14, 263–64
Goetschius, Johannes Martinus, 15
Great Awakening, 214
Guiana, colony at, 153–55
Gunn, Alexander, and Livingston biography, 297–98

Haff, Laurens, 128
Hageman, Howard, 276, 288, 292
Halve Maen, 282
Hamilton, Alexander, 289
Hardenbergh, Jacob Rutsen, 15, 272
Heidanus, Abraham, 123
Hellenbroek, Abraham, 246
Hem, description of, 180–81
Hendricksz, Jan, 121
Hendricxdr, Anthonia, 176
Hendriks, Martijntje, 201
Hoffman, Martinus, 251
Hoffman, Mary, marriage to Archibald Laidlie, 251. *See also* Laidlie, Mary
Hofstede, Petrus, 10
Holt, John, 246
Hoornbeek, Johannes, 123
Houwelijck, 123
Hudson, Henry, 282
Huguenots, in Boston, 222–24; in Carolina, 220–22; in New York, 224–29
Hustaert, Jacob, 179
Huygen, Jan, 43–44, 72

Inglis, Charles, 254, 272-73
Ingoldsby, Richard, 187
Israel, Captain, 188

Jackson, Wilhelmus, 15
Jans, Anneke, 79, 95
Jansen, Harpert, 46
Jansz, Roelof, 95
Jones, Thomas, 254

Kern, John M., 259
Keyser, Dirck, 188
Kieft, Willem, 91-96
Kierner, Cynthia, 296, 299
Klijn, H.G., 327
Koelman, Jacobus, 136, 161, 198-99; and call to New Castle, 201-02
Kranckbesoecker, 38
Kregier, Marten, 126
Krol, Bastiaen Jansz, 37-58, 60, 68, 72; appointment as commissioner, 43; appointment as director, 43-44; as a caffa worker, 50-51; baptism of, 41, 49-52; church discipline of, 46, 56; conversion of, 51; death of, 48; first congregation of, 40; literacy of, 52; pamphlet written by, 52-57; possessions of, 47; remarriage of, to Engeltje Baerents 46-47; return to Holland, 44-47; third marriage of, to Wige (Ytje) Baerents, 48; *Troost der vromen (illus)*, 38
Kuiper, Arie Cz., 330
Kuypers, Gerardus, 312
Kuyter, Jochem, 91

La Garce, 45
Laidlie, Archibald, *(illus)* 240, 13, 239-57, 268, 290, 299, 304; and conflict with De Ronde, 248-51; and revitalization of the church, 248; and Scottish New York, 252; and small group education, 247; and the American Revolution, 253-55; and the Scottish church in Vlissingen, 241-42; and use of English catechism, 246; arrival in New York City, 242; at Red Hook, 255; death of, 255; early life and education, 239-41; marriage to Mary Hoffman, 251; reputation as a preacher, 243-45
Laidlie, John, 240
Laidlie, Mary, death of, 255
Laidlie, William, 239
Lam, Jan Dircksz, 66
Language in worship. *See* Dutch language; English language
Lansman, Jacob, 134
Laud, Archbishop, 151
Leendertse, Denijs, 48
Leiby, Adrian, 267
Leisler, Jacob, 31, 115, 163, 187, 229-30
Leisler's Rebellion, 31, 138-42, 144, 175, 185, 186-91, 194, 204-05, 230-31
Leydekker, Hubertus, 178
Leydt, Johanne 14, 262
Linn, Willia, 305
Literacy in the Dutch Republic, 52
Livingston, Catherine, marriage to Eilardus Westerlo, 287
Livingston, Gilbert, 297-99
Livingston, Henry, 297, 299
Livingston, John Henry, *(illus)* 296, 247-49, 256, 286-88, 290-91, 295-314; and Coeus-Conferentie conflict, 301-02; and historical memory, 312-14; and religious liberty, 300-01, 304-05; and the Articles of Union, 303-04; and the church constitution, 305-06; and the development of the professorate, 307-11; appointment as professor of theology, 307-08; as a professor, 307-12; as president of Queen's College, 311; assessment of, 314; at Utrecht, 299-303; early years, 296-99; on Long Island, 310; ordination of, 303; praise of Laidlie's preaching, 245; return to America, 303; spiritual awakening of, 298-99; supernatural rationalism of, 300
Livingston, Margaret Beekman, 243, 255
Livingston, Philip, 287, 297
Livingston, Robert, 296-97
Livingston, Robert R., 301
Livingston, Sarah, 288, 297
Livingston, William, 254-55
Livingston family, 296-98
Livingston Manor, 297

Index 337

Locke, John, 301
Lott, Abraham, 247
Lovelace, Francis, 134
Lowe, Petrus, 246
Lupardus, Wilhelmus, 141
Lydekker, Gerrit, (*illus*) 260, 14, 259-74; and pietism 264-66; and Toryism, 269-72; assessment of, 274; death of, 274; early life and education, 262-64; in England, 273-74; marriage to Elizabeth Coley, 269; ordination of, 267-68
Lydekker, Gerrit (Sr.), 262
Lydekker, Ryck, 262
Lydekker, Ryck II, 262

Maets, Carolus de, 122
Marinus, David, 14
Mason, John, 252, 254
Mason, John Mitchell, 312
Mather, Increase, 223, 225
Matthew, David, 272
Megapolensis, Johannes, 99, 106, 114, 126, 128, 134
Megapolensis, Samuel, 15
Meijer, Hermanus, 284-85, 309
Meinerts, Samuel, 181
Meusevoet, Vincent, 53
Meyer, Hermanus. *See* Meijer, Hermanus
Michaëlius, Jonas, 4, 39, 59-78; and conditions in New Netherland, 71-72: and conflict with Minuit, 75; and his father, 68; and the organization of the church, 72-73; Eekhof's biography of, 67-69; finding letter of, 63-66; finding second letter of, 66-67; sources for, 69-70; views of native Americans, 73-75
Michaëlius, Jonas Jansz., 181
Michielsz, Jan, 68
Midwest Dutch settlements (map), 323
Milborne, Jacob, 139
Miller, Samuel, 254
Ministers, functions of, 4-5; marriage of, 27-28; mobility of, 11-13; reasons for shortage of, 8-9; social significance of, 5; salaries and status of, 25-27

Ministry, Dutch, after the Reformation, 16; in America, reasons for, 10-11; reasons for success in, 29-30
Minuit, Peter, 43, 59, 72; and conflict with Michaelius, 75-78
Mississippi River, map of the mouth of the (*illus*), 218
Moerdijke, James, 330
Mohawks, 73
Mohicans, 73
Molenis, Justus Wilhelmus, 105
Montanus, David, 200
Montanus view of New Amsterdam (*illus*), 2
Montresor, John, 253
More, Henry, 248
Mouw, Dirk, 280, 301, 313
Murphy, Henry Cruse, 64-65
Muysevoet, Pieter, 85
Muysevoet (Meusevoet), Vincent, 86

Nadere Reformatie, 21-22, 198
Native Americans, 29, 73-75, 163; Bogardus's treatment of, 96, 99; Bogardus's views on, 90, 96, 99; van Twiller's treatment of, 91
Netherlands map (*illus*), xii
New Amsterdam map (*illus*), 33
New Jersey, Apostle of. *See* Bertholf, Guiliam
New Netherland, alcohol use in, 97; conditions in, 71-72, 108; map (*illus*), 34
New Paltz, Walloon church at, 225-26
Nexsen, Elias, 243
Nicholson, Francis, 234
Nijenhuis, J.T. Bodel, and letter by Michaelius, 63-64
Nijmegen, Peace of, 155
Nixon, Elias, 243
Nucella, Johannes, 141

Oggel, Pieter, 324
Orange Colony. *See* Guiana
Orangen Boom, Den, 42
Orange Tree, The, 42
Ordination, first Dutch, in America, 158-59, 168; in Batavia, 158-59; Ordinations in North America, 14-15

Orphans in New Netherland, 128
Orthodoxy, 20–21
Oyapok River, 153

Paget, John, 151
Perkins, William, 53, 86
Pietism, 20–21
Plan of Union, 286; and Albany congregation, 286–87
Polhemius, Johannes Theodorus, 124, 129, 134
Popinga, Marijcken, 142
Predestination, double, 83
Price, John, 152–53
Princess Amelia, 100
Professorate in the Reformed church, development of, 307–11
Purcell, Henry, 291

Queens College, 308–09, 311

Rapalje, Sarah, 42
Reformation, Further, 21-22, 112–13
Reformed Church charter, 140–41
Reiners, Aleijda, 278
Reiners, Arnoldus, 278
Reiners, Eilardus, 277
Reiners, Gesina, 278
Reiners, Hillegonda. *See* Westerlo, Hillegonda
Reiners, Lubbertus, 277
Rensselaerswijck, Patroon of, 7
Reyniers, Agnetie, 105
Riddersbach, Abraham, 48
Ringo, Philip Janse, 45
Ritzema, Johannes, 244, 249, 252, 256, 262, 265, 267–68, 283, 304
Ritzema, Rudolphus, 283
Rodgers, John, 252, 254
Roelants, Adam, 90
Roman Catholic Church, opposition to, 54, 56, 112, 131
Romeyn, Dirck, 15, 304, 309–10
Romeyn, Jeremiah, 312
Romeyn, Thomas Sr., 15
Roosevelt, Isaac, 242n15
Rubel, Johannes C., 259

Schaats, Gideon, 6–7, 18, 103–18, 135, 185; and illegitimate child, 109; and Lutherans, 113–14; and Voetian theology, 110–17; as a Comforter of the Sick, 106; as schoolmaster, 104–05; at Beverwijck, 108–09; death of, 117; in Rensselaerswijck, 107–08; ordination of, 107; theological education of, 105–06
Schenck, Johannes, 189
Schenectady, artist's rendition of (*illus*), 163
Scholte, Hendrik P., 316, 319–21, 323
Schoonmaker, Henricus, 15
Schotanus, Meinardus, 122
Schouten, Petrus, 270
Schuneman, Johannes, 15
Schuyler, Elizabeth, 289
Schuyler, Johannes, 14
Schuyler, Philip, 289
Scott, John Morin, 254–55
Secession of 1834, 324n16
Selijns, Henricus, 7, 9, 14, 119–46, 159, 175, 185–86, 191–92, 194, 199, 204–05, 221, 227, 231–33; and African Americans, 128; and church discipline, 127–28, 131; and Labadists, 136; and Leisler's Rebellion, 138–42, 144; and orphans, 128; and record keeping, 130–31, 142; and Stuyvesant, 126–27; as army chaplain, 132; as voorlezer, 204; at Breuckelen, 124–29; at Leiden, 123–24; at Utrecht, 122–23; at Waverveen, 129–33; clash with Bertholf, 199, 202, 205, 210–13; death of, 143; early years of, 121–22; ordination of, 125; poetry of, 132–33; remarriage of, to Margaretha de Riemer, 137; return to New York, 134–38; secures charter for Reformed Church, 140–41; wedding of, to Machtelt Specht, 128; house (*illus*), 120
Seloivre, Isaac, 202
Seminary, location at New Brunswick, 311
Sewall, Samuel, 223
Slavery, 164. *See also* African Americans
Sloughter, Henry, 187
Sluijter, Peter, 161, 165–67
Smith, William Jr., 254–55

Index

Smout (Smoutius), Adriaen Jorisz, 63, 69
Sonoy, Diederick, 68
Specht, Herman, 123
Specht, Machtelt, 123, 131; marriage to Henricus Selijns, 128
Spiritual vision of Bogardus, 82–84
Stamp Act, 253, 259
Steenwijck, Cornelis, 137
Stiles, Ezra, 291
Stockers, Jan, 1–2
Stoffels, Annetjen, 40, 45
Stuyvesant, Petrus, 92, 108–10, 114–15, 124, 126, 129
Sylvester, Giles, 223
Sylvester, Nathaniel, 223

Tanis, James, 246
Tellner, Jacob, 136, 188
Ten Broeck, Cornelia, marriage of to Laurentius van den Bosch, 227
ten Broeck, Dirck Wessels, 227
ten Broeck, Sara, 229
ten Broeck, Wessel, 227, 229
Tenhage, Annichje, 181
Tesschenmaecker, Petrus, 6–7, 11, 14, 19, 24, 136, 138, 147–70, 184–85, 204, 230; and John Price, 152–55; and slavery, 164; arrival in America, 156; assessment of, 164–69; at Bergen, 166; at Guiana, 153–55; at London, 150; at New Castle, 156, 160–61, 164; at Schenectady, 162–64; at Staten Island, 161–62, 164; at the Hague, 151–52; death during Leisler's Rebellion, 139; death of, 163; early life and education, 149–51; ordination of, 111, 156–58, 169; signature (*illus*), 148; theological orientation of, 166–67
Theological style of Dutch ministers, 20–23
Thibaud, Jan, 189
Thibou, Jacob, 221
Treslong, Count of, 105
Trico, Catelina, 42
Trigland, Jacobus, 69
Trouillart, Florent-Philippe, 221
True Reformed Dutch Church, 272
Twelve-Year Truce, 52, 54

Uiterwijk, Hendrik, 330
Union of Utrecht, 42

van Antwerp, Jakobus, 247
van Breugel, Gerrit Hendricksen, 53
van Bunschooten, Elias, 287
van Coperen, Sara Guiliamse, 200
van Curler, Arent, 109
van de Luyster, Jannes, 324
van den Bosch, Cornelia, 227, 229; remarriage of, 233
van den Bosch, Laurentius, 6, 7, 9, 11, 19, 24, 185, 217–35; and map of the Mississippi, 218, 234; and scandal, 229–33; and variants of his name, 219n2; as an Anglican minister, 233–34; assessment of, 217–19, 234–35; at Boston, 222–24; at Carolina, 220–22; at Kingston, 227–34; at Maryland, 233–35; at New York, 224–233; death of, 233; life in the Netherlands, 219–20; marriage of, to Cornelia Ten Broek, 227; ordination of, 220
van der Donck, Adriaen, 92
van der Linde, Benjamin, 14
van der Meulen, Cornelius, 17, 25, 315–32; (*illus*) 316; and Americanization, 326; and Board of Domestic Missions, 323–24, 327; and church unity, 317; and denominational connection, 324; and education, 325–26; and experiences of death, 318–19, 327–28; and return to the Netherlands, 328–30; and the city, 317; and theology of the Seceders, 320–21, 331; as a tie between East and Midwest, 317, 325–26, 331; assessment of, 330–32; as the glue of the *Kolonie*, 316–17; at Chicago, 327; at Grand Rapids, 327–28; birth of, 318; comparison with Van Raalte, 326; death of, 330; early life and education, 318–20; early ministry, 321–22; immigration to Zeeland, 322–23; marriage of, to Elizabeth Geertrui van de Roovaard, 318; personality of, 318–20; piety of, 317; preaching, 326–27; second

marriage of, to Frouke VanderPloeg, 330; spiritual development of, 319
van der Meulen, Eliza, 318, 330
van der Meulen, Willem, 330
van de Roovaard, Elizabeth Geertrui, death of, 328; marriage to Cornelius van der Meulen, 318
VanderPloeg, Frouke, marriage to Cornelius van der Meulen, 330
van de Vijver, Regaert, 200
van Doornik, Neeltje Voncken, 176
van Driele, Frans, 328
van Driessen, Johannes, 15
van Duijns, Egbert, 179
van Dyk, Arent, 229
van Eeckelen, Johannes, 188
van Eijnhatten, Joris, 300
van Foreest, Joannes, 66, 69
van Gaasbeeck, Laurentius, 111
van G[h]ent, Willem Joseph Baron, 177
van Harlingen, Johannes Martinus, 15
van Leeuwen, Jacob, 45
van Lodenstein, Jodocus, 198
van Markken, Jan Gerritsz, 189
van Nieuwenhuysen, Wilhelmus, 111, 115, 134
van Nist, Jacobus, 15
Van Raalte, Albertus C., 316, 320-21, 324, 326, 332
van Remunde, Jan, 75-76
van Rensselaer, Elizabeth, 291
van Rensselaer, Jan Baptist, 103
van Rensselaer, Kiliaen, 43, 104, 115
van Rensselaer, Maria, 115
van Rensselaer, Nicolaes, 115
van Rensselaer, Philip, 291
van Rensselaer, Stephen II, 287
van Rensselaer, Stephen III, 291
van Schie, Cornelis, 9
van Schuijlenburg, Gerardus, 1-3, 300
van Tienhoven, Cornelis, 56
van Tienhoven, Nicolas, 183
van Twiller, Wouter, 44, 91
van Varick, Cornelia Hesther, 179
van Varick, Jacob Roeloffs, 176
van Varick, Jan, 176, 181
van Varick, Margrieta, 190; household inventory of, 180, 193-94
van Varick, Marinus, 182

van Varick, Rudolphus, 136, 139-40, 173-95, 205, 227; and charges of treason, 188-90; and discipline of van den Bosch, 185-86; as a naval chaplain, 176-77; assessment of, 193-95; at Hackensack, 184; at Hem, 180-82; at Long Island, 182-85; at Malacca, 177-79; at New Castle, 185; children of, 182; death of, 192-94; early life, 175-76; handwriting of (*illus*), 174; marriage of, to Margrieta Visboom, 179-80; preaching along the Delaware, 188; theological education, 176; tombstone of (*illus*), 174
Van Velzen, Simon, 320
van Vleck, Paulus, 15
van Vorst, Cornelis, 91
van Wijngaarden, Jan Florisz, 86
van Zuuren, Casparus, 111, 135-36, 156-58, 189; and Tesschenmaecker, 153
Varick, Richard, 251
ver Brijck, Samuel, 14, 265
Verdieren, Hieronymus, 141
Vergulde Bever, 125, 129
Verhulst, Willem, 42
Vernooy, Elizabeth, 229
Versteeg, Dingman, 66
Vesey, William, 141
Vibo, Josias, 67
Visboom, Dirck Jansz, 179
Visboom, Margrieta, 178-79; marriage of to Rudolphus van Varick, 179-80
Visboom, Sara, 181
Voetius, Gisbertus, 21, 105, 109, 111, 122, 150, 176, 187, 190, 198
Vomelius, Sibrandus, 181
voorlezer, 189
Vrooman, Barent, 15

Walcheren, Classis of, 8
Walker, Robert, 240
Walloons. *See* Huguenots
Washington, George, 289
Waverveen, War in, 132
Webber, Agneta, 121
Weeksteen, Johannes, 135
Westerlo, Catherine, 291
Westerlo, Eilardus 8-9, 13, 255, 275-92; and the American Revolution,

288–89; arrival in Albany, 282–84; as "Dutch Pope," 276, 288, 292; assessment of, 292; birth, 277; call from Albany, 280–82; Common Council award to, 284–85; death of, 292; early life and education, 278–80; honorary degree bestowed, 291; marriage of, to Catherine Livingston, 287–88; poor health of, 291; president of General Synod, 291; spiritual rebirth of, 285–87; writings of, 275–76, 288–89
Westerlo, Hillegonda, 277
Westerlo, Isaac, 277
Westerlo, Johanna, 291
Westerlo, Rensselaer, 289, 291
Willett, Elbert, 182
Willett, Marinus, 182
William of Orange, 68
Wilson, Peter, 305
Witherspoon, John, 302
Wynkoop, Johannes, 233

Ypma, Marten, 317

Zas, Lucas, 81, 84
Zeeland, Michigan, start of, 322–23
Zwemer, Adriaan, 330